SECTARIANISM IN EARLY JUDAISM

BibleWorld

Series Editor: Philip R. Davies, University of Sheffield

BibleWorld shares the fruits of modern (and postmodern) biblical scholarship not only among practitioners and students, but also with anyone interested in what academic study of the Bible means in the twenty-first century. It explores our ever-increasing knowledge and understanding of the social world that produced the biblical texts, but also analyses aspects of the Bible's role in the history of our civilization and the many perspectives – not just religious and theological, but also cultural, political and aesthetic – which drive modern biblical scholarship.

Published:

Sodomy: A History of a Christian Biblical Myth
Michael Carden

Yours Faithfully: Virtual Letters from the Bible
Edited by: Philip R. Davies

Israel's History and the History of Israel
Mario Liverani

The Apostle Paul and His Letters
Edwin D. Freed

The Origins of the 'Second' Temple:
Persian Imperial Policy and the Rebuilding of Jerusalem
Diana Edelman

An Introduction to the Bible (Revised edition)
John Rogerson

The Morality of Paul's Converts
Edwin D. Freed

The Mythic Mind
Essays on Cosmology and Religion in Ugaritic and Old Testament Literature
N. Wyatt

History, Literature and Theology in the Book of Chronicles
Ehud Ben Zvi

Women Healing/Healing Women
The Genderization of Healing in Early Christianity
Elaine M. Wainwright

Symposia: Dialogues Concerning the History of Biblical Interpretation
Roland Boer

Forthcoming:

Linguistic Dating of Biblical Texts: An Introduction to Approaches and Problems
Ian Young and Robert Rezetko

Jonah's World: Social Sciences and the Reading of Prophetic Story
Lowell K. Handy

The Bible Says So!: From Simple Answers to Insightful Understanding
Edwin D. Freed

SECTARIANISM IN EARLY JUDAISM

SOCIOLOGICAL ADVANCES

DAVID J. CHALCRAFT

LONDON   OAKVILLE

Published by

UK: Equinox Publishing Ltd
Unit 6, The Village,
101 Amies St.,
London, SW11 2JW

US: DBBC,
28 Main Street,
Oakville, CT 06779

www.equinoxpub.com

First published 2007

© David J. Chalcraft and contributors 2007

British Library Cataloguing-in-Publication Data
A catalogue record for this book is available from the British Library.

Library of Congress Cataloging-in-Publication Data
Sectarianism in early Judaism : sociological advances / edited by David J. Chalcraft.
    p. cm. -- (Bibleworld)
    Papers from a symposium held at the 2004 International Meeting of the SBL at Groningen.
    Includes bibliographical references and index.
    ISBN 1-84553-083-7 (hb) -- ISBN 1-84553-084-5 (pb) 1.
Judaism--History--Post-exilic period, 586 B.C.-210 A.D--Congresses. 2.
Jewish sects--Congresses. 3. Weber, Max, 1864-1920--Congresses. 4.
Historical sociology--Congresses. I. Chalcraft, David J. II. Society of
Biblical Literature. Meeting (2004 : Groningen, Netherlands)
    BM176.S43 2007
                        296.8'1--dc22

ISBN-10   1 84553 083 7   (hardback)
ISBN-10   1 84553 084 5   (paperback)

ISBN-13   978 1 84553 083 9   (hardback)
ISBN-13   978 1 84553 084 6   (paperback)

Typeset by CA Typesetting Ltd, www.sheffieldtypesetting.com
Printed and bound in Great Britain by Lightning Source UK Ltd., Milton Keynes
and Lightning Source Inc., La Vergne, TN

To the memory of Bryan R. Wilson, who died in 2004,
in acknowledgement of his brilliant contributions
to the sociology of religion

CONTENTS

List of Contributors

David J. Chalcraft is Professor of Classical Sociology at the University of Derby, UK.

Philip R. Davies is Professor Emeritus at the University of Sheffield, UK.

Lester L. Grabbe is Professor at the Department of Theology, University of Hull, UK.

Pierluigi Piovanelli is Associate Professor of Religious Studies, University of Ottawa, Montreal, Canada.

Eyal Regev is Lecturer in the Martin (Szusz) Department for Land of Israel Studies and Archaeology, Bar-Ilan University, Ramat Gan, Israel.

Cecilia Wassen is Assistant Professor in the Department of Religion and Culture, Wilfrid Laurier University, Waterloo, Ontario, Canada.

Jutta Jokiranta is Lecturer in Biblical Exegesis, Department of Biblical Studies, University of Helsinki, Finland.

Albert Baumgarten is Professor in the Department of Jewish History, Bar-Ilan University, Ramat Gan, Israel.

Introduction

Sectarianism in Early Judaism: Sociological Advances? Some Critical Sociological Reflections

David J. Chalcraft

The papers collected here, which result from the invitation of Professor Philip Davies[1] to the authors to take part in a symposium held at the 2004 International Meeting of the SBL at Groningen, have sociology as their main social-scientific subject, with occasional glimpses of anthropology. It is fashionable and now almost a convention to speak in terms of social-scientific approaches to biblical and post-biblical materials and societies, and the intention conveyed is the desire to include all relevant social sciences, including sociology, psychology, economics, political science and anthropology, that might illuminate specific cases (Chalcraft, 1997). When approaching ancient Judaism from the perspective of sociology however, it seems obvious that the enquiry forms a part of the sociology of religion, or more exactly is a branch of historical sociology.

This book is best understood therefore as an exercise in historical sociology, with a close relation to the sociology of religion, given its concern with sects and sectarian movements. The range of methods available to the historical sociologist is not wide, but it is still necessary to acknowledge the theoretical and methodological traditions this collection is rooted in, even if this rootage is at times semi-conscious. This volume locates itself in a more or less Weberian frame of typological and comparative analysis of historical and social data. Even where Max Weber is not the preferred social theorist used as point of departure in the contributions which follow, his methodological legacy can be detected, not least because of the "typological nature" of the approaches adopted. The names of Bryan Wilson and of Rodney Stark and William Sims Bainbridge figure very frequently in the pages which follow, and an important task that remains is an in-depth study of the relations between Weber's sociology of sects and the sociology of sects as developed since Weber in the, often partial, reception of classical sociological ideas in the history of the sociology of religion. However, typological analysis is not the only methodology that is utilized in the contributions which follow, and the reader will encounter sociological observations that are not based in any one particular tradition or method (the author utilizing their "sociological imagination" as they see fit or arguing for eclecticism in the use of the social sciences) as well as contributors using the measures of Stark and Bainbridge, or working in the tradition of "the method of agreement and difference" between pre-selected cases. But in all cases, the data that scholars are seeking to illuminate is located in Second Temple Judaism. And it is perhaps in this overriding interest that a community of purpose can be discovered between the contributors; at the same time, this community of interest means that contributing to historical sociology as such, to the body of concepts and theory that constitutes that sub-specialism within sociology, is not a paramount concern. From the point of view of a sociologist this is regrettable, since for the historical sociologist the individual case and historical sociology as a whole demand allegiance. Historical sociology of ancient Judaism in particular, and historical sociology in general as a discipline, can surely not develop if one is only parasitic on the other.

In the area of biblical and post-biblical studies, it is more common to use the language of models, than the language of ideal types. Clearly there is a very interesting investigation to be undertaken in relation to the similarities and differences between historical sociological studies using models and those rooted in ideal-typical constructions. Alas this cannot be undertaken here; suffice it for us to flag that is not a foregone conclusion that ideal-typical approaches, as practised by Max Weber and Bryan Wilson, for example, are at the same time exercises in model building (nor to imagine that Wilson's method of ideal type construction is exactly what Weber had in mind). Ideal types do not propose to carry predictive and causal qualities. That is, for example, to be able to map "in advance" the trajectories of sectarian movements or the internal degrees of coherence between beliefs, practices and organizational forms. On the contrary such sociological dimensions of sects are the subject of empirical investigation. In most cases in this volume, however, contributors tend to use the word "model" interchangeably with type and ideal type without thereby subscribing to a different methodology. Needless to say, the process of concept formation in historical sociology is an involved and complex process, and one that is plagued by circular reasoning and inhibited by notions of essentialism. I am pleased to report that such pitfalls have been met head-on by the contributors to this volume and all traces of such reasoning removed!

I have taken the liberty of taking advantage of the fact that as editor I have read all of the papers in their finished state not only to introduce the papers but also to offer some (critical) sociological commentary largely relating to matters of concept formation, ideal types and other theoretical issues. The authors themselves have not had the opportunity of reading these comments in their entirety. Where I see an opportunity of making some significant sociological points I have done so, even though this may give the impression that I am more critical of some papers than of others (and I of course have not been critical enough of my own contribution!). Such conclusions should not, however, be drawn.

The first part of the volume provides an extensive interrogation of Weber's writings about sects across a fifteen-year period of his output, beginning with his *The Protestant Ethic and the Spirit of Capitalism* and concluding with his work in the *Economic Ethics of the World Religions* (including *Ancient Judaism*) and the posthumous *Economy and Society*. The first part is not intended as an introduction to the following papers found in Part II in either an historical/chronological or sociological-theoretical sense. Its length derives from the fact that Weber's contribution to the sociology of sects has yet to be examined in the depth required. Whilst I argue that there is further scope for applying Weber's ideas to the sociology of sects in general and in Second Temple Judaism in particular, that application is, in the first instance and within the confines of this book, the future task of the author himself. The second part of the volume provides six independent studies of sects and sectarian movements in Second Temple Judaism, drawing on a range of sociological ideas, concepts, and theories and reaching a range of conclusions. I now turn to introduce both parts of the volume in more detail.

Part I

David Chalcraft's contribution, which constitutes Part I *tout court*, provides the first in-depth analysis of Weber's writing on sects within the context of his writings as a whole. The chapter is a reaction to the treatment normally given to Weber in relation to sects. The reception history shows a lack of engagement with Weber's own texts and how his thinking about sects developed over time and illustrates that in no way can his contribution be adequately summarized as providing a simplistic typological contrast of "church-sect" that can be ignored once noted. On examination of the texts it is found that whilst Weber consistently defines a sect by reference to the voluntary status of its membership that has been admitted to the movement after examination, he not only explores in subsequent texts the sociological ramifications of this feature (in relation to democracy, leadership, economics, and the development of types of personality for example) but also places the church-sect typology within a broader universal and comparative setting where concepts of charisma and virtuosity, and sociological contrasts between voluntary associations and compulsory organizations, take on more significance than the consideration of sect per se, although "churches and sects" are seen as one, and often the most significant, instance of a wider phenomenon or type. In other words, Weber seeks to escape the somewhat culture-boundedness of the concepts of sect and church in his developing sociology. Through these means and on these grounds, it is argued that Weber's sociology of sects is profound and offers many insights for the development of a sociology of sects that have yet to be fully exploited. Within the section on Weber, Chalcraft provides an analysis of Weber's treatment of the Essenes and the Pharisees as found in *Ancient Judaism*, where the emphasis is on showing how Weber made use of his previous conceptual and theoretical findings when thinking about Second Temple Judaism. Since the Dead Sea Scrolls were not discovered until some twenty-seven years after Weber's own death, it was not possible for him to consider the relation between the Scrolls and the community of Essenes described by ancient sources. The placing of Weber's research in the context of discussion of the "inter-testamental period" of his own day, *inter alia*, reminds us that a Weberian approach to second temple Judaism post the discoveries has yet to be carried out. The third section of Chalcraft's analysis seeks to address that gap by proving a Weberian analysis of the Qumran sects which is built upon the close examination of Weber's texts provided earlier. A Weber Bibliography is provided to assist further in the exploration of Weber's sociology.

Part II

In the second part of the book, discussion moves from Weber's time to our own, post the discoveries in the Judean desert and post a good deal of study and debate about the Dead Sea Scrolls and the Qumran community and the Essene movement. Given the nature of the reception of Weber on sects, contemporary work in the sociology of sects and sectarianism in Second Temple Judaism looks to the tradition largely stemming from Ernst Troeltsch and the ways in which his legacy has been taken up, criticized and adapted by scholars such as R. Niebuhr and, in turn, by Bryan Wilson. It is this legacy that provides one context for the further examination of Weberian approaches in the light of this collection. It is of course, however, a valuable tradition of thinking on sects in its own right, and the papers collected here all make at least some reference to the important and seminal work of Bryan Wilson, with Cecilia Wassen and Jutta Jokiranta moving beyond Wilson in their defence of the approach of Stark and Bainbridge, whilst others, notably Lester Grabbe, Pierluigi Piovanelli and Eyal Regev, make use of Wilson's typologies, in differing ways, to illuminate Second Temple religious and social movements. These uses and the other papers in Part II are described in more detail in what follows.

Lester Grabbe's contribution opens Part II with a welcome survey of what is known about movements in Second Temple Judaism, providing a critical guide to the ancient sources. He argues that definitions are an important dimension of research, and that it is necessary to give their formation some critical thought. He argues that a definition of the movements in Second Temple Judaism should all more or less be capable of being defined in a similar way given not only their similar treatment by ancient authorities such as Josephus, but also because the majority of the social movements were religiously orientated. This is not to argue that Josephus was a sophisticated sociologist of his time. Rather, Grabbe states:

> "Although we are not bound to use the terms employed in the original sources…we should take account of the data. One fact to note is that the groups are lumped together: there is no distinction made between the Pharisees and/or the Sadducees and other groups. Thus any attempt to use separate terminology for them would not be supported in the original sources. A common term capable of encompassing the main groups discussed above is desirable."

Grabbe defends the use of the definition of these movements as "sects," on the basis of the sociological advances made by Wilson in moving beyond classical sociological understandings of sects which betray their origins in the European Christian tradition. For example, the use of the definition of sect does not, in the work of Wilson (following Weber in his commitment to freedom from value judgements) imply any sense of opprobrium. For Grabbe, Wilson's highlighting of sects' responses of the world enabled the construction of a series of ideal types that allows for the analysis of sects in a variety of traditions. Interestingly, the application of Wilson's typology to the picture of the movements in Second Temple Judaism provided by Grabbe, results in the Essenes, the Pharisees and so on, being placed into more than one ideal-typical characterization. The ideal-typical sect, labelled as thaumaturgical by Wilson, could apply, Grabbe suggests, to all of the movements! The point where Grabbe's essay finishes leads to the conclusion that further sociological advances, based on Wilson's work, depend upon a close examination of the ideal types and the logic of a complex of attributes, and the degrees of importance to be granted to certain features within the array of attributes, before deciding under which ideal-typical heading the particular sectarian movement, (and to boot, at which stage of its development) is best placed to aid classification. Grabbe rightly reminds the reader that models are not replicas of reality and hence one should not be surprised to find reality escaping the clutches of any one ideal-typical description. Any sect movement will be more or less similar to one or more of the types elaborated by Wilson. That is to be expected. On the other hand, it needs to be noted that the ideal type is a heuristic device, and if the application of the ideal types is such that the careful distinctions elaborated by Wilson distort the "reality" of ancient Jewish sectarian movements (or the ancient data distort the logic of the ideal types) the conclusions to be drawn will be something along the lines of the following alternatives: that the sects concerned are hybrid types or types showing low levels of crystallization or are experimental forms that defy classification since they are very much still emergent and do not have tried and tested social forms to hand to emulate and borrow from. In each case, the development of new ideal types is likely to be helpful. Alternatively, we might conclude that there is insufficient data to make any meaningful distinction in these terms, or that in the case of ancient sectarian movements the observable traits found presented in Wilson's types do not apply. The "lack of fit" (which is an elastic concept in ideal-typical analysis for sure) does not mean that Wilson's ideal types are not heuristically important for the analysis of other sect movements in the past, present or future. The sociological task is less to announce a success or failure of a sociologist's ideal types and more to lead the investigator to study more closely the sectarian movement/s concerned.

Grabbe is very much aware of the limitations of the sources and this is an important factor for all researchers to keep in mind, sociologist or not. It is not without significance that Grabbe begins (at least in the "writing up") with the data before turning to sociology; a sociologist might begin with the concepts to orient the collection of data, or at least work dialectically between concepts and data. That is, perhaps one procedure is to work carefully through each of Wilson's seven types collecting data that might suggest certain second temple movements are best understood as examples of one type in particular; further, it would also be necessary to consider the potential mutual impacts of the sectarian movements on each other within the general socio-cultural and religious milieu, rather than as hermetically sealed ideal-typical movements.

Grabbe also reminds us that it is important to develop a range of sociological concepts, of group, political party, status group, class and association and so on, before we can confidently use the definition of sect in relation to a social movement in second temple times. The choice might not always be an either/or but a both/and. A sect can function as a status group and have political goals and implications, for example. For Grabbe, however, the movements in Second Temple Judaism can be labelled as sects; that is, following Wilson, as "minority religious movements." One of the sociological lessons taught is that there is some gap between agreeing a definition of "sect" and undertaking or applying an ideal-typical analysis of sects. Once a definition has been accepted, the question remains as to what other "baggage" travels with the definition, and it will also soon be asked, what type of sect or sects are we dealing with? With regard to the former, Grabbe rightly highlights that some of the older theological baggage that travelled with the label "sect" has been off-loaded by Wilson. We need to add that Wilson also included within his definition of a sect – that is, prior to the elaboration of the particular types of sect, all of whom share in the over-arching characteristics – a list of attributes held by all sects. Grabbe mentions one of these over-arching characteristics when he notes that one of the things Wilson says about sects is that they demand "total commitment" and that membership in a sect becomes a "master status." Hence when one uses the shorthand "sect" when working in the Wilsonian mode, all of these other features are implied along with it. Equally, when one uses the label "sect" in a Weberian mode, a set of shared characteristics is implied. Followers of Wilson or of Weber can communicate in general about "sect" without always putting the "flesh on the bones," but eventually what precisely is contained within the label "sect" will become a point of issue. Such is the nature of academic discussion. It is quite possible, and more than likely, that scholars can agree to label a religious movement as a "sect," and actually differ markedly about what that implies with regard to origin, organization, belief and practices, and impacts on the wider society and culture. Indeed, the history of research about sects in this period testifies to that truth. Accepting a working definition of "sect" is the point of departure for sociological advances.

Philip Davies, in his *Sect Formation in Early Judaism*, charts a course between the ideographic and the nomothetic tendencies of historical sociology by finding a role for sociological theory whilst retaining the historian's interest in the particular case under scrutiny and in the unique. For Davies, sociological theory is important to the task since the data that is to be interpreted is not only textual in nature, but the texts, in the majority of cases, were produced by the sectarians themselves. Hence, gaining some objective distance from the sources is necessary and Davies reckons that sociology can help "as an exegetical principal to control what will otherwise be either a flat and uncritical exposition of the views expressed or undisciplined scepticisms or imagination."

Rather than utilizing an already established typology or a particular set of criteria for recognizing sects, Davies prefers to state clearly what a sect is for him. Namely, that sects are schismatic and socially segregate from the "parent world." The spirit of Weber (especially with regard to concern with the nature of Judaism and its own peculiar sect-like nature and status) and of Wilson can be felt in Davies' contribution, but he is very much "his own man." Given that sociological theory normally prefers to advance on the basis of engagement with previous conceptual work, such interventions can be harder to appreciate, but they are worth the effort. I prefer to understand Davies' definition of a sect as schismatic as an experiment. That is, it is a heuristic device that argues, for this case and for this enquiry, "let us think of sects" as schismatic. The benefits of such an heuristic tool is, as Davies argues, that studying sect formation can inform as much about the schismatic religious movement as about the parent from which it derives. Davies is just as interested, if not, on this occasion, more interested, in the nature of the parent. On these grounds, Davies positions himself in relation to Wilson typologies, and also the typological contrast between world-affirming and world-denying sects as developed by Roy Wallis, by stating that these distinctions only make sense when understood against the nature of the parent. In this context, it is important to consider what Davies means by "the world" that the sect is rejecting or is recreating in its own image. In a relatively undifferentiated society, of course, where the religious sphere overlaps with the political and economic spheres, to speak of the "world" as Judaism is to speak inclusively of the society as a whole. It is feasible, for example, for a sect to reject the stratification system in a society and socially segregate with its own status system around which is built all the other expected religious and cultural dimensions found within a minority religious movement. On the other hand, if the schism is a break away from a religious tradition, the rejection or affirmation is related not to the social world as such, but to the world of the religious institution being rejected or refined. Further, the aspects of the religious "world" being rejected might, to some minds, be adaphoria. As can be imagined there is an immense sociological literature on the nature of the world that sects reject and how sects might be typologized in relation to that rejection and how it impacts on their own beliefs and organizations.

Another important methodological point is made by Davies when he argues for a distinction to be drawn between the sects' own presentation of its origins, history and central differentiating beliefs, and what may have occurred historically. This can be quite significant in sectarian analysis, if one recalls that Weber tended to examine theological ideas and dogmas for a tendency to sectarianism on the basis of doctrines that differentiated between "the saved" and the "regenerate." From Davies' point of view such a theological distinction might reflect a later rationalization of a split from the religious or social parent/world that was not caused originally by such ideas.

Davies argues that the Qumran documents display, when read with this notion of sect in mind, and read with due knowledge of the layers of redaction that characterize such documents as *The Community Rule*, that there were not one but two sects. The Damascus Community/Sect being the parent of the Qumran sect (the *yahad*). Coming to an understanding of the parent from which the Damascus Community distanced itself takes up the majority of the discussion and is something of a complex task. Davies argues that there must have been a period when the tolerance of difference and variety ceased within Second Temple Judaism, and that this cessation, which was the immediate context or pretext for the formation of sects could have stemmed from the mainstream (refusing acknowledgement of certain differences displayed by other groups) or from the groups that formed sects (wishing to withdraw from the parent): equally possible is that both "sides" reached these positions, albeit gradually, but more or less at the same time. Hence Davies draws a valuable distinction between social segregation (the hallmark and identifying characteristic of the sect) and heteropraxis. Differences in belief and practice, that is to say, do not always and do not necessarily lead to social and religious segregation; clearly, with the existence of sects which do socially segregate from their parent, heteropraxis has apparently become intolerable. For the details of when this might have transpired within the history of Judaism/s I refer the reader to the chapter below. Reaching an understanding of the nature of the parent Judaism(s) from which sectarian movements socially segregated involves something of a long term perspective, and raises the possibility that sectarian tendencies and actual sects have a much longer history than a concentration on Greek-Roman periods of Jewish history might imply.

A long term view of sectarianism in Second Temple Judaism is taken by *Pierluigi Piovanelli* in his contribution to the volume. In his exploration of the variety and origin of Jewish identity/ies there are some interesting parallels with the contributions of Philip Davies and Lester Grabbe that I would like to draw out. Like Lester Grabbe, Piovanelli seeks to think about sectarianism in Second Temple times making use of the ideal-typical work of Bryan Wilson, and briefly introduces the "responses to the world" articulated by Wilson as ways of distinguishing sects from each other. It will be recalled that the responses include the conversion-ist, the revolutionist, the introversionist, the manipulationist, the thau-maturgical, the spiritualistic, the reformist and the utopian. Like Grabbe discovered, applying these ideal types to limited data about religious movements in Second Temple times, means that sooner or later one runs into the problem that the various movements appear to be capable of being placed under more than one category. What is required is suf-ficient detail on either side of the equation: that is, for there to be suf-ficient historical and theological data to view from the perspective of the ideal types and, on the other hand, for the ideal types themselves and the ethnography that supports them, to be given close examination. For example, in Piovanelli's figurative presentation of Wilson's ideal types, the Essenes are said to have features shared with all the ideal types apart from the Reformist and the Utopian. Unlike Grabbe, the Sadducees are not considered a sect at all; neither are they considered to be a denomi-nation, but rather, sociologically speaking (following Weber?) a "church." Piovanelli attempts to deal with these ideal-typical issues by distinguish-ing between secondary sectarian tendencies, implying that, for example, a conversionist stance might be more significant in understanding a sec-tarian movement than some of the other features which, whilst present, are less defining of the essence of that particular movement. Another way of dealing with the application of the ideal types that is presented is to note that the sectarian movements evolve over time, of course, and hence that at different periods, and hence in different documents stem-ming from different times, a movement that was revolutionary becomes reformist and so on.

There are two other methodological points that Piovanelli makes that are worth noting from a sociological point of view. First, he points out that where data is scarce, "historians should pay special attention to every clue that could reveal the existence of sectarian behaviours and/or groups." Perhaps an unintended consequence of this generally good piece of advice is to find evidence of an element of revolution/reform/conver-sion and so on, that whilst slight, in the balance of things generally being slight, can tip the typology willy-nilly. The second interesting method-ological point is to keep in mind the distinction between emic and etic designations of difference and segregation: sometimes the "sect label" is self-imposed and other times it is imposed by those outside the group in a position powerful enough to name names and make labels stick.

What is perhaps ironic is that whilst Wilson's types are often introduced by noting that, unlike Weber and Troeltsch [*sic*] they do not take theological criteria but sociological criteria as significant, analysis in the mode of Wilson rarely, if ever, talks about the types of leadership, membership, rules of admission, means of administration and expulsion and so on, that one might find more in one type of sect than in another, but rather appears to focus on the theological/religious dimensions of the responses to the world to the exclusion of sociological factors per se.

In the second part of his contribution, Piovanelli considers the evidence for observing sectarian processes of group and identity formation including the differences between the returning exiles and those who remained; between the Jerusalem authorities and the Elephantine Jewish community, and finally, between the mainstream Judaism/s and the Enochic groups. Piovanelli's reconstruction should be compared with that of Philip Davies, since they both are concerned with finding the moments when toleration ceased, in the drive to establish an orthodox Jewish religious and ethnic identity. Piovanelli writes that he is convinced that there is a community behind the Enochic literature, who are "clearly proto-sectarian...displaying revolutionist, manipulations, thaumaturgical and spiritualist attitudes." A third methodological point is made in the final part of the essay which reflects on methodological and ethical points. Here, Piovanelli places the interest in Jewish identity into the context of a *long durée* approach to Mediterranean history and culture: that is to say, that ancient Judaism is best approached via an holistic history. The parallels with contemporary social processes are more than implied in the following sentence: "In the end, it seems to me that in such a family, clan, village, and region-based culture sectarianism was a logical centrifugal response to the centripetal pressure exerted by the globalizing ideologies and institutions of the day." Then as now, unravelling sectarian processes is a key part of securing and defending our identities, argues Piovanelli.

The problems that attend the application of ideal types – in these cases those of Bryan Wilson – become readily apparent, and these problems stem not only from the limitation of the sources, but the interpretation of those sources and moreover, from differences in the interpretation of the features identified by Wilson himself. It might be that it is necessary, in order to make sociological advances, to adopt a more Weberian ideal-typical approach where certain features are exaggerated to highlight the presence or absence in terms of degree of a particular dimension of sectarian life. In some ways, I have suggested this is what Philip Davies has done by not seeking to apply a particular set of typologies but by "sticking his neck out" and defining a sect as schismatic and as having a relation to a parent world, as we saw above. We will see below that Regev, and Wassen and Jokiranta (in different ways and on different grounds) also select a particular variable (e.g. tension with the world) or variables (tension with the world as sinful and the quest for atonement) as a focus of analysis rather than work with applying ideal-typical models. It is important to be able to distinguish, to stop the use of ideal types being somewhat arbitrary, between occasions where the ideal type "fails" to illuminate the case, and where the application of the ideal type fails to "illuminate the case": a good sociologist should not blame their tools, especially when they have been chosen by them. To argue that ideal types do not "fit" reality is to forget that the realities Wilson was trying to elucidate did "fit" sufficiently well for him to present the types we have. It would appear to behove sociologists working in Second Temple Jewish history and literature to develop their own ideal types that suit such a relatively undifferentiated society or one in which the logical distinctions which make sense in the contexts studied by Wilson are not required to be consistently present. Of course, not all work in historical sociology has to be in the typological tradition. Another possibility is the employment of a comparative method. The contribution of Eyal Regev to the volume, to which we now turn, raises some of these issues.

It is with such thoughts in mind that we move to consider the contribution to the volume of *Eyal Regev* since, methodologically, there is the prospect that we are moving onto a slightly different plane given the promise found early on that progress in the sociological analysis of the Qumran material will be made via a comparative method. This suggests that, rather than work with set typologies which are "tested" against the data, or against which the data is compared, Regev may prefer to apply what we might call a version of the method of similarity and difference, as first developed by J. S. Mill and supported by historical sociologists such as Barrington Moore in his famous analysis of dictatorship and democracy, for example (Moore, 1966). Through the process of comparison what is shared between different sectarian movements would come to the fore as well as what is not shared, and when these features are placed alongside other present and absence sociological variables a degree of causal explanation can be posited. In many ways, this process of similarity and differences is a method used by sociologists in the construction of types – the method is not usually visible since the results that are presented are the types themselves; moreover, if the construction of types is the aim of the comparison there is less interest in explaining the differences and similarities found in some spheres in relation to their presence and absence in other spheres. For example, one might find that all societies that have experienced a successful liberalizing revolution in their history tended to have a social structure during the crucial period prior to social radicalism, which included a weak aristocracy, an angry and active peasant class, and a politically mature middle class, to act upon an economic, political or military crisis, since where there were no successful bourgeois revolutions, one of these elements and some of these conditions were apparently absent. Barrington Moore, for example, is less interested in the development of types, and more interested in illuminating the cases being considered and postulating some degree of causal explanation.

Regev utilizes an aspect of the method of agreement and difference within his essay, but it is important to note that the majority of the paper analyses and builds upon the typological insights of other sociologists, most notably Bryan Wilson. In other words, one might say that there is a degree of tension between the comparative method and the use of the results of prior ideal-typical analysis. To put the matter slightly differently: should not the agreement that certain sectarian movements are similar and introversionist be a conclusion reached after comparison, rather than being the basis on which the comparison is undertaken? (Comparison of the data being a qualitatively different exercise from assessing some data against an ideal type that has already pre-selected the relevant features of some sects for comparison with a "new" religious movement one is seeking to understand.) Or, perhaps one can say, that one is on stronger ground if the postulated agreement between two or more sectarian movements rests on a variable different from the variable selected for investigation in the case presented? At least it can be seen that there the situation is relatively complex, methodologically speaking.

Regev begins with Stark and Bainbridge, illustrating his approval of the elevation of the notion of "tension with the world" as perhaps the most significant and defining feature of a sectarian worldview, from which other sectarian dimensions follow. Regev is not alone in this regard and many contributors to the volume, and many sociologists (including Weber?) would agree that tension with the world is an important dimension of sectarian life. It seems to me that we need to exercise caution in this regard since it would appear that all movements are in some tension with aspects of the world not represented in the movement since this is the *raison d'être* for the movement in the first place. Further, emphasizing this aspect of tension might lead one to presuppose that there is a degree of consensus "out there" in the world, against which people and movements can pit themselves. It presumes, to use the language of Durkheim, a relative strong sense of a collective conscience, which might not exist in reality. It should also be recalled, as was mentioned above in relation to Davies' paper, that sectarian writings that convey tension with the world, and express this tension in terms of the evil of the world, may well be ideologically dressing up a far more mundane dissatisfaction with the world. Regev is of course aware of the possible range of tension that can persist between sect and world, and the fact that there are differences of degree as well as variety in the content of that rejection and indeed in the consistency with which aspects, tools and techniques as well as ends, of the world are held in suspicion. Leaving aside such factors, it is only necessary for us to note that Regev quotes Stark and Bainbridge with approval and also finds Wilson in agreement with this emphasis on tension (by translating some of his concerns into these terms) with the world as being a central and defining characteristic of the life of the sectarian.

Regev also draws on ideal-typical analysis when he agrees that the Qumran sects were most likely introversionist and revolutionist. When it comes therefore to the comparative part of his paper, he can already restrict the comparison to other so-called introversionist sects. In carrying out this comparison it would, of course, also be important methodologically, if space permitted, to list all those dimensions that these particular instances of introversionist sects did not share, and in this way complete the process of "agreement and difference" and qualm any concerns that one is perhaps not, after all, comparing like with like.

Regev interprets "tension with the world" as an attitude to the "world as evil," which motivates the sectarian to energetically seek atonement. In other words, the sectarian is obsessed with the evil of the world – hence the desire to withdraw from it in seeking salvation. Regev shows how the Qumran writers believed the world outside the sect to be evil and wicked, and hence proves the high degree of tension between them and the world. These beliefs impacted on the manner of joining the sect, since confession of sins was necessary for admittance. Regev shows how the sectarians themselves shared in the guilt of the world, and that their achievement of atonement was a continuous activity. As he writes: "Their [the sectarians] holiness and closeness to God were not only a matter of predestination, but of continuous endeavour of moral behaviour and strict halakhic observance." For those familiar with Weber's depiction of the Calvinist ascetic Protestants in his *The Protestant Ethic and the Spirit of Capitalism*, the type is familiar. Regev is able to draw the conclusion that the sectarian ethos has a deeper rootage than a tension with the world; rather, the rejection of the world is based on a rejection of creation, of human nature itself. Hence the Qumran sectarians share in the fallen nature of the world. This type of tension with the world expressed itself in the quest for atonement via the moral code exercised in the sect, together with its coercive means. It is at this point in his analysis that Regev turns to his comparative data, the purpose of which he defines as an attempt "to comprehend the ideological background and the social function of the Qumranic idea of atonement." Looking at the Amish and the Shakers as an analogous sectarian movement, since, like the Qumran sects, according to the ideal type and Regev's application of it, they were introversionist, Regev establishes that the tension with the world as evil and the concern with the sin of others and their own fallen natures, led the Shakers and Amish to develop public rituals of confession.

In the final part of the paper, Regev considers whether there is a similar sectarian ethos in other literature found at Qumran, namely, in the *Temple Scroll* and MMT. It is actually in this section that a version of the method of similarity and difference can be said to be operating in so far as Regev compares the tendencies in halakhah and sacrificial rites in the *Temple Scroll* with similar texts in the Torah (in the past) and with Rabbinic texts (later in date than the *Temple Scroll* etc.), in order to appreciate the essence of the former. Regev argues that there is a stronger and wider concern with ritual purity in the *Temple Scroll* and so on than in either the Torah or the Rabbinic literature. This occurs in at least four dimensions, including the strengthening of purity boundaries, the elevation of the holiness of sacred food from the realm of the laity to the realm of the priesthood, the extension and intensification of the spatial boundaries of holiness in the Temple Mount and, finally, in the development of special rituals of atonement.

Regev seeks an explanation for the intensification of concerns with ritual purity and the like in the *Temple Scroll* and argues that a sectarian ethos underlies the phenomena since it evidences a growing awareness that the ritual can be corrupted by the world. Drawing on the anthropological theory of Mary Douglas, as later developed by Michael Thompson, Richard Ellis and Aaron Wildavsky, Regev sees the attitude to the world evidenced in the *Temple Scroll* as "Nature Ephemeral." This perspective sees the world "as terrifying and fragile and God as unforgiving." The theorists argue that this attitude to the world is typical of sectarian societies. What this does, of course, is show continuity and possible parentage, from the *Temple Scroll* to later Qumran texts. What cannot be argued at this stage is what caused the sectarian ethos to develop.

Regev concludes, showing the continuity in sectarian ethos between the authors of the *Temple Scroll* and the authors of the *Damascus Covenant* and the *Community Rule*:

The different cultic boundaries parallel the social boundaries of separation from the wicked. Both create an enclave, a restricted social or religious realm. The atoning rituals parallel the penal code, the confessions and the other rituals, since they are all aimed at repairing sin and transgression. They elevate the enclave to a higher degree of sacredness and closeness to God. Both are behavioural means to achieve a spiritual moment of salvation.

Regev, in the space provided, is not able to develop an argument as to why this attitude to the world should intensify during the period when the *Temple Scroll* was composed, nor indeed how the sectarian ethos here expressed in ritual terms developed further to leave behind the ritual dimension in favour of an intensification of the ethical dimensions of atonement: what, to borrow from Max Weber, one might call a "process of disenchantment" that leads to the ritualization of everyday life in an ethical dimension. As noted, these are topics for future work. It is perhaps in answering these sociological and historical questions that Regev will further develop his comparative analysis of sects and employ the method of agreement and difference to isolate causes and provide explanations of similarities and contrasts between sectarian movements separated from each other in time and place. It remains to be seen how far ideal-typical analysis and previously formulated ideal types will figure in a renewed comparative analysis of sects and the extent to which previously formulated ideal types have to be undone to avoid circularity.

The contribution of *Cecilia Wassen* and *Jutta Jokiranta* continues with this theme of using sociological ideas to both suggest and underwrite findings based on redactional analysis of the relevant texts. It could well be that the problems encountered in applying ideal-typical descriptions of sect types finds its exegetical outlet and heuristic value in suggesting that certain configurations – the existence side-by-side of features found in different types of sects – are an indication of stages in the development of sects, witnessed to by redactional levels. However, Wassen and Jokiranta base their sociological analysis, not on ideal-typical approaches, but on the approach argued for by Stark and Bainbridge, who argue that sects are deviant groups characterized by tension with the wider society. Moreover, this tension can be measured through a number of indices. Using this measure Wassen and Jokiranta seek to sociologically demonstrate the degree of sectarianism (the degree of tension) displayed in Qumran texts, and thereby reconsider the extent of "sectual explicitness" (to borrow from Carol Newsom) in texts that hitherto have been considered as not especially (if at all) sectarian in their outlook. In particular, they argue that the *Damascus Document* (and its versions) display more striking sectarian characteristics when viewed from this perspective than has previously been thought. Wassen and Jokiranta note that Wilson's sevenfold typology of sects has proved useful to Qumran scholars and that there is a degree of consensus that the Qumran community by the Dead Sea is an example of an introversionist sect (with some revolutionist overtones). In contrast, scholars such as Regev have seen the Damascus Covenant community as not withdrawn from the wider society to the same extent.

The authors proceed by building on the redactional analysis of D by Charlotte Hempel (who divides the laws and regulations found in D into those dealing with "Halakhah" and those dealing with "Community Organization," with the latter being later and perhaps reflecting the inventions of the community itself rather than what was carried over from other settings) and of S by Sarianna Metso (who distinguishes four layers of redaction). From this basis, the authors turn to consider relevant sociological theory, which in this case means considering what the best way to measure "degrees of sectarianism" might be. As with other contributors to the volume, they find that applying Wilson's seven types to the data, considering differing responses to evil in the world, means that the Qumran data can be understood as exhibiting more than one response to the world, either, as it were, simultaneously or in the course of development of the movement. That is to say, in the final analysis Wilson's typologies cannot be used to answer many remaining questions in Qumran studies and can actually lead to a degree of confusion and conflicting applications. For the purposes of this paper the authors tend to agree with the criticisms made of typological analysis of sects by Stark and Bainbridge who felt that not only were the classical approaches tainted by a western bias (i.e. the church-sect distinction) or failed to clearly distinguish between defining criteria (what exists in every case) and correlates (features which may or may not be present). Clearly, readers will need to immerse themselves in the writings of Weber and Wilson and so on, to determine their degree of acceptance of Stark and Bainbridge's criticisms. What Stark and Bainbridge want to do is introduce a measure that can more or less accurately gauge degrees of sectarianism. The measure they decided upon was tension with the world. This measure of course has to be operationalized: that is, what is to count as an index or instance of tension and how that is to be interpreted and weighted are very important methodological questions to be addressed. Some authors (e.g. Chalcraft in this volume), would argue that Weber not only provided a consistent defining criteria of a sect but also was concerned with degrees of sectarianism, seeing some movements as following the logic of their sectarian tendencies to be more sect-like than others. What Weber resisted – and probably would be resisted by Wilson also – was any attempt to measure such sect-likeness quantitatively with any degree of accuracy. Stark and Bainbridge are against the continual refinement (or rather the exponential expansion) of types and argue instead for procedures that allow for the measurement of degrees of sectarianism, taking a particular variable, in this instance, tension, as an index. It is as if Stark and Bainbridge wish to introduce a higher degree of precision to Weber and Wilson's notion of a particular religious movement being more sect-like or less sect-like than the models worked with.

In contrast to the logic of the approach of Wilson, Stark and Bainbridge appear to believe that they can measure a degree of sectarianism – hence a movement can, as it were, score high on the scale or low – rather than produce a series of ideal types in which some sects display more tension with the "world" and others less so, depending on other beliefs and practices that characterize the sect. One could argue that isolating a variable in this way is to perhaps elevate one feature of sectarianism above others and that in the process the sect is treated atomistically, and that one is left with no appreciation of how one feature of sectarian life might be associated with other features in a variety of configurations. Wassen and Jokiranta, however, are aware of the ways in which the various dimensions of deviance and tension interrelate and possibly reinforce one another. Despite possible disagreements between sociologists about this approach to understanding sectarianism, Wassen and Jokiranta put the method to good use and are able to draw a number of important conclusions regarding not only inner dynamics within the sectarian movements but also in underwriting conclusions reached via redactional analysis.

Wassen and Jokiranta clearly introduce Stark and Bainbridge's approach, and they are convinced of its usefulness for the task in hand. They observe, "Our conviction is that a dimensional model – one in which variables are set on a continuum – allows for a more nuanced and clearer picture than models which distinguish sects based on a variety of characteristics." For them, a "sect movement is a deviant religious organization with traditional beliefs and practices." Deviance corresponds to the degree of tension with the wider society, in so far as tension is measured by "difference" (holding deviant norms), "antagonism" (holding particularistic beliefs and attitudes) and "separation" (manifested in promoting internal social relations at the same time as restricting interaction with outsiders). Wassen and Jokiranta are also aware that it is essential to consider what the appropriate context is for defining the norms of the wider society, and they spend some time delimiting their study accordingly. This latter point is, of course, of interest to Davies and Piovanvelli since it relates to the degree of consensus (the degree of accepted norms of Jewish belief and practice) that they consider significant in viewing the long-term development of sectarianism and the points at which tolerance may have ceased to operate. Wassen and Jokiranta observe: "Despite the pluralism that characterized Jewish beliefs and practices of this time, we believe that deviance from some 'common' norms can be detected." Regev also felt that such "commonality" needed to be accepted in his analysis of sectarian tension with the evil world.

So, armed with this body of sociological ideas and concepts and a sophisticated grasp of the task ahead, Wassen and Jokiranta proceed to analyse the textual data in the light of the sociological theories they wish to apply. Readers will find many insights in the paper, and one of the most significant points is the manner in which separation from the wider society is understood both physically and symbolically: in other words, withdrawal to the desert is not the only way that a Jewish sect can separate itself from the world; one can, so to speak, be in the world and yet not of it, individuals separating themselves from non-sect members through a range of ritual and everyday prescriptions relating to sexual relations, economic interaction and sharing food. That is to say, the sectarian ethos in D can be seen as strong as the sectarian ethos in S, when "withdrawal" is read in this way. The authors also offer some commentary on what I have called the "dark side of sectarian life" (in my contribution here), focusing on the control of sect members and the "spying" of sect members on each other (following Albert Baumgarten), as an example of how the life of the sectarian was "separate" from the life of the non-sectarians (and the role of the Examiner in D which is analysed also brings home the element of control operated by the leadership of the sect over members). Finally, the authors also show how features not shared by D with S – features which have suggested to other interpreters less tension and more integration between sectarians and the wider society (e.g. marriage, owning slaves, economic activities) are not after all indications of a lesser degree of sectarianism. The reasons given for reading the data this way are various but worth considering in depth. The authors conclude that the Damascus Community was not especially integrated with the surrounding society: "Instead, in spite of living among other Jews and gentiles, the members had mechanisms in place to preserve distinct boundaries with outsiders, Jews and gentiles alike." This leads the authors to be able to conclude that "both S and D contain regulations, norms, and ideology that display high tension with the greater society and thus a sectarian stance." We should note that the authors hold that the sectarian stance in D is reflected in the later redactional layers rather than the earlier.

The book closes with the contribution of *Albert Baumgarten*, who has a long association with sociological approaches to Second Temple Judaism and provides us with some welcome, and entertaining, insights into the processes of applying sociology. He brings to our attention the fact that when using the social sciences to interpret ancient materials it is to be expected that our sociological experiments may fail: in fact, that we should expect more failure than success. That is to say, the models we are using, the analogies we wish to draw, might not be very significant and might not apply at all. Since it is normally only the successes that are reported, Baumgarten makes an interesting case for including some reportage of our failures also. This is important, especially since we can learn something about the enterprise of sociological approaches to ancient Judaism in the process, and moreover be reminded of the essential differences between our worlds and the social worlds of the past. Baumgarten reports on his own experience of not "getting very far" in gaining further knowledge of the Qumran sectarians despite utilizing such a well-grounded theory of information processing in sect-like movements and enclaves as developed by Douglas and Mars.

Approaching the Qumran materials from the perspective of information processing would appear to be a good idea, since knowing the answers to such questions as "Who is allowed to know which things, and who is forbidden?" or "Who is reliable as opposed to illicit or discredited sources of information? might well illuminate the dynamics of the group. However, in Baumgarten's own estimation, posing such questions to the Qumran materials teaches very little about the movement than was already known. Moreover, this is not due to the limitations of source, since, he argues, there have been strides made in the past in his own work that were based on a similarly limited textual basis, but whose illumination spread wide. Notwithstanding, Baumgarten concludes that there is little evidence about information processing because, at a crucial period in the sects' development, a strong streak of egalitarianism meant that such matters were not codified.

I have argued elsewhere that a balance needs to be achieved in sociological approaches to ancient Judaism between a sociological imagination on the one hand, with, on the other, a degree of precision in the use of certain theories and the development of certain concepts taken from social science. The same tendencies can be observed in this area of historical sociological approaches to Second Temple Judaism and sectarian movements. On the one hand, there is a need for sophistication in the use of ideal types and concept formation and the application of theory, since to be sloppy in these regards is to court confusion. On the other hand, it must be remembered that ideal types and models are but heuristic devices which need to be used creatively since social realities will never match the logical presentation of phenomena presented in sociology. We have not yet reached a circumstance, I believe, when we can agree with the "quest for imprecision" in sociological method, as recently argued by John Law, despite the wonderful case he makes (Law, 2004). Baumgarten, perhaps in contrast to some of the other papers found in this volume, but in the tradition of the sociological imagination rather than in the tradition of a version of sociological positivism, reminds us of the need for flexibility in our approaches, what he calls an eclecticism. First, we need to remember that "The nature of history is such that one should not expect too high a rate of success in applying ideas from the social sciences to the study of the past." Once we appreciate this fact, our sociological imaginations no doubt will improve. More importantly, Baumgarten observes:

> Some aspects of the social scientific theory will prove beneficial for history, others will not. Those circumstances are effective acknowledgement that notions based on such a different world cannot be transferred whole to another time and place. Eclecticism in employing social scientific insights in writing history, as I see it, is not a flaw, a sign of inconsistency and sloppy thinking. It is not evidence of being misled by superficial similarities that fade on closer analysis. Rather it is a sign of genuine appreciation of difference between the two things being compared, between the source of insight and its application to new material. Indeed, if a historian ever claimed to have found a perfectly consistent and thorough point-by-point equivalence between some historical data and a social scientific model I would take that claim as evidence of history gone awry, that has overlooked important differences.

Hence, the failure to discover more than a few observations about Qumran on the basis of the application of theories of information processes, is, Baumgarten concludes, "a reminder of difference between them [the Qumran sectarians] and the sects of modern times."

Dedication

The book is dedicated to the memory of *Bryan R. Wilson* who died in 2004, in acknowledgement of his brilliant contributions to the sociology of religion, but with specific gratitude from within biblical and post-biblical studies. Students and scholars within the disciplines of Oriental Studies, Biblical Studies and Jewish studies have never failed to benefit from the writings of Bryan Wilson and references to his work are replete in studies that have sought to apply sociology to ancient Judaism. The All Souls Seminar in the Sociology of Religion – a regular meeting of scholars and graduates at Oxford organized and chaired by Bryan Wilson, ensured that for over thirty years the sociology of religion thrived amidst the Ivory Towers. There are still others who had the privilege to study with Bryan Wilson, given the arrangements at the University of Oxford where students in theology were able to consult him or even be jointly supervised by him. The present author in fact transferred from the Faculty of Theology to the Faculty of Social Studies, thus altering the fact of joint supervision to sole supervision (and becoming a sociologist in the process!) whilst preparing my thesis on Weber and the Protestant Ethic. My transfer was achieved only with the support of Bryan Wilson, who, I recall, wrote from the States to secure it. I can still recall the feeling of trepidation that accompanied my visits, as a young graduate student at the age of twenty-two, to All Souls for a supervisory meeting, climbing the stairs of one of the Hawksmoor towers where his rooms were located. We, of course, often discussed matters Weberian and matters sectarian, especially the nature of the ideal type and the meaning of charisma and value-free approaches. Bryan Wilson was always sceptical of the desire to apply sociological insight to historical cases (and even more sceptical of my interest in matters textual), but he nonetheless generously gave of his professional time to help improve the arguments of others and to keep their normative commitments in check. The last letter I wrote to him (actually an email) informed him of the forthcoming Groningen meeting and the planned volume. I would have liked him to have cast his critical sociological eye over the collection presented here, but that is not to be.

Professor David J. Chalcraft
Cumbria, 2006.

Endnote

1. I would like to thank Philip Davies for the invitation to edit the collection and for his continuing interest, support and patience during the completion of the project. It is has indeed been a pleasure for me to edit a volume which contains the essay of a former teacher who I now count as friend and colleague.

Part I
MAX WEBER ON SECTS AND VOLUNTARY ASSOCIATIONS
WITH SPECIFIC REFERENCE TO SECOND TEMPLE JUDAISM

The Development of Weber's Sociology
of Sects: Encouraging a New Fascination

David J. Chalcraft

Despite a long fascination with his seminal contributions to the sociology of religion, Max Weber is often overlooked in the literature when it comes to his ideas about sects and sectarianism.[1] Or rather, on the occasions when he is mentioned his contribution to the sociology of sects is passed over very quickly. His founding figure status, not his ideas, are usually acknowledged before the author swiftly moves on to consider Troeltsch[2] or some later theorist considered more suitable to the task in hand either because they are thought of as faithful followers and extenders of Weber's own "undeveloped" ideas, or as having surpassed Weber's apparent limitations (e.g. Hunt, 2003: 34-35; Johnson, 1971; Jokiranta, 2001: 226; Stanton, 1992; Stark and Bainbridge, 1979: 122). Frequently, when Weber and Troeltsch are treated together as some kind of partnership the analysis is more often based on Troeltsch's ideas than on Weber's, with the result that the exposition of Weber's work is at best limited and at worst inaccurate and often wrong (e.g. Wilson, 1966: 209-10; 1988; Hill, 1973, McGuire, 1997: 142). It is typical for interpreters to suggest that where Weber's work held out potential then that potential was not fulfilled by Weber himself (since he did not apply his ideas in any works or did not return to the distinction and amplify it or some such) or, on an alternative track, to argue that Weber's work actually is severely limited. This is most notably because the church-sect typological distinction, with which he is credited, is seen as culturally specific and time-bound, reflecting a western and even a Christian-centric perspective that was imposed on other non-western cultural and social processes. In such discussions the interpreter often makes reference in passing (i.e. without page citation) to Weber's *Sociology of Religion* or to *The Protestant Ethic and the Spirit of Capitalism*, as if it was solely in these locations that Weber dealt with sects and that somehow or other they were the most significant discussions.

In this essay I intend to show, on the contrary, that there are a considerable number of texts and passages to be considered in reconstructing

Weber's ideas about sects and that doing so provides sufficient evidence that Weber attempted to move the church-sect dimension out of any potential culturally specific orientation. In the process I hope to contribute to the ongoing investigation into the biography of Weber's sociological projects (Tenbruck, 1989; Hennis, 2002a, 2002b) and remind readers of the range of Weber's ideas as they relate to sects. I begin with some observations on Weber's ideal-typical characterization of sects, before providing a survey of key writings that carry Weber's further conceptual and substantive treatments of sects. Throughout the survey I highlight the salient differences between texts that illuminate Weber's development of his sociology of sects.

Weber's Ideal-Typical Treatment of Sects
One way in which Weber's approach to the sociology of sects would appear to be limited to his own horizons is tied up with his ideal-typical methodology.[3] In the course of all his writings Weber does not develop an ideal type of a sect with a number of logically connecting attributes. He develops neither a generic type (under which all varieties of sects can be seen as a variation) nor a series of subtypes[4] (where a defining set of characteristics are firstly developed to identify a sect in general and then to further differentiate between different sects on the basis that the sects classified, whilst sharing the characteristics to "qualify" generally as a sect, vary in other ways to the extent that they are best thought of as a different type of sect). Rather, Weber prefers a polar-type construction, and highlights one feature in particular as essential to understanding the difference between a sect-like religious movement and a church-like religious movement, and for assessing the cultural significance of either.

The defining feature of a sect in Weber's polar type construction is that of *a religious community founded on voluntary membership achieved through qualification.* Why this element is of causal significance for Weber within his own research into the development of central features of Western cultural development is because in order to join a sect the potential member must bring their conduct and lifestyle to the standard demanded by the Sect (if not already plainly of that standard) or have their conduct brought into line through a process of sectarian education. Either way everyday life is affected. Weber is interested in the variable impact of sects on everyday life, in particular on practical conduct, on economic life – or even more precisely, on the development of the unique bourgeois *Lebensführung* of western modernity. Because of this overriding interest it is this feature of the sect he emphasizes most strongly and is often the dominant question Weber is posing to any sect-like religious movement he is considering. This variable is then considered to be the most significant in accounting for the impact of religious movements on cultural and social change; in particular in accounting for the differing impacts of religious movements that are more or less church-like or sect-like.

As his work develops across time, the church-sect typology is placed in a much broader sociological context of comparative historical work, to the extent that the concept of sect and the concept of church become one instance of wider phenomena of a conflict between, for example, virtuosity and mass religion, between office charisma and personal charisma and between the differences between voluntary associations and compulsory organizations. Moreover, it is fairly obvious from the start that the ideal-typical discussion does not mean to imply that a sect can only come into existence if there is a prior parent orthodoxy or church against which it protests. In fact, to read the ideal type in this way is indeed to render the tool culturally specific to the emergence of sects in western Europe during a period when the Church and State were undifferentiated. This latter point becomes clearer in passages in *Economy and Society* and elsewhere which illustrate that Weber rejected one or two common criteria in talking about sects, which clearly indicates that for Weber a sect does not need a parent, nor an orthodoxy or a church to "qualify" as a sect in Weber's sociology.

The definition of the essential feature of the sect as opposed to "church" is consistent across the work, but the implications of this essence are drawn out in differing directions given the context of the discussion at different points in Weber's oeuvre. It is very important to understand how this process unravels in Weber's development, and the manner in which the church-sect typology is transformed. I argue that this transformation renders the church-sect typology of more universal sociological application than the seemingly ethno-centric concepts of church-sect, as first formulated (and as received in the history of the sociology of religion), would seem to imply.[5]

The Texts wherein Weber Discusses Sects
The development of Weber's thinking about sects needs to be traced as it develops over the course of his entire oeuvre in particular texts. The following texts have been selected as being the most significant for purposes of mapping out Weber's central ideas and their development.[6] The "Protestant Ethic writings" are essential, and include the two editions of *The Protestant Ethic and the Spirit of Capitalism* (Weber, 1904b, 1905, 1920a) and all the versions of the essay which eventually became *The Protestant*

Sects and the Spirit of Capitalism (1906a, 1906b, 1920b). The speeches Weber made at the First German Sociological Association's conference in 1910 often relate to our theme (Weber, 1924), and I concentrate on one in particular where, in the second half of his report as Treasurer to the Society (the *Geschäftsbericht*) Weber calls for the development of a sociology of voluntary associations which includes the sect (Weber, 1924: 442-49; Weber, 2002b; Kim, 2002). Attention is then turned to Weber's two major writing projects, both beginning in 1910 and remaining incomplete at his death, namely, the sociology compendium, *Economy and Society* (ES) (Weber, 1968), and the *Economic Ethics of the World Religions* Series (EEWR).[7] In relation to the former the sections most pertinent to Weber's discussion of sects include that entitled, *Political and Hierocratic Domination* (PHDom) (Weber, 1968: 1158-211) and in relation to the latter, I concentrate, albeit briefly, on the two more conceptual essays from the series, the *Introduction* (*Einleitung*) (Weber, 1948c) and the *Intermediate Reflections (Zwischenbetrachtung)* (Weber, 1948b). For reasons of space no mention is made of the individual substantive studies from EEWR – *Ancient Judaism* (Weber, 1952), *The Religion of India* (1958) and the *Religion of China* (1951), although these studies are key to the consideration of the cross-cultural applicability of Weber's conceptualizing of the sect and will be returned to in later expositions.

The Development of Weber's Treatment of Sects: A Survey of Relevant Texts

The Protestant Ethic and the Spirit of Capitalism *(1904–1905 and 1920)*
Although *The Protestant Ethic* (PE) is perhaps Weber's most famous work in the sociology of religion, and although he emphasizes the importance of Calvinism and of the Baptist sects for his thesis, it is not actually in this work that Weber presents his most developed ideas about sects; and this is the case, even though he revised the text of the PE in 1920 (leading one to assume that later findings about sects would be incorporated in the revisions)[8] after further research in the comparative sociology of religion.

It is in the first edition of PE (Weber, 1904–1905), in the second essay that makes up that whole (1905 = 1930: 95-183), that we encounter Weber's first formal statements about the nature of sects and how they should be distinguished from "church." Weber clearly says in the PE that his main concern is not with issues of organization and discipline of either Church or Sect; he is concerned with ethical practical conduct and the reasons for the differences between the practical conduct of various religious groups and what the *dogmatic* as well as the *psychological* factors were that influenced that conduct.

There are two main themes in the treatment of sects in the PE. First, that a sectarian tendency derives from notions of an aristocracy of the religious which encourages differentiation of individuals from each other on religious grounds which is a logical working out of certain theological doctrines; and, second, Weber provides a treatment not of a sectarian tendency but of actual sects, where the sectarian tendency has reached its logical conclusion in the formation of the "believer's church." It is in this latter context that the clearest formulation of the church-sect typology is to be found within the PE. Weber explains as follows:

> This means that the religious community, the visible Church in the language of the Reformation Churches, was no longer looked upon as a sort of trust foundation (Fideikommisstiftung) for supernatural ends, an institution (Anstalt) necessarily including both the just and the unjust...but *solely as a community of personal believers* of the reborn, and only these (Gemeinschaft der persönlich Gläubigen und Wiedergeborenen und nur dies). In other words, not as a "church" ("Kirche"), but as "sect" (sondern als eine "Sekte") (1930: 144; 1920: 152-53).

The contrast church-sect, is here parallel to the contrast between *Anstalt* and *Gemeinschaft* – the terminology used to contrast church and sect will alter across time as we shall see. The footnote discussion to this definitional statement needs a little comment in this connection since Weber adds the important terminological words "Sekte" and "Kirche" to the footnote discussion, since these "technical" terms were not used in the footnote in the first edition (but are in the main text) and it is also clear that the contrast between "voluntary" (already in the first edition) and "compulsory" is made because of the relation between *Verein* (a form not used in the PE, where *Gemeinschaft* was the preferred term) and *Anstalt*, that Weber has developed in-between the two editions of the PE, as we shall see, and which include within them the sect and the church respectively (i.e. the church is an instance of an *Anstalt*). The footnote can be reconstructed as follows (italic indicates addition in 1920)

> such a religious community[9] could only be voluntarily (voluntaristisch) organised *as a sect, not compulsorily as a Church (als Sekte, nicht anstaltsmäs-sig: als Kirche)*, if it did not wish to include the unregenerate and thus depart from the Early Christian ideal. For the Baptist communities it was an essential of the very idea of their Church, while for the Calvinists it was an historical accident (1920: 153; 1930: 254).

Overall however, a comparison of the two editions as they relate to sects indicates that the majority of the variants that exist pertain mainly to the production of the later sect's essay and matters of bibliography. In other words, tracing the later development of Weber's treatment of sects must look outside the PE texts themselves to discover the trends. For the moment, I turn to consider the theme of "sectarian tendencies" that Weber develops in the original PE.

For Weber the Protestant Reformation led to an alteration in the institutional means available for the religiously motivated to address their needs, and led to a fundamental alteration in the organization and prevalence of ascetic practices in everyday life. The other worldly asceticism of the monks (to use terms Weber develops) is replaced by the inner-worldly asceticism of the ascetic Protestants. The motivated laity is increased in Weber's view given the impact of certain theological ideas that developed in the wake of the Reformation. For Weber, it requires the doctrinal developments within Calvinism, above all, and the *psychological* effects of those doctrines on individual believers to bring about the selection of inner worldly asceticism in the pursuit of the calling from a range of alternatives, and a commitment to it. Weber writes of the impact of the Calvinist reformation, following the Lutheran developments, on religious life in the following terms:

> The drain of asceticism from everyday worldly life had been stopped by a dam, and those passionately spiritual natures which had formerly supplied the highest type of monk were now forced to pursue their ascetic ideals within mundane occupations. But in the course of its development Calvinism added something positive to this, the idea of proving one's faith in worldly activity. Therein it gave the broader groups of religiously inclined people a positive incentive to asceticism. By founding its ethic in the doctrine of predestination it substituted for spiritual aristocracy of the monks (geistlichen Aristokratie der Mönche) outside of and above the world the spiritual aristocracy (geistliche Aristokratie) of the predestined saints (Heiligen) of God within the world. It was an aristocracy which, with its character indelebilis, was divided from the eternally damned remainder of humanity by a more impassable and in its invisibility more terrifying gulf than separated the monk of the Middle Ages from the rest of the world about him, a gulf which penetrated all social relations with its sharp brutality (Weber, 1930: 121; 1920: 120).

Weber continues by observing that it is the doctrinal possibility of an "aristocracy of an elect," that is, a sectarian tendency that could result in the development of actual sects.

With the notion of an aristocracy of the elect, Weber is moving towards the notion of *religious virtuosity* (and charisma) but does not use this term at this stage, preferring to use the term Aristocracy.[10] As will be seen, the role of sect membership itself in the formation of character and personality and in turn its impact on social and political change, is not elaborated by Weber in the PE essays: rather, the "aristocratic" observation is not developed in the direction of discussion of *qualification* for an association within the PE but as a description of *personal commitment* as a consequence of doctrinal developments, such as the doctrine of predestination. It should be clear that Weber's sociology of sects finds limited textual discussion in the PE itself. Rather, the "essay" that became, in the course of time, *The Protestant Sects and the Spirit of Capitalism* provides a much richer source.

"Churches" and "Sects" *1906*
The discussion of *"Churches" and "Sects": An Ecclesiastical and Socio-political Sketch* that first appeared in the *Frankfurter Zeitung* and then, almost unchanged, in the journal *Die christliche Welt* (1906b, hereafter CW) takes place through a series of observations about North American society that date back to Weber's visit of 1904, ostensibly to attend the St Louis World Fair, and on which he drew on countless occasions in other work, particularly other work dealing with sects. While it is obvious that in the PE in order to join the "Aristocracy of the Elect" the individual must qualify, it is only in the CW essay that Weber concentrates on the qualities that sects demand of their prospective members and which influence their decision to admit, *after extensive probing*, and concentrates on the fact that the membership must sustain these qualities once they are admitted under the *close monitoring and control* exercised by the sect

Focusing on the selection, probing, monitoring and the threat of expulsion operated by sects in the CW essay, is to highlight how sects maintained *discipline*. This discipline in these sects ensured, Weber argued, that certain ethical dispositions, particularly in economic life, were developed, performed, and expanded. The educative influence of the sects on individuals and through them the wider society is only possible given the nature of the discipline enforced: the two go hand in hand. Moreover, this educative influence ensures the survival in the economic struggle for existence of particular social groups that had a sectarian past, even in the secularizing society of contemporary America. The existence of sects has served to create the proliferation of secular voluntary associations organized on similar lines in contemporary America and the development of individual autonomy and responsibility through close involvement in these organizations.

In this manner Weber treats the topic of discipline in the sects that he announced in the PE would be discussed later. In the PE, the need for objective proof of election that motivates the individual to perform is for oneself and is not performed for the benefit of self through the eyes of others. Weber was interested in locating the forceful psychological energy that led Calvinist individuals to devote themselves with such commitment to the pursuit of a rational calling, which he found in their salvation anxiety. The ascetic sects also became committed to the rational calling as Weber will demonstrate, but the interest in the Baptist movement in the PE was to ascertain whether any new theological grounds for understanding the origin of the calling could be traced to that source. Weber answered in the negative. It is in the CW essay that the processes that led to the fostering of the commitment to the calling in the non-Calvinist ascetic Protestant movements is discussed.[11]

In the CW, Weber explains how the achievement of objective proof is obtained not only internally for the individual through their actions but externally through the approval of others who agree to admit the individual to the sect on the grounds that they have demonstrated their quality, and moreover continue to do so whilst a member. It is with the notion of *Selbstbehauptung* – of holding one's own in the midst of one's peers, and being able to affirm oneself and assert oneself within the association that Weber most fully captures the educative processes brought about by the sect, in its processes of selection and breeding that ensure the survival of the fittest types of characters and personality for success in the developing capitalistic way of life. The importance of self-assertion (Selbstbehauptung) that Weber describes in the CW becomes a constant feature of his writing about sects from this point on and is arguably one of his most important contributions to a renewed sociology of sects.

It is in the second part of the essay that Weber returns to a formal definition of the sect in contrast to the church, and he has carefully avoided any technical use of the terms "Sect" and "Church" until this point.[12] He writes

> A "church" claims to be an institution (Anstalt), a kind of divine gift in trust (Fideikomissstiftung) for the salvation of the souls of those who are *born into it*. These people are, as a matter of principle, the object of its ministrations, which are tied to its "office." A "sect" – according to the terminology used adopted here ad hoc, one that of course would not be used by the "sects" themselves – is, by contrast, a free community of individuals who *qualify* for membership on purely religious grounds. They are *accepted* into this community on the basis of a decision freely entered into by both sides (1906b, 210) (freie Gemeinschaft lediglich religiös qualifizierter Individuen, in welche der einzelne kraft beiderseits freier Entschließung aufgenommen wird).

The italics are Weber's own, and they highlight precisely the points Weber is making in the CW essay as compared with the PE (note there is no *Verein–Anstalt* contrast, but an *Anstalt–Gemeinschaft* contrast). The emphasis then is on qualification and acceptance with both parties making voluntary decisions: voluntary decisions to apply, to join and a voluntary decision to admit. Weber uses the idea of "office" in speaking of the *Anstalt* – irrespective of the officer the official of the Church has jurisdiction. Weber has yet to speak in terms of a contrast of the charisma of office versus personal charisma, but elements of what becomes a central sociological contrast under which the church-sect distinction eventually is subsumed (see further below) can be observed, since Weber emphasizes the qualities of the personal believer as the main element in sectarian thought: what counts is personal quality, and the individual succeeds and fails in relation to God, revelation, the community, the state and so on, on the basis of their own abilities and achievements. The leadership of the sect is selected not on the basis of an office already held, but on the basis of "the religious qualities already held" (215).

The Protestant Sects and the Spirit of Capitalism *(1920)*
As the first footnote to this essay indicates, the text is an expanded and revised version of the original 1906 "Churches and Sects" essays as appeared in the *Frankfurter Zeitung* and *Die christliche Welt*. Compared with 1906, certain elements remain but have been re-ordered, whilst some elements appear in a different context. Some of the themes of 1906 have been taken up and explored in more depth, whilst there is also a range of new material and by far a better documentation of the trends Weber is exploring. The origin of the sects essay in the "travel report" of Weber's visit to America in 1904 can still be seen clearly in the revision, and Weber is at pains in the new version to present his observations sequentially in the guise of a reconstructed ethnography, where original impressions are further tested against further data for confirmation or disconfirmation.

As we have seen, the PE focused on the process of proof with which the individual reassured themselves with regard to their own state of grace, and the 1906 essays focused on the processes of qualification and admittance of the individual to the sect and the educative influence of the sect, through the exercise of its discipline, on the individual and potentially and indirectly on the society as a whole. In continuity and contrast, the 1920 version, in terms of emphasis, *brings the actual community that carries out the admittance and discipline of the sect member into view.* The workings of the sectarian community include observations relating to the requirements of "brotherhood" within the sect. The most significant feature driving the community as a whole is to protect the purity of the sect, and this purity is the responsibility of the community itself with all individuals working together. Given Weber's stress in other texts on the rise of the autonomous and responsible individual, schooled in the hard discipline of the sects, this community focus stands out in contrast.

It is also in the 1920 essay that the two strands of Weber's analysis of the motivation of the ascetic Protestant that we have identified as being treated separately in the PE and the "Churches and Sects" essays respectively, are brought together. Namely, the proof to oneself and the proof to others that characterized the ascetic sectarian Protestant drive for assurance of salvation. Weber does this as follows:

> The premiums were placed upon "proving" oneself before God in the sense of attainting salvation – which is found in all Puritan denominations – and "proving" oneself before men in the sense of socially holding one's own within the Puritan sects. Both aspects were mutually supplementary and operated in the same direction: they helped deliver the "spirit" of modern capitalism, its specific *ethos*: the ethos of the modern *bourgeois middle classes* (Weber, 1948a: 321).

Weber, at this stage in 1920, is thereby able to bring these two strands together and effect an integration of the original PE essays and the original sects essays, without thereby loosing the central thrust of either with regard to the role of psychology and sect discipline respectively. It is surely significant that he does not alter the text of the PE itself in 1920 in these ways, relying only on indicating that these matters are discussed "in the following essay," by which he means the following essay in the first volume of the *Collected Essays in the Sociology of Religion*, namely: *The Protestant Sects and the Spirit of Capitalism*. In fact, in 1910, in the second and last reply to Rachfahl, Weber had already indicated the mutually reinforcing nature of these two strands which, all the while the PE remained unrevised or only supplemented by the early "Churches and Sects" essay was not widely acknowledged. Clearly, by 1920 Weber still holds to the mutually reinforcing nature of the two strands of the argument, but is perhaps even more committed to the fact that the original essays dealt with the psychological dimension of motivation, whereas the "sects essays" had as their subject the sociological impact of sect organization and discipline on the personality, character and motivation of the sect member.[13] Of course, sect discipline does not apply to those ascetic Protestants who remained "in the Churches."

In the 1920 presentation of *The Protestant Sects and the Spirit of Capitalism* the definitions of sect are not presented formally, but in a more discursive fashion such that Weber's thinking in this respect needs to be reconstructed from various points in the essay. One of the reasons for this difference is perhaps given by Weber in the first footnote where he says that, given the work of Troeltsch, formal discussion of sect is unnecessary, and he refers the reader "back" to PE(!).[14] He writes,

> It is crucial that sect membership meant a *certificate* of moral qualification and especially of business morals for the individual. This stands in contrast to membership in a "church" into which one is "born" and which lets grace shine over the righteous and the unrighteous alike. Indeed, a church is a corporation which organises and administers religious gifts of grace, like an endowed foundation. Affiliation with the church is, in principle, obligatory, and *hence proves nothing with regard to the member's qualities*. A sect, however, is a voluntary association of only those who, according to the principle, are religiously and morally qualified. If one finds voluntary reception of his membership, *by virtue of religious probation*, he joins the sect voluntarily (1948a: 305-306).[15]

Weber uses the fact that in American society there is a "convergence of the sects" (that is, they increasingly avoid discussing their dogmatic differences to promote the ethical dimension which they all share) as a way of entering the point that what the sects all share, sociologically speaking, is the system of admittance. Of course, as above, Weber retains the all important and forever constant conception of the voluntary nature of the organization, but he adds more detail to the process – including now, the *ballot and the probation*. These two latter features have a communal point: the ballot means that all members vote on the admittance in the light of the probation that is performed in full view, as it were, of the entire congregation. Weber writes:

> It does not matter whether one be Freemason, Christian Scientist, Adventist, Quaker, or what not. What is decisive is that one be admitted to membership by "ballot," after *examination* and an ethical *probation* in the sense of the virtues that are at a premium for the inner-worldly asceticism of Protestantism and hence, for the ancient puritan tradition. Then, the same effect could be observed (1948a: 307).

Once again the distinction between the compulsory and the voluntary can be seen – (*Anstalt* and *Verband* – note *Verein* is not used and neither is *Gemeinschaft*). The distinction between the charisma of the office and personal charisma and the perennial conflicts between their claims for authority can be detected in the distinction between *Anstalt* and *Verband* but the elaboration of these types is not to be found here, but elsewhere (see further below).

Weber on Sects at the First German Sociological Conference, Frankfurt 1910

Thus far we have considered the body of writing that is directly concerned with the discussion of sects within branches of Protestantism. We now turn to consider a different body of writing that serves to extend Weber's ideas about sects beyond their original confines. We begin with the Business Report Weber made to the German Sociological Association in 1910.

It is in this piece, more than any other, that the analysis of sects is placed firmly in the context of the sociology of associational life (taking further the observations made in 1906 about the sectarian origin of American associational life). The sect is now considered alongside other forms of associations, thus rendering the sect one form of association. The emphasis is less on the process of joining and acceptance of an individual by a sect or association. It is now almost taken for granted by Weber that membership of a sect, club or association, especially where examination and/or rigid testimonials are required – is a certification of whatever values are esteemed by the organization. The emphasis is *now more on what types of transformation of individual and society might occur through membership of an association*: the implication being that a range of character formations and a range of social implications are possible given the array of associations in any one modern society. That is, Weber is not only concerned with the formation of ascetic Protestant characters at the hands of the protestant sects. Weber has established to his satisfaction that ascetic Protestant sects played a significant role in the education of the Puritan and the spread of capitalistic ways of being, notably a commitment to rational work in a calling; and that American associational life is a secularized version of sectarian life: hence membership in one type of voluntary association – namely, the sect – has been shown to have had an impact on character and on social change. Weber is now interested in extending the purview to consider the variety of impact of an array of associations, including further sects, on character formation and cultural development. Not only will the individual develop the skills required to "hold one's own" – and whatever these skills are will impact significantly on the character development of the individual within the organization – but will also make adjustments in their own personality and values in order to retain self-esteem: Weber suggests asking how this psychological equilibrium is achieved by individuals in differing associations. Or rather, Weber is concerned to persuade his colleagues in the Sociological Association that they should devote some of their energies and resources to developing sociology of voluntary associations (Vereinswesen).

The speech is important for a number of reasons, especially for us because it is on this occasion that the contrast between "Church and Sect" is subsumed under the wider generic and more significant contrast of *Anstalt* and *Verein*. Indeed, *Kirche*, makes only one appearance in the whole speech, whereas *Sekte/Sekten* occurs more frequently in accordance with a speech about voluntary associations. There are two consequences at least of Weber's "extension" of the concept of Sect to be one instance of a *Verein* (a *Verein* based on qualification after examination which involves withdrawal from the non-qualified): first, literary, artistic and professional movements can be understood as sects and, second, the realization that not all sects are of the type of ascetic Protestant sects which provided Weber with the original data for the construction of the polar typology.

As an example of the extension of the concept of sect to include non-religious movements, read what he says about Freudian psychoanalysis:

> ...a particular theory created by a famous Viennese psychiatrist, has led to the founding of a sect, which has gone so far as to close its meetings to non-members and hold its meetings in secret. The "complex-free" person as the ideal, and a form of life conduct through which such a complex-free person can be created and preserved, is the object of this sectarian activity, and almost all aspects of life can be regulated according to those ideals (Weber, 2002: 206).

In the course of the presentation, Weber reminds his audience of the definition of sect, and we meet once again an articulation of important points.

> For the nature of a sect lies in its being a combination of specifically qualified people and not an "institution" (Anstalt), and its socio-structural principle involves a rejection of those sanctions typical of an authoritarian organisation (Zwangverbände) such as the state or the church. It *has* to be a "voluntary association" (2002b: 201, cf. 1924: 442).[16]

Once again the importance of qualification and the voluntary dimension of the sect is stressed. Now, of course, the nature of that qualification – whether of business ethics or other particular religious or ethical virtues – are not mentioned, since it is now, as compared to the writings of 1904, 1905 and 1906, possible to speak of Verein in general, and hence of sects considered more generally too. Weber extends the notion of sect to include non-religious, artistic or other worldview/professional associations, and in the process not only makes a methodological point about *Wertfreiheit* but shows how his thinking has moved beyond thinking of the sect as existing only in the religious sphere (and in some ways echoes the wider use of sect/sectarian in the Russia essays of 1906 where partisan political movements were said to have sect-like characteristics; see Weber, 1995)

> At this juncture, I feel compelled to mention that, as always, the term "sect" is employed here in a manner quite free of value-judgement. The term seems to have a particularly negative connotation for no reason other than it is linked to ideas of "narrowness." Specific, firmly articulated ideals can be brought into life in no way other than in the founding of a sect whose enthusiastic followers strive to realise them fully, and who therefore unite with one another and set themselves *apart* from others (Weber, 2002b: 206-207).

This statement is one of the few in which Weber does not utilize the criteria of an association based on the voluntary membership of individuals who have proved themselves after examination to qualify (though clearly an individual most show the appropriate skills and attributes in order to join the relevant association – as he has mentioned in this speech already); Weber also does not imply that a sect follows from a desire to separate the saved from the unsaved, the qualified from the unqualified, but rather points *to the sect as the only vehicle for systematically pursuing certain ideals in everyday life*. It is the holding of the ideals that qualifies the individual for membership in a sect, and this holding of the ideals differentiates them from those who do not, and this differentiation is followed to the conclusion that the ideals cannot be pursued or enacted unless the "qualified" withdraw from the "unqualified." It is clear to see how Weber's sociology of the sect begins to address the problem – one not encountered with the Baptist sects – that certain ideals when pursued in a sectarian organization, will not impact on the wider society and whose achievement may not entail the "type of education for public rational life" Weber has in mind. Some ideals lead to the formation of sects that promote mystical flight rather ascetic rationalism. Not all sects, from Weber's point of view, so to speak, are "good," but Weber was always impressed with attempts to articulate firmly-held beliefs rather than to hold no beliefs at all. The more sectarian movements Weber includes the more likely the fact that some sects will not carry out the educative role seen in the ascetic Protestant sects.[17]

The Einleitung *(1915)*

The development of the church-sect typology and the analysis of sectarian movements is not a central concern of the two key essays to be considered here from Weber's series, *The Economic Ethics of the World Religion*

(EEWR), the *Einleitung* and the *Zwischenbetrachtung*. Rather, the church-sect typology reappears in continuity with previous analysis, but is placed in a comparative context (continuing the widening of the concept that we observed in the 1910 *Business Report*) that has important implications for our understanding of its meaning and development.[18]

The theme of the "aristocracy of believers" (found in the original PE) is given firm expression, and extended to include the comparative framework of the EEWR, even though the term "aristocracy" as such is not utilized (to avoid confusion with the *social* status group). The ascetic sectarians we have encountered previously are now to be understood as "virtuosos," and as virtuosos can be compared with similar heroic pursuers of particular sacred values in different times and religious traditions. The *Einleitung* is the *locus classicus* of the presentation of specific social classes as carriers of types of practical religious ethics in Weber's sociology; in this regard the following statement is striking and should perhaps stand at the beginning of any analysis of Weber's sociology of sects. He writes:

> The empirical fact, important for us, that men [*sic*] are differently qualified in a religious way stands at the beginning of the history of religion (Weber, 1948c: 287).

The central point in this "stratification of charisma" is, that whatever the sacred values might happen to be, they "could not be attained by everyone"; rather, "the possession of such faculties is a 'charisma,'" and this can cut across all other ascriptive and achieved titles. We recall that the predestined sectarians of Calvinism had to demonstrate their worth. Their worth is their charismatic ability. It is clear, however, that Weber in the *Einleitung* is not talking only or restrictively of the ascetic Protestants but of all religious movements that value particular charismatic gifts that lead to redemption, whether that be dancing, healing, magic, prophecy, self-denial, feats of endurance, spiritual insight, or ritual cleanliness and fulfilment of the prescriptions of ritual law. Weber's observation has universal application. It is meant as a comparative device not restricted to any specific culture or time period or religious tradition. Further, the charismatic gifts are not restricted to either the ascetic or mystic aspects of religious rejections of the world, but the powers of the mystic are also seen as charismatic.

The main difference Weber is seeking to convey is between the religiosity of the charismatically endowed (and the followers of the charismatic must too demonstrate their charisma, thus forming a charismatic community – a term not actually used by Weber, be it noted, in *this* essay) and those who are not. Hence the typological contrast here is not one between ascetic/mystic, nor one of social organization of the religious community as church-like or sect-like, nor between priest and charismatic magician or prophet, between institution and voluntary association, but rather *between the virtuoso religion and the religion of the masses* (those who do not display the charismatic qualities valued in the movement); a contrast, that is, between virtuoso religiosity and the religiosity of the everyday (Alltagsreligiosität). As Weber, observes, "It follows from this that all intensive religiosity has a tendency toward a sort of status stratification, in accordance with differences in the charismatic qualifications. "Heroic" or "virtuoso" religiosity is opposed to mass religiosity" (1948c: 287).

Weber provides a list of carriers of charisma/virtuoso religiosity which serves to place "sect" in a comparative framework which takes it strictly outside of any culture –bounded, church-sect typology, since it is but one incarnation of a wider trend or of other typical conflicts. Weber illustrates who the "status carriers of a virtuoso religion" have been, and they include, the leagues of sorcerers and sacred dancers, religious status groups of the Indian Sramana, early Christian ascetics, Pauline and Gnostic pneumatics, Pietist ecclesiola, and – Weber says explicitly – "all genuine sects." "That is, sociologically speaking, associations (Verbände) that accept only religiously qualified persons in their midst." And finally, Weber concludes the list by including "monk communities all over the world" (Weber, 1948c: 287-88).

Just as a sect is now treated as one instance of much broader and universal typological contrast, so too is the contrasting type of elite, the "church." For the church is defined by Weber, in a non-culturally specific way as, "a community organised by officials into an institution which bestows gifts of grace" (1988: 260: "einer anstaltsmässig mit Beamten organisierten gnadenspenden Gemeinschaft").

He continues:

> This means that the church stands for a universalism of grace and for the ethical sufficiency of all those who are enrolled under its institutional authority. Sociologically, the process of levelling constitutes a complete parallel with the political struggles of the bureaucracy against the political privilege of the aristocratic estates (ständischen Aristokratie) (1988: 288).

In many ways, this definition of the Church is not at odds with what we have encountered previously, and the idea of the church as an institution (Anstalt) that administers grace to all, is a direct continuation of earlier definitions (as indeed there is continuity with the definition of sect); yet, its context renders the concept universal and comparative: the specific form of any specific Church in Western Europe (e.g. the Catholic Church during the Middle Ages) is but one example of a "community organised by officials" and hence can be contrasted not only with sect, but also with monastery and any other religious movement that is not organized by officials into an institution which bestows "gifts of grace." It seems to me that through talking of virtuosity as the ground for social status differentiation with regard to religion, Weber has taken the sectarian tendencies he observed within Protestantism, and universalized them to be part of a tendency to virtuosity that characterizes all religions. Just as sect was one form of voluntary association it is also one form of virtuosity. Hence sects can develop in any tradition that tends towards virtuosity, just as sects can develop in theological traditions that develop doctrines of the just and the unjust, the saved and the reprobate, and the withdrawal of the elect from the non-elect. Yet this tendency to virtuosity does not have a simple one-to-one relationship with the pre-existent class and status structure of any society since the membership of the virtuosity, in theory at least, elevates the individual beyond that stratification system and transcends it.

Zwischenbetrachtung *(1915)*

We can only touch the surface of the essay, since I only need mention those aspects that are directly relevant to the discussion of sects. Sects are not directly treated within the essay, but it is important to note that Weber utilizes fully the mysticism/asceticism typological contrast, which also appeared in the *Einleitung* and in the earlier reply to Troeltsch's presentation at the German Sociological Association's first conference in 1910, in which Troeltsch spoke of three typological developments in Christianity, Church, sect and mysticism (Weber, 1924). The association between mysticism and Troeltsch's typology of sect and church can lead interpreters to see Weber's conception of mysticism in similar terms. However, Weber typologically contrasts church and sect, and asceticism and mysticism, but there can be mystic churches and mystic sects and so on. We are led to consider, therefore, what might happen to the conception of a sect when mystic religiosity can frame the typological treatment of the church-sect continuum.

The main concern of the essay is the exploration of the conflicts between religion and various "world orders." Weber's interest is how the "religion of brotherliness" comes into conflict with values, principles and goals that characterize the operation of the economy, or of the state. The essay is notable, amongst other things, for describing the experience of the modern world as a disenchanted environment. But most significantly, this essay, taking up where the *Einleitung* leaves off, develops the distinction between asceticism and mysticism into four types of abnegation of the world, and it is within these typologies that the formation of sects, and of groups of virtuosos, of both mystical and ascetic varieties, can be understood.

Since Weber began, back in 1904–1905, with the *Protestant Ethic* study, it is clear that by this stage of the development of the sociology of religion, the ascetic Protestants are but one type of a range of possible responses to the world; but they are, of course, of great significance in Weber's account of the rise of western rationalism. Some of the reasons for this reside in the fact that the rationalism of their system of thought and action meant that consistent answers to theodicy issues and to the tensions between religion and other value spheres of the world, were provided. Herein lies its power over individuals and its appeal for those searching for meaning: the search for meaning being a fundamental drive for the individual in Weber's anthropology. But ascetic Protestantism was not the only response to the world that was capable of consistency or of forming sects of virtuosos. For example, in terms of the conflict between the ethic of brotherliness and the sphere of the economy (especially the modern rationalized capitalist economy), mysticism also has a consistent response (but if widespread would have totally different consequences for society than those brought about by Protestantism), as follows: "Mysticism is a unique escape from this world in the form of an objectless devotion to anybody, not for man's sake but purely for devotion's sake, or, in Baudelaire's words, for the sake of 'the soul's sacred prostitution'" (1948b: 333/1988: 546). The mystic gives away all she has irrespective of who asks for it.

Just as in 1910 Weber extended the purview of his ideas about sects to include voluntary associations, which could be organized on the basis of a range of differing values and have variable impacts on the development of ascetic personalities, the *Zwischenbetrachtung* brings out clearly that not all associations in the religious sphere will be ascetic Protestant sects, but a variety of forms is possible along the whole gamut of ascetic-mystic configurations. In other words, even though Weber will never abandon the centrality of the ascetic Protestant sects for the education of the modern individual required by capitalistic culture, and even though non-ascetic sects will often be considered in relation to the nature of the ascetic Protestant sects, Weber's comparative historical sociological vision is not compromised to the extent that he cannot "see" alternative forms of significance and importance.

Economy and Society (1914–1920)

By far the most involved discussion of sects in ES is in the section, *Political and Hierocratic Domination* (Weber, 1968: 1158-211) which closely follows, thematically and chronologically, the discussions of Charisma (Weber, 1968: 1111-57) (itself one of three types of domination). The thematic connection between these sections is also anticipated in the *Basic Sociological Terms*.[19] It is significant that it is not in the *Sociology of Religion* (Weber, 1968: 399-634) but within the wider discussion of types of domination (the *Herrschaftssoziologie*) that Weber mostly draws on his knowledge of sects.

Political and Hierocratic Domination

Turning to the PHDom chapter itself we find that Weber repeats, as he has so often before, the typological contrast between church and sect; in this instance he is fleshing out the relation between the church and office charisma on the one hand, and of the sect with personal or virtuoso charisma, on the other. In this way, the development of the concept of sect from the PE through to the EEWR series, where virtuosity was a key focus, reaches its final embellishment (to which it has been logically progressing throughout Weber's thinking), namely: *that the sect is a community of charismatic individuals.* Those ascetic Protestants who formed themselves into a sect and admitted only qualified members, were virtuosos, and their virtuosity was a sign of their charisma. In the case of the ascetic Protestants the charisma proved itself through the ability to successfully and continually devote oneself to a calling. In the following definition, the centrality of charisma to the conception of sect, is quite visible. Indeed, it is here for the first time that the concept of "charisma" and the concept of "sect" are explicitly mentioned together (by name).

> Sociologically, the church differs from the sect by considering itself the trustee of a "trust fund" of eternal blessings that are offered to everyone; as a rule, it is not joined voluntarily, like an association, but its members are born into it; hence, even those who lack religious qualification, who are heretical, are subject to its discipline. In one word, the church is the bearer and trustee of an *office charisma, not a community of personally charismatic individuals,* "als eine Gemeinschaft rein persönlich charismatisch qualifizierter Personen" [my italics] like the sect (Weber, 1968: 1164 ; cf. Weber, 1985: 692).

The essential point of Weber's analysis therefore, which colours all of the later discussions, is not a church-sect distinction as such, but rather a focus on the differential nature of charisma and the tendency to form groups of aristocratic ways of life. When a sect is considered as a prime example of charismatic virtuosity that forms communities to which only the qualified, after proof, can belong, the possibility and existence of sects in cultural environments that lack an orthodoxy or a developed organization of hierocratic domination is probable.

As such one does not necessarily need an orthodoxy or a church to have a sect since the sect is made up of groups of persons who happen to have the qualities revered in the society or the specific social group in greater degree than others, hence forming an aristocracy of virtuosos. The "church" is not to be thought of as "the remainder" nor the "mass." What is required is the existence of sacred values that are esteemed and sought after. Sects then clearly emerge in a context; the charismatic gifts need only be "out of the ordinary" and a challenge to everyday life.

This relates also to Weber's major distinction between asceticism and mysticism: or various forms of world negation which was introduced in the *Einleitung* and further developed in the *Zwischenbetrachtung*. The virtuosos could be mystical or ascetic. Where asceticism is not present the aristocracy of *ascetic* virtuosity can not emerge: hence one is less likely to find ascetic sects or ascetic monks; equally, where mysticism is not present as a religious value or is not highly esteemed, then an aristocracy of mysticism is less likely to emerge. Further, it is more likely for ascetic virtuosity (especially of the inner-worldly type) to develop into sectarian organizations since inner-worldly asceticism proves itself in the world, and in association; mysticism proves itself individually, and hence does not often occasion sects.

It is important to note what Weber says towards the end of the quotation above, since he explicitly mentions where a "church" may exist in non-western, non-Christian traditions. The quotation continues: "In the full sense of the term, churches have arisen only in Islam and Lamaist Buddhism, apart from Christianity: in a more restricted sense, because of the *national* delimitation, churches were also created by Mahdism, Judaism and, apparently, the ancient Egyptian hierocracy" (Weber, 1968: 1164).

Conclusion

The analysis above argues that there is much more to Weber's treatment of sects within in his sociology than the reception history of Weber in the sociology of religion and related sub-disciplines would suggest. On these grounds, it is time we renewed our fascination with a Weberian approach to a sociology of sects and began to undertake renewed analysis of sects from a Weberian point of view. Not only are there a significant number of texts in which Weber writes about sects but these texts, when closely examined, exhibit elaborations and developments that demand attention. Moreover, the developments that can be observed demonstrate a continuity in Weber's emphasis on the role of voluntary membership after proven examination as an essential ideal-typical characterization of sects at the same time as the church-sect distinction is subsumed within and articulated alongside Weber's development of concepts of asceticism and mysticism, virtuosity and mass religiosity, personal and office charisma and the organizational distinction between voluntary associations and compulsory organization. These developments, it is argued, serve to make Weber's ideal-typical characterization of sects applicable in a comparative historical sociology. It also needs to be appreciated however, that Weber's project was a specific one and directed to answering a central cultural issue of his own time: namely, the rise of western rationalism and the impact of various social forms on the formation of types of character and personality. It is on account of these specific enquiries that Weber chooses to accentuate the feature of voluntary membership after examination as central to his ideal-typical characterization of sects. When we do not share Weber's particular questions it is probable that Weber's ideal types appear less suited to our purposes. But then, Weber knew that. However, it is possible to adapt Weber's specific question about the rise of personalities suited to the economic rationalism and life-style of modern capitalistic culture into a more general question that Weber had to pose whilst researching his specific question: namely, to ask what types of personality are formed in a variety of movements and organizations including sects and voluntary associations. In other words, with respect to a sociology of sects to develop an historical comparative sociology concerned with the nature, formation, types and significances of sectarian personalities.

Endnotes

1.　*The Max Weber Dictionary: Key Words and Central Concepts* (Swedberg, 2005) is a good place to begin to gain an overview of Weber's work, and Kaesler's *Max Weber: An Introduction to his Life* and *Work*, follows closely the development of Weber's texts and has a valuable chapter on Weber's biography. *Max Weber: A Comprehensive Bibliography* (Sica, 2004), provides an essential guide to works in English. Also worth consulting are the introductions to Weber in various dictionaries and encyclopaedias, including Chalcraft (2006), Scaff (1998) and Whimster (2001). Freund's *The Sociology of Max Weber* (1968) is still useful, and for the sociology of religion the reader cannot fail to benefit from Schluchter's *Rationalism, Religion and Domination: A Weberian Perspective* (1989). For definitive German texts the on-going critical edition of the Max Weber Gesamtausgabe is indispensable.

2. The precise relation between Weber's and Troeltsch's projects in the sphere of the sociology of protestant ethics and the typologies of church, sect and mysticism are not discussed in this essay, nor do I discuss the complex friendship that existed between them in relation to their professional lives. For the moment see Graf (1987, 2004) and Drescher (1992). It is also of interest to compare Weber's treatment of sects with those of both previous and contemporary writers (theologians, historians, novelists, etc.) other than Troeltsch to gain a measure of Weber's uniqueness.

3. One of Weber's first references to the church-sect distinction is actually in the course of presenting his account of ideal types and concept formation, in his essay that predates "The Protestant Ethic," namely, "Objectivity in Social Science and Social Policy," published in 1904 (Weber, 1949). The quotation brings out clearly the way in which the feature highlighted in one type of religious movement/organization is highlighted precisely in relation to the absence or presence or difference of that same feature in other religious movements. He wrote "...the ideal type is an attempt to analyse historically unique configurations or their individual components by means of genetic concepts. Let us take for instance the concepts 'Church' and 'Sect.' They may be broken down purely classificatory into complexes of characteristics whereby not only the distinction between them but also the content of the concept must constantly remain fluid. If however, I wish to formulate the concept of 'sect' genetically, e.g., with reference to certain important cultural significances which the 'sectarian spirit' has had for modern culture, certain characteristics of both become *essential* because they stand in an adequate causal relationship to those influences." Weber, 1949: 93-94 (his italics; original, 1904).

4. Bryan Wilson provides the most sophisticated version of a multiple typology. The relation between the work of Wilson (1959, 1963, 1969, 1973, 1990) and Weber is a complex one which deserves a separate analysis. Wilson's work is certainly neo-Weberian (in spirit if not in letter), and is a highly significant contribution to the reception history, but the extent to which they would have agreed in relation to the former's analysis of secularization or of the process of concept formation is open to debate, especially since Wilson's reception of Weber took place during the period of the dominance of the appropriation of Weber for American sociology by Talcott Parsons (1902–1979) and his structural-functional/social-action type of analysis. In other words, we might need to "de-Wilsonise" the reading of Weber on sects, much like others have argued for "de-Parsonising Weber."

5. Since Weber, when first formulating the ideal-typical contrast – in the Objectivity essay as an example, and then, soon afterwards, in PE – did not have any context in mind other than medieval and post-Reformation Christianity, it is reasonable to suggest that he was not consciously envisaging a comparative historical application of the concept and hence was very much thinking within the confines of trajectory in western Euorpe. I am conscious that there are various features of Weber's analysis of sects that could be taken as being more or less culturally specific, even when full cognizance is taken of the fact that Weber knowingly interrogated the historical record with a particular set of (culturally relevant) research questions. For example, it is clear that the ascetic Protestant sects are a constant source of comparison for any other sect movement in history in Weber's account and hence no other sect movement is ever considered, as it were, on its own terms but always in relation to

a pre-established finding. Further, the emphasis Weber gives to the development of character by means of "holding one's own in the presence of one's peers," could well reflect a range of cultural experiences that were specific to a particular class and gender Weber was familiar with. For reasons of space these dimensions of the continuing legacy of Weber's sociology of sects will have to await a future occasion to be discussed.

6. What is not discussed here includes: passages in the Sociology of Religion (in ES) which overlap with passages in the EEWR; the treatment of sects in Weber's examination of the Russian revolutions of 1905 and 1917 (see Weber, 1995, but note that the English edition does not carry all the relevant sections dealing with Russian sects) nor the treatment of sects in his sociological studies of India and China; I have also excluded Weber's discussion of sects in the Anti-kritiken, namely, those Replies to the first critics of the PE (Weber, 2001; Chalcraft 2001, 2002), in particular the exchanges with Rachfahl (Chalcraft, 2005), and I have chosen not to discuss the important exchange with Toennies and Troeltsch that took place at the first German Sociological Association's conference in 1910 (Weber, 1924: 462-69). Analysis of these texts must await a later occasion as does Weber's attitudes to contemporary sectarian movements, such as those associated with Freudian analysis, the cult of the poet Stefan George, or other counter-cultural artistic, ascetic and mystical movements.

7. The EEWR series includes the studies of the religions of India (Weber, 1958), of China (Weber, 1951), and the study of Ancient Judaism (Weber, 1952). The texts, *The Protestant Ethic and the Spirit of Capitalism*, and *The Protestant Sects and the Spirit of Capitalism* are also part of the series in so far as they are collected together with the other studies in the three volumes of the *Collected Essays in the Sociology of Religion* (*Gesammelte Aufsätze zur Religionssoziologie*). The series also includes an introductory essay, the *Einleitung* (known in English as "The Social Psychology of the World Religions" (Weber, 1948c) and the "Intermediate Reflections" (Weber, 1948b). For the collection of the essays together, Weber also added a *Vorbemerkung* (known in English as the Author's Introduction and found in translation in Weber, 1930: 13-31).

8. Weber actually felt it unnecessary to revise the second edition of the PE with regard to sects in any significant manner because the very next essay to follow the PE in the first volume of the *Collected Essays in the Sociology of Religion* was The Protestant Sects essay in which the importance of the sects to the thesis was clearly presented.

9. In 1905 Weber had "als Kirche" changing it to, "religiöse Gemeinschaft" in 1920, apparently to avoid the echo in the added portions, and of course to create agreement in the use of *Gemeinschaft* between the main text and the footnote.

10. Weber means an aristocracy by "achievement" and not by "ascription," as we would say today, and in this way is using the term far more sociologically than Troeltsch, as he himself points out (Weber, 2002a: 218). "Virtuosity" is not used in this connection until post 1914.

11. I think it right to say that Weber already knew by the time of writing of the second PE essay that the sects operated in this fashion, since he had already visited America and he constantly indicates that the matter will be discussed. The idea for the CW essay, and before it, the FZ version, would have been in his mind from his return, and he wrote it up as soon as he could given all his other commitments.

12. It is noteworthy that Weber has avoided the use of the noun *Kirche* as much as possible in his exposition up to this point; and it is now at this juncture that he introduces the concept of Sect. Since the religious movements themselves do not call themselves sects but churches, one can used *Kirche*-like vocabulary but it is not appropriate to use the noun *Kirche*, or as it were, Church with a capital C, since America has no established Church. Weber will use a series of compound nouns, which in English require the separation of Church and community into discrete nouns, for example, but which in the original German indicate a different meaning. (In the FZ version the only times *Kirchen* appears, is once in the title, and twice in inverted commas: that is, in the sections dealing with the formal conceptual definition of the polar-type Church-Sect). *Kirche* equally appears in the majority of cases in inverted commas, illustrating a technical usage: the other occasions, are in the speech of the iron-goods tradesmen, and in the paragraph dealing with the statistics and the attitudes of the "populace" to their religious community, that is, their church. Overall then, we can say that Weber carefully chooses his vocabulary, and in this way the ideal-typical momentum of the piece is contained.

13. To turn to the relevant section (Weber, 2001: 109-12) of Weber's second reply to Rachfahl of 1910. First Weber reminds us (and Rachfahl!) of the aim of the PE essays: "I first had to explain the *characteristic* features of these [methodical life practices] practices and then their inner consistency and the absolute seamlessness with which they were lived out by every individual who grew up in the atmosphere these religious powers created-even if not *consciously* of course." Weber then proceeds to show where the second important dimension, that of the sects, fitted in relation to the preceding. "That these motives also found powerful supports in the various social institutions of the churches and in other institutions influenced by the churches and sects *I partly sought to indicate* briefly in my Archive essay and *partly* sought to illuminate more clearly in my outline in Christliche Welt. Let me *recapitulate*" (109, my italics).

14. It is comments such as these which invite interpreters to follow Weber's advice, and take his word at face value, and ignore Weber's own ideas about sects in favour of those Troeltsch or an earlier less sophisticated version of his own position. Such comments, in my view, are regrettable.

15. My italics. The original German reads: "Daß also die Sektenmitgliedschaft – im Gegensatz zur Mitgliedschaft einer Kirche, in die man 'hineingeboren' wird und die ihre Gnade über Gerechte und Ungerechte scheinen läßt – ein ethisches, insbesondere auch ein geschäftsethisches, Qualifikationsattest für die Persönlichkeit bedeutete. Eine 'Kirche' ist eben eine Gnadenanstalt, welche religiöse Heilsgüter wie eine Fideikommißstiftung verwaltet und zu welcher die Zugehörigkeit (der Idee nach!) obligatorisch, daher für die Qualitäten des Zugehörigen nichts beweisend, ist, eine 'Sekte' dagegen ein voluntaristischer Verband ausschließlich (der Idee nach) religiös-ethisch Qualifizierter, in den man freiwillig eintritt, wenn man freiwillig kraft religiöser Bewährung Aufnahme findet." It is significant to note that *Gnadenanstalt* (and *Fideikommissstiftung*) stands in typological opposition to "voluntaristischer Verband" showing the continuity with previous definitions we have examined. The note of obligation will be taken up in the context of Weber's discussion of domination and made a central concern (see below).

16. "Deshalb, weil die Sekte ihrem Sinn nach ein Zusammenschluss von spezifisch qualifizierten Menschen ist und nicht eine 'Anstalt', weil sie nach ihrem soziologischen Strukturprinzip die Sanktion der autoritaeren Zwangsverbände – Staat, Kirche – ablehnt und 'Verein' sein muss."

17. What is regrettable is that given Weber's concerns, and the fact that the German Sociological Association did not in the event support his proposals, the sociology of types of personality and leader and led that might develop in particular sects and voluntary associations were not studied in any depth by Weber, and, with only few exceptions, this aspect of his sociology has not received the attention it deserves. Indeed, the reception history of Weber on might read differently if the centre-piece of his enquiries was located, not in a dichotomous church-sect distinction, but as part of a general concern with personality types existing in various social orders, organisations and institutions. Work within the sociology of organizations and total institutions (e.g. Goffman, 1961), and the rise of the bureaucratic personality (Merton, 1968; Whyte, 1958) and so on, would then be seen as part of the legacy to encourage a theory of "the sectarian personality" for example. Considered in this way there is a line of continuity from Gerth and Mills earlier work (1954) to the examination of character in modernity undertaken by Riesman (1961) and more recently, by Richard Sennett (1973, 1998, 2003, 2004). Hennis (2002a, 2002b; Chalcraft, 2002) has tried to remind Weber scholars of this tradition.

18. In a later section I consider those sections of *Ancient Judaism* that deal with the Pharisees (published posthumously) and other movements in Second Temple Judaism, given our interest. But I will not be considering the substantive treatment of sects in either the China or the India study due to considerations of space. But we should note that Weber applies the sect typology to the analysis of Indian and China religious movements. Since the *Einleitung* and the *Zwischenbetrachtung* provide the main theoretical and conceptual "introduction" and "intermediate reflections" on Weber's project in the EEWR series, it is more than adequate as a means for discussing the treatment of sects within the whole series given our interest in developing an understanding of a Weberian Approach to the Sociology of Sects.

19. I do not have space to discuss here Weber's definitions of Church and Sect found in the Basic Categories (Section 17) section of Economy and Society or its relation to the earlier 1913 Logos version. These discussions are important not least because Weber becomes apparently more aware of the dimensions of physical coercion and domination in religious organizations but applies this to understanding the "Church" rather than the sect. The fact that an *Anstalt* is a compulsory institution is common across Weber's texts; the implications that "compulsory" involves the *coercive compulsion* of members who should belong and *de facto* do belong to the "church" becomes starker across the development of Weber's thinking about church-sect. "An organisation which *claims* authority only over voluntary members will be called a *voluntary association* (Verein); an organisation which *imposes*, within a specifiable sphere of operations, its order (with relative success) on all action conforming with certain criteria will be called a *compulsory organisation* or *association* (Anstalt)" (my italics; Weber, 1968: 52). Since for Weber the sect has a close relation to the development of individual autonomy, responsibility and democratic processes the possibility of physical coercion, and even the possibility of "damaging psychical coercion" does

not appear to figure in his sociology. In the section dealing with Church, Sect and Democracy (a subsection of PHDom [Weber, 1968: 1204-11] that we also cannot examine in detail here, Weber writes: "Rather, the sect is a group whose very nature and purpose precludes universality and *requires the free consensus of its members,* since it aims at being an aristocratic group (Aristokratisches Gebilde) an association of persons with full religious qualification" (Weber, 1968: 1204). The notion of the "aristocracy" that was present in the original PE essays can be seen echoed here, but there is no sense of the dark side of sectarian life to be sure.

Weber's Treatment of Sects in *Ancient Judaism*: The Pharisees and the Essenes

David J. Chalcraft

This chapter considers Weber's treatment of sects in Second Temple Judaism as found in his text *Ancient Judaism*.[1] In distinction to the analysis undertaken thus far, the concern, given the nature of the case, is less with uncovering Weber's further development of conceptual distinctions (though when these occur they will be noted) and more with approaching the text as an example of Weber, as it were, applying his knowledge and theories to a particular example. Given that our interest in developing a Weberian approach to the sociology of sects has as one of its main intentions a reconstruction of sects and sectarian movements within the society of Second Temple Judaism, it is of great interest to see Weber's sociology, so to speak, "in action." This seemed to be an appropriate place to begin before moving on to apply our own reconstruction of Weber's approach to sects to individual substantive cases. It is surely important to move towards the goal of a sociology of sects in Second Temple Judaism only after witnessing how Weber himself went about the task. Analysing Weber's approach to sects in ancient Judaism should alert us to the limitations as well as to the prospects of applying Weber. One essential difference between the context in which Weber worked and the context in which we find ourselves, is the fact that in Weber's day there was no knowledge of the Dead Sea Scrolls. The discovery of the scrolls in the late 1940s (Edmund Wilson, 1969) and their gradual publication and translation – a process that continues today (Davies, Brooke and Callaway, 2002) – presents an hiatus of great import. Before we can undertake a Weberian analysis of Second Temple Judaism and its sects it is necessary to appreciate what a Weberian analysis looked like prior to the discovery of the scrolls before moving on to produce a Weberian analysis post the discovery of the scrolls. It is with the former that this chapter is concerned. In the following chapter I develop a Weberian approach to the Qumran materials post 1947.

Approaching Ancient Judaism

One of the problems with reading *Ancient Judaism* is the feeling of a lack of anchorage that would be provided by knowing the methodological procedures, the conceptual apparatus, and the thematic issues that Weber was exploring in this study which is but one in the series of the EEWR. That is to say, that these preparatory elements are to be found, but outside of the text itself. This assessment applies equally to the section on the Pharisees and Essenes, even though this text was actually left unfinished at Weber's death, published separately and then included by Weber's wife, Marianne Weber, as an appendix to *Ancient Judaism*, the third volume to appear in the *Collected Essays in the Sociology of Religion*. One will not find, for example, a definition of sect within *Ancient Judaism*. Now that we have mapped the development of Weber's treatment of the concept of sect in his writing overall, and familiarized ourselves with other central features of his sociology of religion and domination (see above), we are in a better position to approach the specific treatment of sects in *Ancient Judaism*.

Weber on Pariah Status as a Sectarian Phenomena

Approaching *Ancient Judaism* as an example of Weber applying his sociological understandings of sects is to go against the grain of his intentions. Weber appears to be overwhelmingly concerned with arriving at the sociological essence of the phenomena of Jewry, and tracing the significant moments in its historical development that leave an indelible imprint on the religion. It was the emergence of the Jewish people as a collectivity with pariah status that most intrigued Weber, rather than the examination of the Pharisees and the Essenes, or any other movement for that matter, being an exercise in applying his concept of the sect to a variety of historical circumstances, or seeking out all examples of so-called sectarian behaviour and organization to formulate a universal typology and history. The latter types of sociological approach were not championed by Weber. There is a relation between sectarian tendencies and pariah communities, however, about which Weber was not unaware. The pariah community cannot be a sect in the ways Weber distinguished the sect, precisely on account of membership being *ascribed* in the former rather than *achieved*, through free will and acceptance after examination in the case of the latter. One might say that sectarian communities that have withdrawn into vicinal segregation, either intentionally or as an historical accident, have themselves turned into "castes of the reborn," as Wilson had observed, whilst still remaining sectarian. But apart from this question of membership it appears that the in-group/out-group mentality and economic ethic is similar to certain sectarian tendencies Weber has discussed hitherto, as we have noted. The segregation from the world and from non-members that is practised by the pariah community is, for sure, a sectarian tendency. Weber does underline that the segregation and the ghetto was *voluntarily* undertaken. In terms of a sociology of sects, Weber understands the principles of segregation that became operative and dominant in Jewish life, as leading to the sect-like existence of a whole religious faith *vis à vis* the wider world. However, it is not the case that a pariah status is the same as a sectarian status considered sociologically. The sectarian tendencies in Judaism – leading to separation from the world and, in the days of the Second Temple, to increasingly caste-like divisions within Judaism between the various movements that wanted to be segregated not only from the non-Jews but also from other Jews as well – finally led to the pariah community of Jews after the destruction of the Temple up to and including Weber's own day.

Weber's *Ancient Judaism* is organized teleologically to the extent that he wants to explain the emergence and characteristics of the pariah status of Judaism in the world. The study opens with these ideas – for example, Weber states plainly, "Hence we ask, how Jewry developed into a pariah people" (1952: 5). Indeed, the opening sentence reads, "Sociologically speaking the Jews were a pariah people, which means, as we know from India, that they were a guest people who were ritually separated, formally or de facto, from their social surroundings" (1952: 3).

A Pariah group is based on ritual segregation from the surrounding peoples. It was voluntarily undertaken and people are born into the group; others can join subject to a number of ritual prescriptions. Here we have a whole nation, as it were, taking on a sect-like structure, apart from the fact that birth (hence ethnicity) rather than a way of life or moral conduct is a qualification. There are continuities between a pariah status and a sectarian way of life in the ideology of in-group and out-group mentality and the keeping of distance. But the pariah group is based on ethnic lines, hence the majority are born into the community (there are converts), and hence do not volunteer: so a pariah community is a church-like association, with sect-like tendencies, but is neither a church nor a sect. Part of Weber's point is that it is unlikely that Judaism can develop sectarian or monastic movements since in its very nature as a religion the separation from the world has already been accomplished. Of course, one can witness the development of sectarian breakaways within the "pariah church" – here the definition of sectarian is *vis à vis* an orthodoxy of faith/doctrine/practice/organization rather than as a withdrawal on the grounds of purity/morality from the "world." Also, of course, the tendencies to become a pariah people are, for Weber, located in the workings out of longer term sectarian tendencies.

Weber's interest in the pariah status of the Jews was an aspect of his wider concern with the rise of western rationalism and the role of Jewish rationalism in that process. For Weber, because of the double-ethic practised by pariah Jews, the origin and spread of those attitudes to work and money contained in the Puritan idea of the calling, could not be traced back to Judaism. Whatever types of economic rationality did develop within Judaism, the pariah status and the corresponding double-ethic could not provide a basis for the spread of a worldview that demanded psychological commitment from across a wide range of classes and communities. For Weber, the contribution of Judaism to western rationalism resided more in ethical and prophetic rationality: in short, to disenchantment of the world through the emphasis on individual moral behaviour. Weber would trace this element of Judaism not to the interests and influences of the priests or to the maintenance of ritual, but to the example of the prophets. An asceticism of the type displayed by ascetic Protestantism, which found its most energetic and influential setting within the ascetic sects, continuing where the ascetic monks had left off in pre-Reformation times, Weber felt, was not to be found in ancient Judaism, especially after the fall of the Second Temple. It is in the light of Weber's assessment of ancient Judaism, which was made prior to the discovery of the Dead Sea Scrolls (and, of course, prior to many other material discoveries and the development of new perspectives in biblical studies) that any prospect of evidence being turned up that might suggest the wider existence of such ascetic or sectarian ideas and movements is significant. This is the case since the existence of such movements might have led, and could lead, to a rethinking of Weber's assessment. A key point to underline, however, is the fact that Weber's interest in ancient Judaism derives from these wider themes and issues articulated across his work considered as a whole. Weber cannot always direct us in our own enquiries since his own particular interests lay elsewhere, often with more universal and comparative problems relating to the nature of western modernity.

Given the ethnic qualification of Jewry, all Jews come under the jurisdiction of the Temple and its priesthood, and in this sense, under the jurisdiction of the Jewish "Church." Church is used here in the Weberian sense as a compulsory organization. To escape the contradiction of talking of Judaism in terms more commonly associated in everyday speech with Christianity, and following Weber's own development of the concept of a compulsory organization to be an *Anstalt*, it is best to talk sociologically about the ancient Jewish church as an *Anstalt* in the religious sphere: namely, a hierocratic institution. To be clear, though, Weber does call the Jewish religion a Church (Weber, 1968: 1200), as indeed did many other contemporary commentators. Weber describes the Jewish religion as of the church type rather than as the sect type, and moreover reiterates on numerous occasions that there is a lack of asceticism and a lack of monasticism within it. In order to be clear about the nature, degree and type of asceticism to be encountered in ancient Judaism, and in the period of the Second Temple in particular, it is necessary to examine Weber's presentation in *Ancient Judaism*.

Weber on the Pharisees and the Essenes

1. *Sources pre Dead Sea Scrolls*

Since Weber provides a sociological reconstruction of Second Temple Judaism and after, *before* the discovery of the Dead Sea Scrolls, his analysis of the Essenes is restricted to the ancient authorities of Josephus and Philo, and his analysis shares many similarities with contemporary scholarship, which was similarly reliant on these sources, which were accorded a good deal of credence (Callaway, 1988: 64). Weber's treatment of the relation between the Pharisees and the Essenes shares many similarities with the scholarship of the time. The similarities in the treatment of the Essenes – their organizational structure and beliefs – stems from the use of the ancient sources, with authors selecting which features to retell, whilst trying not to merely repeat the accounts found in Philo and Josephus. It is important to ascertain the degree to which Weber's work follows contemporary trends, if any grasp of the importance of his formulations, especially as regards the nature of sects in Second Temple times, is to be achieved. It is not remarkable, for example, for Weber to hold to an opinion like that expressed by Bousset, that "later Judaism is through and through Pharisaism" (Bousset, 1892: 32), since this was more or less commonly shared. Weber notes that, after the fall of the Temple, all Judaism became Pharisaic and the Sadducees became a heterodox sect.

Weber cites just one scholarly source in his text – Ismar Elbogen (1874–1943), *Die Religionsanschauungen der Pharisäer* (Berlin, 1904) – and does not indicate his opinion regarding the respective reliability of either Josephus or Philo or Pliny. It is possible that aspects of his reconstruction are supported by the more introductory books he lists for the project as a whole: for example, Marti's history: *Geschichte der Israelitischen Religion* (3rd edn, 1907). Weber obviously selects from Philo and Josephus, but does not always share the process nor the principles of selection with the reader. Given Weber's interest in the Quakers, for example, it is somewhat remarkable that he does not comment on those passages in Philo, that speak of a rational ethic of the Essenes, especially their commitment to honesty in economic life, and the refusal to take oaths and so on. Either Weber did not see an analogy, or did not know of the passage. The Essenes are not mentioned outside of the *Ancient Judaism* study.

Weber considers the Pharisees to be a sectarian brotherhood, and the Essenes to be a sect of the Pharisees. In particular, for Weber, the Pharisees segregated themselves from the ritually impure "people of the land." There are other contemporary authorities who also viewed the Pharisees in this fashion, and also saw the Essenes as "ultra-Pharisees." For example, Ewald in the fifth volume (1867) of his *Geschichte des Volkes Israel* shared this view. Also, Kohler, in the *Jewish Encyclopaedia* of 1906, concluded: "A careful survey of all the facts here presented shows the Essenes to have been simply the rigorists among the Pharisees, whose constant fear of becoming contaminated by either social or sexual intercourse led them to lead an ascetic life..."

Scott, writing in Hastings' *Dictionary of Christ and the Gospels*, observed: "The Pharisees formed a fraternity with peculiar vows, which separated them from the heathen, the common people and the Sadducees" (H. M. Scott, 1908: II, 352). However, there were others, most notably, Friedländer, who, in his *Die Religiösen Bewegungen innerhalb des Judentums im Zeitalter Jesu*, thought the opposite to Weber's position with regard to the relationship between the Pharisees and the Essenes: "Aber nicht nur nicht pharisäisch ist der Essenismus, er ist sogar streng anti-pharisäisch" (1905: 130).

Labels for Essenes in the Literature of the Time
The Essenes were called a variety of types of organization in the academic literature of the time. Scott, for example, selects ascetic community from a range of choices, thus: *"The Essenes were an ascetic community among the Jews...they seem to have corresponded more closely to a monastic order than to a sect or a religious party"* (C. A. Scott, 1906: 536). Labels for the Essene movement include: philosophical mystics, a community of ascetics, an exclusive society of like-minded men, a secret society, a brotherhood, an esoteric brotherhood (Fairweather, 1908: 204), a monastic order, "a pre-Christian order of Jewish monks," and a sect. After Josephus they are named a school, party or sect. Often these terms are used interchangeably by the same authors. That some scholars when using the term "sect" had examples of sects from Christian times, (rather than simply repeating Josephus's use of the word), is shown by the loose comparisons often made. For example, Holtzmann, in his *Lehrbuch der Neutestamentlichen*

Theologie (1897: I, 109) compares patriotic attitudes of the Essenes with similar sentiments held by the Mennonites and Quakers in the American war, whilst Fairweather (1908), although he does not explore the affinity at all, considers them similar in the peculiarity of their "manners and customs," to the "curious modern sect of the Doukhobors (a position he supports by quoting a long passage from a contemporary account of travel in Canada!). It is in such a context that Weber's account is to be placed. It is somewhat disappointing, therefore, to find that Weber seemingly oscillates between a variety of labels himself when speaking about the Pharisees and the Essenes.

Dominant Interpretative Issues in Weber's Time about the Essenes

The dominant issues at the time when Weber was writing in relation to the Essenes revolved around the extent to which their beliefs and organization could be seen as outgrowths of Jewish tendencies and to what extent they were attributable to foreign influence. The position, as phrased by Scott, had to be considered by all: "While it is impossible to deny the Jewish foundation on which it [Essenism] rests, it is equally impossible to overlook the presence of foreign elements" (C. A. Scott, 1906: 536). Again, "while they are distinguished by exaggerated adherence to the Jewish law and by special reverence for Moses as lawgiver, they betray at the same time certain ideas and practices which are foreign to Judaism, and seem incompatible with its spirit" (1906: 536). Throughout the debates there is central concern about the relationship between Essene teaching and organization and those of emergent Christianity. In considering the relation between Christianity and the Essenes, Weber wrote: "Essenian ethic like the Early Christian in many points represents Pharisaic ethic intensified. The nature of this intensification, however, differs between the cases" (Weber, 1952: 410). There are many overlapping ideas and institutions between the Essenes and early Christians. However, "what matters more than all else is that the epiphany of a present personal saviour and his cult, as well as the tremendous and specifically Christian significance of the 'spirit' pneuma, as far as known, remained alien to the Essenes" (Weber, 1952: 411).

There was little disagreement about the Jewish elements to be found in Essenism. Fairweather's comment is typical: "In respect of their belief in Providence, which was more absolute than that of the Pharisees; in respect of their veneration for Moses and the Law; and in respect of their Sabbath observance, which was of the strictest possible type, they were Hebrews of the Hebrews" (1908: 207). The Jewish nature of the Essenes was often understood as a developed and extreme form of Pharisaism (with the unspoken idea that the sect "split off" at some point from the home Pharisaism).

Foreign Influences on the Essenes

The candidates for foreign influence on the Essenes, included, Zoroastrianism as argued by Lightfoot and Cheyne, or, as Zeller and Schürer argued, Pythagorenan and Hellenic influence. For Friedländer (1905), the Hellenic influence is far more significant than any Jewish element. Fairweather summarizes his position as follows: "According to this scholar… the fundamental idea of Essenism is the crucifixion of sense through the observance of the greatest possible abstinence with a view to the ennoblement of the soul. Perfection is the end aimed at, and strict abstinence the means of attaining it" (1908: 212).

Social Origins Proposed for Essenes in the Literature of the Time

When the origins of the Essenes cannot be traced to pietistic movements within Judaism itself, or are not linked to the Pharisees, scholars speak of withdrawal from "the distracting bustle of the world," from social corruption, along the lines of a principle of analogy that "like causes bring about like results." The author in the *Encyclopaedia Britannica* (T. K., 1879: 552), for example, observes with confidence: "Certain conditions of civilization have favoured the formation of secret societies, with analogous institutions, in all ages." In Judaism, "misrule, corruption, and fanaticism were everywhere gathering head: good men despaired of controlling such a headlong and turbulent movement; what could they do but withdraw from it, and cultivate, a purer life under such conditions as secured or admitted it, in the exclusive society of men like-minded with themselves."

In both of these examples, it is clear that there is a need for some sociological precision. Weber roots his understanding of the motivations to be an Essene, if I read him aright, on the religious motivation to gain a gift of grace, illustrating the fact that, for Weber, the theological context and the nature of religious needs and ideal interests must be taken seriously in any sociological account of religious movements, including sects.

Weber and the Dead Sea Scrolls

The relation of the Pharisees to the Essenes, and the whole problem of whom they were, has been complicated by the Dead Sea Discoveries. As Filson remarks, "Our understanding of the Essenes will be greatly affected by the view we take of the ancient ascetic group that lived at Qumran" (1964: 53).

What difference knowledge of the scrolls would have made to Weber's analysis is a question of great interest, but which cannot be speculated upon here at any length. We do not know the answer as to how Weber would have responded to Filson's point. To gain a sense of that impact one would need to appreciate how scholars re-wrote their understandings of the Essenes as the Qumran texts came to light. Moffatt, writing in Hastings' *Encyclopaedia of Religion and Ethics* in 1912, following Lightfoot, who had called the Essenes, "the great enigma of Hebrew history," speaks of the mystery of the Essenes. "They appear and disappear in a mist" he writes, "leaving barely a clue to their existence. None of their sacred books has survived..." (Moffat, 1912: 400). One can imagine the excitement that was caused when Moffatt and others like him realized that the Dead Sea Scrolls could be Essene. A key issue, of course, would be whether Weber would have accepted the scrolls as being Essenic and whether he would have equated the Qumran settlement with the Essene communities described by Philo and Josephus. His analysis of the Pharisees as a sect-like religiosity would probably not have been revised *on these grounds*; if any revisions were to be made they would probably have related to the relation between the Essenes and the Pharisees, and the degree to which the "sect within a sect" line of argument – that the Essenes were extreme Pharisees to all intents and purposes – based on a deeper knowledge of their doctrines and practices, was still supportable. Weber undoubtedly would have been intrigued to discover traces at Qumran of Jewish asceticism and mysticism and to consider the extent he would have needed to revise his overall assessment of the presence of these virtuosities in ancient Judaism and indeed the subsequent possible legacies of Judaism through these routes.

Even with the discovery of the Scrolls, though, it is difficult to reach any certainty about the relation between the Essenes and the Pharisees. As Fitzmyer (1992) observes, there is no certainty whether, for example, the "seekers after smooth things" are to be identified with the Pharisees, and the self-identification of the community as "sons of Zadok" would tend to suggest that the problematic relationship is more likely to be with the Sadducees rather than the Pharisees (which does not necessarily mean that they did not once have a close relationship). As we have seen, Freidländer already questioned the relation with the Pharisees, and one does not need the Dead Sea Scroll materials to do so. For sure, Weber would have had considerable more data to assess, and would have formed a firmer opinion regarding the nature of the "foreign elements" to be found in the movement; perhaps even to establishing the full extent of the "Indian connection" he posits. Weber, although he was aware of the discovery of the Hebrew manuscript of the book of Jesus Sirach (and revised the relevant section in the PE accordingly), his treatment of the Essenes in *Ancient Judaism* makes no reference to the Damascus Document; its connection to the Dead Sea Scrolls had to await the discovery of fragments of the former in the latter. As Callaway observes, "the attribution of this document to Essene composition was scarcely entertained until the discovery of several fragments of it in Qumran Caves 4–6" (1988: 89). The one exception that is noted, one Riessler, did not publish in Weber's life-time (1927). Weber does mention the medieval ascetic sect of "the weepers of Zion," who are attested in the same body of texts as ben Sira uncovered at Cairo, but dismisses the example as not relevant to his current concerns.

Weber's Sociology of Sects and the Analysis of the Pharisees and the Essenes
The Pharisees (but not the Essenes) in relation to sects are explicitly mentioned by name in Weber's sociology in the following comparative paragraph about religious virtuosity, found in the Sociology of Religion section of *Economy and Society*.[2]

> The earliest Christian sources represent [these] religious virtuosi as comprising a particular category, distinguished from their comrades in the community, and they later constituted the monastic orders. In Protestantism they formed the ascetic sects or pietistic conventicles. In Judaism they were the perushim (Pharisaioi), an aristocracy with respect to salvation which stood in contrast to the am ha 'arez. In Islam they were the Dervishes, and among the Dervishes the particular virtuosi were the authentic Sufi's. In the Skoptzi sect, they constituted the esoteric community of the castrated (Weber, 1968: 539-40).

The paragraph illustrates how, for Weber, the Pharisees are one example of the universal phenomena of the tendency to virtuosity, which can hold different qualities as virtuoso values and organize into various social forms. Like the early Protestants, the Pharisees applied to their own lives the demands normally made only on a certain section of the religious, in the processes creating a "priesthood of all believers" which both secularized the ethic by expanding the circle of the virtuosos and sacralized everyday life.[3] In *Ancient Judaism* Weber attributes social significance to the Pharisees, and considers them to be a sect that played a significant role in transforming Second Temple Judaism. The Essenes, in comparison, are a sect of the Pharisees (a sect of a sect), and did not have the social significance he attributes to the latter.[4] The Pharisees are, for Weber, a trans-local sect. The Essenes he sees as a separate order. In what follows, I pick out the sociological aspects of Weber's presentation in an effort to connect the analysis with Weber's conceptual apparatus as we have encountered it hitherto. I also make some critical comments along the way indicating where Weber might have applied his sociological ideas in more depth, had that been his intention.

The Pharisee Brotherhood, the Trans-local Sect and Economics

Weber calls the Pharisees a sect, a brotherhood and an order. There is little difficulty, given the discussions in the *Zwischenbetrachtung* and of sects in American society, of conceiving of the sect simultaneously as a brotherhood, since the ethic that guided relationships between sect members was an ethic of brotherhood. An "order" would appear to relate more to a monastic group of virtuosos, but Weber does not describe the Pharisees again in these terms.

Indeed, it is the notion of the Pharisees as a trans-local sect that recalls the network created by sect brothers Weber described as a social possibility once qualification for a sect was certificated and an individual's moral standing became transferable from place to place. As we have seen this network developed and functioned especially in the "frontier society" of developing America. Weber summarizes: "Thus we are faced here with the sect, indeed the inter-local sect. It permitted the *chaber* coming to a strange place with testimonials of his brotherhood at once to become a denizen in a community of like-minded persons" (Weber, 1952: 387).

Weber does not develop in any depth an analysis of the workings of that network in Second Temple Judaism, or of the social securities provided by the brotherhood, which might enable postulation of some of the more material interests that may have motivated individuals to join. Weber only draws attention to the brotherhood functioning as a communal network for urban dwellers torn from agricultural settings and their "home" communities. "The chevra, the Pharisaic order, was indeed a substitute for the rural neighbourhood for landless city dwellers and as such it corresponded to their external and internal interests" (Weber, 1952: 390). Further, Weber does not dwell on how a trans-local sect might have implications for economic activities, nor indeed, why mobility as such was an issue in Second Temple times.

Weber, on the basis of Philo and Josephus, might have made similar comments about the functioning of the network of brothers of the Essene movement. For example, Philo in his *Quod omnis probus liber*, draws attention to the care of the sick members by the Essenes drawing on the common fund for those no longer able to work; Philo makes a similar point in his lost

Apology for the Jews as excerpted in Eusebius. Josephus draws attention to the consequences of the expelled member, which shows the dependency of the member on the sectarian brotherhood. The with-holding of the material and ideal benefits of the sect from the "fallen brother" is perhaps an example of what Weber meant by coercion in the sphere of religion. It was for the "Jewish church" not for a "Jewish sect" to publicly execute the guilty, although Josephus implies the death of the expelled.

For Weber, the attitudes of the Essenes to economic life derived from their strict interpretation of the law. He observes, for example, that:

> The commandment not to steal was tightened; one was not to burden his conscience with any sort of gain. The legitimacy of all gain seemed problematic. The Essenes, therefore, shunned trade even as war; they rejected the possession of money and slaves; they restricted permissible possessions to the necessities of a handicraft or tillage livelihood. Correspondingly, they pushed the old social commandment of brotherliness to the length of an unworldly love communism of consumption (Weber, 1952: 407).

One might expect Weber to spend longer considering the Essene way of organizing and its impact on economic life in general, along the lines developed in the analysis of Protestant Sects. From Philo's accounts, for example, an impression can be gained of how the Essene way of life – at least in the towns – intertwined with everyday economic life, and provided both a corporate way of accumulating gain, and a security against ill-health and old age. Moreover, Philo appears to describe an attitude to work in various occupations for the profit of the order, of an ascetic and devoted type akin to the protestant devotion to work for the greater glory of God.

It is the attitude to money that Weber argues constituted one of the main differences with the Pharisees. Weber does not provide a sociological analysis of the economic and social benefits to be gained from joining the Essenes, although the existence of the trans-local sect and the community formed in urban areas was mentioned in relation to the Pharisees. Whilst the Essenes had strict attitudes to economic activity, Weber observes that, "No closed corporate organisation of this form with the prohibition of profitable pursuits is known to have existed on the basis of *ordinary* Pharisaism of the time" (Weber, 1952: 409; my italics). For Weber, it was probably the ideal interest in the receipt of charismatic gifts that played a more significant role in motivating the Essene, than the material and ideal interests surrounding everyday life. As Weber wrote: "The true motive for the special Essenian way of life is apparently to be found in the gift of grace conveyed by the secret teaching and the quest for this reward" (408).

For the Pharisees, Weber observes, the material and ideal concerns of everyday life were not to be denied on the grounds of some doctrine of the fallen state of matter. Actual, "rejection of the world" was "just as alien to ordinary Pharisaism as were the respective rules of the Essenes and in turn may well be explained by non-Jewish influences" (1952: 410).

Public Estimates of Sectarian Virtuosity

Similarly, in a manner reminiscent of Weber's comments concerning the esteem for the practices of the Quakers that developed in England and America, to the extent that their ethical and business practices led to an admiration that might extend to emulation, the Essenes, according to Philo, met with the support and admiration of many contemporaries. Philo observed, with obvious national pride in the ethical accomplishments of some of his fellow Jews, that: "Their moral excellence triumphed, and everybody treated them as independent and free by nature, praising their common meals and their indescribable good fellowship..." (quoted in Moffatt, 1912: 397). If this account can be trusted, a Weberian point about the wider impact of sects on everyday life could be postulated in the case of the Essenes.

Sect Membership Achieved and Not Ascribed

Philo also reports, via Eusebius, on the principle of achieved rather than ascribed status with regard to joining the sect. A criterion that goes to the heart of the essence of the sect, it will be recalled, that Weber establishes as the key note in the polar typology of church-sect. Philo observed: "Their sect is formed not on family descent, for descent is not reckoned among matters of choice, but on zeal for virtue and philanthropy" (Moffatt, 1912: 397). Given the limitations of the sources, Weber does not speculate on the processes of application, probation and the grades of membership in the Essene movement beyond what is provided in the standard accounts. Clearly, the discovery of the *Community Rule* and related documents at Qumran would add greatly to the data Weber would have considered in this regard.

Sectarian Tendency and the Tendency to Virtuosity

Weber posits the origin of the Pharisees, and by implication the Essenes, to the Hasidic movement stemming from Macabbean times. In terms of Weber's sociology discussed above, this "purity movement" developing in a period of military heroism and continuing into civil society, provides a tendency to virtuosity that obviously, and eventually, led to a sectarian tendency. In other words, purity and its heroic pursuit became a highly prized sacred value, the achievement of which would lead to the status of virtuosity within the society. The demands of heroism, whether of a military or of a "muscular piety" type, demands the assertion of self. Even though the Hasidim were not a sect, both they and the Pharisees segregated themselves from impure persons and objects. The sectarian tendency of drawing distinction between the in-group and out-group is taken further by the Pharisees through their introduction of the organizational dimension of "separateness"; this they did through making the movement into an order/brotherhood (*Chaburah*). This brotherhood developed sectarian tendencies, Weber argues, since joining the exclusive brotherhood was very strict and onerous. However, Weber does note that not all followers of the Pharisees were formally brothers in the brotherhood. For sure, the brotherhood was the kernel of the movement. The major innovation – which recalls the hatred of the damned expressed by the Calvinists – was utter contempt for the ritually impure. Hence, the sectarian tendency to separate from others leads to the formation of the Pharisaic brotherhood and its attitude to the people of the land and the Sadducees. The sectarian tendency was based on the virtuoso pursuit of ritual purity according to the law.

In so far as they strove for Levitical purity – which, Weber argues, was a fundamental element of the Essene sect – they are to be seen as "a radical Pharisaic sect" (1952: 406). Weber goes on to speak about the Essenes, not in terms of sect, but in terms of order and brotherhood; like their parent, but much stricter.

> The Essenes were, like the larger Pharisaic *brotherhood*, an *order*. But their affiliation prescriptions were far stricter and comprised, above all, a solemn vow, a novitiate, and years of probation. The organisation of the order was quite strict and *monk-like*. The head (mishmar) of the local chapter had unconditional authority. Excommunication lay in the hands of a council of 150 full members (my italics; 1952: 406).

The Essenes were stricter since than the Pharisees in so far as they "segregated themselves from the less pure by excluding not only connubium and commensality but all contact" (406); they also shared – as a logical corollary of their sectarian tendencies, a rejection of priests in general. The intensity of ritual and purity prescriptions extended to strict interpretations of Jewish law, and had a significant impact on their attitudes to economic life.

Aristocracy of Saints and Personal Charisma

The Pharisees saw themselves as the aristocracy of the faithful, as the "saints" within Judaism – recalling Weber's language of "aristocracy" in relation to sects – in distinction to the "people of the land." Since the

purity sought after by the Pharisees was the responsibility of the individual, and not all members of society could achieve such ritual purity,
it followed sociologically that personal charisma, as displayed in (ritual)
conduct, had far more authority than any charisma of office. Personal
charisma has more worth than the charisma derived from position. The
charisma is earnt and not ascribed. It is understandable then that the
ritual rules that were to be followed were very strict and, by definition,
extraordinary. One demonstrated one's charisma, one's legitimacy as a
Pharisee, through the ability to perform these duties. Weber writes that
the member of the Pharisaic brotherhood should "shoulder the yoke of
the commandments." There was strict training, and the member was
expected to lead a holy life. Separation laws were considered very important indeed, as was the strict observance of the Sabbath.

It was conduct, not the occupation of an office, that was paramount
and which demonstrated the charismatic qualification to be a member
of the brotherhood (not all "Pharisees" were members). In these ways,
the Pharisee sect has similarities to the sects of the ascetic Protestants.
The assertion of the self in ritualistic terms often needs to take place in
the view of other brothers. The circle of brothers is significant since holiness and purity is more easily achieved in the company of like-minded
and like-purified persons; but the circle can also play the function Weber
underlined in the sect, of the individual being seen to carry out the
prescriptions in the presence of fellow members, and thereby proving
their qualification and affirming and asserting their membership of the
brotherhood. However, the nature of the conduct demanded, and hence
the nature of the virtuosity to be displayed was not, as it was with the
ascetic Protestants, an inner worldly asceticism, but rather a living in the
world observing the demands of ritual purity. Such a sacred value could
be achieved only through types of segregation from others.

The Charisma of the Community

A further sociological development, that we have been led to expect, is the
way in which the community, the brotherhood itself, becomes the most
significant social organization for its members and gains an autonomy
and power thereby. Weber writes of the Pharisees that "the community
now became the bearer of the religion" (1952: 388).

The community, the "aristocracy of the saints/holy" desires a good
degree of independence from other social formations; just as personal
charisma leads to the rejection of office, so the charisma of the community looks to create institutions that conform to a standard and reflect
the needs of the members. Indeed, Weber traces the strong community

nature of Judaism in various diasporic places back to the work of the Pharisees. The benefit of being Pharisee – as it were in the balance of material and ideal interests that motivate individuals and social groups in Weber's sociology – can be found in this mutual recognition and support that a brotherhood offers to those who have been admitted, after proof and examination to the sect. To be sure, Weber does not spend any time elaborating on the process of application and admittance to the Pharisaic brotherhood.

The charisma of the community Weber sees evidenced in the growth of community institutions, which would have led to degrees of self-direction and a degree of democracy, and community involvement. Weber mentions the Pharisees' development of love feasts, the synagogue, the Sabbath and the festivals in this regard. Weber does not delve into the types of personality, of leadership and of "the led" in his analysis. Limitations in the data are no doubt partially responsible for this lack, but we have noted above that Weber's sociology of sects rarely goes down this track, however desirable Weber once thought such an analysis would be. Nonetheless, in the discussion of the Pharisees and of the Essenes, Weber does not look into "the dark side" of sectarian life. Once again the aspect of the origin of democratic institutions and individualism are of more significance. It is of some surprise therefore that Weber does not comment on the hierarchal nature of the Essene movement as described by Josephus, which Weber seems to accept as normal as the grades one might find in a monastery (which is not a sect). In this way, Weber does not consider the lack of democracy that might obtain in certain parts of the Essene movement. Indeed, in Josephus's account the fact that a longer serving member can be ritually defiled by a member of a lower rank would lead to social divisions of a caste-like nature within the sect, which, following Weber's analysis of sects, would appear to render the movement unsect-like.

The Social Carriers of Religious Worldviews and Ethics

Weber's sociological concern to establish the particular affinities between certain groups of social strata and types of religiosity and ethic, to the extent that religions come to bear the stamp of the material and idea interests of those social strata to whom the beliefs and practices appeal and are subsequently "carried" by them, can be observed. As with many sectarian movements, Weber places the "carriers" of Pharisaism, within urban centres, with the movement appealing to the civic strata: artisans and petty bourgeoisie. The "people of the land" are considered impure, incapable of following all the ritual prescriptions required; prescriptions that are easier to follow in the urban areas. In this way, Weber argues, the brotherhood becomes something of a replacement for the lost communal ties that once existed for many civic strata who perhaps had migrated to the towns. For example, Weber writes that the brotherhood of the Pharisees appealed to the petit bourgeois, and their interests meant that the practical-ethical dimensions of the teaching were stressed. By this, Weber refers to the tendency to want to perform the necessary rituals and practical duties rather than to cultivate philosophic speculation as characteristic of the petty bourgeoisie. On the other hand, the development of theological notions of messianic hope, the resurrection of the dead and accommodation to foreign angelogy, which, Weber argues, were all achieved under Pharisaism, he sees as concessions to the demands of the plebeian strata, as typically occurs. With regard to the Essenes, however, Weber does not offer any sociological thoughts on their social composition. Rather the motivation to be an Essene is located less in systems of social support, and less in degrees of social status, and more in the pursuit of the ideal of the achievement of a virtuosity of grace and prophetic insight.

Types of World Rejection

Weber, in the *Zwischenbetrachtung*, distinguished between types of world rejection in a fourfold typology of inner and other worldly asceticism and inner and other worldly mysticism. These distinctions are utilized by Weber in *Ancient Judaism* and differences between the Pharisee sect and the sect of the Essenes correspond to differing forms of world rejections entertained by either. For Weber, the Pharisees pursued Levitical purity, which was the essence of its asceticism and was carried out "within the world"; the Essenes also pursued Levitical purity, but withdrew from the world. Their asceticism, such as it was, was therefore, in Weberian terms, an other – worldly asceticism. Because Weber believed that since such other-worldly types of asceticism were not "natural" to Judaism, these tendencies must have derived from foreign influences. However, matters are not so straightforward in Weber's account as this would appear and this is because, for Weber, this particular other-worldly asceticism was forged within Essenism, with a mystic seeking after charisma and prophetic insight. Weber does not resolve the possible tension between the ascetic and mystical dimensions of Essenism with regard to the processes of applying and qualifying for the Essene sect. The tension resides in the fact that admittance in the first instance cannot be on the basis of a gnostic knowledge of the sect's secrets, but rather on the basis of a type of ritual yet benevolent conduct that was esteemed by the sect, or on the basis of the demonstration of possession of charismatic gifts of prophecy and healing, since it appears that the knowledge of the secrets was granted only after admission. It will be recalled that Weber argued that a sect had an educative influence not only on the applicant but also indirectly on the society as a whole, so this dimension is significant in any sociological assessment of a sect in ancient Judaism. These considerations relate to Weber's ongoing concern with the relative and intertwining roles of material and ideal interests in understanding individual action and social change. It would appear that, for Weber, the motivation to join the Essenes would have had both material and ideal interests at heart, and moreover, the desire to share the secrets and the mysteries of the sect would be a considerable motivation to prove oneself in terms of conduct, during the novitiate. It was because of the "mixing" of ascetic and mystical elements, that Weber concluded that Essenism would have had a limited impact on the development of a rational Jewish ascetic ethic of the sort found amongst the ascetic Protestant sects, even had the movement not been, to all intents and purposes, destroyed by the Romans.

In this assessment of the mix of ascetic and mystical elements in the Essene movement, Weber follows Josephus, as he acknowledges. The secret teaching, Weber writes, "appears to have consisted of an allegorical re-interpretation of the holy legends, a pronounced faith in divine ordainment, and a more than usually explicit angelogy, various acts of sun-worship...a promise of immortality with conceptions of heaven and hell" (1952: 408).

Herein Weber detects elements that are non-Jewish in origin and not found in Pharisaism either: Hellenic, Persian and even Indian sources are posited, as Weber moves to final summation of the nature of Essenic religiosity:

> The inclination towards celibacy, the ranks of the order, and the rejection of animal sacrifice may represent Indian influence – through some sort of mediation – but, like washings and sacraments, these elements could also stem from Hellenistic-Oriental mysteries. Probably the elaboration of secret doctrine was derived from the same source. In fact, the order of the Essenes represents *a fusion of sacramental mystery religion with Levitical purity ritualism* (1952: 408-409; my italics).

The gifts that are bestowed – and hence, one presumes, applying a Weberian logic, highly sought after and the qualities that mark off this aristocracy of believers from others – were the gifts of prophecy, and to some extent therapeutics – knowledge of the powers of minerals and roots.

Besides these markings, Weber writes that their "religiosity" was one of "prayer characterized by intense devotional attitudes" (408).

It would appear that Weber's assessment of the Essenes as a "sect of a sect," belies the fact that he often speaks of the Essenes more in terms of mysticism than asceticism (for example, their communism and under-standing of brotherly love is nearer to Baudelaire's sacred prostitution of the soul, than it is to a Calvinist impersonal charity) and more in terms of being an order (novitiate, ranks in the movement, the role of the *mishmah*, celibacy, withdrawal from society; Weber, 1952: 406) on an analogy with a monastic movement of virtuosos rather than as a sect as such. It would appear, therefore, that sociological accounts of the Qumran community that look to a typology of monastic movements to understand the textual remains of the Dead Sea Scrolls, may find a good deal of support from Weberian sociology.[5]

The Asceticism of the Pharisees and the Essenes

The main reason why Weber posits a non-Jewish origin for these Essene ideas rests on his assessment of the type of asceticism practised by the Pharisees and the degree to which it rested on a abnegation of the world. It is very important to realize that whilst the Essenes are a sect of the Pharisee sect, for Weber neither Judaism per se nor the Pharisees preached an abnegation of the world; the conflicts with economics, art, eroticism that "religious brotherhoods" can experience, especially if their theologies are strongly dualistic, did not occur in Pharisaism according to Weber. Weber's refrain is that Pharisaic ideas did not lead to a rejection of the world: such rejection and flight from the world is not natural to Judaism in Weber's estimation. As he writes, "the idea was quite remote that withdrawal from the world be prerequisite to religious salvation" (1952: 401).

On the contrary, for the Pharisees, as for Judaism in general, health, wealth and happiness are all accepted as God's gifts and form part of the natural Jewish ethic. This aspect is essential to grasp the differences between the Pharisees and Essenes, and indeed between the Pharisees and the ascetic Protestants, as presented in Weber's sociology. As he underlines:

> there was lacking precisely any point of departure for an economically ordered methodical or inner-worldly asceticism as well as for a sexual asceticism...we must by no means seek a principled, ascetic way of life at the basis of Pharisaic Judaism. It required strict ritualism as did the official religion of India. For the rest, Judaism was a religion of faith based on trust in God and his promise of living in fear of sin as disobedience toward

him and in fear of its consequences. Judaism certainly did not present an ascetic way of life. To be sure in one point its way of life resembled the rational ascetic principles: in its commandment of vigilant self-observation and absolute self-control (Weber, 1952: 401-402).

In this sense, any such flight from the world, and any elaborate dualistic conceptions, must stem from non-Jewish sources, and hence the Essenes, to the extent that they can be characterized this way, are, for Weber, a non-Jewish, heterodox sect. They were tolerated within Judaism, Weber argues, on the account of continued communion with the Temple and the observation of the Mosaic Law.

The Path to Pariah

Essenism did not contribute to the development of the pariah status of the Jews, although their sectarian nature was an index of the process of segregation taking place within Judaism at the time, and between Judaism and the wider world. Pharisaism, on the other hand, did play a very important part in the development of the distinctive pariah status of Judaism. Even though the brotherhood/order of the Pharisees was replaced in time after the destruction of the Second Temple, with the Rabbi taking over the mantle of religious leader, the "spirit" of Pharisaism, Weber opines, "was all dominant in Jewry." In particular, ritual purity, which continued to characterize Judaism – and moreover was increasingly intensified, owed its characteristic stamp to Pharisaism Nonetheless, these segregating processes, including the Essenic experiment, extended well beyond Pharisaism, and were endemic.

> Pharisaic purity ritualism brought about higher ritual barriers against both outsiders and in-group members. The barriers precisely against in-group members were important. The Essenian community segregated itself out of fear of defilement from the intermarriage, commensalism, and close contact with the rest of the Jews, and it is questionable whether they were the only *conventicle* of this kind. The Pharisaic brotherhood segregated itself likewise from the *am ha aretz*, Jerusalemite Jewry and those influenced by the Jerusalem priesthood segregated themselves from the Samaritans and other survivals of the old Jahve prophets and the Jerusalem priesthood after the Samaritans had been formally excluded from the sacrifice in Jerusalem which they were inclined to honour. Thus there emerge a firm and, due to its ritualistic condition, a caste-like structure of the old Yahwe believers. Alongside this hereditary privileges of the priest and Levite sibs continued to live on within Jewry. They were not completely excluded from intermarriage with other Jewish sibs, but were, indeed, under the commandment of hypergamy. To this was added the ritualistic rejection, in part tabooing, in part disapproval of certain occupations as an element of religious status formation (Weber, 1952: 415-16).

Final Comment

Weber, then, applies his sociological understanding of sects and voluntary associations, of sectarian tendencies and the tendencies to virtuosity to the case of Second Temple Judaism. In the process he provides an analysis of the sectarian tendencies of the pursuit of ritual purity – a relatively new phenomenon in his sociology given the concentration previously on the ascetic rational actions of the Protestant sects, but one which needs to be considered in the context of Weber's other writings in the EEWR series, namely, the China and, above all, the India studies. It is perhaps regrettable that he did not examine further, in the light of his sociology, elements of Pharisaism and Essenism that the classical sources he was utilizing might have enabled him to do. No doubt this "lack" is partly attributable to the unfinished nature of his work on ancient Judaism, in part to the limitations of the classical sources and in part to his overriding interest in the formation of the pariah community of the Jews within his comparative sociological history of the rise of western rationalism. Because Weber assessed the Pharisees and the Essenes in the way he did, he was unable to find a way of applying his interest in the formation of sectarian personality to the materials: since the movements were not ascetic in the sense of the ascetic Protestant sects, and hence allowed little room for the types of self-assertion Weber considered significant, he was not led to develop this aspect of his sociology of sects in his study of ancient Judaism.

Now that Weber's treatment of sects across his writings have been considered, and his application of those principles to the study of the Second Temple has been examined, it is now possible to move forward with a Weberian approach to the sociology of sects and apply Weber's ideas (including those he did not apply himself) to the analysis of Second Temple Judaism, making full use of the Qumran materials that were not available to Weber but are available to us.[6]

Endnotes

1. The new critical edition of *Ancient Judaism*, produced for the Max Weber Gesamtausgabe and edited by Otto Eckart should now be consulted as the definitive text. The volume, alas, was unavailable to me during the writing of this piece.

2. That Weber had long held the view that the Pharisees were a sect can perhaps be seen in the first edition of the PE (1904–1905) where he discusses Bunyan's *negative* attitude to them, in his *Sermon on the Pharisee and the Publican*. Weber comments on Bunyan as follows: "Why is the Pharisee condemned? He does not truly keep God's

commandments, for he is evidently a sectarian (Sektierer) who is only concerned with external details and ceremonies, but above all because he ascribes merit to himself, and at the same time, like the Quakers, thanks God for virtue by misuse of his name" (1930: 272 n. 60).

3. In 1909, there is a passage in Weber's *The Agrarian Sociology of Ancient Civilizations* (1976: 254), dealing with conditions in Palestine in Hellenistic times which treats the conflict between the Sadducees and the Pharisees as akin to a conflict he later would have described as a conflict between office and personal charisma and in which an affinity between the Puritans and the Pharisees is alluded to: "a conflict between the rule of an aristocratic theocracy and the rule of a theology that regulated all life's activities and was taught by professionals, 'the separated ones' (Pharisaioi), and which gained the support of the petty bourgeoisie. The rural population was considered immoral by the Pharisees, and in fact country folk have at no time and at no place (with a single exception: the Donatists) supported Puritan doctrines."

4. We gain an intimation of the nature of the Essenes – as a sect within a sect – at an early stage in *Ancient Judaism*, when Weber considers the universal historical importance of the "adoption" of the Old Testament in the development of Christianity:

> In order to assess the significance of this act one needs merely conceive what would have happened without it. Without the adoption of the Old Testament as a sacred book by Christianity, gnostic sects and mysteries of the cult of Kyrios Christos would have existed on the soil of Hellenism, but providing no basis for a Christian church or a Christian ethic of workaday life. Without emancipation from the ritual prescriptions of the Torah, founding the caste-like segregation of the Jews, the Christian congregation would have remained a small sect of the Jewish pariah people comparable to the Essenes and the Therapeutics (1952: 4-5).

5. I have not been able to include any analysis of Weber's sociology of monasticism in this account. For the moment see, Silber (1995); Kaelber (1998); Collins (1986: 45-76); Stock (1990) (cf. Chalcraft, 1992). For work on asceticism and virtuosity at Qumran see Ling (2004) and Lawrence (2005).

6. I do not mean to imply that significant sociological work has not already been undertaken in Qumran studies, nor that scholars have so far failed to address the types of questions Weber would pose. The point, rather, is that there has been no systematic and planned Weberian analysis of Second Temple Judaism based on his oeuvre.

Towards a Weberian Sociology of the Qumran Sects

David J. Chalcraft

The previous chapters have shown how Weber's thinking about sects developed in the course of his career and how Weber "applied" his ideas to the analysis of the Pharisees and the Essenes in the appendix to *Ancient Judaism*. This chapter provides a synthetic treatment of Weber's sociology of sects and applies a number of his concerns and perspectives to the analysis of the Qumran sect(s).

1. *Ideal Types and the Central Question of the Development of Types of Personality as Carriers of Social and Cultural Change*

Weber's church-sect distinction is an ideal-typical construct in which the church is a polar counterpart to the sect. A Weberian sociology does not develop a definition of a sect with a list of attributes, nor try and establish a range of types of sects with their own list of attributes, but rather highlights an essential feature of the sect from the perspective of the sociological and cultural questions being posed. Weber was aware of other standard definitions of the sect put forward by previous and contemporary scholars, but dismissed them as not getting at the essence of a sect; these other criteria include relations to the state and the size of the community. Weber does not postulate that sects are schisms from parent orthodoxy although he shares the idea that when orthodoxy exists any religious group that is unorthodox is probably labelled as a sect/heresy by the orthodox. Equally, of course, there are movements, such as the Qumran movement, that present themselves as the "true" version of the faith in distinction to a parent body or bodies.

The dominant way of defining a sect in distinction to a church is by reference to the mode of belonging. A sect's membership is constituted by volunteers who have freely applied to join and who have proved themselves worthy after examination to be admitted according to the criteria laid down in relation to certain personal qualities or attributes. This ideal-typical definition of a sect does not alter across all of Weber's texts.

Hence one of the central features of a Weberian approach to sectarianism to be employed in the analysis of Qumran materials involves pursuing the nature of the process of application, admission, monitoring and disciplining of the individual that takes place in the movement and the manner in which the personal qualities esteemed by the sect bring about personal and, in turn, social and cultural change within and outwith the sect. Overall, Weber is concerned with the types of personality that are created by various sects and associations and the impact of these character-types and the ethics they carry for understanding social and cultural change.

In contrast, a "church" is characterized by compulsory membership. The implications of the definition of the sect and the contrast with "church" are spelled out differently in Weber's various texts as principles of charisma, or coercion and domination, or of size become the topic of discussion or where Weber's focus is on the transformation of character and personality or the impact of the sect on social and economic change. Weber does not mean to suggest that other features of sects are not relevant to grasping the total picture but rather that the key difference between the functioning and the sociocultural impacts of a "sect" or "church" resides in the principle of membership and the importance given to personal qualification.

In ideal-typical fashion, a religious movement is either more or less church-like or sect-like. Hence, degrees of "sectness" are possible. Weber utilizes this notion of "sectness" to assess the variable impacts on social and personal and cultural change of particular sects and it is possible to utilize the typological contrast in similar fashion in our own work. A Weberian sociology of sects seeks to develop concepts and theories that have universal applicability in the comparative historical study of social life. To this end, in the course of his sociology Weber sought to universalize his concepts of sect and church through showing how they were one instance of wider sociological processes (see previous chapter).

Nonetheless, Weberian sociology of sects is firmly rooted in Weber's analysis of the ascetic sects of Protestantism and their influence on the rise of western economic and cultural rationalism. Hence, despite Weber's attempts to universalize his concepts and apply church-sect distinctions to non-western religious movements, the example of ascetic Protestantism is a constant source of reference that can at times make the analysis appear culturally specific. In particular, it leads the researcher to constantly talk in terms of "lack" which privileges the examples of the ascetic Protestant sects. This phenomena stems from Weber's own research project and it is only the degree to which these research questions are shared with Weber that fidelity to this incarnation of his method is required. Nevertheless, working within the Weberian tradition does serve to raise important questions about each and every sect we may wish to understand.

The central theme of Weber's enquiries can be seen as being less about one particular type of personality that was essential to the rise of modern western rationalism and more about the variety of the types of personality that social organizations have moulded across time and space (Hennis, 2000a; 2000b). In this way, a Weberian sociology of sects becomes at the same time an enquiry into the formation of types of sectarian personality and their contrast to non-sectarian types of personality moulded by alternative modes of social organization. The Qumran materials can be approached with questions relating to the manner in which the Qumran sects selected and bred particular types of character and personality and how these transformations impacted in general on social, cultural and economic life as well as the manner in which these very processes of admittance and disciplining impacted on the social history of the sect itself and how it developed across time.

2. *Theological Doctrines of Predestination and Sectarian Tendencies*

The most significant features of *The Protestant Ethic and the Spirit of Capitalism* (1904–1905; 1920) reside in the role Weber accords to theological ideas in the evolution of sectarian tendencies which can develop into the creation of sects. The theological ideas that are of concern in the latter text are Calvinist notions of predestination, which create a division between individuals on the basis of their state of grace. Such divisions are at the root of sectarian tendencies just as social divisions based on other criteria are at the root of many dynamics in society since differentiation between individuals and groups is the fundamental building block of social structure. For Weber the consequences of the doctrine of predestination for the individual believer was an intense salvation anxiety which could not be relieved by any other means than by proving one's state of grace through the performance of an "effective calling." In other words, through being able to demonstrate a state of grace through objective signs relating to everyday tasks, and most significantly through objective signs of success in the sphere of business. The impact on the personality and the type of ethic carried by the ascetic Protestants is directly related to the values esteemed by the sects on the basis of their beliefs. Since an effective calling could be demonstrated via business activities, business activities were more highly esteemed than hitherto. Other sects might develop other means of demonstrating election, and the Weberian point is that when this is the case motivation to commit to those means is increased where salvation anxiety is intense.

The social and psychological benefits that might accrue to gaining the status of elect are not a central concern of this text (though Weber may have already been aware of this dimension). However, it is possible to observe, with the benefit of hindsight (gathered from knowledge of how Weber's sociology develops), that the motivation to excel in spiritual life or to find a satisfactory outlet for an intense spiritual or ascetic nature is a significant feature to consider in understanding the activity of "virtuosos" (who are, on these grounds, potential sect members). In the PE Weber does not utilize the terminology of virtuosity (preferring "elect" or "aristocracy of the elect"), since virtuosity is developed later as a significant concept. For example, Weber observes in the PE that with the closure of the monasteries those individuals who are motivated by their "intense religious natures" had to seek another means of putting their needs and desires into practice. As Weber writes, speaking of the impact of Protestantism and the "priesthood of all believers,"

> The drain of asceticism from everyday worldly life had been stopped by a dam, and those passionately spiritual natures which had formerly supplied the highest type of monk were now forced to pursue their ascetic ideals within mundane occupations (1930: 121).

Such motivated individuals will re-appear in Weber's sociology of religion and take on a central role. Already it can be seen how Weber's model of the individual sectarian partakes of a process of, on the one hand, selection of individuals, many of whom seem predisposed to want to join a demanding religious movement and, on the other hand, of a process of breeding, where those individuals and others are moulded by the discipline of the sect itself. We shall return to this contrast below.

The PE introduces us to the notion of an Aristocracy of the Elect – a high standing status group whose status is acquired on the basis of their religious qualifications to form *an elite of equals*. When presented in these ways, membership of a sect would not appear to be something that has a stigma of deviance attached to it, but rather, in the given context Weber is analysing, a goal that one is driven to achieve. In PE the achievement to join the elect/the sect, as analysed by Weber, is driven less by a desire to share social benefits and more by a need to alleviate a state of anxiety that derives from the insecurity associated with a particular theological set of ideas.

Weber clearly accords original theological conceptions with a good deal of independence as a causal factor in explaining the development of sectarian tendencies and of sects. Qumran scholars will not need any extra encouragement to study the theological backgrounds to the development of the Qumran Community or indeed for sectarian tendencies in the Second Temple Period. Whilst we need to be wary of reading foundation distinctions in the later writings of sects where ideological justifications and self-understanding are provided but retrospectively placed at the origin of the movement (see Davies in this volume), it is certainly the case that the *Community Rule*[1] provides theological reflection on the predestination of those who walk in the light compared with those who are walking in darkness (Fitzmyer, 1992: 52): a dualistic presentation of the distinction between degrees of grace that has sectarian implications in its elitist differentiation between individuals. Moreover, as in Weber's understanding of the ascetic sects, the relative standing of an individual can be gathered from "the signs identifying their works during their lifetime" (1QS 3, line 14; cf. 4Q373). These theological dualistic ideas – which run like a *leitmotif* through much of the Cave 1 material and also in materials from Cave 4, do not appear to be so far removed from the phenomena Weber was highlighting when he took the doctrine of predestination as the fundamental point of departure for the ranking of individuals on religious grounds in Calvinism and other similar ascetic sects. This ranking, in Weber's sociological explanation, has social status implications and provides a context for reconstructing individual motivation to adopt ascetic (and sectarian) lifestyles. Whether any evidence can be found at Qumran to confirm if there were high degrees of religious insecurity caused by these doctrines themselves (or whether the insecurities stemmed from other sources, e.g., a concern with the corruption of the cult and other core beliefs in the light of Hellenizing activities) is a moot point.[2]

Within the *Community Rule*'s exposition of the "doctrine of the two spirits," elements of the doctrine that might have caused a "salvation anxiety" can be identified. The Teacher, in the closing verses of the Rule, sees it as part of their role to counsel the faint-hearted. They vow to "distribute," "loving kindness towards the oppressed, encouragement to the troubled heart, and discernment to the erring spirit, teaching understanding to those that murmur" (1QS 10.29–11.2). Further, regulations designed to deal with those who "betrayed" the Community and its teaching, or "murmured" against the authorities indicate that the sect did not work for everyone, and that such failure could relate to failure to provide assurance of the achievement of religious goals. To be sure, the treatment meted out to those who displayed such doubt and anxiety ("stubbornness of heart") hardly encouraged its articulation. For example, the *Community Rule* stipulates: "Should a man return whose spirit has so trembled before the authority of the community that he has betrayed the truth...he shall do penance for two years" (1QS 7.23-24).

It could be that, in the course of the development of the sect, what was once a doctrine that led to confidence in one's own standing before God could develop into a tendency that worked to decrease and lessen that confidence. For example, the sect could at one time have operated as a community of equals with all individuals who were members being understood by self and others to have the requisite amount of "light" to qualify for membership. Once the sect operates a doctrine that this degree of light can vary, even between sect members (though too much darkness would result in either non-admittance or eventual expulsion: "by their fruits ye shall know them!") then membership of the sect could actually increase self-doubt in the religious sphere rather than working to alleviate it. Equally, such a development could lead to further differentiation within the sect, including ranking and the identification of an inner core of the "most holy." As is often the case, a sectarian tendency can harden into a sectarian reality which, in turn, leads to further differentiations on religious grounds. The doctrine of the two spirits contained in Column 3 of the *Community Rule* appears to be far more straightforward in the dualistic handling of the matter than the more complex treatment found in Column 4: the former clearly drawing a distinction between the sons of light and the sons of darkness, with the latter expounding that darkness and light strive within each individual including sectarians. The implications of differentiating sect members from others, and leaders from led, on this basis are obvious and may well be one of the reasons such a doctrine developed over time. In the *Community Rule* only fragmentary remnants of a one-time community of equals can be uncovered, for the text is replete with hierarchy, ranking and control. All the latter being elements that reduce the "sect-like" impact on personality and social change that Weber was interested in locating.

Finding textual support for developments such as these in the *Community Rule* undoubtedly revolves around the manner in which the redactional levels are reconstructed. For example, at times the *Community Rule*, in its "final form" in 1QS seems to equate the "Council of the Community" with the Community itself, whilst at other times the Council appears as an elevated grouping within the larger community (1QS 6). Moreover, it is not clear (at least to me) whether those "men of perfect holiness" in Columns 8 and 9, setting up a "House of Holiness," are not yet a further elite group within the movement as a whole that developed over time (rather than being the original body who established the sect in the desert). It would appear that given the lack of apparent consistency in the labelling of various organizational features of the sect that the redactional activity in the text has obscured and confused sociological realities that pertained at different times.[3] I return to consider these points in more detail below.

This information is of sociological interest from a Weberian point of view, since it not only allows for a measurement of salvation anxiety but is also suggestive of motivations that drove actors to commit to the strict regime of the sect itself. The latter commitment could be considered even stronger if it is allowed that there are passages in the *Community Rule* that speak of the achievement of perfection. For sure, there is an equal emphasis on the saving work of Yahweh (e.g. "He will refine for himself the human frame by rooting out all spirit of injustice from the bounds of his flesh" 1QS 4.21-23), but as we know from Weber's analysis even if the believer could not change the mind of the deity or force his/her secrets, they were nonetheless motivated to *convince themselves* of their status. In Qumranic terms, this would mean becoming assured that the "portions" of the light they carried outweighed the "portions" of darkness they were seeking to overcome.

Given the teaching in the *Community Rule* the expectation is that actual behaviour and attitude will be transformed through membership of the sect. Examination of the sectarian is not restricted to testing of knowledge, but includes examination of their behaviour over time (the sectarians' "spirit and deeds" and "understanding and practice of the law" are explicitly mentioned 1QS 5.22, 30). In a manner somewhat analogous to the processes reconstructed by Weber in the PE, a link can be traced from the theological doctrines held, to the motivation to perform in particular ways, to the translation of those doctrines and motivations into actual behaviour against which the individual and their own state of grace in the eyes of God and their standing in the community as a whole are at stake. If there were indeed differing degrees of "lightness" and "darkness" in each sectarian, the goal of the sectarian, through following the teaching of the sect and learning its secrets and through being accorded a higher rank in the course of time within the sect, would be to increase their portions of light before the final "Visitation."

3. *Ideal and Material Interests: Motivations to Join Sects and the Role of Economic Considerations*

For a Weberian sociology of sects it is necessary to ask what material and ideal interests might be motivating particular individuals in particular social settings to join sects, and what the personal as well as the social and cultural advantages might be for becoming a member and, on the reverse side, what were the personal, social and cultural consequences, if any, of not being allowed to join, or of being expelled. If we were to call Weber's interest in these processes an interest in "conversion" as such, it would be clear that for Weber material and ideal interests have a role to play in any convincing account.[4] We have already learnt from the PE that the ideal interests include the theological doctrines and religious ideas and needs that may develop as a consequence of those doctrines. That is, an individual may wish to join a sect on the grounds that the doctrines and way of life it espouses appear to be precisely what they themselves hold to be the case. Such a conscious commitment to the ideas of the sect, however, will, of course, vary depending on the degree of openness operated by the sect with regard to doctrine. Indeed, at Qumran, what is required is not exact knowledge of the sect's teaching on application, but an inclination to "inquire." Even with limited knowledge of the exact beliefs and practices of a sect an individual supplicant can be seen as making something of a cognitive choice based on information and hence be motivated by more ideal interests. Further, an individual may wish to have their subjective experiences confirmed and their grace assured, or indeed, in the case of virtuosos, to have their spiritual gifts recognized. All of these latter possibilities would come under a heading of ideal motivations.

From the PE text we know that for Weber psychological motivations to gain assurance of salvation was a major force in the life of the individual to adopt certain lifestyles. For sure, the need for assurance of salvation and grace would be a significant motive for joining a sect as well. But Weber is clear to point out that gaining such assurance is a "religious good" and needs to be placed alongside the other "goods" that are gained by virtue of attainting sect membership. In other words, what Weber calls material and ideal interests work together and are difficult to unravel. The *Community Rule* promises the sect member the material and ideal rewards of "healing, great peace in a long life, and fruitfulness together with everlasting blessing and eternal joy in life without end, a crown of glory and a garment of majesty in unending light" (1QS 4.5-8). To be sure, quite an attractive set of "religious benefits" for this life and the next. Such an observation though should not lead the researcher in the Weberian mode to cynically consider all seekers after sect membership as somehow motivated solely by material concerns nor as being hypo-critical when those concerns are expressed in non-material ideal terms.

In this connection it is important to dwell for a moment on Weber's treatment of the episode of the baptism that took place in Mount Airy,

North Carolina. He travelled here in 1904 to observe the baptism with his American cousins (Weber, 1920a). Whilst it would appear that Weber accepts the explanations given by his informants that individuals have sought sect membership for purposes of self-advancement in society, especially in relation to economic transactions, it soon becomes clear that Weber himself does not consider the individuals to be hypocritical. Moreover, the very processes that the individual is subjected to are sufficient for Weber to consider a good deal of sincerity. First, this is because the sect probes deeply into the life of the individual to the extent that any pretence would soon be exposed. Indeed, it was knowledge of this "inquisition" that led non-sectarian members to accept the credentials in business of sect members. As Weber writes: "This was because of the *thorough scrutiny* of the candidate's moral and business conduct (Lebensführung) that preceded admission" (2002a: 207); secondly, once within the sect, the sect works not to free the individual to cease from the type of behaviour with which they qualified but rather works to increase it given the strict discipline enforced. Weber observes: "Throughout their history, all the sects that grew up on the basis of the Baptist movement, especially the Quakers, exercised a ruthlessly rigorous *control* over the conduct of their members, paying particular attention to their *business* probity" (2002a: 208; Weber's italics); but thirdly, and just as importantly, the material interests do not dominate the ideal interests, given how the social reality of the group works on the individual themselves. Weber writes: "The individual seeks to make his mark *himself* by integrating himself into the social group" (2002a: 213). Which is to say that the individual is not freed by membership to perform, as it were, as he/she likes within the wider society with guarantees of moral and business probity, but is required to constantly demonstrate that probity within and outwith the sect, and moreover to further their own standing and the standing of the community itself in the eyes of the world and the eyes of God through continual proving of their worth, as is demanded of each and every individual within the sect.

From the description of the length of probation necessary to be fully admitted to the Qumran sect, it can be seen that joining the movement was no easy matter, but required considerable perseverance and strength of will. Moreover, the commitment to the sect did not ease off over time, but rather increased and was subject to annual review. It remains to be seen to what extent the Qumran movement promoted such expression of individuality and indeed provided opportunities to promote the movement in the eyes of non-members.

It is in this connection that we can begin to consider Weber's notion of self-assertion (Selbstbehauptung) since it conveys his idea that membership of a sect does not provide a haven in which one can hide from the demands of group-life, but rather an arena in which personal qualities need to be displayed (I will return to consider this concept further below). The arena in which the sectarian performs is most often the gaze of his immediate associates and frequently the membership of the sect as a whole. In this context the following passage is very significant:

> The cool objectivity of sociation encourages the individual to find his precise place in the purposeful activity of the group – whether this be a football club or political party – but it does not in any way diminish the necessity for the individual to be constantly looking for ways to assert himself (Selbstbehauptung). On the contrary, it is precisely *within* the group, in the circle of his companions, that the task of "proving" himself becomes most urgent. For this reason, too, the association to which the individual belongs is never something "organic" and all embracing that mystically hovers above him and surrounds him. Instead, it has *always* been quite consciously a mechanism for his own *purposes*, whether material or ideal (Weber, 2002a: 213-14; his italics).

The feeling of being a member does not come from some increase of comfort and support for weaknesses and suffering the "trials of life," for example, but rather from being able to achieve the goals valued by the organization. When those goals involve material success as a sign of ethical ability, and constitutes proof of grace, material interests and ideal interests would appear to go hand in hand. In situations where the qualities esteemed by the sect relate to economic abilities as indications of moral standing it is clear that economic behaviour will be affected but if a sect values other qualities the impact will be less in the sphere of the economic and more in other spheres, perhaps in areas in which impact is far harder to trace.

Weber was interested in the variety of impacts on personality and social and cultural change that could be affected by the values esteemed by various sects and associations. But it is fair to say, as noted above, that Weber's dominant question in his sociology overall relates to types of economic rationality. Hence a Weberian sociology is very interested in determining the degree to which "economic qualities" were considered in admittance to the sect and, in turn, what type of "economic philosophy" was promoted within the movement and, further, what then was the impact of that approach to money, business and property within the sect itself and in the society beyond the sect. Were the economic ethics of the wider society at extreme odds with those practised within the community itself? Did the society beyond the sect, for example, "learn" new attitudes to economic life from the sect members, either through observation or direct contact, or was a potential influence affected by lapsed members applying the approach to their activities once they had left the movement and were operative in the society at large? These and other questions suggest themselves and before moving on to consider the non-economic impacts on character and society that the Qumran movement achieved, it is necessary to spend some time briefly considering the relevant data in this dimension (see Murphy, 2002).

In order to provide some answers to these Weberian questions it is important to understand the role of the "community funds" operated by the sect (i.e. each sect member surrenders their "wealth" on full admittance, and all economic gains belong thereafter to the community and not the individual), and the degree to which business transactions took place between members of the sect themselves (members of the sect in other locations?) and between members and non-members. In the process of admittance to the sect, one's property is as it were frozen in the first instance, being recorded by the Bursar but not merged with the communal property. Whilst the individual was preparing for sect admission, it would be unlikely that they could continue to utilize their property for economic ends, if they indeed had that type of estate or business. Only after a further period of probation and testing was the individual property fully merged with the community property. When that occurred the individual was able to partake of the common property too. Lying about the extent of one's property is a "crime" against the community and its leaders. One of the "errors" legislated for in the documents is damage to/loss of community property: the sectarian is entrusted with the care of his comrades just as he is entrusted with the care for the sect property (the punishment for negligence is, however, less for the latter than for the former). All the property of non-sectarians is "unclean" and should not be merged.

The sociological work of Goffman on "Total Institutions" (Goffman, 1961) may be instructive here (if we can step outside the Weberian frame for the moment), since he theorizes the common practice in monasteries, prisons and mental hospitals of taking the personal belongings away from inmates during the process of admission. The purpose of doing so, is not to increase the wealth of the institutions (since the property is kept untouched until their release) but to gain control of the new member. Their identity – in terms of their self-identity and their connection with the "outside world" are taken away in one blow through this regime. At Qumran the surrender of property no doubt functions as a measure of commitment of the sectarian (and during probation may have involved financial loss), and a loss of connection to the outside world, but also serves the purpose of generating the self-sufficiency of the community and its general segregation from the wider society.

Also in these regards, the fragments of information like the ostraca found at Khirbet Qumran (which may be a record of a deed of a gift including a slave, an estate and its produce; see Cross and Eshel, 1997; cf. Vermes, 1997: 596-97), or 4Q 344, 346, 348 and similar examples (e.g. 4Q 351–58) become very precious. Also of significance are the wisdom texts found at Qumran (4Q 415–18, 424). The type of advice they contain and the manner in which economic "common-sense" appears as an index of sectarian knowledge of the mysteries of life, would suggest not only that there are economic/business dealings with both sectarian and non-sectarian members, but also that a good deal of duty and ethic surrounds "best practice." It is surely the case that "treasures" buried in 64 different locations, listed in the curious *Copper Scroll* (3Q15) are fictional, even though it can be imagined how a committed and ascetic group of sectarians, might, over many decades, be able to accumulate at least some "capital." It was traditionally the case that the life of the sectarians "in the camps" were considered to have had somewhat closer interactions with non-sectarians than the "segregated" community at Qumran, but recent doubts about the interpretation of the archaeological data at Qumran, for example, raises the possibility of significant relations with nearby settlements (Davies, Brooke and Callaway, 2002: 168-73) and, moreover, as Wassen and Jokiranta argue (in this volume) attitudes in the *Damascus Document* do not necessarily exhibit less "tension with the world" than the *Community Rule*. In the contrast of the righteous world of the sect and the fallen world of the wider society it is clear that certain ways of making money and a commitment to accumulating certain types of wealth are frowned upon. The "men of injustice" are "zealous for wealth." On the other hand, taking something from a non-sectarian is permissible on the grounds that "it must be bought with a price": the medium of money easing the transaction and restricting ritual impurity (cf. Davies, 2004). It is not the gaining of wealth in itself that is tainted and a temptation, but incorrect attitudes towards its acquisition and use.

It could well be that elements in the *Community Rule* can be read as evidence of continued social and economic exchange between sect members and non-sect members (and hence revising the notion of the Dead Sea Community as segregated). If such exchanges were not taking place, why legislate for the nature they should take? It would not seem necessary to advise as follows unless certain sectarians were mobile outside the confines of the "community walls" and unless they were dealing with non-sectarians: "These are the ways in which all of them shall walk, each man with his companion, *wherever they dwell*. The man of lesser rank shall obey the greater in matters of work and money" (1QS 6.4-6; my italics). If there were a series of interactions, including financial, business and produce exchanges, the specific attitude to these matters displayed by the sectarians, if strikingly different from the non-sectarian, would at least draw comment, and might, as in the proverbial case of the Quakers (which Weber never tired of quoting) impact on a general attitude to business and exchange. This would happen the more successful the sectarian "economic practice" appeared to be to outsiders. There is clearly much work to be carried out on the "economic data" from a strictly Weberian point of view.

A major problem with any interest in tracing the impact of sectarian ways of life on the wider society, apart from the limited knowledge held about ways of life in Second Temple times before the emergence of sects and after the destruction of Qumran in CE 68 by the Romans, is whether there was any "afterlife" to sectarian ideas, or carriers of sectarian ideas, or whether the whole experiment died out finally in the destruction at Masada. If, for example, a greater degree of continuity could be established from the sectarians to certain persons and ideas recorded in the New Testament (e.g. John the Baptist; see Fitzmyer, 1992: 106-108; 140-41) or in the later various "ascetic-monastic" movements in Egypt and Sinai (Fitzmyer, 1992: 141-42) and so on, then a historical tradition could be traced from Qumran to later examples of ascetic and economic practice that Weber was interested in. As it were, "a missing link" between earlier and later forms of rationalism could be provided and a way of assessing the impact of the sect on character and behaviour in general could be provided. The dualistic treatment of sect member and non-sect member, which carried over into the economic realm, would, for Weber, be something of an intensification of the double ethic he identified with Jewish economic practice, where different rules were operative whether the "client" was Jew or Gentile.

4. Benefit of Membership and Social Consequences: *The Support of Sect-Brothers,* Gemeinschaft *and the Trans-local Sect*

One of the material benefits for sect members and for elements of the society as a whole, Weber postulates, is the network that sectarian membership could provide, connecting disparate groups that shared the same beliefs and ethical principles (though different from each other on other grounds, such as kinship, ethnicity and cultural-linguistic heritage). These trans-local connections were a significant factor in providing support and social contact, and basically operated by connecting sect members from one part of the country with another. Such mutual support networks were of importance in frontier environments or in contexts where kin-relations were either stretched to the limit or were no longer operative. In a rapidly developing society the building blocks of social relations provided by the sect were sought after. Since it could be demonstrated that an individual was a member of the sect, was a sect brother, and qualified for support and was to be trusted, sectarianism impacted significantly, Weber argued, on American life to the extent that secular clubs and associations emulated the organization of the sects for similar ends. Membership of the association was a guarantee of the individual's moral status and functioned as a badge of brotherhood.

The credit worthiness of the sect brother included the fact that if a sect member, through circumstances beyond their control, found themselves in difficulties a reputable sect would make every effort to support the distressed member. The main function of the sect in the society is, however, to guarantee the *character* of the sect member and that the trust of the sectarian in business shown by other sect members and other non-sect members rested less on the fact that his sect would "bail him out" than on those personal qualities. Nevertheless, Weber's observations about the nature of sect brotherhood and the benefits such a social network provided for members and, moreover, the manner in which non-members are treated differently in social life because they are not part of the brotherhood, are of great importance. Weber's interest in brotherhood would appear to stand in some tension with his general attitude to the sect as a *Gesellschaft* rather than as a *Gemeinschaft*.[5] The notion of brotherhood would appear to support a *Gemeinschaft* type of reading of the character of the sect, one based on emotional bonding and familial personal relations. Since, as we have seen above, Weber sees secular clubs and associations in American society as direct descendents of the sect, basing membership on qualification after examination, it would be a significant bulwark against modernity's isolating tendencies if those associations were examples of brotherly support. Also, in periods of instability in Second Temple times a sect could be seen as a haven from the ravages of social change. Where identity is insecure and ethnicity not sufficient as an index of belief and behaviour, movements that provide opportunities for the development of character and the carrying of an external badge (e.g. the Essenes' white garments as mentioned by Josephus) as a symbol of that nature have an attraction that should not be overlooked. Establishing "trust" requires the ability to assess the stranger and neighbour for their "trustworthiness" and external badges of character have a clear function in such circumstances.

Weber's point though, needs to be correctly understood. The spirit of brotherhood[6] claims exclusive allegiance and provides exclusive support and the social and personal relations are based on the "cool objectivity of sociation." For sure, those outside of the fraternity are not extended any brotherly support but this does not mean that those inside are emotionally supported by the brotherhood. The degree of emotional support – the extent to which "family life" might be replicated amongst the "brothers and sisters" of the sect would depend, Weber might argue, on whether the sect based its values on a mystic religiosity rather than on the ascetic and ritual achievement of holiness. The mutual support found in the ascetic Protestant sects does not pertain to the emotional sphere of life. The advantages were often economic and the distinction between in-group and out-group members demonstrated itself most often with respect to the charging of interest on loans. When the Quakers extended the principles of "honesty as the best policy" to dealings with all – both fellow sect members and non-sect members – what was extended was the same degree of impersonal impartiality that operated within the sect.

What Weber finds noteworthy is that, following an individual's admittance to a sect, they could have a formal written guarantee of their moral worthiness that would be accepted by others as legitimate, thus resulting in mobility and networking. Transferring moral and business status in such a way that it could transcend a particular social location – by implication a relatively small scale, socially isolated social location – is the root of possible significant social change.

A Weberian sociology of sects is equally concerned to observe similar arrangements wherever sects have grown in size and can be found in more than one location, or in cases where perhaps original separate sectarian movements have merged or formed something of an alliance. The certification of personality and moral qualities provided by the sect allows for mobility and transfer of individuals from place to place, from one community to another and facilitates mutual exchange of ideas and goods. For the individual sectarian, the guarantees of sectarian membership provide elements of security in an insecure world, where central authority is weak and cannot be relied upon. In these ways, new connections are established and counter-orders become emergent. Sectarian membership can be a dynamic force rather than a bulwark to the *status quo ante*.

It is conceivable that the Qumran movement functioned as a translocal sect from time to time. It would seem likely that any relations between the sectarians in the "cities and camps" and those housed by the Dead Sea at Qumran would function in this manner. It could well be that the reference in the *Community Rule* to "Wherever there are ten men of the Council of the Community there shall not lack a priest among them" or the mentioning of at least two fellow sectarians "wherever they dwell" (1QS 6.7-9) allude to small conventicles of sectarians related to the parent sect from whom they are separated more or less permanently in their own settlement or whilst on a journey away from the main body. Furthermore, the ranking of sectarians in the movement meant that a more senior sectarian could guard against the moral and ritual activities of a junior member being forgotten during a journey: every Jedi has his paduan (spelling = Padawan), as we have learnt from *Star Wars*. In both cases, the regulations are developed to ensure continuance of the discipline of the sect and monitoring of its exercise. These regulations operate both within a larger settled community and between sect members who happen to be mobile for a duration, perhaps for purposes of economic exchange, for recruitment of members or for visiting fellow sectarians.

It is in this connection, following Weber, that we can consider the extent to which the Qumran materials suggest a social grouping similar to a *Gemeinschaft* or one nearer in type to a *Gesellschaft*. From a Weberian point of view, the more a community resembles a *Gesellschaft*, the more likely the community provides an avenue for, and even demands, the "assertion of self" since status within the group is achieved rather than ascribed. From the evidence of the *Community Rule* it is possible to conceive of elements of both *Gemeinschaft* and *Gesellschaft* in the sense of the terms as used by Weber above. It is in those instances in the *Community Rule* that appear to describe a community of equals that a feeling of *Gemeinschaft* can be gathered, and where value is placed on a supportive environment, like when the *Community Rule* observes the static manner of life in the community: "No man shall move down from his place nor move up from his allotted position. For according to the Holy design, they shall all of them be in a Community of truth and virtuous humility, of loving kindness and good intent one towards the other and [they shall all of them be] sons of the everlasting Company" (1QS 2.24-26). This description stands in striking contrast to the ranking celebrated elsewhere in the document and the chances of promotion and demotion within the movement on an annual basis. The same impression of a *Gemeinschaft* is gained from those regulations relating to caring for a sect brother and the sect's property and for having a joint and corporate responsibility for each person's spiritual welfare. "Let no man address his companion with anger or ill-temper, with obduracy or with envy prompted by the spirit of wickedness." The latter stipulations no doubt function to create an atmosphere of social wellbeing, but it needs to be remembered that to act opposite would be to betray one's fallen nature (1QS 5.25-27). Also the fact that the community as a whole often appears to be the court of appeal for decisions relating to admittance and re-admittance to the sect suggests a communal sharing of tasks and decision-making. Toennies, within his study, distinguished between the various bases upon which individuals might feel a bond with a community: a community of blood, a community of residence/place and a community of ideas. The last of these can extend over time and distance but must be subject to a ritual of renewal at periodic intervals for it to be a reality. The sharing of property at Qumran (including land) suggests a "community of place." Further, the sharing of sectarian beliefs might constitute a "community of ideals." If all members were, ethnically speaking, Jewish, a "community of blood" might be arguable, but in the sect it is the community of ideas that was dominant.

What works against the impression of *Gemeinschaft* at Qumran are the aspects of hierarchal control that are dominant within the Rule, (see further below) and the onus placed upon an individual to prove themselves: when it comes to examination of the sectarian, being a member of the community does not render their personal records insignificant. Clearly many of the rules and their infringement relate to relations between fellow sectarians, with the strictness of guidelines for in-group and out-group relations turned inwards to the sectarians themselves, perhaps in the absence of regular in-group/out-group interactions. Being a member of the sect does not excuse one from faults but rather heightens their importance and the opportunities for the observation of infringement. The individual sectarian must show themselves dedicated to the life of the sect and prepare for the annual examination of their "nature, deeds and knowledge" of sect beliefs and practices. The reward for such proving of self is elevation in the ranks of sects. The commitment to the community as a whole raises the significance of infringement of rules by individuals. Individuals are encouraged to secure and maintain the holiness of the community as a whole through subjecting themselves and their associates to close monitoring and to the reporting of infringements. The fact that the *Rule* legislates for how members might chastise or falsely accuse a fellow sectarian is evidence that such practices took place and are a further example of how the activities of in-mates in "total institutions" does not reflect mutual brotherhood but protection of self through the instrument of the community. In these ways, the Qumran sect is nearer to Weber's conception of a *Gesellschaft* than a *Gemeinschaft*.

5. Admittance to the Sect, Selection and Breeding, Sectarian Discipline and the Development of Types of Personality

5.1. Processes of Application, Probation and Continued Monitoring

A Weberian approach to the sociology of sects, includes seeking for data to answer questions relating to the processes of application for joining a sect, the method of probing carried out by those responsible for admittance and the structures and processes in place for the continued monitoring of the religious ideas and practical activities that are held at a premium by the sect concerned. For Weber these variables stamp the sect and the membership and hence variation in these processes is of sociological significance for assessing the nature, type and degree of educative influence of sect membership and so on. It is essential to know not only what the qualities were that needed to be demonstrated by sect members but also the various ways in which discipline of those qualities was organized and administered.

5.2. Sectarian Discipline and Education and its Impact on the Individual and on the Wider Society

It is through discipline that sects were capable of educating members in ethical and practical dispositions especially as they related to economic life. This education was also highly effective in promoting individual autonomy and responsibility and thereby had a major impact on social life in general, especially once the principle of admission and discipline were adopted by secular organizations based on the sect model. When looking at sectarian movements a Weberian approach wants to evaluate critically the degree to which the sect operated in ways that effected social changes of this nature and, if not, to seek to locate the variables that appear to have hindered that type of impact, whether these are internal to the sect or external to it. In any Weberian approach to the sociology of sects a concentration on the nature of discipline and its impact on the development of individual autonomy and responsibility, firstly *within the group* and then subsequently in the wider society will be on the agenda. Where the religious values are not deviant but sought after the sect can influence the society from within, since individuals seek to "live up to" those standards in a similar way, perhaps, to how the medieval laity, especially the upper echelons of society, valued the religious life of the monks and supported their work through generous gifts without wishing to be actual monks themselves (Southern, 1953: 150-54). The educative influence of the sect, therefore, is not to be restricted in all instances to the internal operations of the sect itself, but can impact on the lifestyles of non-sect members who become aware of the sect's principles. We have already discussed aspects of this dynamic when considering the possible impact of sectarian economic attitudes.

The manner in which an individual proves themselves in the company of the sect and the avenues available for assertion of self will vary and the possibilities for doing so need to be established by the researcher. Since for Weber sects play a significant role in the "break-through" to modernity, it is important to keep before us the degree to which individualism was "a possibility" within smaller scale and relatively undifferentiated societies in the past. Different types of discipline and the rigour with which it is enforced can be a significant variable in the development of types of personality and types of rationality. It is important to recall a comment by Weber about the discipline in the sects, and discipline in religious movements/institutions in general, which he made in the original PE essays. These comments concern the existence of "too much discipline:"

> the effect of church discipline was by no means always a similar one. On the contrary, the ecclesiastical supervision of the life of the individual, which, as it was practised in the Calvinistic state churches, almost amounted to an inquisition, might even retard that liberation of individual powers which was conditioned by the rational ascetic pursuit of salvation, and in some cases actually did so. The mercantilist regulations of the State might develop industries, but not, or certainly not alone, the spirit of capitalism; where they assumed a despotic, authoritarian character, they to a large extent directly hindered it. Thus a similar effect might well of resulted from ecclesiastical regimentation when it became excessively despotic. It enforced a particular type of external conformity, but in some cases weakened the subjective motives of rational conduct (PE, 1930: 152).

5.3. Selection and Breeding of Individuals and the Phenomena of Self-Assertion
Weber speaks of the educative role of the sect in relation to the individual byprocesses of both selection and breeding. It is not insignificant that Weber utilizes Darwinian language in this context. The ascetic Protestant sect brings about the "survival of the fittest" in terms of the necessary personality traits and beliefs required by the way of life of the spirit of capitalism. When voluntary associations, such as clubs, demand the same demonstration of similar characters, they too select and breed the individual members in certain directions. In this fashion, the sect and similar voluntary associations become major vehicles for personal transformation and in turn for social change. The selection of individuals – namely that not all those that apply are admitted, or rather that in order to be

sure of admittance individuals cultivate those characteristics esteemed by the sect – serves to impact on everyday life since individuals must alter their beliefs and actions in accordance with the sect principles. Similarly, once a member of the sect, the qualities esteemed by the sect are further bred. Indeed, excelling in those qualities appears to be demanded. This latter tendency relates to Weber's notion of *Selbstbehauptung*: a process of gaining self-esteem and maintaining a position within the sect by almost out-performing other sect members with relation to particular deeds and achievements, but always for the good of the sect community.

Weber's stress on the sect as an arena where a person is forced to "hold one's own" and to assert themselves in relation to the values and goals held dear by the association, betrays his own belief that personal development and cultural change is dependent on agonistic struggle. Whilst a Weberian sociology might wish to distance itself from such a conception, it is certainly the case that the impact of the sect on the personality of the individual is of utmost significance. It is important to ask, however, whether certain cultural and social developments in a particular social setting have occurred or are occurring to allow the individual qua individual to put their head above the communal parapet.[7]

For the moment, we can observe that various elements of sectarian organization might work against these very principles of self-assertion and indeed consider such individuality as tantamount to rebellion within the sect. For example, the existence of a novitiate, levels of membership, and strict control by a ruling inner group of leaders or priests would tend to work against such assertion of the self. Rather, it would suggest a "mortification" of self before the leaders of the movement and the community as a whole was in order. That is, one affirms one's suitability by disavowing one's individuality. Clearly, it is with movements that promote self-assertion that Weber locates the types of social and personal change he considers significant for the rise of western rationalism.

5.4. *What Types of Personality Are Developed in Sects and Voluntary Associations?*

What is absolutely central to a Weberian approach to sects, is the need to ask what happens to the personality of the individual applying to, joining and proving themselves within the sect or voluntary association, and what type of leadership and what type of domination develops in such organizations. The variables that are of significance and cannot be predicted are those relating to the core values – the qualities esteemed by the voluntary association or sect – that one must demonstrate to be a member of the association. (We must presume that these values can develop and alter across time and such development can cause further conflicts and divisions.) What these values are and what personality traits one must display or cultivate can, of course, run the whole gamut of possibilities, from an aggressive display of cunning and violence to the carrying out of ethical actions of sincere generosity to the weak. In other situations, one can imagine a set of values held dear by the association which, like the example of the choral society Weber uses, rather than encouraging action in the world, serve to channel energies and emotions down tracks that do not precipitate personal or social change. One gains the impression that the Pharisaic and Essenic pursuit of ritual purity (*sic*), that Weber examines in *Ancient Judaism*, is one example of such an abre-action of material and ideal interests that does not lead to an impact on society and culture akin to the impacts he traces back to ascetic Prot-estant sects. It will be recalled that, for Weber, the ascetic Protestants could only abreact their psychological anxiety about their own state of grace through rational action in the world in a calling: other avenues for release, such as a private confessional, were unavailable because of theo-logical ideas. In pursuing a Weberian approach to the sociology of sects it is not enough to describe the beliefs and ideas, nor only the processes of recruitment and retention, but also to enquire as to the impact on the personality as such of those ideas and those processes. What types of character are created by sects? Clearly, the nature of the individual personalities formed through the workings of the association/sect will impact on the nature of the movement as a whole of which they are a part. Especially, as Weber opined, the nature of the leadership.[8] All of these impacts, in turn, can impact on the wider society, and serve to promote or undermine themselves.

5.5. The Development and Type of Sectarian Personality at Qumran

In the light of the above remarks about Weber's approach to these ques-tions concerning processes of admittance to a sect, sect discipline and the impact on the personality of disciplinary processes in accordance with the values esteemed by the movement, I turn now to consider these issues at Qumran.

Given Weber's emphasis on voluntary membership as an essential feature of a "sect" in contrast to a "church," it is satisfying to record the numerous occasions where the *Community Rule* mentions the fact that the community is a voluntary one: the community is made up of "all those who have freely pledged themselves." On these grounds alone we can say that the movement appears to be a sect from the perspective of Weber's own polar typological definition. A Weberian sociology, however, wants to move beyond applying a label to consider the personal, social and cultural consequences of these processes for the types of development and impacts Weber had in mind. Before doing this, it is necessary to preface to our remarks some observations concerning the sociological history of the community as possibly reflected in the *Community Rule*, since decisions made about its redactional levels impact significantly on which data in the document relate to the processes we are seeking to understand. At this stage of my enquiries, I can only tentatively suggest ways in which we might move towards a Weberian sociological history of the Qumran sect.

5.5.1. *The History of the Community in Sociological Perspective.* Scholars are agreed that the *Community Rule*, in the version we have from Cave 1, is the result of a number of redactions. It is also agreed that the history of the movement is connected with the history of the redaction to the extent that reconstructing the levels of redaction is at the same to unravel the diachronic development of the sect(s). It would appear sensible for a sociological reconstruction of the history of the movement to be attempted and to question whether the levels of redaction identified to date have had sociological criteria in mind in dating texts and their relations to one another. It would be an interesting experiment to bracket out questions of palaeography, carbon dating and other non-sociological factors in attempting a sociological reconstruction of the history of the movement. Sociological attention would be focused on the nomenclature utilized in the document for various social groupings, roles and institutions in the movement, and also the various processes of admittance and discipline recorded in the text.

In such an experiment it could well be that those elements of the text that are currently considered to be a reflection of the original nucleus of the movement are in fact a reflection of the latter stages of the movement. Commentators often see the description of the group of priests and laity in Column 8 tasked with "making a way in the desert" as a record of the first stages of the movement. If, however, a sociological trajectory is imagined in which such gradations of rank and perfection are the result of a longer process of sectarian history and that this trajectory might be reconstructed from the sociological data in the text, it could be that this move to the desert is an event that takes place later, rather than earlier, in the community's history.

Without controlled examination of the data in the light of the histories of a number of sectarian movements in history, it is a hostage to fortune to be confident about any particular reconstruction that might be offered

here in the absence of such work. Suffice to say at this stage, that a sociological imagination can, perhaps, more readily envisage a development
of a religious movement from a communal semi-democratic origin to
a closely controlled, hierarchical movement dominated by priests, than
a movement from an original kernel of priests and laity which expands
to become a communal affair. Indeed, other versions of the Community
Rule from Cave 4 indicate that the priests did not always figure in the
hierarchy of the movement. Further, Weber's concern with the processes
of self-assertion as a driving dynamic on the part of sectarians as virtuosos driven by salvation anxiety within religious movements of this type
suggests that where such processes of self-assertion and their control can
be observed, that an analogous trajectory might be probable.

Aside from his interest in the self-assertion of the sectarian, Weber's
own contribution to an historical reconstruction such as this is to be
found in his analysis of charisma and its routinization. Later sociology
of religion built on Weber's contribution in a manner that was too posi-
tivistic in the light of Weber's intentions and which was moreover, as
Wilson pointed out, rather historically and culturally specific: namely,
the theories post- Weber elaborated a somewhat rigid model of development of the sect as it developed into a church. The model predicted
a transition from church to sect and sect to church along a continuum
which now included the denomination, as something of a half-way house.
I cannot elaborate further this dimension of Weber's sociology of religion
here. What can be said, is that Weber's characterization of the sect is
of a voluntary movement made of charismatic individuals who together
form a charismatic community. In the charismatic community the onus
is less on hierarchy and control, and more on democratic principles. For
Weber, the more coercion and control that one finds in the movement
the more "church-like," and the less "sect-like" that movement is seen to
be. It would appear that at Qumran, despite the role of the community in
making decisions, that democratic processes were not writ large. Where
the ability to speak (and if allowed to speak, for the point to be taken
seriously) is directly associated with one's rank within the organization,
and where decisions finally reside in the priestly executive (to which one
is born) it will be quite unlikely for a political and social education to
be taking place within the sect of the same quality of the education that
takes place regarding the sect's beliefs, rules, ritual and mysteries. Weber's
interest in the role of self-assertion and the manner in which status within
the sect might be acquired thereby, offers further sociological reasoning
as to how the Qumran sect, as reflected in the *Community Rule*, developed over time, since further gradations based on achievement can be

seen as emerging in the course of time as the very result, if unintended consequence, of their practice. When possibilities for further differentiation emerged, all parties had a vested interest in defending their own status and ring-fencing what positions could be achieved and which were ascribed. The harder achievement could be made to be, and moreover finding ways of making achievement of rank appear not to be simultaneously an indication of respective levels of light as opposed to levels of darkness, would function to keep the status quo operative. It is possible, within this process of development, that a move to the desert by a core group of men and priests of "perfect holiness" might be postulated.

5.5.2. *Admittance to the Qumran Sect and Processes of Discipline.* The sect would select from the populace those natures who were attracted to what they had heard about the movement and who were motivated to explore "the right way of living" and to place themselves as virtuosos under a strict regime. For the sect, it was sufficient that a person "inquire" "that they might know the hidden things, in which they have sinfully erred," and not treat "with insolence" those "matters revealed." Clearly the supplicant cannot have known about the secret things, and it is a general behavioural disposition and record of past behaviour that leads the Guardian and those responsible for admittance to recommend embarking on the first period of probation. The sect placed a premium on certain actions/deeds and it was these types of attitude and behaviour that would recommend the selection of a member and would be the substance of their further training and education within the sect. The dispositions include, "a spirit of humility, patience, abundant charity, unending goodness, understanding and intelligence; [a spirit of] mighty wisdom which trusts in the deeds of God and leans on his great loving – kindness..." and so on (1QS 4). The meaning given to "understanding" and many of the other qualities, of course, is open to interpretation and what would constitute an example of its operation would be decisions that would need to be made by the "gate-keepers" to the sect, who, no doubt, had become reasonably experienced in these procedures.

The novitiate was subject to further monitoring during their probation. Once they had been allowed to embark on their sectarian career, they would be instructed in the ways of the sect, and then brought before the congregation and the Council of the Congregation and they together would decide whether to continue to support the individual in their quest to join the sect. If answered in the affirmative the individual was still not a full member and was excluded from the Meal of the Congregation and had no share of community property. After passing this year of probation the individual was again examined "with regard to his understanding and observance of the Law." If successful his property was merged but not utilized by the Community, and he was admitted to the Meal of the Congregation but not to the Drink of the Congregation. After a further year of probation was successfully completed he would be admitted to the Drink of the Community, have his property fully merged, would be ranked according to his abilities and be able to participate in the meeting of the congregation and make contributions (1QS 6).

Once a full member of the community, the sect member was under the full gaze of those under whom they had been placed, under the gaze of the community as a whole and the priests and the elders. The *Community Rule*[9] describes how once joined to the holy Congregation, the Community will, apparently at an occasion where more than one individual is being admitted, write down the names of the new members, "in order, one after the other, according to their understanding and their deeds, that everyone may obey his companion, the man of lesser rank obeying his superior. And they shall examine their spirit and their deeds yearly, so that each man may be advanced in accordance with his understanding and perfection of way or moved down in accordance with his distortions" (1QS 5). In order for the latter to take place a record of the "understandings," ways of life, interactions, responses to examination on points of detail and following of ritual prescriptions, would need to have taken place.

Behaviour within the sect and right knowledge of sect teaching were the paramount concerns. Such expectations kept the moral career of the sectarian within relatively narrowly defined tracks. A sectarian proved themselves and gained self-esteem apparently from the development of right knowledge and the performance of right behaviour. Indeed, elevation through the ranks of the sect depended upon it, and lack of appropriate progress or backsliding could result in temporary or permanent exclusion, especially from the communal meal. Despite this element however, it would appear that the sect was organized in such a manner that would not allow individuality to appear, nor had the levels of self-assertion Weber observed as operative in the ascetic Protestant sects become apparaent. Part of this situation no doubt stemmed from the lack of a modernist attitude to individual identity (of course!). Where deviance from the sect rules and rituals and beliefs is reported it can safely be assumed that there is significant individuality in existence to rebel against sect principles. The fact that members will inform against a fellow-member is not a sign necessarily of a heightened sense of corporate identity in the society in general, but surely is an indication of commitment to the purity of the sectarian community itself. At the same time, perhaps a zealous regard for reporting others was also a means of rising in the ranks of the sect and in this way a manner of asserting the self and gaining prestige and personal self-esteem. During the "interviews" that took place periodically to establish levels of understanding of the law and its practice, it can be imagined how the individual needed to assert their own levels of success and performance, without at the same time indicating any over-blown sense of pride. The atmosphere in the *Community Rule*, however, smacks more of control and surveillance than the development of responsible and autonomous self-monitoring on the part of virtuoso individuals.

If it was the case, as 4Q186 might lead one to think, that individuals were assessed for their respective "parts" of light and darkness, not on the basis of records of their past lives, but on the basis of their physical appearance and their "star-sign," it would follow that the selection of individuals to be bred for sectarian membership and for membership of the Holy House of Israel was somewhat arbitrary: with personal qualities of character and behaviour only becoming operative once admitted to the sect. Indeed, on the basis of these physical characteristics, an individual could be placed in a very low rank indeed within the movement and strive to prove to themselves and others that they had more "parts" light than "parts" dark, achieved through the grace of Yahweh and the direction of the Teacher. However, even where this arbitrary system was not used (if it ever was) the sectarian was motivated to assert their own "levels of light" given the ranking and promotion system operating within the movement.

One way to think about the type of character that the sect might be developing is to consider an individual who has left the sect. For this portrait we draw on our imaginations. One can imagine that a member of the sect who had subsequently left the movement would display a character that was suspicious of individuals, but whose interactions with others was coloured by the reserve and humility learnt as appropriate behaviour between sectarian brothers when a member of the sect. Perhaps an overriding concern with washing and the status of the tools and utensils to be utilized would be observable. They would probably prefer to eat alone. An awareness of living in-between at least two ways of calculating the annual year and its seasons and religious significance, could lead to a feeling of being in a cultural "no-man's-[nor yet woman's]land" – an anomic experience for sure. To the extent that the "sapiental teaching" had been imbibed by the individual, the ex-sectarian would be armed for life with attitudes to oaths, loans, witnessing, trusting others and having an ascetic and utilitarian attitude to money and property. But perhaps the most conscious emotion would be one of being free from a social movement that had organized itself hierarchically into ranks, where one's standing depended not on a range of practical skills or claims to descent, but on the basis of knowledge of the sect's own teaching. In life outside of the sect, these forms of social status did not operate, and other ways of asserting self and connecting with others was expected. What the experience of the sect may have taught in general terms was that the relation between ascribed and achieved status within the sect was as ideologically coloured as social life outside the sect: whilst within the sect the promise of advance on the basis of achievement seemed to act as a counter-balance to the ascribed bases of social status in the 'world outside', the reality in the sect was that charisma itself was stratified. Perhaps when the lapsed sectarian re-entered non- sectarian life, he or she felt more strongly than previously that all forms of ascription were objectionable though hardly capable of challenge.

6. *Virtuosity and the Heroism of Everyday Life*

The most significant factors to emerge for a Weberian approach to the sociology of sects from the *Einleitung* are to do with Weber placing the analysis of sects into a broader historical–comparative framework. It is important not only to search for sectarian tendencies in the theological and religious ideas of the time, but also to search for any "tendency to virtuosity" that may exist in the culture and can find expression in religious movements. What constitutes virtuosity will vary from case to case. For Weber, the variation is not unrelated to other cultural dimensions that are operating, including religious ideas, types of prophecy and the conception held of the deity. Moreover, a Weberian sociology takes very seriously material and ideal interests, and attempts a multi-dimensional treatment of these factors, without reducing one to be a reflection of the other. Taking material interests seriously means being conscious of the class and status stratification systems and groupings in any society and seeking affinities between the stratification and the development of religious ideas and movements. But in no way is a Weberian sociology of sects interested in reducing the attraction of virtuosity to any one particular stratum, even though typical affinities may be observed in the historical record. One reason why the situation is more complex is the very fact that achieving the status of virtuoso on the basis of religious gifts esteemed either by the society as a whole or a section of it, or a particular class within it, can serve to transcend all current status attributes to provide a new status. Therein, perhaps, lays a major motivation to join a group of virtuosos. But it must be remembered that the virtuoso performance is a taxing and demanding one, and not for the faint-hearted. So, any material rewards that might be gained need to be placed in the balance of the ideal demands placed upon the sectarian. A Weberian approach searches for the examples of virtuosity within a complex set of status relations; it asks what the sacred values are that underpin virtuosity and considers who might and who might not be able to "raise their game" to qualify; these virtuosos may or may not be ascetic, and the presence of virtuosity may or may not lead to the formation of sects – a community of virtuosos. Joining a sect and remaining an esteemed member of a sect is something of an "extreme sport": the conquering of the self and the heroic achievement is channelled in directions that are available to it. It is important to ask within the context which undiscovered continents of human life are available in which to demonstrate one's excellence as explorer? When military struggle, for example, is no longer possible the heroic impulse might be sublimated in the direction of ascetic and pious practices which themselves slowly gathered the approval of the wider culture, since it provided an avenue for heroism. One thinks of the nature of Jewish resistance to colonial power in the period of the Macabbees and thereafter. In the light of such a consideration it would not be remarkable to find members of the Qumran community taking part in the final stand in 74 CE at Masada. In both cases the heroism was constituted by resistance and personal sacrifice. It hence is important for a Weberian sociology to consider the nature of heroism in a culture and the opportunities for its expression, accolade and achievement. Weber appears to be working with an anthropology of human nature that allows for and to a degree expects to discover in each culture persons who are motivated to be heroic: indeed, discovering the sphere in which one might be heroic is a fundamental constitutive of vocation. Again, an issue to consider is the degree to which this is a phenomena of modernity, itself traceable to the impact of Protestant ideas of vocation and the extent to which the will to be heroic is more ancient. Once a community of virtuosos comes into existence, the prospect of conflict with the bearers of official charisma, in whatever state and/or "church" guises may pertain to the social context, is increased. A Weberian sociology of sects is concerned with analysing the constitution of virtuoso and office charisma in a particular social setting and examining the nature and degree of the conflicts that may occur. The latter is a topic for a later discussion, but one must surely begin with the *Halakhic Letter* (4QMMT). But it might also be the case that a conflict between virtuosity and office charisma was taking place within the Qumran movements themselves, and that controlling the self-assertion of the charismatic individual was but one instance of that perennial sociological reality.

Conclusion

For Weber, sects were not for the weak-minded; and, moreover, sects pro-vided the social and psychological context for the creation of the strong minded, of the self-reliant who have acquired self-esteem (Selbstgefühls) through sectarian belonging and self-assertion (Selbstbehauptung). Strong-minded enough, he felt, to survive in, and even to carry, the processes of modernization. After our consideration of some Qumran material above from a Weberian point of view, what kind of conclusions can be drawn concerning the development of types of personality in the Qumran sect(s)? The sectarian at Qumran seems to be caught between the need for self-assertion and the maintenance of self-esteem. In other words, elements of the features of the ascetic sect that Weber was most interested in can be detected in the sources, but the overall impression is that the virtuoso would soon tire of the system (which may have been the intention of the group in charge). The Qumran sectarian could have been motivated by feelings of salvation anxiety in the light of the doctrine of the two spirits, and the fact that the sect operated a strict system of hierarchy in which the individual sectarian could advance or be demoted as their "deeds and knowledge" were assessed each year provided a context that would encour-age effort. Indeed, the out-performance of fellow sectarians for one's own advancement was facilitated by the "league table" of ranking within the movement. On the one hand, this system of discipline and education could motivate the individual to perform, and this performance would be a per-sonal achievement for which the individual was rewarded. The develop-ment of knowledge of sect teaching and ritual was an important part of the progress of the individual sectarian, but not all of these aspects of sect belief impacted on ethical standpoints and actual behaviour. In those cases where personal dispositions and attitudes were cultivated and influenced social interaction within the sect, a transformation of character can be postulated.

On the other hand, maintaining self-esteem in this environment may well have been difficult. Given the close monitoring of the individual by their immediate superiors in rank, and the chance that one might remain in the same rank or be demoted, the individual was not in control of their own destiny. The system of ranking and the existence of priestly control of the sect overall, render the sect less an example of the democratic ascetic type of sect Weber championed in his account of social change.

Foucault (1979) reminds us that the best form of discipline into ways of thinking and acting are those that operate within the person, whether they are being monitored or not. The trick is to get the individual to internalize self-discipline as if they were being observed. Weber would agree that unless the individual is led to make an assessment of their own performance and state of grace, self-reliance and autonomy and responsibility are slow to develop. It appears that this type of character development was not encouraged at Qumran. Perhaps one reason was that with such development demands for personal and political rights within the movement also find an anchorage. The last thing the priests wanted was a questioning of their grip on the movement.

The close control, the gaining of esoteric knowledge, the distribution of reward from the controlling priests, the lack of apparent opportunity to weigh one's own soul in the balance of one's knowledge and self-monitoring, the loss of personal property and other forms of identify and the insecurity concerning rank and the state of one's "portions" of light and darkness would work to undermine the processes of self-assertion that the sect had always seemed to promote, but was probably more successful in promoting during the time, if it ever existed, when sect members were of equal standing: a charismatic community of virtuosos who had the same high degree of "parts of light."

Endnotes

1. All references to the *Community Rule* and other Qumran documents are taken from Vermes' *The Complete Dead Sea Scrolls in English* (Complete edition, 1997).

2. There are a number of important issues to be addressed in this connection. For example, if the Qumran sects "withdrew" on the grounds that they subscribed to a different calendar it would appear that the sequence of development might be less from dualistic doctrines of predestination and more from such ritual and liturgical differences with the distinction between "sons of light" and "sons of darkness" being a secondary ideological explanation of the differentiation. The correct interpretation of 4QMMT is not without significance here. Of course, once strict differences between elect and non-elect (sect members and non-sect members) has developed, all manner of corollaries can be worked out, even to the extent of how people look and how fat or otherwise their thighs happen to be! (e.g. 4Q186, frag. 1). The "background" to differentiation between the qualified and the non-qualified may have an even longer history, and hence be something of a standard procedure in everyday life, when we consider Weber's interest in *Ancient Judaism*, in the taking of "vows," of shorter and longer duration, for the purposes of military activity. Such vows involve "ascetic" practices, such as the way of life of the Nazarenes, or of Samson. Indeed, in the *War Scroll* it is clear that the "troops" for the final holy war are not only "volunteers" but must be pure in deed and bodily form (1QM, Column 7). In such cases,

the individual has to be "qualified" to take part and must have their qualification examined by the relevant "authority." The *Damascus Document*, on the other hand, and to a certain extent the *Community Rule*, indicate the corruption, as they see it, of the wider (Jewish) society, including its profanation of the Temple and its rituals,, and how relations between persons are characterized by greed, deceit, and evil. The "apostates" have "wallowed in ways of whoredom and wicked wealth" (CD 8.5-6). Indeed, signs of having a "spirit of darkness" include: "greed and slackness in the search for righteousness, wickedness and lies, haughtiness and pride, falseness and deceit, cruelty and abundant evil..." and so on (1QSL 4.9-15). These lists of the ways of the non-sectarian provide a set of judgements about the "wider society" that can be read as reflections of reasons for withdrawing from the society in the first place. Reflection on why such differences pertain in society could lead to theological articulation of a doctrine of "two spirits."

3. Clearly these observations require further work to render them robust in the light of the available evidence. It seems to be that there is sufficient textual evidence for reconstructing a sociological history of the sect from the redactional levels in the Community Rule. See further below.

4. For a recent (non-Weberian) attempt to use sociology to understand conversion in relation to the Qumran documents see Brooke (2005).

5. Within classical sociology a distinction between so-called traditional and so-called modern societies is made through the typological contrast of communities and societies or associations respectively. Durkheim subscribed to a version of this story of the rise of modernity through his types of mechanical and organic solidarities (Durkheim, 1893). Labelling these types *Gemeinschaft* and *Gesellschaft* is a tradition going back to Weber's contemporary Toennies whose study, *Gemeinschaft und Gesellschaft* (1887) contrasted the types of social relationships in communities (as *Gemeinschaft* was translated) with relationships in associations (as *Gesellschaft* was translated) as a major difference between personal, face-to-face, supportive social relations, on the one hand, and impersonal, contract-based types of social relations on the other. Weber is, somewhat counter-intuitively, claiming that sect communities are not based on close, emotional mutually supportive ties, but rather resemble impersonal associations, and hence "anticipate" aspects of modernity, and help bring it about.

6. In using Weber's terms it is, of course. very difficult to escape the implicit sexism in the language of "brotherhood." Indeed, one might agree with Bologh (1990) that Weber's approach to social and ethical questions is masculinist. Such would be her opinion of Weber's stress on agonistic struggle and the drive to "assert oneself" (cf. Sydie, 1987).

7. In Durkheim's sociology, of course, there is little room at all for the development of modern conceptions of individuality in so-called (pre-modern and industrial) mechanical societies.

8. There are, of course, studies of the psychological and leadership dimensions of sectarian life that are valuable (e.g. Faris, 1937; Barker, 1986; Aberbach, 1986). Adorno *et al.*'s *The Authoritarian Personality* (1950) is not without relevance to this type of interest. My point is that this interest could be, but often is not, traced back to Weber.

9. I am presuming that the processes of admittance to the sect can be pieced together from various sections of the *Community Rule*, and that for the moment what might appear as two processes of admittance, one to the community as a whole, and one to the inner sanctum of the community, that is the Council of the Community (which was not open to all, but only those who had "risen through the ranks" to a state of perfection), can be ignored given that I have not yet established that difference. I only note that there is repetition in the Rule and that at times the Council and the Community are synonymous whereas on other occasions the labels appear to apply to differing social arrangements.

A Weber Bibliography

Aberbach, David. 1986. *Charisma in Politics, Religion and the Media: Private Trauma, Public Ideas.* Basingstoke: Macmillan.

Adorno, T. W. *et al.* 1950. *The Authoritarian Personality.* New York: W. W. Norton.

Albrow, Martin. 1990. *Max Weber's Construction of Social Theory.* Basingstoke: Macmillan.

Barker, Eileen. 1986. *The Making of a Moonie: Choice or Brainwashing.* Oxford: Blackwell.

Beetham, David. 1987. *Bureaucracy.* Milton Keynes: Open University Press.

Blaikie, Norman. 1993. *Approaches to Social Enquiry.* Cambridge: Polity Press.

Bologh, Roslyn. 1990. *Love or Greatness. Max Weber and Masculine Thinking: A Feminist Enquiry.* London: Unwin Hyman.

Bousset, J. W. F. 1892. *Jesu Predigt in ihrem Gegensatz zum Judentum.* Göttingen.

Broch, Hermann. 1984. *Hugo von Hofmannsthal and his Time: The European Imagination 1860–1920.* Ed. and trans. M. Steinberg. Chicago: University of Chicago Press.

Brooke, George. 2005. "Justifying Deviance: The Place of Scripture in Converting to the Qumran Self-Understanding." In Kristin De Troyer and Armin Lange, eds, *Reading the Present in the Qumran Library: The Perception of the Contemporary by Means of Scriptural Interpretation.* Leiden: Brill.

Callaway, Philip. 1988. *The History of the Qumran Community: An Investigation.* Sheffield. Sheffield Academic Press.

Chalcraft, David J. 1992. "Review of *Listening for the Text*, by Brian Stock." *History of the Human Sciences* 5.2: 141-44.

—2001. "Introduction." In D. J. Chalcraft and A. Harrington, eds, *The Protestant Ethic Debate: Max Weber's Replies to Critics of the Protestant Ethic*: 1-19. Liverpool: Liverpool University Press.

—2002. "Reconstructing Max Weber: The Contribution of Wilhelm Hennis." *Max Weber Studies* 2.2: 233-42.

—2004. "Nineteenth Century Comparative Sociology on Israel: The Contribution of Herbert Spencer." In Lawrence and Aguilar, 2004: 29-45.

—2005. "Reading Weber's Patterns of Response to Critics of *The Protestant Ethic*: Some Affinities in and between Replies to Felix Rachfahl and Werner Sombart." *Journal of Classical Sociology* 5.1: 31-51.

—2006. "Max Weber." In John Scott, ed., *Key Sociologists: The Formative Theorists*: 203-209. London: Routledge.

Chalcraft, D. J., ed. 1997. *Social Scientific Old Testament Criticism: A Sheffield Reader.* Sheffield: Sheffield Academic Press.

Cheyne, T. K. 1898. *Jewish Religious Life after the Exile.* New York: Putnam.

Collins, Randall. 1986. *Weberian Sociological Theory.* Cambridge: Cambridge University Press.

Conybeare, F. C. 1903. "Essenes." In J. Hastings, ed., *A Dictionary of the Bible*: I, 767-72. Edinburgh: T&T Clark.

Cross, F. M., Jr, and Esther Eshel. 1997. "Ostraca from Khirbet Qumran." *Israel Exploration Fund* 47: 17-28.

Davies, D. 2004. "Purity, Spirit and Reciprocity in the Acts of the Apostles." In Lawrence and Aguilar: 259-80.

Davies, Philip R., G. Brooke and P. Callaway. 2002. *The Complete World of the Dead Sea Scrolls*. London: Thames & Hudson.

Dawson, Lorne. 1997. "Creating 'Cult' Typologies: Some Strategic Considerations." *Journal of Contemporary Religion* 12.3: 363-81.

Drescher, Hans Georg. 1992. *Ernst Troeltsch: His Life and Work*. London: SCM Press.

Durkheim, Emile. 1893. *The Division of Labour*. Basingstoke: Macmillan.

Elbogen, I. 1904. *Die Religionsanschauungen der Pharisäer*. Berlin: Itzkowski.

Eliaeson, S. 2002. *Max Weber's Methodologies*. Cambridge: Polity Press.

Ewald, H. 1866. *Geschichte des Volkes Israel*. Göttingen: Dieterichischer Buchhandlung, 3rd edn.

Fairweather, William. 1908. *The Background of the Gospels or Judaism in the Period between the Old and the New Testaments*. Edinburgh: T&T Clark.

Faris, Ellsworth. 1937. *The Nature of Human Nature*. New York: McGraw Hill.

Filson, F. V. 1964. *A New Testament History*. London: SCM Press.

Fitzmyer, J. A. 1992. *Responses to 101 Questions on the Dead Sea Scrolls*. London: Geofrey Chapman.

Foucault, M. 1979. *Discipline and Punish*. New York: Vintage.

Freund, J. 1968. *The Sociology of Max Weber*. Allen Lane: Penguin.

Friedländer, M. 1905. *Die Religiösen Bewegungen innerhalb im Zeitalter Jesu*. Berlin: Reimer.

Gerth, Hans, and C. Wright Mills. 1954. *Character and Social Structure: The Psychology of Social Institutions*. London: Routledge, Kegan Paul.

Gerth, Hans, and C. W. Mills, eds. 1948. *From Max Weber*. London: Routledge.

Goffman, Erving. 1961. *Asylums: Essays on the Social Situation of Mental Patients and other Inmates*. New York: Anchor.

Graf, F. W. 1987. "Friendship between Experts: Notes on Weber and Troeltsch." In W. Mommsen and J. Osterhammel, eds, *Max Weber and his Contemporaries*: 215-33. London: Allen & Unwin.

—2004. "Ernst Troeltsch's Evaluation of Max and Alfred Weber: Introduction and Translation of Letter by Ernst Troeltsch to Heinrich Dietzel." *Max Weber Studies* 4.1: 101-108.

Hastings, J. ed. 1906–1909. *A Dictionary of Christ and the Gospels*. 2 vols.; Edinburgh: T&T Clark.

Hekman, Susan J. 1983. *Max Weber and Contemporary Social Theory*. Oxford: Martin Robertson.

Hennis, W. 2002a. *Max Weber's Central Question*. Newbury: Threshold Press, 2nd edn.

—2002b. *Max Weber's Science of Man*. Newbury: Threshold Press.

Hill, Michael. 1973. *A Sociology of Religion*. London: Heinemann.

Holtzmann, H. J. 1897. *Lehrbuch der Neutestamentlichen Theologie*. 2 vols.; Freiburg: Mohr Siebeck.

Hunt, S. 2003. *Alternative Religions: A Sociological Introduction*. Aldershot: Ashgate.

Johnson, B. 1971. "Church and Sect Revisited." *Journal for the Scientific Study of Religion* 10.1: 124-37.

Jokiranta, J. 2001. " 'Sectarianism' of the Qumran 'Sect': Sociological Notes." *Revue de Qumran* 20: 223-39.

Kaelber, L. 1998. *Schools of Asceticism: Ideology and Organisations in Medieval Communities*. Pennsylvania: Pennsylvania State University Press.

Kaesler, D. 1988. *Max Weber: An Introduction to his Life and Work*. Cambridge: Polity Press.

Kalberg, S. 1994. *Max Weber's Comparative Historical Sociology*. Cambridge: Polity Press.

Kim, Sung Ho. 2002. "Max Weber and Civil Society: An Introduction to Max Weber on Voluntary Associational Life (Vereinswesen)." *Max Weber Studies* 2.2: 186-98.

—2004. *Max Weber's Politics of Civil Society*. Cambridge: Cambridge University Press.

Kohler. 1906. At www. Jewishencyclopedia.com.

Law, John. 2004. *After Method: Mess in Social Science Research*. London: Routledge.

Lawrence, Louise J. 2005. "Men of Perfect Holiness (1QS 7.20): Social Scientific Thoughts on Group Identity, Asceticism and Ethical Development in the Rule of the Community." In J. Campbell, W. Lyons and L. Piererien, eds, *New Directions in Qumran Studies*: 83-100. Edinburgh: T&T Clark.

Lawrence, Louise J., and M. I. Aguilar, eds. 2004. *Anthropology and Biblical Studies: Avenues of Approach*. Leiden: Deo Publishing.

Lightfoot, J. B. 1916. *St. Paul's Epistles to the Colossians and to Philemon*. London: Macmillan, 7th edn.

Ling, Timothy J. 2004. "Virtuoso Religion and the Judean Social Order." In Lawrence and Aguilar, 2004: 227-58.

Lohse, Eduard. 1976. *The New Testament Environment*. London: SCM Press.

Marti, Karl. 1907. *Geschichte der Israelitischen Religion*. Strassbourg: Freidrich Bull, 5th edn.

Martindale, D. 1959. "Sociological Theory and the Ideal Type." In L. Gross, ed., *Symposium on Sociological Theory*: 57-91. New York: Harper & Row.

McGuire, M. B. 1997. *Religion: The Social Context*. Belmont: Wadsworth, 4th edn.

Merton, Robert K. 1968. *Bureaucractic Structure and Personality: Social Theory and Social Structure*. New York. The Free Press, enlarged edn.

Moffatt, James. 1912. "Essenes." In J. Hastings, ed., *Encyclopaedia of Religion and Ethics*: V, 396-401. Edinburgh: T&T Clark.

Mommsen, W. 1989. *The Political and Social Theory of Max Weber*. Cambridge: Polity Press.

—2000. "Max Weber's 'Grand Sociology': The Origins and Composition of Wirtschaft und Gesellschaft." *History and Theory* 39: 364-83.

Moore, Barrington, Jr. 1966. *The Social Origins of Dictatorship and Democracy: Lord and Peasant in the Making of the Modern World*. Harmondsworth: Penguin Books.

Murphy, Catherine M. 2002. *Wealth in the Dead Sea Scrolls and in the Qumran Community*. Leiden: Brill.

Orihara, H. 2003. "From 'A Torso with a Wrong Head' to 'Five Disjointed Body-Parts without a Head': A Critique of the Editorial Policy for the Max Weber Gesamtausgabe 1/22." *Max Weber Studies* 3.2: 133-68.

Otzen, Benedikt. 1990. *Judaism in Antiquity: Political Development and Religious Currents from Alexander to Hadrian*. Sheffield: Sheffield Academic Press.

Parsons, Talcott. 1937. *The Theory of Social Action: A Study in Social Theory with Special Reference to a Group of Recent European Writers*. Glencoe: The Free Press.

—1966. *Societies: Evolutionary and Comparative Perspectives*. Engelwood Cliffs, NJ: Prentice Hall.

Riesman, P. 1961. *The Lonely Crowd: A Study of the Changing American Character*. New Haven, CT: Yale University Press.

Riessler, P. 1927. *Altjüdisches Schriftum ausserhalb der Bibel übersetzt und erläutert*. Heidelberg: F. H. Kerle.

Roth, G. 1979. "Charisma and the Counter-Culture." In G. Roth and W. Schluchter, eds, *Max Weber's Vision of History: Ethics and Methods*: 119-43. Berkeley, CA: University of California Press.

Scaff, L. 1998. "Max Weber." In R. Stones, ed., *Key Sociological Thinkers*: 34-45. Basingstoke: Macmillan.

Schluchter, W. 1989. *Rationalism, Religion and Domination: A Weberian Perspective*. Berkeley, CA: University of California Press.

Schürer, E. 1908. *Geschichte des Jüdischen Volkes im Zeitalter Jesu Christi*. 3 vols.; Leipzig: Hinrichs, 4th edn.

Scott, C. Anderson. 1906. "Essenes." In Hastings, 1906–1909: I, 536.

Scott, Hugh M. 1908. "Pharisees." In Hastings, 1906–1909: II, 351-56.

Sennett, Richard. 1973. *The Uses of Disorder: Personal Identity and City Life*. Hardmondsworth: Penguin.

—1998. *The Corrosion of Character: The Personal Conseqences of Work in the New Capitalism*. New York: W. W. Norton.

—2003. *The Fall of Public Man*. Harmondsworth: Penguin, 2nd edn.

—2004. *Respect. The Formation of Character in an Age of Inequality*. Hardmonsworth: Penguin.

Sica, A, 2004. *Max Weber: A Comprehensive Bibliography*. New Brunswick: Transaction.

Silber, I. 1995. *Virtuosity, Charisma and Social Order: A Comparative Sociololgical Study of Monasticism in Theravada Buddhism and Medieval Catholicism*. Cambridge: Cambridge University Press.

Southern, R. W. 1953. *The Making of the Middle Ages*. London: The Cresset Library.

Stanton, G. 1992. *A Gospel for a New People*. Edinburgh: T&T Clark.

Stark, R., and W. Sims Bainbridge. 1979. "Of Churches, Sects and Cults: Preliminary Concepts for a Theory of Religious Movements." *Journal for the Scientific Study of Religion* 18.2: 117-33.

Stock, Brian. 1990. "Max Weber, Western Rationality and the Middle Ages." In Brian Stock, *Listening for the Text: On the Uses of the Past*: 113-39. Baltimore: The Johns Hopkins University Press.

Swedberg, R. 2005. *The Max Weber Dictionary: Key Words and Central Concepts*. Stanford: Stanford University Press.

Sydie, R. A. 1987. *Natural Women/Cultured Men: A Feminist Perspective on Sociological Theory*. Milton Keynes: Open University Press.

Tenbruck, F. H. 1989. "The Problem of Thematic Unity in the Works of Max Weber." In K. Tribe, ed., *Reading Max Weber*. London: Routledge.

Toennies, F. 1887. *Gemeinschaft und Gesellschaft*. Berlin.

T. K. (no name given). 1879. "Essenes." In *Encyclopedia Britannica*: 550-52, 9th edn.

Vermes, Geza. 1997. *The Complete Dead Sea Scrolls in English*. Harmondsworth: Penguin Books.

Weber, Max. 1904b. 'Die protestantische Ethik und der 'Geist' des Kapitalismus. I. Das Problem." *Archiv für Sozialwissenschaft und Sozialpolitik* 20.1: 1-54.

—1905. 'Die protestantische Ethik und der 'Geist' des Kapitalismus. Die Berfusidee des asketischen Protestantismus." *Archiv für Sozialwissenschaft und Sozialpolitik* 21.1: 1-110.

—1906a. *"Kirchen" und "Sekten" Frankfurter Zeitung*. (In two parts) 13th April/15th April.

—1906b. *Die christliche Welt*. (In two parts) 14th and 21st June.

—1920a [1915]. *Zwischenbetrachtung in, Gesammelte Aufsätze zur Religionssoziologie II*.

—1920b. "Die protestantischen Sekten und der Geist des Kapitalismus." In *Gesammelte Aufsätze zur Religionssoziologie*: I, 207-36. Tübingen: J. C. B. Mohr (Paul Siebeck).

—1924. *Geschäftsbericht und Diskussionsreden auf den deutschen soziologischen Tagungen, in Gesammelte Aufsätze zur Soziologie und Sozialpolitik*: 431-83. Tübingen: J. C. B. Mohr (Paul Siebeck).

—1930. *The Protestant Ethic and the Spirit of Capitalism*. Trans. Talcott Parsons. London. George, Allen & Unwin

—1948a. "The Protestant Sects and the Spirit of Capitalism" (original German, 1920). In Gerth and Mills, 1948: 302-22.

—1948b. "Religious Rejections of the World and their Directions (= Intermediate Reflections/Zwischenbetrachtung)." In Gerth and Mills, 1948: 323-59.

—1948c. "Social Psychology of the World Religions (Einleitung)." In Gerth and Mills, 1948: 267-301.

—1949. *The Methodology of the Social Sciences*. Ed. and trans. Edward Shils. Glencoe: Free Press.

—1951. *The Religion of China: Confucianism and Taoism*. Ed. and trans. H. Gerth. New York: The Free Press.

—1952. *Ancient Judaism*. New York: The Free Press.

—1958. *The Religion of India: The Sociology of Hinduism and Buddhism*. Ed. and trans. H. Gerth and D. Martindale. New York: The Free Press.

—1968. *Economy and Society*. Ed. G. Roth and C. Wittich. 2 vols.; Berkeley, CA: University of California Press.

—1976. *The Agrarian Sociology of the Ancient Civilizations*. London. Verso.

—1981. "Some Categories of Interpretative Sociology." Trans. Edith Graber. *The Sociological Quarterly* 22: 151-81 [original published in German, 1913].

—1985. *Wirtschaft und Gesellschaft: Grundriß der verstehenden Soziologie*. Ed. J. Winckelmann. Tübingen: J. C. B. Mohr (Paul Siebeck), 5th rev. edn.

—1988. "Einleitung." In *Gesammelte Aufsätze zur Religionssoziologie*: I, 237-75. Tübingen: J.C.B. Mohr (Paul Siebeck).

—1995. *The Russian Revolutions*. Ed. and trans. G. Wells and P. Baehr. Cambridge: Polity Press.

—2001. *The Protestant Ethic Debate: Max Weber's Replies to his Critics, 1907–1910*. Ed. David J. Chalcraft and Austin Harrington; trans. Austin Harrington and Mary Shields. Liverpool: Liverpool University Press.

—2002a [1906b]. " 'Churches' and 'Sects' in North America: An Ecclesiastical and Sociopolitical Sketch." In C. Wells and P. Baehr, eds and trans., *Max Weber: The Protestant Ethic and the "Spirit" of Capitalism and Other Writings*: 203-20. Harmondsworth: Penguin.

—2002b. "Voluntary Associational Life (Vereinswesen)." *Max Weber Studies* 2.2: 199-209.

Whimster, Sam. 2001. "Max Weber: Work and Interpretation." In G. Ritzer and B. Smart, eds, *Handbook of Social Theory*: 54-65. London: Sage.

— 2004. *The Essential Weber: A Reader*. London: Routledge.

Whyte, W. H. 1957. *The Organisation Man*. London: Jonathan Cape.

Wilson, Edmund. 1969. *The Dead Sea Scrolls 1947–1969*. London: W. H. Allen.

Wilson, Bryan R. 1959. "An Analysis of Sect Development." *American Sociological Review* 24.1: 3-15.

—1963. "Typologie des sects dans une perspective dynamique et comparative." *Archives de sociologie des religions* 16: 29-63.

—1966. *Religion in Secular Society: A Sociological Comment*. Harmondsworth: Pelican.

—1969. "A Typology of Sects." In *Types, dimensions et mesure de religiosite*: 31–56. Rome: Acts of the 10th International Conference for the Sociology of Religion.

—1973. *Magic and the Millennium*. London: Heinemann.

—1976. *Contemporary Transformations of Religion*. Oxford: Clarendon Press.

—1982. *Religion in Sociological Perspective*. Oxford: Oxford University Press.

—1988. "Methodological Perspectives in the Study of Religious Minorities." *Bulletin of the John Rylands University Library* 70.3: 225-40.

—1990. *The Social Dimensions of Sectarianism: Sects amd New Religious Movements in Contemporary Society*. Oxford. Clarendon Press.

Zeller, Eduard. 1882. *Die Philosophie der Griechen*. Leipzig: Fues's Verlag (R. Reisland).

Part II

SOCIOLOGICAL APPROACHES TO SECTARIANISM
IN SECOND TEMPLE JUDAISM

WHEN IS A SECT A SECT – OR NOT?
GROUPS AND MOVEMENTS IN THE SECOND TEMPLE PERIOD

Lester L. Grabbe

You can waste a lot of time with definitions. Scholarship is littered with the impotent offspring of sterile debates over definitions, and yet definitions can be important for clarity and common argument. They can also do great harm by canalizing all subsequent interpetation and debate in a wrong or unhelpful way. There is the old conundrum of whether a tree falling in the forest makes a sound if there is no one there to hear it. I remember as a schoolboy listening to a science teacher explain that of course it would not make a sound because a sound was "a noise that causes the sensation of hearing." He did not seem to notice that the outcome of the question had already been determined by his initial definition. However, one clever lad brought the whole discussion to an abrupt halt by noting that God would always be able to hear it.

The present paper is concerned with asking the question, What do we call the various groups in Second Temple Judaism? There are several ramifications to this: first, although the discussion will have implications for a wider debate about definitions, it will not go further than considering appropriate terminology for Second Temple Judaism; secondly, the ultimate aim is pragmatic – finding usable term(s) – not a lengthy theoretical discussion from first principles; thirdly, the decades-long discussion among sociologists will provide the background and context. We shall proceed by first looking at some of the main groups known from the Second Temple period, as examples of the issues that must be addressed when considering definitions. Only then will the specific question of definition be examined in light of recent sociological discussion.

The Empirical Data: An Examination of Second Temple Movements

We have some knowledge of many different Jewish groups from this period, though in a number of cases the actual information is very skimpy. Only a selection can be given here, but these examples should be sufficient to provide the necessary empirical data for the discussion in the next section.

The Qumran Group

The Jewish religious group of antiquity that we know most about is the group at Qumran. There is much about it that could be debated, but space does not allow that here (see Grabbe, 2000: 201-206). I shall simply note a fairly wide consensus among specialists. First, the settlement at Qumran was responsible for depositing the manuscripts in the surrounding caves, that is, the Scrolls represent in some way the library of the Qumran community. Secondly, although it is widely accepted that many of the texts among the Scrolls were not written by the Qumran group, there is also general agreement on a core of texts which are the product of the community and its ideology. There is some confidence, therefore, that we have a means of determining the perspective and many of the beliefs of the Qumran community.

This central core of documents include some of those found in the first discovery of Cave 1 (the *Community Rule* [1QS], the *Habakkuk Commentary* [1QpHab], *Rule of the Congregation* [1QS^a]) plus the *Damascus Document* (CD; 4Q266–73 = 4QD^{a-h}). The salient points about these documents can be summarized:

1. The group responsible for the writing were founded and led by a particular individual, the *Moreh ha-Zedeq* (מורה הצדק) or Teacher of Righteousness (CD 1.5-12//4QD^a 2.2.10-16.
2. 1QS and some of the *Damascus Document* are given over to a description of a community or communities which resemble those of a monastery.
3. There is some suggestion that parts of the movement were celibate (cf. 1QS); however, other parts married and had families, the main evidence being the statement at CD 7.6-8 (not paralleled in 4QD): "And if they live in camps according to the order of the land and take wives and produce children, they shall walk according to the Torah."
4. Property was held in common by the community rather than individuals.
5. The community saw itself as being persecuted, among the persecutors being the "Wicked Priest" (probably the high priest in Jerusalem).

Essenes

The relationship of the Qumran group to the Essenes requires careful consideration. The Essenes are one of the best documented Jewish groups in literature from antiquity. This literature is still not the same as primary evidence, but for most such groups we depend on secondary sources (i.e. much later literary sources). Before tackling the thorny question of their relationship to the Qumran group, if any, our concern here is to consider the group as they are described in the classical sources. According to Philo and Josephus, who are our main sources for the Essenes,[1] the basic characteristics of the group were as follows:

1. Number about 4000 males (*Ant.* 18.1.5 §20; *Probus* 75).
2. Live in many towns and villages (*War* 2.8.4 §124; *Probus* 76; *Hyp.* 11.1).
3. No wives, women, or marriage (*War* 2.8.2 §§120-21; *Ant.* 18.1.5 §21; *Hyp.* 11.14-17).
4. Community of goods and communal meals (*War* 2.8.3 §122; *Ant.* 18.1.5 §20; *Probus* 85–86; *Hyp.* 11.4-5).
5. Work at agriculture and crafts (*Ant.* 18.1.5 §19; *Probus* 76; *Hyp.* 11.6, 8-9).
6. No swearing of oaths (*War* 2.8.6 §135; *Probus* 84).
7. No changing of clothes (*War* 2.8.4 §126; *Hyp.* 11.12).
8. No slaves (*Ant.* 18.1.5 §21; *Probus* 79).

This has a number of characteristics that we would associate with a distinctive group: (a) small numbers, (b) customs that differ from society as a whole, (c) community organization. However, they do not seem to have physically withdrawn from society since they live around the country in towns and villages.[2] It is possible, of course, that in each of these towns and villages there is one or more community houses where the Essenes live and spend much of their time. Our impression, then, is of a movement that has partially but not wholly withdrawn from society. Anyway, the group also depends on society to provide new members since there is no propogation of membership through marriage and children. This is the minimum picture; however, if we are prepared to go further and add details from Josephus's accounts that have no parallel in Philo's writings, we come up with the following additional information (from both the *War* and the *Antiquities*):

9. Election of overseers and officials (*War* 2.8.3 §123; *Ant.* 18.1.5 §22).
10. Belief in the immortality of the soul (*War* 2.8.11 §§154-58; *Ant.* 18.1.5 §18).

The *War* makes a number of addtional points which do not occur in the *Antiquities* (or in Philo):

11. Oil defiling (*War* 2.8.3 §123).
12. Prayers to the sun (*War* 2.8.5 §128).
13. Daily schedule of work (*War* 2.8.5 §§128-32).
14. Bathing before eating (*War* 2.8.5 §129) and if touched by an outsider (*War.* 2.8.10 §150).
15. Speaking in turn (*War* 2.8.5 §132).
16. Study of the writings of the ancients and medicines (*War* 2.8.6 §136).
17. Regulations for admission to (*War* 2.8.7 §§137-42) and expulsion from the order (*War* 2.8.8 §§143-44).
18. Preservation of angels' names (*War* 2.8.7 §142).
19. No spitting in company or to the right (*War* 2.8.8 §147).
20. Strictness in observing the Sabbath (*War* 2.8.8 §147).
21. Foretelling the future (*War* 2.8.12 §159).
22. Existence also of a group that marries (*War* 2.8.13 §160).

This additional information, if accepted, considerably complicates the picture. Many of the practices mentioned might set the Essenes off from the rest of society in certain beliefs but would not affect its overall standing, since there were differences between Jews in beliefs about angels, eschatology, keeping the Sabbath, and the like. These differences in belief could also affect practice, but not generally in such a way as to cause problems with the rest of society. However, when one had to bathe after touching someone outside the community, it would mean a greater restriction on contact with society as a whole. Such contact would not be prohibited, but washing at some point soon afterward would be required, perhaps creating a tendency to restrict contact with outside society to certain members or certain times. The picture presented to us, if we simply compile these data, is of a community that lives in its own community dwellings with narrow internal rules about organization and conduct. Although contact with external society is not at all forbidden, it would tend to be restricted in certain ways.

However, if part of the movement was permitted to marry, this might suggest a greater diversity within the movement than suggested up to now. For although it would certainly be possible to be married and still live in a community house, with separate quarters for men and women, or some sort of apartments for couples, this would create problems. We might rather expect that those portions of the movement with married people would live in ordinary houses in the local community, even if within their homes they observed Essene rules. Even though we do not know how they lived, we have to consider the consequences of this statement by Josephus.

Josephus also mentions a few individual Essenes, which may give us further information to characterize the Essene movement: Judas, who was noted for his successful foretelling of events in the time of Aristobulus I (*Ant.* 13.11.2 §311); Manaemus, who predicted Herod's rise to rule and was rewarded by him (*Ant.* 15.10.5 §373); Simon, who interpreted a dream of Archelaus (*Ant.* 17.13.3 §§347-48); John, who was one of the commanders during the war against Rome (*War.* 2.20.4 §567; 3.2.1 §11). These confirm some of the pictures we had already gained from the descriptions of Philo and Josephus. Members of the movement seem to have access to the outside world and to have communicated not only with members of the upperclass but even rulers such as Herod and Archelaus. One Essene became a military commander. Was the designation "Essene" a reference to his past which he had left behind, or was he a practising Essene at the time of military command? The text does not help us, and either is a possibility.

Finally, we consider the statement of Pliny the Elder who mentions the Essenes in his *Natural History* (5.73). He places the Essenes in one location (on the shores of the Dead Sea between Jericho and En-gedi) and confirms that they are celibate. This description makes the group look very restricted, but it also contradicts the testimony of Philo and Josephus. They can be reconciled only if we assume that Pliny had information on only one group of Essenes and was not aware of the wider movement though, interestingly, neither Philo nor Josephus mention a special community on the shores of the Dead Sea. It is this last passage that forms one of the strongest arguments for linking Qumran with the Essenes, since Pliny's description puts the Essenes at or very near the site of Qumran. Some other characteristics seem to link the two, such as evidence of celibacy on the part of some of the community but also some indications of marriage on the part of some sections of it.

Revolutionary and "Messianic" Movements

When certain sections of Josephus are read, they leave the impression that particular periods in the history of Judah were characterized by revolts. The extent to which this is Josephus's own invention or represents a genuine increase in revolutionary movements at particular times can be debated.[3] From his descriptions, though, these groups show a good deal of diversity. After the Hasmonean dynasty was overthrown by Herod with the help of the Romans, Aristobulus and his descendents managed to rally an army of followers and raised a revolt against Herod on several occasions. In this case, the movement centred on the question of the legitimate ruler and probably involved a lot of ordinary Jews who were otherwise normal members of society. In other words, those who participated in these revolts were not members of an exclusivist group but represented a significant portion of the population of the country.

When we come to the various rebel leaders at the time of the "War of Varus" (just after the death of Herod in 4 BCE), however, the leaders in some cases seem to have "messianic" pretensions.[4] By "messianic" I have in mind the fact that at least some of these particular rebel leaders, who were usually of the *hoi poloi* or *ammei ha-aretz*, considered that they had a divine anointing – that they had been chosen by God to lead their people. The basis of the legitimacy of the leadership, and therefore of the group, was a calling from God. There may well have been an attempt to connect these individuals with the Hasmonean house in some way – unfortunately, the data are too sparse to know one way or the other – but their followers were likely to be aware that they were not in the same category as members of the direct Hasmonean family. Calling on God for legitimacy created a different sort of rebel group, a much smaller and more exclusive one.

Josephus tells us that in 6 CE, at the time Judea became a Roman province, a fourth sect or philosophy sprang up alongside the Sadducees, Pharisees, and Essenes (*Ant.* 18.1.1 §§4-10; 18.1.6 §23), whom Josephus calls the "Fourth Philosophy." This was a militant group, supposedly like the Pharisees in all respects except that they acknowledged no sovereign other than God. Their main characteristic was to refuse to recognize Roman rulership and to fight against the new provincial government.

Josephus states that the "Fourth Philosophy" gave rise to the *Sicarii*, a group that specialized in assassinating Jewish officials who cooperated with the Romans. There is some question whether this connection was based on reliable evidence or was only Josephus's own inference without any basis in reality. Regardless of whether there was an organic relationship with the Fourth Philosophy, the *Sicarii* made their presence felt in the mid-first century CE. In order to finance their activities, they did two things that modern terrorists have done: (1) they kidnapped family members of high officials, including the high priest, and threatened to harm them if not paid a ransom; (2) they sold their services to those who could afford to pay for them, a sort of Assassins for Hire. Astonishingly, their customers supposedly included some of the Roman procurators and even one of the high priests.

Perhaps one of the most puzzling but also interesting situations is that of the different revolutionary groups during the 66–70 war. The *Sicarii* were active at the beginning but were driven out of Jerusalem and spent the rest of the war at Masada. Another group seems to have come into existence toward the beginning of the war, called the Zealots. This was not the group at Masada, despite Y. Yadin,[5] but one in Jerusalem. However, the Zealots and a couple of other groups fought among themselves for control of Jerusalem until it was invested by the Romans. Only then did they unite and fight with great courage a battle that they could not hope to win. Here are groups that drew boundaries to the extent of trying to maim and kill one another, yet they fought a mutual enemy and seem to have similar goals and ideals. It is also difficult from Josephus's description to keep up with the shifting membership and relationship.

In sum, we have little information on most of these groups, and some may have been simply revolutionary groups and thus not religious movements. Yet it seems clear that at least some, if not all, had messianic or other religious beliefs and thus qualify as religious movements, however transitory.

The Pharisees[6]

We now come to the Pharisees. A common view is that the Pharisees were akin to a "church," *a là* Troeltsch. That is, while Josephus's other groups were "sects," sect is a "bad" word; since the Pharisees are "good," they could not be a sect. What is more, the Pharisees were in charge of religion – against those nasty priests who opposed them but still had to follow their diktats.[7] The fact is that we know little for certain about the historical Pharisees. There are major problems of source analysis, choice of sources, relationship of sources, and the theoretical framework in which sources are interpreted. But what we do know tends to go contrary to the view above which nonetheless is still widespread.[8]

Most would accept that Josephus is an important source on the Pharisees, even if there are some sharp disagreements on how to interpret some passages in his works. Two of his works begin discussion of the Pharisees' activities in relationship to events around 100 BCE. In the earlier work, the *War*, this is the reign of Alexander Janneus (103–76 BCE) during which time the Pharisees are among the opposition to Alexander (though Josephus does not particularly stress the Pharisees, suggesting that at the time he wrote the *War* he did not see them as especially significant among the opposition). In the *Antiquities* the Pharisees are given much greater prominence, including interaction with the ruling Hasmonean family at an earlier time, namely, the reign of John Hyrcanus (135–104 BCE). How to explain the differences in emphasis between the *War* and the *Antiquities* is an important issue, but for present purposes we need only note that already under the Hasmoneans the Pharisees are presented as a group seeking political power. In the *Antiquities* John Hyrcanus was actually a Pharisee at one point but broke with them over the punishment of an individual for speaking out against the ruler (*Ant.* 13.10.5-7 §§288-99). Both John and his son Alexander Janneus were enemies of the Pharisees after that. However, Alexander's wife Alexandra Salome (Shelomzion), who succeeded him, allowed the Pharisees great power and influence in her government (we can debate the anecdote about Alexander's dying advice to his wife,[9] but the great influence – whatever its cause – seems well attested).

After the reign of Alexandra, Josephus says nothing about activity by the Pharisees as a group for about half a century. Then suddenly under Herod we find some Pharisees trying to insinuate themselves into Herod's household to influence some members of his family. When he found about this, he had some executed. Later, about 6000 Pharisees refused to swear an oath of allegiance to Augustus Caesar and were fined (*Ant.* 17.2.4–3.1 §§41-47). Certain individual Pharisees (Pollion and his disciple Samais) were honored by Herod because of predictions allegedly made in his youth and also in his early career (*Ant.* 15.1.1 §3; 15.10.4 §§368-71). Nevertheless, between the Pharisees as a whole and Herod there seems to have been little love lost. The Pharisees appear under Herod as they did under the Hasmoneans: a group desirous of gaining political power, though in this case without success.

Although Josephus mentions Pharisees here and there after the time of Herod, he does not discuss any further collective action. Simon, son of Gamaliel, was a Pharisee at the time of the first revolt but does not seem to have held his office because he was a Pharisee. If the Pharisees as a group were politically active after the time of Herod, Josephus does not tell us. One can ask why this is the case. The answer is not necessarily simple. It could be that Josephus does not have any information, or possibly his aims caused him not to refer to such group activity. But there is another possibility, and that is that the Pharisees as a movement had changed their approach to politics. This is the thesis put forward by Jacob Neusner on the basis of rabbinic literature. If we accept that Hillel and Shammai were Pharisees (which might be debated), the early traditions associated with them indicate an inward-looking religious group, not a party seeking political power. Why is this? Is it because they were a pacifist faction of the Pharisees? Is it because Hillel and/or Shammai changed the direction of the movement? Is it that the tradents were interested only in the legal traditions? Were they in fact not Pharisees? Neusner's suggestion is that the movement realized that, under Herod, it was dangerous to be political and changed their orientation. What better individual to carry out this radical alteration of aims than the famed Hillel?

The Pharisees, according to Neusner's analysis based primarily on the pre-70 traditions about rabbinic figures and the "schools" of Hillel and Shammai, were a table fellowship group. That is, they were essentially a lay group that tried to replicate the temple and priesthood in the home. Their focus on matters of purity, the sabbath and festivals, tithing and the various agriculture laws, marriage and the family, all indicate a group which had control over its own internal affairs but did not control the wider society. This interpretation is to a large extent supported by the New Testament picture. Josephus's data emphasize only that they had "traditions of the fathers not written in the Book of Moses"; unfortunately, he never gets round to telling us what these traditions are. Josephus's picture can be, but does not have to be, reconciled with Neusner's thesis. The thesis is plausible, but there are so many fundamental questions that a number of possibilities remain. Not the least of our problems is trying to relate two quite different sources when we cannot even be sure that one of them is talking about the Pharisees as such.

To summarize a lengthy study and argument made elsewhere, one of the things I think we can say is that the Pharisees were not the ones who ran the country. They did not have control of the temple. The people did not live their lives by Pharisaic precepts. The Pharisees may have had a reputation for piety, and some individual Pharisees appear to have held important offices, but the Pharisees as a group were a small group, alongside other groups. So how do we characterize them from the point of view of our concern?

As far as their interaction with society is concerned, we see no evidence of withdrawal. At least some of the time in their history the Pharisees were looking for political domination – they wanted to run the country, and they practically did during the nine-year reign of Alexandra. We are not told what membership of the group was, but we know that some priests and even a few officials were members; on the other hand, there is no evidence that it was especially associated with these groups (unlike the Sadducees). Yet as A. I. Baumgarten (1987) has pointed out, the one consistent characteristic of the Pharisees is their adherence to traditions not written in the Torah. They are not just a political group but a religious one, and their political manoeuvrings may have been only a means to a religious end. If the early laws of the Mishnah and other Tannaitic literature represent Pharisaic law, this would suggest that the observances of the group would set them off in certain ways from other Jews such as, for example, their regulations about eating tithed and untithed food or some of their purity observances.

The Sadducees[10]

We have little information on the Sadducees, and almost all of it is hostile to the group. First is Josephus who discusses the Sadducees as a whole in two places. In the *War* he hardly ever mentions the Sadducees (or the Pharisees, for that matter). His only real discussion is at *War* 2.8.14 §§164-166. Here Josephus focuses first on the Sadducean belief in fate and their rejection of life after death. He then states that, contrary to the Pharisees, the Sadducees "are, even among themselves, rather boorish in their behaviour, and in their intercourse with their peers are as rude as to aliens." This last statement clearly represents a biased perspective and cannot be taken as an objective description.

In Josephus's *Antiquities* the Sadducees are mentioned alongside the Pharisees in the time of John Hyrcanus, when the latter moved his allegiance from the Pharisees to the Sadducees (*Ant.* 13.10.5-7 §§288-99). Subsequent references to the Pharisees in Josephus's narrative do not include the Sadducees until much later. In *Ant.* 18.1.3 §§4-23 he characterizes them, first of all, by stating that they do not believe that the soul survives death. They observe only the laws, by which he seems to mean only the "written laws" (and not tradition, contrary to the Pharisees). Only a few follow their beliefs but these are "men of the first merit" (ἄνδρας...τοὺς...πρώτους τοῖς ἀξιώμασι). Yet they accomplish almost nothing because, even when they assume a public office, they are forced to follow the Pharisees or the crowds would not tolerate them. This last statement is matched in its peculiarity only by modern scholars who take it at face value. When Josephus's own narrative is read, it gives no support for it, apart from the brief reign of Alexandra Salome in the mid-first century BCE. The Sadducean high priests and others seem to have had no trouble getting their way. This is indicated by the one example that Josephus mentions when the Sadducean high priest Ananus managed to effect the execution of James the Christian even though some opposed it (*Ant.* 20.9.1 §§199-200).

The significant New Testament references are mainly in the Acts of the Apostles. Acts 4:1-2, while not identifying the Sadducees with the temple authorities, certainly associates the two quite closely: "the priests and the captain of the temple and the Sadducees." A similar picture is drawn in Acts 5:17: "when the high priest arose and all those with him, the sect (αἵρεσις) of the Sadducees..." Toward the end of the book, the apostle Paul is brought before the Sanhedrin. He perceives that part of the members are Pharisee and part Sadducee, who differ over the question of the resurrection and the existence of angels and spirits (Acts 23:6-9). The Sadducees reject all three. Despite the alleged division of the membership between the opposing groups, the Sadducees seem to get their way. There is no evidence that the Sadducees lacked power or were dominated by the Pharisees.

This quick survey has not given us much that we can get our teeth into, but we are left with the impression that the Sadducees – or at least some of their number – are involved in government or administration, not only of the province but also the temple. At least some of their number are apparently wealthy or prominent in society. But they have certain beliefs that seem to make them a religious group rather than just a social club.

Sociological Discussion

As so often, Max Weber introduced the question of sects, but he in fact made little use of the model in his work.[11] Discussions about what to call such groups, therefore, still often begin with E. Troeltsch (1931) and his model of a church/sect dichotomy. Unfortunately, his discussion – like that of many subsequent sociologists – depended on assumptions and data from a particular Christian context: the European situation with state churches. If Troeltsch had drawn on the North American religious scene, his ideal type might well have been quite different.[12] It is not my purpose to review the debate in detail but to look at more recent discussions that show better promise of addressing the specific issues of concern here.[13] I shall concentrate on the one sociologist whose work is at the forefront of the debate and who has seemed to me to be most helpful in addressing the question, the late Bryan Wilson.[14]

Wilson's work is especially important because of extension study of actual movements in various parts of the world. His analysis first dealt primarily with Christian groups, for which he noted a number of their characteristics, their procedures for organization, the ways in which they originated and the elements of the conditions under which they emerge (1967: 1-45). These various lists of attributes are the sort of thing that non-sociologists tend to latch on to and try to apply to a quite different context. But while the lists might be helpful in giving a context to sectarian origin and development, they are not definitive but, as Wilson made explicit, they vary from group to group. An important step made, however, was to begin to develop a typology of sects that depended on "mission," of which he identified four types (1967: 25-29). He soon refined his analysis to propose seven ideal types based on the various views on how to achieve salvation (Wilson, 1970: 36-47), finally developing his discussion to encompass non-Christian groups (Wilson, 1973).

At this point, I wish to note some of the points made by Wilson that seem to be relevant to my questions, drawing on his various works, especially his *Magic and the Millennium* (1973). Please note that this is my formulation, not an explicit list found in a particular place in his work:

- "Sect" should be used with none of the negative overtones often associated with the term in a standard Christian context (1970: 14; 1973: 17-18). The term (or its translation equivalent) is widely used in other areas of the world without opprobrium (1973: 11, 31, 34; 1990: 1-3).

- The term "sect" does not imply a corresponding "church" but is roughly equivalent to "minority religious movement" (1970: 24-26; 1973: 34). Nor does it imply a movement on its way to becoming a "denomination" or "church" (1967: 22-23).

- Definitions of "sect" based on organization and/or doctrine are defective, especially outside the Christian context (1973: 14-16).

- Any analysis needs to be sociological, not theological. "Response to the world" seems to provide the most useful analytical tool because it involves a variety of characteristics, including belief and ideology, lifestyle, organization, form of association, social orientation, and action (1973: 18-30).

- Membership in a sect usually implies total commitment (1967: 24; 1973: 32-33). Unlike large communities (churches, nationalities, ethnic groups, and the like), membership is not just nominal and casual. Sect activity usually dominates the member's life.

As noted, Wilson's main criterion for distinguishing the various sorts of sect was originally that of their "mission" (1967: 25-26), but this was capable of misunderstanding since it might imply recruitment to membership. His final refinement discussed the different sectarian types in terms of "response to the world," which included the element of salvation (1973: 18-28). Salvation encompasses a number of possible approaches: achieving personal redemption for the individual in this life or a life to come, changing the world for the better, saving a group or race or even all mankind from destruction, fulfilling some sort of divine destiny.

However, they all involve overcoming evil. Again, "evil" is used in a broad sense to mean anything that is negative or bad, not just evil in a moral or religious sense. All sects know that something is wrong and they set out to correct it: this is salvation from evil; this is their response to the world.

Wilson created seven ideal types of sect, with the idea of covering the main possibilities of their reaction to the world. These were

1. Conversionist: God will change human beings.
2. Revolutionist: God will overturn the present world.
3. Introversionist: humans must withdraw from the world.
4. Manipulationist: humans must learn the right means of living in the world.
5. Thaumaturgical: humans must call on divine or magical powers.
6. Reformist: humans must reform the world, with God's help.
7. Utopian: humans must completely change society, with God's help.

What one must remember is that ideal types are theoretical models that one employees as a means of interrogating the real world. The pure ideal types are not necessarily found in reality.[15]

How might we apply these insights to the Jewish groups of antiquity? Do they work? We first need to consider the references to Jewish groups in antiquity. When we look at the ancient sources, we find a variety of terminology. Josephus refers to the main ones as "philosophies" (φιλοσοφίαι: *Ant.* 18.1.1-2 §9, 11; 18.1.6 §23); however, he also uses the term *hairesis* (αἵρεσις). Although it is the origin of the English word "heresy," the Greek word in fact referred to a "sect, faction, party, school" in a more neutral sense. The word sometimes means "choice" (cf. *War* 1.10.3 §199; *Ant.* 1.8.3 §169; 7.13.2 §§321-22), and perhaps the idea that someone has "chosen" to belong to a sect or faction is implied, but it is not clear that such an etymological meaning has to adhere to the word when it refers to a "sect" or "party." Josephus refers to the *hairesis* of Judas the Galilean (*War* 2.8.1 §118), the Hasmonean Antigonus (*Ant.* 15.1.2 §6), the Essenes (*War* 2.8.3 §122; 2.8.7 §137, §142), the Pharisees (*War* 2.8.14 §162; *Ant.* 13.10.5 §288; *Life* 2 §12; 38 §§191; 39 §197), and for the Sadducees (*Ant.* 13.10.6 §293; *Life* 40 §199). The same word is used in the book of Acts to refer to the Sadducees (5:17), the Pharisees (15:5), and the Christians (24:5: "Nazarenes").[16]

Although we are not bound to use the terms employed in the original sources (or their common English translation), we should take account of the data. One fact to note is that the groups are lumped together: there is no distinction made between the Pharisees and/or Sadducees and other groups. Thus, any attempt to use separate terminology for them would not be supported by the original sources. A common term capable of encompassing the main groups discussed above is desirable. Part of the problem is finding a definition that is not question begging – that does not make a priori assumptions about certain groups. This is where Wilson's approach turns out to be very helpful.

Some have wanted to treat the Pharisees separately (e.g. Sanders 1990: 236-42). Curiously, it is not the Pharisees who are a problem. As noted, the Sadducees have been a special problem and have sometimes been more or less ignored in the discussion.[17] The quick survey above has not given us much in the way of solid data, but we are left with the impression that the Sadducees (or at least some of their number) are involved in the government or administration, not only of the province but also the temple. At least some of their number are apparently wealthy or prominent in society. This might suggest that we are not dealing with a religious sect but a social class or even a club of some sort. But such a conclusion would ignore data equally well attested: the Sadducees have specific religious beliefs and practices. This makes them a religious group, as much as the Pharisees.

Potentially, we could use a number of words to refer to Jewish groups, but most of them do not work as generic terms. We have to be aware also that a number of potential terms have already been taken up by sociologists and others with particular connotations. I have used the term "group" so far through much of the present study, but "group" has had a significant place in sociological study, with interest in such aspects as group dynamics (Holy, 1996; Homans *et al.*, 1968). Yet "group" has a wide meaning, much wider than religious identity.[18] The same applies to "movement" ("social movement") which is also a term discussed by sociologists (Tarrow, 1996). The terms "party" and "faction" tend to be used in reference to political groups (Lijphart, 1996; Vincent, 1996). "School" implies a particular mode of thought and thus seems inappropriate for some of the more revolutionary groups; also, we tend not to use "school" of religious groups. "Denomination" and "church" tend to work best in a Christian context. The term "cult" has sometimes been used, but apart from the negative – even nefarious – connotation given to it in popular usage, sociologists now tend to avoid the term (cf. Melton, 2004). It really refers to a mode of worship or devotion: scholars of the Bible and Judaica conventionally use it to apply to many of the activities within the temple. In Christianity it does not usually refer to a particular religious group so much as a subgroup with a particular object of veneration (e.g. "the cult of Mary"). The one word that works for all the groups considered here and also carries religious implications is "sect." Some will still feel it bears a negative connotation, but there is no reason why it must. Wilson comments that he is using "sect" as essentially a synonym of "minority religious movement."[19] It can be a neutral designation meant to characterize pre-70 Jewish groups when there was no official church but the temple, priesthood, and common practice across the scattered Jewish communities set the general norm for living as a Jew.[20]

It will no doubt be asked: How do the various Jewish sects fit into Wilson's model? In the light of some of the caveats expressed above, considering how little we know about some of them, I hestitate to put them into his ideal types at the moment. As an exercise, it might be useful; however, the cautions already expressed must be assumed. One of the things that stands out, though, is the extent to which most of the groups can fit more than one category:

1. Conversionist (God will change human beings).
2. Revolutionist (God will overturn the present world): various apocalyptic and "messianic" groups.
3. Introversionist (humans must withdraw from the world): Qumran, Essenes.
4. Manipulationist (humans must learn the right means of living in the world): Sadducees? Pharisees?
5. Thaumaturgical (humans must call on divine or magical powers): most or all of them!
6. Reformist (humans must reform the world, with God's help): Sadducees? Pharisees?
7. Utopian (humans must completely change society, with God's help): Pharisees?

Regardless of whether these identifications are cogent, as far as I am concerned the various groups are best described as "sects." Only some of the revolutionary groups might be excluded, if they were purely political, but even here there seems reasonable evidence that at least some of them had religious motivations. Those with religious motivations would certainly be "sects" in my analysis.

Conclusions

This study has looked at two sides of the same problem: How do we designate the Jewish groups in the Second Temple period, and how is whatever term we choose situated in the sociological study of religious movements? As so often, we begin with the "father of sociology," Max Weber, though in this case it is his friend Ernst Troeltsch who has most influenced the debate. Troeltsch's model was irretrievably conditioned by its base in the contemporary Christian situation in Germany and other European countries. In certain contexts it was no doubt helpful, but it has long skewed the debate.

It was the important recognition, in the second half of the twentieth century, that the existence of a "sect" does not imply a corresponding "church" which helped to free the discussion to address the situation found in many parts of the world. Bryan Wilson's work, first on minority Christian groups in the UK and the USA and then on Third World and other "new religious movements," provided the new model. This was being developed some three or four decades ago at the same time that specialists were realizing the true situation in Second Temple Judaism and starting to reject the "orthodoxy" model.[21]

Models are models. They only help us to examine the empirical evidence, but among other things Wilson's model of seven ideal types provides the valuable insight that we do not need to come up with new terminology (cf. Wilson, 1973: 9-11). Once "sect" is shorn of its negative attitude and seen to indicate a "minority religious movement," without necessarily implying a split from a "church," it can serve the useful function of designating most and perhaps all the movements we know of in Second Temple Judaism. The group most difficult to characterize is not the Pharisees, as some have thought, but the Sadducees. Yet even here the little knowledge we have about them is that they are a religious group and not just a social class. They can also be labelled a sect.

Endnotes

1. Philo, *Quod omnis probus* (75–91) and *Hypothetica* 11.1-18, as quoted by Eusebius, *Praep. evang.* 8 (LCL 9.437-43); Josephus, *War* 2.8.2-13 §§120-61; *Ant.* 18.1.5 §§18-22.

2. This assumes that Philo and Josephus do not mean that they live in strictly isolated dwellings in these towns and villages. The indication is that they have contact with other members of society in the towns and villages.

3. Cf. McClaren (1998) and the comments in Grabbe (2000: 285).

4. See further the discussion and references in Grabbe (1992: 511-14, 552-54).

5. Yadin (1966); on the question, see Grabbe (2000: 287-88).

6. For a full study, see Grabbe (1999a); a similar but shorter treatment can be found in Grabbe (2000: 183-209).

7. Cf. Moore (1927–30), whose views became a consensus until the idea became undermined in the 1970s (cf. especially Neusner, 1973).

8. See Neusner 1973; also Grabbe 1977.

9. According to Josephus (*Ant.* 13.15.5–16.1 §§398-406), Janneus told her to turn some of the powers of state and also his body over to the Pharisees to do with it what they would, after his death. When she did so, instead of desecrating the corpse, they gave Janneus a magnificent funeral.

10. For a full study, see Grabbe (1999a); a similar but shorter treatment can be found in Grabbe (2000: 183-209).

11. Troeltsch (1930 [1931 in refs]: 144-45); Hill (1987: 155).

12. This was pointed out by B. Wilson (1970: 22-25). I found Wilson's comment interesting because not long after he wrote – but long before I had read him – I also used the American denominational picture as an analogy for understanding Jewish sects in Second Temple times (Grabbe, 1977).

13. See p. 114 above. Some useful discussions and surveys include O'Dea (1968); Hill (1987); Melton (2004).

14. See Wilson (1967, 1970, 1973, 1990). I also found the discussion by Baumgarten (1997: 1-41) helpful and am mostly in agreement with it. I should point out, however, that I had been thinking about the question quite some time before I saw his treatment (cf. Grabbe, 1992: 465), so that our conclusions have been reached independently for the most part. See also my review of Baumgarten (Grabbe, 1999b).

15. A perusal of M. Weber's writings quickly demonstrates the difference between the ideal type and real examples in the world. See, e.g., his study of the city in which real cities usually cut across the various ideal types (Weber, 1958).

16. My focus is on the terms used in the original sources, not on assuming that some sort of etymologizing will necessarily give us insight into which term to use. "Sect," it seems to be agreed, comes from Latin *secta* "school" (e.g. Quintilian 3.1.18; 5.7.35; 5.13.59). The basis of this, in turn, is *sequi* "to follow"; derivation from *secare* "to cut" has been proposed but is probably to be rejected, though one cannot rule out some influence (Simpson and Weiner, 1989: XIV, 842).

17. Baumgarten (1997: 11 n. 29) acknowledges that he has problems with accommodating the Sadducees, and they tend to be omitted from his discussion (cf. Grabbe, 1999).

18. Holy (1996: 351) comments on the term as follows: "Group has been used in many different ways, but it commonly refers to a plurality of individuals bounded by some principle of recruitment and by a set of membership rights and obligations."

19. Wilson (1973: 34).

20. On the question of what it meant to be a Jew, see my discussion (Grabbe, 2000: 292-311). One work that I have found very helpful in the debate is Cohen (1999).

21. Following G. F. Moore (1927–30), it was widely accepted that the Pharisees (and rabbis, projected back to the Second Temple period) represented some sort of orthodoxy among Jews.

References

Baumgarten, Albert I. 1987. "The Pharisaic *Paradosis*." *HTR* 80: 63-77.

—1997. *The Flourishing of Jewish Sects in the Maccabean Era: An Interpretation.* JSJSup, 55; Leiden: E. J. Brill.

Cohen, Shaye J. D. 1999. *The Beginnings of Jewishness: Boundaries, Varieties, Uncertainties.* Hellenistic Culture and Society, 31; Berkeley, CA; Los Angeles; London: University of California.

Grabbe, Lester L. 1977. "Orthodoxy in First Century Judaism: What Are the Issues?" *JSJ* 8: 149-53.

—1992. *Judaism from Cyrus to Hadrian.* I. *Persian and Greek Periods;* II. *Roman Period.* Minneapolis: Fortress Press. (Pagination continuous; British edition in one-volume paperback.) London: SCM Press, 1994.

—1999a. "Sadducees and Pharisees." In Jacob Neusner and Alan J. Avery-Peck, eds, *Judaism in Late Antiquity: Part Three. Where We Stand: Issues and Debates in Ancient Judaism*: I, 35-62. HdO; Erste Abteilung, der Nahe und Mittlere Osten, 40; Leiden: E. J. Brill.

—1999b. "Review of A. I. Baumgarten, *The Flourishing of Jewish Sects in the Maccabean Era.*" *JSJ* 30: 89-94.

—2000. *Judaic Religion in the Second Temple Period: Belief and Practice from the Exile to Yavneh.* London/New York: Routledge.

Hill, Michael. 1987. "Sect." In Mircea Eliade, ed., *Encyclopaedia of Religion*: 154-59. New York; London: Macmillan.

Holy, Ladislav. 1996. "Groups." In Kuper and Kuper, 1996: 351-52. London; New York: Routledge.

Homans, George Caspar, *et al.* 1968. "Groups." In Sills, 1968: VI, 259-93. New York; London: Crowell Collier & Macmillan.

Kuper, Adam, and Jessica Kuper, eds. 1996. *The Social Science Encyclopedia.* London; New York: Routledge.

Lijphart, Arend. 1996. "Parties, Political." In Kuper and Kuper, 1996: 589-91.

McClaren, James S. 1998. *Turbulent Times? Josephus and Scholarship on Judaea in the First Century CE.* JSPSup, 29; Sheffield: Sheffield Academic Press.

Melton, J. Gordon. 2004. "An Introduction to New Religions." In James R. Lewis, ed., *The Oxford Handbook of New Religious Movements*: 16-35. Oxford: Oxford University Press.

Moore, George F. 1927–30. *Judaism in the First Three Centuries of the Christian Era.* 3 vols.; Cambridge, MA: Harvard University Press.

Neusner, Jacob. 1973. *From Politics to Piety.* Englewood Cliffs, NJ: Prentice-Hall.

O'Dea, Thomas F. 1968. "Sects and Cults." In Sills, 1968: 130-36. New York; London: Crowell Collier & Macmillan.

Sanders, Edward P. 1990. *Jewish Law from Jesus to the Mishnah: Five Studies.* London: SCM Press; Philadelphia: Trinity Press International.

Sills, David L., ed. 1968. *International Encyclopaedia of the Social Sciences.* New York; London: Crowell Collier & Macmillan.

Simpson, J. A., and E. S. C. Weiner, eds. 1989. *Oxford English Dictionary.* Oxford: Clarendon Press, 2nd edn.

Tarrow, Sidney. 1996. "Social Movements." In Kuper and Kuper, 1996: 792-94.

Troeltsch, Ernst. 1931. *The Social Teachings of the Christian Churches.* Trans. Olive Wyon. 2 vols.; London: George Allen & Unwin; ET of *Die Soziallehren der christlichen Kirchen und Gruppen.* Tübingen, 1911.

Vincent, Joan. 1996. "Factions." In Alan Barnard and Jonathan Spencer, eds, *Encyclopedia of Social and Cultural Anthropology*: 222-23. London; New York: Routledge.

Wallis, Roy, ed. 1975. *Sectarianism: Analyses of Religious and Non-Religious Sects.* London: Peter Owen.

Weber, Max. 1930. *The Protestant Ethic and the Spirit of Capitalism.* Trans. Talcott Parsons. New York: Charles Scribner's Sons; London: Allen & Unwin.

—1958. *The City.* Trans. D. Martindale and G. Neuwirth. London. ET of *Die Stadt* (1921) = 1978 [1968]; G. Roth and C. Wittich, eds, *Economy and Society*: 1212-1372. Berkeley, CA; Los Angeles: University of California.

Wilson, Bryan R. 1970. *Religious Sects: A Sociological Study.* World University Library; London: Weidenfeld & Nicolson.

—1973. *Magic and the Millennium: A Sociological Study of Religious Movements of Protest among Tribal and Third-World Peoples.* London: Heinemann.

—1990. *The Social Dimensions of Sectarianism: Sects and New Religious Movements in Contemporary Society.* Oxford: Clarendon.

Wilson, Bryan R., ed. 1967. *Patterns of Sectarianism: Organisation and Ideology in Social and Religious Movements.* London: Heinemann.

Yadin, Yigael. 1966. *Masada: Herod's Fortress and the Zealots' Last Stand.* New York: Random House.

Sect Formation in Early Judaism

Philip R. Davies

The manuscripts from Qumran have not only revealed to us something of the "inner life" of Palestinian Judaism in the late Second Temple period, but have also provoked new ways of understanding the nature of Second Temple Judaism itself. In this essay I want to clarify, with reference to the Qumran material, the nature and origin of "Jewish sects" by posing a distinction between social segregation and heteropraxis. This distinction will in turn become useful in exploring the nature of ancient Judaism itself. The existence of a sect implies the existence of a "parent," from which the sect obtains some of its identity but against which it matches its identity also. (This, to my mind, distinguishes a "sect" from a "movement"; in my own definition, a sect is schismatic.) What *was* that "parent" Judaism? Three issues in particular that arise from recent scholarship on this "Judaism" are (a) when can we first speak of "Judaism"? (b) should we more accurately speak of "Judaism" or "Judaisms"? and (c) what kind of processes best describe the development of this "Judaism" – centrifugal, centripetal or both?

While reasons for the social segregation of the Qumran sect(s) – and thus their sectarian formation in the strict sense – can in fact be plausibly reconstructed, the polemics the texts display do not reveal why, of the range of ideas and practices that Second Temple Judaism exhibits, and the variety of process of accommodation, the particular issues specified (which often amount to differences in halakhah, understanding of scriptural law, and notably calendar and purity) should have generated sects.

Method and Approach

In discussing any particular case of "sect formation" a balance is needed between theoretical considerations, such as those drawn from sociology, which are themselves extrapolated from a comparison of numerous specific instances, and a historian's reverence for the specific. Most of the sociological research on sects has been conducted on Christianity (Weber, Troeltsch, Durkheim, Wilson) and on New Religious Movements

(Wallis). In the case of ancient Jewish sects, however, the approach is hampered by the lack of reliable sources as well as a critical appraisal of the religion itself (though Weber produced some excellent insights). In the case of the Qumran scrolls, our major evidence for ancient Jewish sectarianism, the evidence is skewed: a great deal of texts, many sectarian, but little reliable history from external sources and archaeological data that in fact do disappointingly little to illuminate the texts or the sects that wrote them. The only possible approach, then, is a textual one, but, given the one-sidedness of the evidence (we have no guaranteed external descriptions unless we identify the sect[s] as Essene), this requires great care. Sociological theory can function – and in my view *must* function – as an exegetical principle to control what will otherwise be either a flat and uncritical exposition of the views expressed or undisciplined scepticism or imagination.

The taxonomies suggested by sociological theory (e.g. world-affirming, world-denying, introversionst, reformist) to my mind make sense only when seen against what is the essential character of a sect: its relationship to its parent, to which sects generally relate, and not to the world in general. Judaism itself (insofar as we can generalize: it is now common, though hardly universal, to speak of "Judaisms" before the triumph of the rabbis) displays features of assimilation, accommodation, rejection and uneasy co-existence with "the world," for which indeed, it has a word: "peoples" or "gentiles." And Judaism is not a world-religion; whatever its occasional strategies of conversion, its ideology was generally strongly ethnic and exclusivist, its outward symbols those of difference (circumcision, Sabbath, dietary laws, rejection of religious images). Indeed, Judaism itself displays many of the characteristics of a sect. Here it differs considerably from Christianity, on which many sociological models are built. But this is not to reject the assumption that even ancient Jewish sects display features and mechanisms common to sects of other religions and other times, for sectarian formation, whatever its religious grounds, is also a social movement and as such amenable to sociological explanation. Indeed, that principle is, I think, fundamental to our definition of what a sect is.

On Defining a Sect

The problem of defining "sect" still dogs our research into ancient Judaism, and probably always will, because we are unlikely to reach agreement on how to use the term. One can therefore only state the definition being used and adhere to it. Perhaps, in the end, use of the word "sect" does not matter: rather, the phenomenon I have in mind is of a social group that finds it impossible (for whatever reason) to inhabit the same social world as the rest of society. Many Jewish groups (Pharisees, Sadducees, Zealots) held different views and observed different practices, perhaps strongly condemning other such groups: but from descriptions of these groups it does not seem that they segregated except for the performance of their distinctive routines. Rejection of some features (aspects of identity) and rejection of all can, of course, be a matter of degree (Shakers, Amish, Jehovah's Witnesses, Mormons, all show this); and hence the term "sect" depends on discernment of a crucial degree of separation. Given this, I recognize a sect as a social group that has socially segregated itself from its wider social matrix. A sect does not regard itself as merely a *part* of a wider society, but as the only legitimate representative, a microcosm. Other sects or groups within the same matrix are rejected. One of Wilson's criteria (Wilson, 1959: 1973) for sectarian identity is that dual membership (of the sect and of the society outside it) is not permitted; and this makes the same point. The segregation of a sect may be in part symbolic but will always be visible and, to the sectarian, real and distinct: the boundaries are not merely ideological, interior or private. A sect need not in principle be religiously defined: one may plausibly speak of a philosophical or even political sect, but in such cases philosophical schools and political movements are acting rather like religions, demanding adherence to a worldview that shapes the beliefs and practices of its adherents, and implicitly or explicitly opposing all other views. Ancient Judaism was, indeed, often presented and understood in the ancient world as a philosophy (and Moses compared to Plato). On this definition, the communities described in the Qumran texts are sects, and the texts themselves can be considered, in Ricoeur's words, as "texts of redescription" (Ricoeur, 1995; *what* the texts are "redescribing" will be the theme of much of this essay). However, as I shall argue below, the task of redescription develops from the sectarian schism: it is not a prerequisite; and that redescription can in fact contradict factors that historically generated the schism (as, for example, a formally dualistic wordview can be superimposed on a view of divine election that initially legitimizes adherence to a sect, as seems to be the case in the Qumran scrolls).

A sect's social segregation obviously entails ideological alienation. But the ideology may not be the primary cause. Differences of belief or behaviour within a society are always present, and do not in themselves produce sects. As long as society as a whole and those exercising those beliefs and practices are mutually tolerant, differences will coexist in the form of parties, associations, or denominations. While these formations will possess a degree of ideological independence, they will also participate in the larger social identity.

There is an important implication of this observation. We do not necessarily find the reason for sectarian formation in the actual beliefs or practices that a sect describes. The task of "redescribing" an alternative identity presupposes sectarian status, and even if the actual reason for segregation is political, the sect will justify its existence on ideological grounds. In other words, the sect will (re)write its origins with the aim of establishing its identity claims, from a sectarian vantage point. Hence, many sectarian beliefs and practices *postdate* the moment of segregation but are nevertheless retrojected to the beginnings. After all, where a sect claims the identity of its parent, that identity must go back to the very beginnings.

This is illustrated in the *Damascus Document* (see below) by the claim that after the depredations of Nebuchadnezzar, a new "Israel" was formed by divine initiative, with a new lawgiving and a new covenant:

> But with those who survived and adhered to the commandments of God,
> God established his covenant with Israel, even for ever... (CD 3.13-14).

Here, as with several other late Second Temple period writings, including Daniel 9, the present era begins after the exile, the earlier history of the "old Israel" being written off. Indeed, the so-called "Deuteronomistic History" itself does precisely that, cataloguing an occasionally relieved history of disobedience leading to final doom. The renewed covenant and lawgiving in Ezra-Nehemiah (Nehemiah 8–9) similarly recapitulates the beginning of "old Israel," based on a new community of "children of the golah" (Ezra 4:1; 6:19-21; 8:35 etc.). Sectarian claims to be the "true Israel" will therefore not extend back to that "pre-exilic" era (CD's "covenant of the 'first ones'": 1.4; 3.10), and the exile thus becomes the time of birth of all "Israels" of the Second Temple period (on the *topos* see, e.g., Knibb 1976; 1983). In the *Community Rule*, however, a bolder claim is made: a new history (or non-history) is fashioned through a myth of predestination in which the "children of light" were chosen from the beginning of creation. It can be argued that far from predating the foundation of the sect responsible this starkly dualistic mythology developed as a means of creating an identity older than that of "Israel" itself.[1]

Consequently, it is important not to blur the ideological and social components of sect formation into a single explanation. Ideological differences do not explain sects: they provide both an element of precondition, and a *post hoc* rationalization – which, ideally, we should try to unravel and distinguish. Sects actually become sects for other reasons. Separating the ideological differences from the process of social segregation has two important consequences for an understanding of the Qumran texts: it allows us to state unequivocally that the texts contain descriptions of two *sects*, not parties or movements, because physical separation from the religious and cultural environment is clearly entailed. But it also creates a problem in identifying the role of ideological difference: which aspects provided the pretext, or condition, for segregation, and which developed later as the sectarian worldview expanded to embrace the definition of a distinct "Israel"?

Qumran Sects

At this point it is probably helpful to sketch the Qumran sects and suggest something of their distinctive ideologies, but also possible reasons for the formation as segregated entities and as self-contained "Israels." By "Qumran sects" I do not mean to imply sects necessarily housed at the settlement of Qumran, but as shorthand for "sects described in the Qumran manuscripts."[2] Whether any of the manuscripts in the caves were written at Qumran or refer to its inhabitants does not need to be settled here.[3] However, Qumran scholarship as a whole is not agreed that we are dealing with two sects: they are often thought to be different versions of the same sect (e.g. García Martínez, 1988). What follows is informed by my literary analysis and on my comparison of the ideological structures of the two sects in the *Damascus Document* and the *Community Rule* respectively (Davies, 2000a; 2000b), using the categories of "Israel," "Torah," "temple" and "messiah."

The "Damascus" Sect

The "Damascus Community," as described in the D texts (chiefly CD, the most complete, but non-Qumranic version, and the Qumran Cave 4 [4QD] mss.)[4] was organized in two kinds of settlement, "cities" and "camps" (CD 12.19, 23; 13.20; 14.3). This arrangement is also implied in 4QMMT (4Q394 frag. 3-7, 17-18 = 4Q397 frag. 3.2-3, and it is likely, from these references, that the chief settlement was in Jerusalem (cf. CD 12.1-2 *'ir hammiqdash*).[5] It described its members as being in a "new covenant" made in the "land of Damascus" (CD 6.19), which required them not to "enter the sanctuary to light his altar vainly" (CD 6.12), and thus the sect maintained a limited connection with the Jerusalem temple (CD 11.17-21). It held that "all Israel" had erred, especially in the matter of observing Sabbaths and other sacred times (CD 3.14); other disagreements about the torah are cited in 4.13–5.11. From this and from numerous other Qumran texts it can plausibly be inferred that the sect observed a calendar of 364 days. Further disagreements over matters of purity law occupy much of the contents of the *Halakhic Letter* (4QMMT), and it has been suggested (e.g. by Schiffman, 1994) that differences over the interpretation of torah constituted the main item of contention between this "Damascus" sect and its parent society, or at least the religious leaders of that society.

For this group we have no self-designation other than "Israel" (cf. "cities of Israel," "seed of Israel," CD 12.17, 22).[6] This sect claims for itself the title "Israel," possession of the true covenant and the assurance of deliverance at the final divine visitation; its boundaries are with "Israel" as a whole, although certain groups within Israel ("builders of the wall," "seekers of smooth things," CD 4.19; 1.18) may indicate specific groups. Its "camps" and "cities" (which, together with the rules of initiation and discipline, show its self-contained social organization) were apparently subject to distinct sets of regulations, and possibly only in "camps" were married members to be found (CD 7.6-7); there is a least an implication that this was not the case for all. Although there were priests in this sect (CD 9.13-16; 13.2; 14.7), the senior rank seems to be that of *mebaqqer* (CD 14.9-12). The members are divided into priests, Levites, Israelites and *gerim*.[7]

The *Damascus Document* is the only text that includes an account of the origins of this sect. It claims to have originated after the punishment of the first "Israel" by exile, with the granting of a renewed covenant; whether or not this is an explicit response to the stories of Ezra and Nehemiah (the latter not preserved among the Qumran manuscripts, the former represented possibly by a small fragment) it offers the same general outline as these books in seeing "Israel" as reborn from the ruins of an old one, by means of a second covenant and lawgiving, that is, founded by *direct divine initiative*. It also regards "Israel" (i.e. Jewish society beyond the sect) as in error, either as a continuation of the old, failed Israel, or as another new "Israel" that has repeated the mistakes of the old.

Thus, halakhic and calendrical differences are evident in the texts and in D are made a basis for contention. Indeed, the title given to the founder of this sect is "Interpreter of the Law" (*doresh hat-torah*). But calendrical differences at least are apparent in texts that do not appear to emanate from a sect (such as *1 Enoch* and *Jubilees*). Hence they predate sectarian formation. The implication of these other texts is that at one time these differences could be accommodated within the society of Palestinian Judaism without the adherents of either system requiring to segregate from the other.[8] If they are a pretext for the formation of the sect, then it is the ending of toleration on one side or the other that constitutes the actual reason.

The Yahad

What we know of the *yahad* is derived mostly from 1QS and the 4QS manuscripts (= S), constituting various recensions of what we call the *Community Rule*. The name *yahad* appears at the very beginning and the contents seem to indicate a celibate group, though there is no explicit statement to this effect. The goal of the members (or at least the *maskil*, which apparently designates a teaching office) is to follow the commandments of God "as commanded by the hand of Moses" (1.2). There are also several references to a "covenant" (such a ceremony is described in 1QS 1.16–2.18). However, a doctrinal section in 3.13–4.26 describes esoteric teaching, revealed apart from the Torah, that divides humans into "light" and "darkness" (and finally allows a mixture of the two in each person). Authority is (sometimes) accorded to the "sons of Zadok" and there is also reference to a "council of the *yahad*," the role of which remains unclear and disputed. A section of disciplinary rules is also included, governing life within the sect, and in some respects quite similar to those of the "Damascus" laws. But unlike D, these rules are not derived from the scriptural torah. The material in Columns 8 and 9, which many interpreters have taken to represent the earliest layers of the document, appear to reflect the foundation of this sect, proposing the establishment of a "council of the *yahad*" of twelve men and three priests, who will function as a "holy house." In this connection the phrase "making a way in the wilderness" (9.19-20) is used, though whether this is literal or metaphorical use cannot be known. The stated aim of this group is to "atone for the guilt of iniquity and rebellion of sin, for grace for the land, without the flesh of burnt offerings or the fat of sacrifice" (1QS 9.4).

Taken by itself, this document (especially in its varying recensions) gives little help in explaining why the sect was formed. That it was a sect is evident from the rules of admission (which are similar to those of the "Damascus" community) and segregated lifestyle. Several other points of ideological comparison with the *Damascus Document* (predestination, lack of [full] communion with the Jerusalem temple, intense study of the law of Moses) can be found. There are three major lines of interpretation open, all of them assuming that the *yahad* springs from the "teacher of righteousness." If one is to take 1QS 8–9, following Murphy-O'Connor (1969) as a "Manifesto" proposing a move to the desert and the foundation of a small group, from which a larger community grew; the reasons for this proposal, however, is not given in the text.[9] A second line is to rely on clues in D. In CD 1 and in manuscript B he is connected with the history (though not the foundation) of the "Damascus" sect. In CD 6.11 "one who will teach righteousness" is expected at the "end of days" and it has been argued (Davies, 1981; 2000b) that this title, identified with the "messiah of Aaron and Israel," was claimed by an individual. A third way is offered via the *Pesharim*, who portray the "teacher" as persecuted by a "wicked priest." The "wicked priest" does not appear in D or in S texts.[10] The suspicion lingers that this scenario is secondary and unhistorical, obliterating the "Damascus" community entirely and presenting the founder of the sect as an opponent of the Jewish high priest. Two of these lines of interpretation assume that the *yahad* was brought into being by followers of a charismatic individual; only the second theory offers a precise reason for his appearance and his behaviour. Hence, this is the interpretation followed here, though the evidence is not sufficient for certainty. Once independent of the "Damascus community," however, the *yahad* developed its ideology in distinctive directions, while fundamentally continuing to share several of the ideological elements of the parent sect. The death of its charismatic founder (alluded to in CD 20.13-15?) no doubt prompted some ideological adjustment if (as a figure of the "end of days") his appearance was thought to herald the eschaton. However, since the *yahad* does not appear to have been a sect of Judaism, but a sect of a sect of Judaism, study of its origins contributes only indirectly to our theme.

The question of what precipitated the Damascus sect to form remains as yet unanswered. But for the moment let us leave it and consider the nature of that "Judaism," or rather that "Israel" to which the sect claimed sole possession.

Ideological Variety within Second Temple Judaism

The central question here – how do we understand the formation of the "Damascus sect" (and its splinter) – involves us in an analysis of Second Temple Judaism as a whole. Here we shall primarily consider ideological differentiation, but the issue of possible sect formation at other times and places will also be borne in mind.

Ideological differences characterize the whole of Second Temple Judaism, which was rather pluriform. This pluriformity is attested not only in the different expressions (and sects) of Judaism observable in the late Second Temple period, but even in earlier times: in fact, from the beginning. The "beginning" I take to be the moment when "Israel" and "Judah" ceased as political entities and "Israel" was born as a religious community. That phrase may seem redolent of the scholarship of the late nineteenth century, with its distinction between a "pre-exilic" and "post-exilic" character. But we have progressed some way beyond Wellhausen and his contemporaries – without entirely dismissing their insights.

Several different models have been proposed for the development of "Judaism." The model inherited from the nineteenth century (and not abandoned until well into the twentieth) was of a fairly monolithic religion, introduced by Ezra and Nehemiah, centred on law, temple, priesthood and cult. The spontaneous "prophetic" religion apparent in earlier times was lost or submerged, to be rediscovered in Christianity. That model was modified by several scholars into a dualistic scheme, in which the "prophetic" religion did not disappear but continued, alienated and repressed, but visible. It gave rise to an apocalyptic movement or theology, traces of which are evident in the biblical literature and which gave birth, among other things, to Christianity which was, in Käsemann's famous phrase (Käsemann, 1960), the "mother of Christian theology" (though one should not deny Schweitzer his contribution). Among these scholars, Plöger (1968), Steck (1968) and Hanson (1975) all proposed schemes of this kind, which effectively distinguished an "establishment" from a "protest" movement (or "protest movements": such entities often splinter into smaller units or, as Plöger called them, "conventicles").[11] For Plöger, such eschatologically-minded cells, culminating in the *Hasidim* of 1 Maccabees 2:42-44 (and standing behind the authorship of Daniel) opposed a hieratic and non-eschatological establishment, while for Hanson, similarly, prophetic groups deprived of power and allied to Levites developed an apocalyptic worldview that can be tracked through the development of a distinct prosodic style and mythological motifs in certain late prophetic biblical texts.

This model might be called "centrifugal," implying a "centre" from which dissent spreads. A rather opposite view is implied (if not argued for) by Sanders, who believes that despite obvious variety, a "common Judaism" emerged, centred on common values and practices (such as festivals, tithing, but, of course, also circumcision, dietary customs, Sabbath observance) (Sanders, 1992). This view implies, perhaps, a kind of centripetal development, though Sander's description does not include a historical investigation, and he includes "belief" as well as "practice" in his description. We may doubt whether common belief can be deduced from common practice (if such were the case), but Sanders's point seems to be that "Palestinian Judaism" was by and large a coherent and widely-accepted religious system.

Somewhere between these two extremes, it has also become common to speak of "Judaisms" rather than "Judaism." Prominent in this usage is Jacob Neusner, for whom "Judaism" in any kind of normative sense, or expressing a coherent religious system, is hard to discern before the efforts of the rabbis to create it. Without necessarily identifying a number of "sects," Neusner sees different "Judaisms" with their own belief systems and to some extent practices also. Whether these emerge by differentiation or coexist from the origins of Second Temple society is not Neusner's issue.

It is perhaps unwise as well as unnecessary to choose clearly between these options; all have their evidence and arguments in favour and all encounter objections. Cumulatively, they simply underline how little we understand of the dynamics of a society that was to generate two world religions and stimulate a third. But in order to understand sectarianism we do have to understand whatever it was that sects separate *from*. If we cannot pretend to offer a comprehensive answer here, some widely-held assumptions can be set aside.

First of all, the centrality of the Jerusalem temple and the Mosaic law seem to constitute a widely-agreed nucleus of Second Temple Judaism (the phrase itself betrays such an opinion!). But while we can document the importance of that temple by the second century BCE, at any rate, we do not know how it grew. The accounts of Ezra and Nehemiah are still generally regarded as reliable descriptions of how law, covenant and temple were re-established in the mid-fourth century. But there are good reasons to doubt that Ezra, at least, is a contemporary description. I have set out the arguments elsewhere (Davies, 1995; but see also the well-known thesis of Torrey).[12]

Ezra and Nehemiah together offer an account of the origins of (Second Temple) Judaism: Nehemiah mainly in respect of the restoration of Jerusalem as capital of Judah and Ezra in respects of law and covenant. Their combination may be due to purely historiographical motives (a desire to reduce two accounts of the same period to one), but even so the existence of originally separate stories and heroes suggests different versions preserved in different circles, each with different interests in the character of "Judaism." Given the doubts about the antiquity of Ezra, it is precarious to assume that the portrait given corresponds to the historical reality. Rather, the portrait itself reflects the existence of certain interest groups at a later period. Weber's characterization of " 'post-exilic' Judaism" as a "confessional community" (Weber, 1952; 1978) aptly recognizes the "semi-sectarian" character of the Ezra-Nehemiah narratives if not their origin. In retrojecting such interests onto the canonized legend of Jewish origins, they give the impresson that Judaism itself behaved very much like a sect: hence Weber's notion of a "pariah" religion (intended, of course, as a technical description, without prejudice).[13] He also argued, however, that sects proper did not arise in Judaism until the Graeco-Roman period (if only the Qumran material had been available to him!)

With doubt thrown upon the historical context and reliability of Ezra (Nehemiah as a character is better attested, though the date of compilation of the book may also be later than the period assigned to its hero), it becomes necessary to reconsider how Judaism began, if we assign that beginning to the Persian period (c. 530 BCE–330 BCE). Here we have little direct evidence, but a number of clues. To begin, the recent revival of interest in the Neo-Babylonian period has highlighted the fact that for at least a century the centre of Judean life was in the territory of Benjamin, formerly part of the kingdom of Israel. Its chief sanctuary was Bethel, seat of the God of Jacob. The replacement of Mizpah as capital and Bethel as sanctuary by Jerusalem, and the introduction of a policy of one sanctuary only in Judah are processes that we know happened, but which are not described – and not reliably dated:[14] rather, we can see echoes of a fairly traumatic power shift throughout the Hebrew Bible in stories of the transfer of the ark from Benjamin to Judah, of kingship from Saul to David, of extensive critiques of the cult and sanctuary of Bethel, and of the appropriation of Benjaminite historiographical traditions.[15]

The political, religious and social differences – even antagonism – between Judah and Benjamin were to an extent mitigated by the merging of the identities of Israel (= Jacob/Bethel) and Judah, a process especially evident in the book of Isaiah,[16] and possibly the absorption of an "Aaronite" priesthood (Blenkinsopp, 1998). To this profound upheaval and religious contention we should add the differences between those entering from Babylonia and the indigenous inhabitants – religious, social, linguistic, economic – and also those who had immigrated from neighbouring lands after the fall of Jerusalem and the deportation of the ruling class. A further element is introduced by the Yahwistic population of Samaria. Nehemiah suggests early conflict engendered by opposition to his rebuilding of Jerusalem. This feature may well reflect local hostility to the moving of the capital from Mizpah (though it is now concealed): the implication of a rift between Judah and Samaria, however, is now widely regarded as anachronistic (pointing to a possibly later date for the composition of the book). As part of the process of opposition/negotiation between Samaria and Jerusalemite Judah, the former kingdom of Israel was vilified (Kings) or virtually erased (Chronicles), while the theory of a "twelve-tribe Israel" was elaborated to embrace both Judah and Benjamin, to assert (through the invention of a historiographical tradition about a "united monarchy") the legitimacy and hegemony of Judah, and in some circles to sustain the hope of a restoration of the "lost tribes." Finally, while Ezra-Nehemiah suggests a single process of "return" from Babylonia, that portrait may also be ideologically driven: continual immigration throughout the Second Temple period is just as likely, and probably also emigration back to Babylonia, given the economic and social ties between Judean communities in both places. Such a two-way population transfer will explain the broad compatibility between the two religious systems that was apparently maintained.

It is therefore inadvisable to consider a "normative" Judaism established as early as the fifth century BCE as a starting point. The highly variegated set of mainly Greek writings called the Pseudepigrapha and the calendrical and halakhic practices of the Qumran scrolls may well, in principle, represent elements as old as the views they oppose; the model of a stable ideological core against which various groups vigorously protested is not at all obvious. Indeed, the question of why the evidence for such protest is now found embedded with writings subsequently canonized in the Jewish scriptures suggested rather that such protests emanated from within scribal establishments and were to a degree tolerated. The model that the evidence suggests as a whole for the beginning of "Judaism" is, if not volatile, at least vigorously pluriform and characterized by processes of both differentiation and accommodation. In short, it does not indicate a climate in which sects, in the sense defined earlier, are likely to have formed: on the other hand, the ideological preconditions for sectarian formation, under the appropriate social and political instigation, are abundantly evident. In that qualified sense, Jewish sectarianism has roots that are more ancient than often conceded.

The variety within Second Temple Judaism just outlined is partly recognized in the work of Boccaccini (Boccaccini, 1998; 2002), though his approach is primarily that of an historian of ideas and not a social historian. His reconstruction basically follows the contours of previous portraits in postulating two rival priestly schools: the Zadokite and the Enochic, which differed doctrinally over the origin and nature of sin. The Enochians believed that evil originated from above and could not be removed from the earth; the Zadokites that sin could be avoided by following the Mosaic law. Other differences between them lay in their calendar, and in the espousal by Enochians of "apocalyptic." The fact that the Qumran texts preserve features of both Judaisms, including compromises between the two views is explained by him as a process of compromise, initiated by some Enochians.

More precisely, Boccaccini traces from *1 Enoch*, through Daniel, *Jubilees* and the *Temple Scroll*, a merging of the Enochic and Mosaic (Zadokite) traditions that occurred in the wake of the Maccabean war. In the *Halakhic Letter* (4QMMT) he sees a manifesto of the Enochic priesthood against a now disenfranchised Zadokite priesthood, and in the *Damascus Document* an attempt by followers of the "teacher of righteousness" to control the Enochic movement which was accommodating its views to those of the Zadokites. The failure of this enterprise led to the founding of a community at Qumran which broke with the main Enochic movement, producing a dualistic and strongly predestinarian ideology.

Unfortunately, Boccaccini suggests an "Enochic" Judaism *arising in opposition* to an entrenched Zadokite one. But there seems no reason to suppose the invention of a new tradition when several conflicting traditions already existed. It is also unfortunate that he seems at times, like many predecessors, to reproduce a binary model of Second Temple Judaism. But there are also strengths to this thesis. One is to take seriously the problem of the Enochic literature and the fact that the Qumran manuscripts seem to combine Enochic and Mosaic models of Judaism that are otherwise rather distinct. Another is to recognize a process of negotiation and not simply opposition between representatives of different kinds of Judaism (or different "Judaisms"). Last, but not least, and however briefly, he identifies a number of other "opponents" of the Zadokites: Samaritans, prophets, and the sapiential movement; and he observes that the sapiential movement denied the covenantal basis of Judaism. Here he hints at the rather broader and more diverse picture that has been suggested above.

Should we continue to regard "Zadokite" or "Mosaic" Judaism as the original "foundation" of our reconstruction of Second Temple Judean culture and religion? We can detect several quite diverse traditions in the canonized scriptures, and to a large degree we can see harmonizing processes between them. The laws of Deuteronomy were (secondarily?) identified with Moses and present a programme for an idealized "Israel" that is nevertheless incumbent on individuals, and not the king as representative of a political state (calling into question the usually scholarly dating of its composition), inventing the idea of a treaty between deity and "Israel," and specifying social and political rather than cultic matters. But the laws of Leviticus (P) reflect a quite different portrait of "Israel," in which cultic matters, and the maintenance of "holiness" are paramount. The two bodies of writing are not contradictory, but neither are they entirely compatible. However, both in the process of editing the Mosaic corpus (the Torah, Pentateuch) and in later attempts at rationalizing them (*Temple Scroll*, Talmud) we can see how a single system incorporating both covenant and holiness, emerged.

A similar process of assimilation and accommodation can be seen in the fusion of wisdom and torah, observable above all in certain "wisdom" psalms (including Psalm 1), and also evident in ben Sira. Again, this is a gradual process, and was never entirely completed: the wisdom tradition itself embraced the culture of manticism (also responsible for the genre of apocalypse) and, as the *Instructions* texts from Qumran show, shifted towards the notion of an eschatological recompense for both righteous and wicked, as well as redefining the social categories that corresponded in biblical instructional wisdom of "wise" and "foolish," promoting "poor" to an ethically positive position (see Harrington, 1996; Collins, Sterling and Clements, 2004). In the Talmud we still see torah adorned with all kinds of legend, myth, superstition and folklore that testify to an extremely rich repertoire that was never digested into a normative "torah piety."

The social processes corresponding to these literary and ideological negotiations are largely invisible to us, but should be inferred. Nevertheless, certain differences could not be overcome. Calendrical calculations, with their corresponding implications of different priestly castes and festival cycles, are one such case. As mentioned earlier, there is evidence within the prophetic literature of the formation of distinct groups in the early centuries of the Second Temple period. A number of commentators have pointed to the material in Isaiah 56–66 as revealing the existence of such groups (see, e.g, Hanson, 1975; Blenkinsopp, 2003). Where strong differences of ideology and practice existed, where reconciliation was impossible, then either such groups would be obliged to form sects or there would be a sufficient degree of toleration to allow such differences to be observed without undue discrimination. For our purposes, then, the key question is whether such indications of protest or heteropraxy point to the formation of sects – and if so, when. Much of the evidence for such groups comes from Isaiah 56–66, the dating of which remains disputed. Blenkinsopp (1990; 1995; 1997) has argued for a sect of *haredim* ("Quakers") in the Persian period, in some way connected with the "servant" figure. Blenkinsopp makes an excellent case for the continuity of this Isaianic tradition through the book of Daniel and into the Qumran manuscripts. He also points to a strong "insider-outsider" mentality evidence in these texts. While reserving judgment on whether such a group or groups should be called a sect, as defined above, Blenkinsopp has made a very powerful case for the continuity of traditions and practices – and a sense of community – that continued for several generations.[17]

As a final illustration of this thesis of a tolerant Second Temple Judaism, and a clue to the point at which this toleration ceased, I suggest that the distinctive Enochic doctrine of sin is, far from being any kind of reaction or innovation, embedded in the Priestly literature of the Pentateuch (in this case, in Genesis and Leviticus). According to *1 Enoch* 6–36, sin entered the world through a descent of heavenly beings who copulated with human women and produced a race of giants; the resulting bloodshed led to divine intervention, imprisoning these divinities and obliterating their offspring in the Flood. The sin thus brought into the world continues, nevertheless, until the final judgment. This story is quite different from the narrative of Genesis 1–11, but the division of that material into "J" and "P"[18] is important, for the "P" material contains no account of the origin of evil, while "J" has a story of disobedience by the first humans, murder by their son and thereafter increasing wickedness, even after the Flood. In fact, the Flood, as this story acknowledges, makes no difference to anything: the "wickedness" of the human imagination persists (Gen. 6:5/8:21). "J" also preserves a truncated account of the heavenly descent (6:1-4), but decouples it from the ensuing Flood, and turns its murderous giants into heroes ("Mighty men, men of repute"). The covenant that follows the Flood in the Priestly source (P) dwells on the shedding of blood, and in the P antediluvian geneaology (ch. 5), Enoch is mentioned as having lived 365 years and walked with God, after which "he was not, for God took him" (5:21-24). Finally, the "P" material in the Flood is predicated on months of 30 days, in conformity with the Enochic (and Qumranic) calendar.

The conclusion must be that everything in "P," including the Leviticus reference, is not only consistent with the *Enoch* account but betrays an acceptance of those traditions. It seems very likely that the "Enochic" theology of the origin of sin is precisely that of the major Pentateuchal source: the flood resulting from corruption of the *earth* (not humans) and leading to a ban on the shedding or eating of blood, and awareness of a connection between the figure of Enoch and the solar calendar, and of his immortality. If we add Leviticus to the circle from which this "P" source emanates, we can also note the scapegoat ritual in chapter 16, which refers to "Azazel," one of the names given in later versions of the story to the leader of the heavenly group,[19] and the fact that the goat "for Azazel" is sent into the wilderness makes sense of the imprisonment there of this heavenly being.

This is not to say that "P" is a text of "Enochic Judaism," but that the most distinctive aspect of "Enochic" theology is not confined to "Enochians." The acceptance of Enoch as a prominent figure is also apparent in ben Sira (44:16; 49:14), though here he is not singled out to the degree that he is in the Enochic literature. Ben Sira is perhaps a crucial witness in the case being made here about the formation of Jewish sects, for he also indicates a certain animosity towards the Samarians (15:26), who perhaps should already be regarded as a sect, though hardly of a religion that they would call "Judaism"! The reasons for this development are unclear but almost certainly result from a difference over the legitimacy of the sanctuaries of Jerusalem and Shechem (see Purvis, 1965). Since both communities share the Pentateuch, in which the issue is not addressed, we may regard the Pentateuch itself as evidence of a period of toleration over this matter.

The End of Toleration

The theory being proposed here for the origin of ancient Jewish sects implies an end of toleration, on the part of either those who formed the sects or those who rejected them. We have just seen ben Sira's evidence for the formation of the Samari(t)ans as a sect; and this schism may also be reflected in 2 Kings 17:24-41, in which the Yahwistic beliefs and practices of Samarians are acknowledged, but alongside idolatrous practices, "and their descendants continue to do as their ancestors did" (17:41).[20]

But a more dramatic proof of lack of toleration is in the material reviewed earlier. While the "P" material in Genesis 1–11 accommodates "Enochic" ideology, the "J" material removes almost every trace. As already observed, in Genesis 6:1-4 the episode of heavenly descent is converted into a benign or inconsequential occurrence, detached from the Flood and from the origins of sin, while sin itself is defined as (increasing) human disobedience to divine commands. The figure of Enoch himself (Gen. 4:17) is accorded no special treatment whatsoever,[21] while two important features of the descent story as contained in *1 Enoch*, the shedding of blood and the transmission of knowledge of arts and sciences, are assigned to Cain, who then becomes a substitution for Azazel. Cain's mark, his reprieve from death, and his wandering in the wilderness also adopt key features of the fate of the scapegoat.[22] Here Enoch and the mythology connected with him are overwritten rather than accommodated (see further Davies, 1986).

One objection to this interpretation, of course, is the traditional sequences of Pentateuchal sources, by which P is later than J. The argument that this order – at least for Genesis 1–11 – should be reversed has been made by Blenkinsopp, and not in pursuit of the thesis being pursued here, for Blenkinsopp has a different understanding of P's view of the origin of sin: see Blenkinsopp, 1992, especially 79.

Other religious practices that show clear signs of being rejected are divination, idolatry and prophecy. The first two of these hardly need documentation: the third, however, is less clear-cut, since prophecy seems to be celebrated. Yet the legislation in Deuteronomy 13 makes it clear that prophecy is genuine only when it is already fulfilled; and, if fulfilled, only true if its content does not entail idolatry. Effectively, prophecy, like monarchy, is redundant. In its turn, Chronicles mutates prophets into Levites (e.g. 2 Chronicles 20). No doubt "prophetic" movements continued, but the canonized literature at least makes it clear that the true prophets are all dead ones.

It is, therefore, possible to trace the removal of toleration as well as the toleration itself, to follow in the literary relics the footsteps of social and political developments. But with the exception of ben Sira, the literary evidence is undatable. The destruction of the temple at Gerizim by John Hyrcanus in 128 BCE constitutes a fixed point, but the motives for that act are disputed and the animosity between the Shechem and Jerusalem communities is probably somewhat older.

Several important political and social changes occurred following the conquests of Alexander. One may deduce that the unification of Palestine under the Ptolemies changed the social and cultural situation in important ways; certainly it restored political integration to Palestine for the first time since the previous period of Egyptian control in the Late Bronze age. In the following century loyalties were divided between those who leaned toward Egypt and those with connections to Mesopotamia. A century or so later a dynastic power struggle within Jerusalem and its sphere of influence initiated a series of political manoeuvres that led to Seleucid intervention and a resistance among Judean groups led by the family of Mattathias. In this struggle it has often been claimed that a Jewish group – perhaps a sect – known as *Hasidim* participated in the resistance. But this has been challenged, though it is virtually certain that the resistance was composed of several of the differentiated interest groups that we have indicated existed side-by-side (see Sievers, 1990).

The success of the Hasmoneans did not resolve the issue of Hellenistic agendas, which were not only pursued outside Palestine but adopted in large measure by the rulers and their subjects. However, the formation of an independent Jewish state posed challenges and offered opportunities. The struggles had polarized a number of groups and opinions, both between the collation that had gained power and others, and within the coalition itself. What were formerly mutually tolerant groups became less so. The huge enlargement of the formally "Jewish" population in Palestine posed further questions of orthopraxy and allegiance. Schwartz (2001: 41) has estimated a two to five-fold increase.

Baumgarten has analyzed why Jewish groups – the Sadducees, Pharisees, Essenes and the Dead Sea Scroll sect – flourished during the Maccabean era. He concludes that the major factors were an encounter with
an outside culture, Hellenistic, that seemed to be weakening the external
national perimeter, the impact of expanded literacy, urbanization, and
eschatological hopes aroused by the Maccabean victories. In general
this analysis seems correct, especially in its elucidation of a complex of
factors. We may disagree on whether the Sadducees or Pharisees were
"sects," in the definition we have given, for we do not know that either
denied the identity of "Israel" to other Jews or regarded themselves as the
exclusive bearers of that identity. But undoubtedly the ideological differences that had long characterized Jewish society seem to have formalized
into politicized groups.

The "Qumran" sect of "Damascus Covenanters," however, does not
seem to have constituted a political group; its texts strongly suggest an
antagonism towards Pharisees (if these are the *dwrshy hlqwt*), but strongest of all an aversion to the priests in control of the Jerusalem temple.
Clearly these were following a different calendar. The calendrical issue,
however, as has been argued above, was of long standing and even the
Book of Jubilees, which strongly endorses the 364-day calendar, and may
date from around 100 BCE, does not seem to reflect a sectarian stance,
though perhaps it betrays some sharpening of the debate. The Dream
Visions of *1 Enoch* 83–90 and the visions of Daniel 7–12 reflect the polarization within Judah that the Hasmonean war (and its preceding conflict)
generated, but do not indicate a withdrawal from Judean society. Daniel's
maskilim may constitute a special group, but their social segregation is
not yet apparent, while *1 Enoch* 89:73 insists that from the beginning, the
bread on the altar of the post-exilic temple was impure. In *1 Enoch* 92–
105, the "Epistle of Enoch," we perhaps come to a point where the logic
of imminent eschatological expectation and the connection between
the misfortunes of the people and their past errors leads (as in Daniel)
to a dualistic distinction between those who have not angered the deity
(and will be rescued at the time of divine intervention) and those who
will be punished for having behaved in a way that has brought on the
misfortunes.

It is tempting to see in this theological reasoning the core of the sec-
tarianizing process, when a group identifies itself as the ones who are
about to be saved from the wrath that is upon them and receive the
imminent divine salvation. For here the self-identity of the "true Israel"
is obviously at hand. And indeed, it would be perverse not to appreciate how much the traumas of the second century (and indeed the first)

BCE induced in many groups an explanation in terms of theodicy and imminent divine intervention. But how far such a psychology would itself necessarily lead to social segregation is doubtful. Creating a community that is self-contained and socially distinct points rather to the expectation of a rather longer future. Undoubtedly many elements of a sectarian self-consciousness exist in these texts from the Hasmonean period. But does this explanation account for the social organization?

Such a solution is feasible if we propose that the "Damascus" community separated itself in expectation of imminent reconstitution as the true Israel. In the realization that the god of Israel was not in fact content with the pluralism of Judean society, did it insist on rejecting the alternative calendar and festivals and rules of holiness and go off to be its own Israel? But it is also possible that other groups felt the same about them, and with the support of the Hasmoneans barred them from participation in the temple cult on their own terms, insisting rather that they follow the practices of the remainder.

Unfortunately, we have only the writing of the sects themselves about their own formation. Even Josephus, in his account of the three *heireseis* does not bother to explain why or even exactly when they came into existence. Indeed, he implies that Judaism was in his day much as we have argued it was earlier: tolerant of many different expressions of "Judaism." Perhaps the manuscripts at Qumran show us the only Jewish groups that became sects. But whatever the truth of the matter, whether or not the pluralism of Judaism continued much as before, further political upheavals would lead to greater fissures. At all events, the more we examine the nature of Jewish sects, the more eloquently it emerges that the real problem, with which we still grapple, is the nature of the "Judaism" from which they came.

Endnotes

1. An earlier stage of the process of claiming "parental" identity for this sect may perhaps be found in CD 1, where its founder, the "teacher of righteousness," is inserted into an existing history (compare the absence of this figure from parallel histories in CD 2.14–4.12 and 5.16–6.11). The pre-"teacher" era is now dismissed as a time of "groping for the way like the blind" (1.9).

2. The debate about the relationship between caves, scrolls and ruins continues to generate a huge amount of secondary literature. Still in favour of Qumran as the sectarian settlement is Jodi Magness (2002); a case against has been developed by Norman Golb. See, most recently, Hirschfeld (2004).

3. Indeed, strictly speaking, it does not need to be assumed that these sects actually existed, or at least exactly as described. The texts describing the sects may well contain a degree of utopian fantasy or idealizing: see Davies (1992).

4. An excellent recent account of these texts and their interpretation is given in Hempel (2000).

5. This observation tends to support the contention of Fraade (2000) concerning the addressees of the (original) document.

6. "Zadok" or "sons of Zadok" (CD 4.1-4) is not (*pace* Schiffman and others) a self-designation of the sect, but only used midrashically, together with other terms from Ezek. 44:15. It is worth bearing in mind, however, that many of the names of Jewish groups we have from this period were given by others. The title "Damascus sect" is perhaps open to question, since "Damascus" itself may refer to the city of that name or stand as a cipher for elsewhere; and while it appears in CD seven times (six if we discount a parallel in ms B) it is found only once among the Cave 4 fragments and never in the *Laws* section; see further Hempel (2000: 58-60).

7. The precise meaning of this term in CD is uncertain: biblically it means "resident alien," but in Mishnaic Hebrew, "proselyte".

8. The suggestion by Murphy-O'Connor (1974) that these differences are due to different calendrical and halakhic observances among Babylonian (or some Babylonian) Jews has not been widely adopted, but remains possible. However, the evidence of a "solar" calendar, and other Enoch traditions, within the P material of the Pentateuch (see below) suggests that these ideas were familiar, and even acceptable, within Palestinian Judaism at some relatively early stage in the Second Temple period.

9. It is not strictly necessary, of course, to assign this proposal to the "teacher," who appears nowhere in the S manuscripts. If the expression *moreh hayahid* ("unique teacher") in CD 20.14 should be emended to *moreh hay-yahad* (teacher of the *yahad*), that would presumably settle the matter.

10. Another opponent of the "teacher," the "man of the lie" or "spouter of lies" (*kzb*) does appear in CD 2 as the "scoffer" (*'ish hallazon*) who "dripped lying (*kzb*) waters" (CD 1.14-15), contrasted by the Teacher, *moreh*, which also means "rain" (see Hos. 10:12: *wyrh zedeq lahem*). This "scoffer" leads those who "backslide from the way" (1.13), probably referring not to "Israel" at large but to those within the "Damascus" community who rejected the Teacher: according to CD Israel has already backslid and is effectively out of the picture. Within the *Pesharim*, scholars are undecided whether this figure is to be identified with the "wicked priest" – confusion is perhaps already present in the *Pesharim* themselves.

11. Also "dualistic" is the scheme of Morton Smith, but he envisages a different division, between a syncretist and "Yahweh-alone" party (Smith, 1971; however, he also noted the presence of different groups within each coalition). On "early sectarianism" see also Smith (1961).

12. Recent studies have revived the contention of Torrey that the figure of Ezra is historically suspect. Nehemiah is known to ben Sira (49:13) as a wall-builder and to the author of 2 Maccabees (1:20-29) as one who had the fire of the altar returned. Neither reference includes Ezra. The implication may be that Ezra and Nehemiah represent originally independent stories of the origin of Judaism, of uncertain date though Ezra is probably no earlier than the second century BCE, and secondarily combined in a single scroll. That scroll represents the view, and the Judaisms, of one or strictly two Jewish factions that have socially and ideologically merged, symbolically in the single scene of Ezra standing next to Nehemiah. If this is right, we accept the contents of these books to create the origin of a normative Judaism.

13. Weber notes ritual segregation, circumcision, dietary laws, sabbath observance, endogamy and ethnic and physical disqualifications (Weber, 1978: 413) Weber has been closely followed in recent times by Talmon (1986; 1991: 16-43).

14. The reports in the books of Haggai and Ezra about the (postponed) rebuilding of the Jerusalem temple may be partly the result of an attempt to suggest that it commenced very shortly after a "return." For a recent detailed analysis of this problem, see Edelman (2005), suggesting that the restitution of Jerusalem as capital of Judah, and temple city, belongs to the late fifth century and to a Persian initiative.

15. These issues are well covered in the contributions to Lipschits and Blenkinsopp (2003). It is, of course. to this period that many of the so-called "northern" traditions identified among the biblical material is most obviously to be assigned.

16. This process, interpreted in a different way, is extremely well illustrated in Kratz (forthcoming).

17. Blenkinsopp accepts the essential historicity of Ezra, and thus dates the *haredim* (mentioned in 9:4 and 10:3) to the fifth century, suggesting that Ezra himself may have been one of its members, or at least supported by them. On the view that Ezra reflects a later historical context, we cannot be certain when this group originated. Also problematic is the question of how the book of Isaiah came to be transmitted in a sectarian format (if Third Isaiah is essentially sectarian literature). It may be better to think of a Judean society in which a higher degree of toleration of differences was exercised than is often supposed.

18. The division represents a recognition of clear stylistic and ideological differences between parallel episodes: the sigla are conventional only and do not imply any view of the "New Documentary Hypothesis" beyond the simple fact of two distinct compositional styles, reflected in different vocabulary and ideology.

19. The form ʿAzazel is used in the Qumran Aramaic fragment 4QEnGiants[a] (=4Q203). Shemiḥazah, ʿAzazel and ʿAsael are all given in *1 Enoch.*

20. The entire question of the anti-northern prejudices of 1–2 Kings (plus sections of Joshua–Samuel) and Judean-Samarian relations suggests either that the "Deuteronomistic History" was composed at a time when relations were deteriorating or that the work is to be attributed to anti-Samarian attitudes predating any formal breach. The focus of the books of Kings on Jerusalem may suggest a breach over the issue of the legitimacy of Shechem (which is apparently not contested in Joshua 24). A recent review of the entire question of Samarian and biblical origins is Hjelm (2000).

21. It has nevertheless been pointed out on several occasions that Enoch's son Irad might allude to the "descent" (*yrd*) of heavenly beings.

22. In particular, his statement that "my sin is too great for me to bear" is a poignant affirmation of the feeling of weight of sin ritually laid upon the goat.

REFERENCES

Baumgarten, A. I. 1997. *The Flourishing of Jewish Sects in the Maccabean Era: An Interpretation.* Leiden: E. J. Brill.

Blenkinsopp, Joseph. 1990. "A Jewish Sect of the Persian Period." *CBQ* 52: 5-20.

—1992. *The Pentateuch: An Introduction to the First Five Books of the Bible.* New York: Doubleday; London: SCM Press.

—1995. "The 'Servants of the Lord' in Third Isaiah." In R. P. Gordon, ed., *The Place Is Too Small for Us: The Israelite Prophets in Recent Scholarship*: 392-412. Winona Lake: Eisenbrauns.

—1997. "The Servants and the Servant in Isaiah and the Formation of the Book." In C. C. Broyles and C. A. Evans, eds, *Writing and Reading the Scroll of Isaiah*: I, 155-75. Leiden: E. J. Brill.

—1998. "The Judean Priesthood during the Neo-Babylonian and Achaemenid Periods: A Hypothetical Reconstruction." *CBQ* 60: 25-43.

—2003. *Isaiah 56–66*. Anchor Bible; New York: Doubleday.

Boccaccini, Gabriele. 1998. *Beyond the Essene Hypothesis: The Parting of the Ways between Qumran and Enochic Judaism*. Grand Rapids, MI: Eerdmans.

—2002. *Roots of Rabbinic Judaism: An Intellectual History, from Ezekiel to Daniel*. Grand Rapids, MI: Eerdmans.

Collins, John J., Gregory E. Sterling and Ruth A. Clements, eds. 2004. *Sapiential Perspectives: Wisdom Literature in Light of the Dead Sea Scrolls. Proceedings of the Sixth International Symposium of the Orion Center for the Study of the Dead Sea Scrolls and Associated Literature, 20-22 May, 2001*. Leiden: E. J. Brill.

Davies, Philip R. 1981. *The "Damascus Covenant": An Interpretation of the "Damascus Document."* Sheffield: JSOT Press.

—1986. "Sons of Cain." In J. D. Martin and Philip R. Davies, eds, *A Word in Season: Essays in Honour of William McKane*: 35-56. JSOTSup, 42; Sheffield: JSOT Press, 1986.

—1992. "Redaction and Sectarianism in the Qumran Scrolls." In F. García Martínez, A. Hilhorst and C. J. Labuschagne, eds, *The Scriptures and the Scrolls*: 152-63. Leiden: E. J. Brill.

—1995. "Scenes from the Early History of Judaism." In D. V. Edelman, ed., *The Triumph of Elohim*: 145-82. Kampen: Kok Pharos.

—2000a. "The Judaisms of the Damascus Document." In J. Baumgarten, Esther G. Chazon and Avital Pinnick, eds, *The Damascus Document: A Centennial of Discovery*: 27-43. STDJ, 34; Leiden: E. J. Brill.

—2000b. "Judaisms in the Dead Sea Scrolls: The Case of the Messiah." In T. Lim, ed., *The Dead Sea Scrolls in their Historical Context*: 219-32. Edinburgh: T&T Clark.

Durkheim, E. 1915. *The Elementary Forms of the Religious Life*. Trans. Joseph Ward Swain. London: Allen and Unwin.

Edelman, Diana. 2005. *The Origins of the Second Temple: Persian Imperial Policy and the Rebuilding of Jerusalem*. London: Equinox.

Fraade, Steven. 2000. "To Whom It May Concern; 4QMMT and its Addressee(s)." *Revue de Qumran* 19: 507-26.

García Martínez, F. 1988. "Qumran Origins and Early History: A Groningen Hypothesis." *Folia Orientalia* 25: 113-36.

Golb, Norman. 1994. *Who Wrote the Dead Sea Scrolls? The Search for the Secret of Qumran*. New York: Charles Scribner's Sons.

Hanson, Paul D. 1975. *The Dawn of Apocalyptic*. Philadelphia: Fortress Press.

Harrington, D. J. 1996. *Wisdom Texts from Qumran*, London; New York: Routledge.

Hempel, Charlotte. 2000. *The Damascus Texts*. Sheffield: Sheffield Academic Press.

Hirschfeld, Yitzhar. 2004. *Qumran in Context: Reassessing the Archaeological Evidence*. Peabody, MA: Hendrickson.

Hjelm, I. 2000. *The Samaritans and Early Judaism: A Literary Analysis*. Sheffield: Sheffield Academic Press.

Käsemann, E. 1960. "Die Anfänge Christliche Theologie." *Zeitschrift für Theologie und Kirche* 57: 162-85.

Knibb, Michael A. 1976. "The Exile in the Literature of the Intertestamental Period." *Heythrop Journal* 17: 253-72.

Kratz, Reinhard Georg. Forthcoming. "Israel in the Book of Isaiah." *JSOT*.

—1983. "Exile in the Damascus Document." *JSOT* 9: 99-117.

Lipschits, Oded, and Joseph Blenkinsopp. 2003. *Judah and the Judeans in the neo-Babylonian Period*. Winona Lake, IN: Eisenbrauns.

Macchi, J.-D. 1994. *Les Samaritains: histoire d'une légende. Israël et la province de Samarie*. Genève: Labor et Fides.

Magness, Jodi. 2002. *The Archaeology of Qumran and the Dead Sea Scrolls*. Grand Rapids, MI: Eerdmans.

Murphy-O'Connor, Jerome. 1969. "La genèse littéraire de la Régle de la Communauté." *RB* 76: 528-49.

—1974. "The Essenes and their History." *RB* 81: 215-44.

Plöger, Otto. 1968. *Theocracy and Eschatology*. Trans. S. Rudman. Oxford: Blackwell.

Purvis, J. D. 1965. "Ben Sira and the Foolish People of Shechem." *Journal of Near Eastern Studies* 24: 88-94.

Ricoeur, Paul. 1995. *Figuring the Sacred: Religion, Narrative, and the Imagination*. Minneapolis: Fortress Press.

Sanders, E. P. 1992. *Judaism: Practice and Belief 63 BCE–66 CE*. London: SCM Press; Philadelphia: Trinity Press International.

Schiffman, L. H. 1994. *Reclaiming the Dead Sea Scrolls*. Philadelphia: Jewish Publication Society.

Schwartz, Seth. 2001. *Imperialism and Jewish Society 200 BCE–640 CE*. Princeton; Oxford: Princeton University Press.

Sievers, Joseph. 1990. *The Hasmoneans and their Supporters: From Mattathias to the Death of John Hyrcanus I*. Atlanta, GA: Scholars Press.

Smith, Morton. 1961. "The Dead Sea Sect in Relation to Ancient Judaism." *NTS* 7: 347-60.

—1971. *Palestinian Parties and Politics That Shaped the Old Testament*. New York; London: Columbia University Press.

Steck, O. H. 1968. "Das Problem theologischer Strömungen in nachexilischer Zeit." *Evangelische Theologie* 28: 445-58.

Talmon, Shemaryahu. 1986. "The Emergence of Jewish Sectarianism in the Early Second Temple Period." In idem, *King, Cult and Calendar in Ancient Israel*. Jerusalem: Magnes Press.

Talmon, Shemaryahu, ed. 1991. *Jewish Civilization in the Hellenistic-Roman Period*. Sheffield: JSOT Press.

Torrey, C. C. 1910. *Ezra Studies*. Chicago: University of Chicago Press.

Troeltsch, E. 1981. *The Social Teaching of the Christian Churches*. Trans. Olive Wyon; introduction by H. Richard Niebuhr. Chicago: University of Chicago Press (German original 1923).

Wallis, Roy. 1984. *Elementary Forms of the New Religious Life*. London: Routledge & Kegan Paul.

Weber, Max. 1952. *Ancient Judaism*. New York: Free Press.

—1963. *The Sociology of Religion*. Boston, MA: Beacon Press.

—1976. *The Agrarian Sociology of Ancient Civilizations*. Atlantic Highlands, NJ: Humanities Press.

—1978. *Economy and Society*. Berkeley, CA; Los Angeles: University of California Press.

Wilson, Bryan. 1959. "An Analysis of Sect Development." *American Sociological Review* 24: 3-15.

—1973. *Magic and the Millennium*. New York: Harper & Row.

Was There Sectarian Behaviour before the Flourishing of Jewish Sects? A Long-Term Approach to the History and Sociology of Second Temple Sectarianism

Pierluigi Piovanelli

The last decade has witnessed a growing interest in the study of the formation of Jewish identity in Antiquity. Thus, Albert I. Baumgarten has explored the paradox of *The Flourishing of Jewish Sects in the Maccabean Era* (1997), while Shaye J. D. Cohen has made a strong case for *The Beginnings of Jewishness* (1999) in the same context. These and other contributions – we could also mention those of Philip R. Davies (1998), Martin Goodman (1994), Lester L. Grabbe (1995), George W. E. Nickelsburg (2003), or the late Anthony J. Saldarini (1988) – highlight the social and ideological constructions of such new political and/or cultural realities in the aftermath of the Maccabean victory. The new and stimulating way these authors look at old and much debated topics is immediately perceptible when we compare their works with, for example, a great classic such as Morton Smith's *Palestinian Parties and Politics That Shaped the Old Testament* (1971).[1] The main difference consists in a new and acute sensitivity to social-scientific, anthropological, and cross-cultural approaches, methods, and models. Such new perspectives, allied to the more traditional philological and literary skills, have been applied to long known documents, such as Josephus's works, and to newly published sources, such as the Dead Sea Scrolls, with the result of a modification of our perception of Second Temple history and culture.

The reflections that I offer here will be about three different aspects of such processes and will concern the following points: (1) the social-scientific definitions of what is a religious sect and their usefulness in the case of Jewish sectarianism, (2) the identification of some possible sectarian behaviour during the early period of the Second Temple and (3) some methodological and ethical consequences for the historians and specialists of ancient Judaism.

1. *Religious Sects and Jewish Sectarianism*

The definition of any ideal type – or of any ideal model – invariably differs from one author to another, and its applicability to concrete historical cases of the past is often either enthusiastically advocated or drastically rejected. In the case of the charismatic model of leadership, for example, some social historians of early Christianity still use the very wording of the original Weberian definition, while others simply refuse even to pronounce the word "charisma" because of the Weberian, German and therefore – supposedly – authoritarian and imperialistic origins of such a concept.[2] Only a few seem to realize that the perception of the charismatic phenomenon has undergone a complex evolution since Weber's days, and that the "great man" approach has made room for a much more sophisticated "transformational" perspective (Piovanelli, 2005a).[3] The same is probably true for the use – and abuse – of the sectarian concept, model and typology. In my opinion, the fact that originally Max Weber and Ernst Troeltsch elaborated the first draft of it in the context of Western Christianity and its Protestant renewal movements[4] does not justify the too skeptical conclusion of those who refuse to transpose and to adapt it to other environments and periods. On the contrary, I am convinced that we can persist to use it – we *have* to use it – not as a mathematical formula but as *a flexible and heuristic tool*.

Among the contemporary elaborations on religious sectarianism, Bryan R. Wilson's typology seems to be the most sensitive and operationally useful. Wilson's sociological interest for sectarianism grew up from his fieldwork carried out in the 1950s on some British "sects" such as the Elim Foursquare Gospel Alliance, the Christian Science Movement, and the Christadelphians (1961). Progressively he took into account an increasing variety of religious groups, not only Western present-day sects but also "Third-World" millennial movements of protest (1970; 1973). Ultimately this enormous empirical endeavour paved the way to the elaboration of a theoretical framework for an "alternative," no longer theological but truly sociological understanding of contemporary New Religious Movements: how they arise, evolve, change, flourish, decline, or fail in different contexts and situations (1982; 1990).

> [Wilson] characterises the sect as a voluntary association with a strong sense of self-identity. Membership depends upon merit or some kind of qualification such as knowledge or acceptance of doctrine or of conversion evidenced by some form of religious experience. The sect is exclusive and regards itself as an elite in sole possession of the truth. It is separated from the wider society and at odds with prevailing orthodoxy. Certain standards

of behaviour are required of members and expulsion may follow any serious or persistent failure to live by them. Regular procedures for expulsion will exist. The commitment of the sectarian is always more total than that of the non-sectarian and he or she is always more distinctly characterised in terms of religious affiliation. The sect has no distinct or professional ministry (Wilson, 1970: 26-34; as summarized by Hamilton, 1995: 197-98).[5]

According to Wilson, non-sectarian persons accept the world as it is, with its mainstream culture and values, leaders and institutions. By contrast, sectarian groups reject the world as evil and can be classified according to the variety of their responses to it:

Conversionist sects seek to change the individual's hearts and are especially concerned with the recruitment of new members (e.g. the revivalist offshoots of Methodism and the various schismatic groups that emerged from Pentecostalism).

Revolutionist (or *transformative*) sects are waiting for a supernatural intervention that will change the world (e.g. Seventh Day Adventism, Jehovah's Witnesses, Rastafarians and, more generally, every millennial movement).

Introversionist sects tend to withdraw from society and to found isolated communities (e.g. the Hutterites, the Doukhobors and the Amish Mennonites).

Manipulationist sects claim to possess special or esoteric knowledge that enable them to influence the world (e.g. Christian Science, Theosophy and Scientology).

Thaumaturgical sects believe in oracles and miracles dispensed by supernatural agencies (e.g. the French and Belgian Antoinists, the American "snake handlers" and the "Zionist" churches of South Africa).

Spiritualistic sects emphasize communication with the dead (e.g. Kardecism and Umbanda cult in Brazil).

Reformist sects try to provide a moral and ethical example for the rest of the society (e.g. contemporary Quakerism).

Utopian sects are committed to rediscovering an ideal way of life that has been corrupted by the existing society (e.g. the Oneida Community, the Brotherhood of the New Life, or the Bruderhof) (Wilson, 1967: 24-29; 1970: 36-47; 1973: 18-28).[6]

In each sectarian group the discourses about God, the faithful and the world are also radically different.

The objectivists focus on the world, saying:
God will overturn it (revolutionists);
God calls us to abandon it (introversionists);
God calls us to amend it (reformists);
God calls us to reconstruct it (utopians).

The subjectivists say:
    God will change us (conversionists).
The relationists, if we may call them that, say:
    God calls us to change perception (manipulationists);
    God will grant particular dispensations and work specific miracles
(thaumaturgists) (Wilson, 1973: 27).

It is heuristically interesting to put the different Second Temple Jewish movements and groups that are normally considered to be the best candidates to receive the sociological label of "sect" into Wilson's ideal classification.[7] Specialists of ancient Judaism have already eclectically used some of these categories.[8] A more exhaustive map is proposed in the following on the following page.

The first striking finding is that the Sadducees – in spite of the label of "sect" that they traditionally receive in scholarly literature[9] – cannot be considered as sectarian group from a purely sociological point of view. They lack such a basic prerequisite for sectarianism that is the rejection of the existing society. In fact, with the only exception of Shelamzion's reign (76–67 BCE), they were constantly associated with Judean political and religious power all through the late Second Temple period. On the one hand, they do not seem to fit in any of the sectarian categories of Wilson's typology. On the other, their aristocratic elitism does not contribute to make them suitable for being considered as a "denomination," that is, a voluntary, informal, and tolerant association of members who are socially compatible (Wilson, 1967: 25).[10] The only reasonable alternative would be to consider the Sadducees as the group that actually represented – sociologically speaking – the mainstream and dominant "church" movement of Second Temple Judaism.[11] In such a role, they were among the preferred targets of the revolutionary factions before and during the First Jewish War (66–70 CE).[12]

The sociological profile of the Pharisees is more delicate to draw. Their sectarian characteristics largely depend on the evaluation of their historical trajectories – and of the written sources that provide such information.[13] Obviously, as with every social phenomenon, sects are not static, but evolutionary realities. Thus, the Pharisees could have begun their career as a sectarian group – if we judge from the surname of "separatists" they earned and their possible, but not demonstrated, Hasidim lineage – and subsequently transform themselves into a much more ecumenical movement. Nonetheless, after a period of fiery political opposition during the reigns of John Hyrcanus (134–104 BCE) and especially Alexander Janneus (103–76 BCE), they seem to have accepted the general rules of Judean society. In any case, they were able to exert their reformist

	Enochians	Hasidim	Sadducees	Pharisees	Essenes	Qumranites	Millennialists	Zealots
Conversionist					×	×	×	
Revolutionist	×	×		×	×	×	×	×
Introversionist						×		
Manipulationist	×				×	×		
Thaumaturgical	×				×	×	×	
Spiritualistic	×				×	×		
Reformist		×		×				
Utopian					×		×	×

influence inside and outside the official institutions of the Jewish State. In the end, two of their leaders, Yohanan ben Zakkai and Rabban Gamaliel II, created in Yavneh the inclusive conditions for the reunion and the rebirth of Judaism beyond the previous dissensions.[14] Therefore, a reformist attitude seems to be the main feature of the Pharisees as a sectarian group,[15] even if it would probably be more exact and advantageous to consider them either as a religious party,[16] or a religious voluntary association,[17] or – adopting a sociological terminology – a religious denomination.

Clearly revolutionist – or simply revolutionary – and probably utopian were the Hasidim and the Zealots, the two sectarian movements involved in the great liberation wars at the two ends of the late Second Temple spectrum.[18] This is also true for the different millennialist movements – including the groups of John the Baptist and Jesus of Nazareth[19] – that intermittently arose after the death of Herod the Great in 4 BCE. In their case, we should also stress their conversionist and thaumaturgical tendencies. Both Theudas and the anonymous Egyptian prophet promised wondrous signs to those who would leave all and follow them to the Jordan river or to the Mount of Olives. Usually, after the repressive intervention of the authorities the majority of the millennialist movements merely disappeared or entered in an introversionist phase.[20]

The precise nature of the relationships existing between the Enochic groups, the Essenes, and the Qumran community are still hotly debated. We shall deal with the Enochians in the second part of our essay. Concerning the Essenes and the Qumranites, Florentino García Martínez has convincingly argued that the former were the parent movement from which the second withdrew (1988; García Martínez and van der Woude, 1990; García Martínez and Trebolle Barrera, 1995: 77-96, 239-49). Even if the addressee of the famous *Halakhic Letter* on *Some of the Works of the Torah* (4Q394–399) was more probably a Jewish ruler – perhaps Alexander Janneus – than an Essene leader, the utopian attitude that Josephus ascribes to the Essenes stridently contrasts with the introversionist proclivities of the members of the Qumran community. The latter's schismatic trajectory is now confirmed by Gabriele Boccaccini's systemic analysis of the *Damascus Document*, the *Community Rule*, and other "sectarian" documents (1998: 119-62; 2002a: 89-103).[21] Accordingly, the Qumranites seem to have formed a new religious group that appeared, lived its life and then disappeared as an introversionist sect without major changes.[22] Among the sectarian secondary features shared by the Essenes and the Qumranites there are conversionist, manipulationist, thaumaturgical and spiritualist aspects that emerge from the examination of the available data.[23] All these point to the truly sectarian nature of the Essenes and the Qumranites in comparison with their non-sectarian colleagues, the Sadducees and the Pharisees.

Finally, we should also remember that sects are not only – or not always – objective realities that we can identify, study and describe according to some specific features. More often than not a sect – like a dialect – is the product of a social construction, the result of discrimination from the outside. Accordingly, we should distinguish between primary and secondary sectarian phenomena. In the first case, the formation of a sect results from a consciously assumed foundational act such as a split, secession, and/or any other creative initiative according to an emic logic, "we are different and better than them." While in the second case, it results from a contraction, a withdrawal under the external pressure of an etic discrimination, "they are different and worse than us."

In this connection, Early Christianity offers a telling example of both primary – the Matthean and Johannine communities[24] – and secondary sectarianism – the more socially friendly Lukan and Valentinian communities[25] – for the reason that the Roman authorities were unable to make the difference between each of them and collectively considered all of them as a single, bizarre and harmful *superstitio*. Of course, this does not mean that the Matthean and Johannine communities did not see themselves as persecuted minorities – in this case, as victims of mainstream Judaism – or that Lukan and Valentinian communities were not, to a certain extent, already sectarian. After all, historical objects and realities always are more complicated than theoretical models.

The point that I would make is that, in historical research, when we deal with sectarian phenomena in Antiquity, especially when the surviving evidence is mainly literary and coming from the religious elites and/or institutions – as is often the case for the Second Temple period – historians should pay a special attention to every clue that could reveal the existence of sectarian behaviours and/or groups.

2. *Early Second Temple Sects and Sectarianism*

A long-term exploration of the history of the early Second Temple period – in the Persian Achaemenid and Hellenistic Ptolemaic periods – easily demonstrates that earlier phenomena of polarization between "us" and "them" had already begun to crack the apparently monolithic Judean community. To quote just the most significant episodes of such a largely unknown history, we will briefly refer to (1) the conflicts between the exiles and those who stayed in the country, (2) the lack of assistance provided to the Elephantine community, and (3) the appearance of the first Enochic groups.

The books of Haggai, Zechariah, Third Isaiah and Ezra-Nehemiah provide the main clues pointing to the social and political difficulties that the Babylonian exiles experienced on their return to the land of Israel. As for the book of Ezekiel, its author(s) proposed a new theocratic program for the city of Jerusalem, its institutions, its prince and its clergy. Even if we do not need to follow Paolo Sacchi's dramatic interpretation of the events behind such literary texts as the result of a civil war between the exiles and those who stayed (2000: 61-68),[26] it is true that, after the rather mysterious disappearance of Zerubbabel, apparently no other governor of Davidic descent ruled over Judea. As a possible consequence of such a troubled state of affairs, it is extremely likely that some social groups were marginalized. In the case of the local, not-exilic priests and other religious practitioners, such loss of status could have provoked some sectarian reactions.[27]

The progressive publication of the Torah and Ketuviim – Rishonim as well as Aharonim – contributed to establishing and reinforcing a new, stronger and stricter Judean identity by providing Judean men and women with a new set of specific discourses, beliefs and practices. However, if we consider such a long process of codification as an attempt to reform and update Judean religious life according to the perspectives of the new ruling classes, we can legitimately wonder if the totality of the Judean population did actually and automatically accept such a new program.[28]

This is not a purely theoretical question, because, even if we do not have any evidence from the land of Israel itself, thanks to the discovery of the archives of the community of Judean mercenaries and their families in Yeb, the Elephantine of the Greeks, we actually know that some peripheral people, who considered themselves as members of the Judean ethnos, got into troubles with the Jerusalem religious authorities at the end of the fifth century BCE.[29] Their antiquated Yahwism probably ended up as being too distant from the new standards in vogue in Jerusalem. Thus, in spite of Hananiah's recommendations to properly celebrate the Feast of Unleavened Bread (Cowley letter #21, sent in 519 BCE), when some years later the local shrine was destroyed by the Egyptian mob, apparently (according to Cowley #30, sent in 407 BCE) the Jerusalem priests did not use their influence to support the request made by the Elephantine leaders for the rebuilding of their temple of YHW in Yeb. Moreover, in the same years, the "Deuteronomist" editors of what should be considered as the first more or less achieved edition of the book of Jeremiah clearly expressed their distaste for – from their point of view – illegitimate worship of the "Queen of Heaven" among the Judean refugees in Egypt

(Jr^a [LXX] 50:8–51:30 // Jr^b [MT] 43:8–44:30). The fact that the well-known administrative list Cowley # 22 mentions the Aramaic god and goddess "Eshem-Bethel" and "Anat-Bethel" just after "YHW the God" makes such a coincidence rather suspicious (Piovanelli, 1995).[30]

Among the many questions that such intriguing evidence stirs up, one could ask if the Elephantine tritheistic worship was a syncretistic novelty or an archaic form of Yahwism. If we judge from the pillar-figurines that the archeologists found almost everywhere in the Jerusalem buildings of the last days of the First Temple period, the answer is that the worship of a Judean goddess – the famous Asherah – probably was a common pre-exilic feature.[31] One could also speculate about the reaction of the Judean population in Elephantine discovering that, according to the Jerusalem religious authorities, their good old Yahwism was no longer tolerated as if, in a certain way, their Judean identity had become problematic. Were they ready to separate themselves from Jerusalem in order to preserve the specificity of their faith? We know that they tried to get in touch with the Judean governor Bagohi and, more interestingly, with Delaiah and Shelemiah, the sons of Sanballat, the governor of Samaria. However, they were probably swept away by the Egyptian mob before being able to make any decision. Even if they did survive, would this group have been strong enough to give birth to a new sectarian movement? In spite of its hypothetical nature, this question is not so gratuitous. After all, the great Italian Semitist Ignazio Guidi was of the opinion that they could: he suggested that the persecuted members of the Judean colony of Elephantine were the ancestors of the Falasha nation, the Ethiopian Jews (1932: 95-97 n. 2)![32]

Be that as it may, the most important element to retain is that a strong process of reinvention of the Judean identity was already at work during the first two centuries of the Second Temple period. As for the side effects of such an undertaking, the possibility that some groups were progressively pushed back into the margins of the Judean society and reacted in a sectarian way seems to be very high. Positive evidence for early Second Temple sectarianism has been detected, especially in the prophetic texts.[33] However, the reasons invoked to explain such a fragmentation need to be reconsidered. This situation was not the result of an evolution from the "homogeneity" and "uniformity" of the late First Temple period to the "multicentricity" and "heterogeneity" of the early Second Temple (as argued by Talmon, 1986: 179, 186; 1991a: 22, 28-29).[34] On the contrary, the building of a new Judean entity and identity (Joel Weinberg's "citizen-temple community") shaped by the exilic experience and the codification of a more rigorous "monotheism" (Morton Smith's "YHWH-alone" party), along with the new claim to represent the "true

Israel" against those who stayed in the country (both Judea and Israel) and had supposedly had their religion and bloodline corrupted, would ultimately lead to a variety of sectarian responses.

This could also be the case of the people who expressed their dissatisfaction with the religious situation of the day under cover of the earliest Enochic writings, written as early as, at least, the third century BCE. It is almost always problematic to reconstruct a picture of the real authors and audiences from what we can read in a literary text. Yet, the possibility of the existence of one or more Enochic communities is suggested by the uninterrupted sedimentation of the Enochic traditions and texts. Such works seem to follow a coherent path of development. The same foundational myths – the different versions of the story of the Watchers and the Giants that serve as a pretext for Enoch's heavenly journeys and revelations – provide the narrative storylines for the first episodes (the *Book of the Watchers* and the *Book of the Luminaries*) as well as for their subsequent rewritings (the *Book of Giants*, the *Book of Dreams*, the *Epistle of Enoch*, the *Book of Parables*, as well as *2 Enoch* and the constellation of texts called *3 Enoch*).[35] Also at the interior of the main literary units of the Enochic cycle previous texts and traditions have been reprocessed and newly interwoven into the actual texture. Thus, in *1 Enoch* 6–11 the final editor of the *Book of the Watchers* added some elements taken from the story of Asael to the original myth describing the angelic rebellion lead by Shemihazah. An originally independent *Animal Apocalypse* (*1 Enoch* 85–90) was inserted into the *Book of Dreams*, and similarly, the *Apocalypse of Weeks* (*1 Enoch* 93:1-10; 91:11-17) found its way into the *Epistle of Enoch*. To this we could also add that the language, namely, Aramaic, is another special feature of at least those texts whose fragments were found in Qumran caves.[36]

The people beyond the ancient Enochic texts – to paraphrase the title of a fascinating recent monograph of James R. Davila (2001) – seem to have had a special interest in supernatural matters. More precisely, if we are entitled to transfer to them Davila's conclusion about their late heirs responsible for the so-called *3 Enoch*, they seem to have been involved in some kind of "magic" and/or "shamanic" activities. Therefore, it is difficult to imagine that the authors of – or the group(s) behind – such early texts as the *Book of the Watchers* and the *Book of Astronomy* are to be located among the members of the Jerusalem clergy that precisely rejected – at least, if we judge from the Deuteronomist interdictions that they were supposed to follow[37] – such an approach to the sacred. In fact, both David W. Suter (1979; 2002; 2003) and George W. E. Nickelsburg (1981; 2001: 238-47) were able to detect in *1 Enoch* 6–16 a criticism directed against the Jerusalem Temple and priesthood. They also found geographical clues

– the mention of the waters of Dan, Abel-Main, Lebanon, and Senir in *1 Enoch* 13:7-9 – that would point, in the case of *1 Enoch* 12–16, to an origin in Northern Galilee, in the area of Mount Hermon.[38]

This juxtaposition of alternative mythologies and regionalist peculiarities could be the best indicator of a sectarian milieu. As a matter of fact, the *Book of the Watchers* and related Enochic texts continue to play a major role in the studies on the beginnings of Second Temple apocalypticism. According to García Martínez, it is precisely such a pre-Maccabean apocalyptic tradition that supplied the second-century BCE Essene movement with its ideological roots. While in Boccaccini's opinion, the Essenes and the group that produced the earliest Enochic literature would be but one and the same movement. Passing from one more or less sectarian movement to another, the Enochic heritage would finally reach the Qumran community, the most representative sectarian group of the late Second Temple period besides the different Christian groups.[39]

If we are not falling into the classical trap of circular reasoning, it seems to me that such a close connection between Enochic literature and sectarian attitudes was already there from the beginning. As Albert Baumgarten wisely acknowledges, quoting the authoritative opinions of Giambattista Vico and Elias J. Bickerman, "Successful ideas or institutions [...] rarely (if ever) spring full-born into the world" (1997: 23).[40] He adds a few pages later,

> Works such as the early sections of 1 Enoch or the book of Jubilees fall into the category of forerunners. They are the focus of some social action, in response to new situation created by the encounter with Hellenism. They lead more or less directly to the Qumran community, as attested by fragments of the works in their library and the citation of Jubilees in the Damascus Document (CD xvi, 4). Nevertheless, works such as Jubilees have not yet generated true social effectiveness. Can one confidently write of a community behind the Enoch literature, or Jubilees? (Baumgarten, 1997: 25).

Leaving aside the question of the "social effectiveness" of *Jubilees*, I am convinced that we can not only "confidently write of a community behind the Enoch literature" but also envision such a group as a clearly proto-sectarian one displaying revolutionist, manipulationist, thaumaturgical, and spiritualist attitudes.

3. *Final Methodological and Ethical Reflections*

To appreciate all the implications of Second Temple Jewish sectarianism one has to make use – with Baumgarten or Saldarini – of social-scientific models that are heuristically useful in the study of ancient societies and cultures. Yet to understand religious phenomena in the Second Temple period one needs to adopt – with Boccaccini or Grabbe – a "holistic perspective" encompassing all the aspects of the Persian, the Hellenistic, and the Roman episodes of the Judean and Jewish history. In this connection, it is clear that "[t]he significance of the Persian period for the succeeding centuries cannot be overemphasized" (Grabbe, 2000: 317).

Another illustration of the continuity existing between early and late Second Temple periods is the progressive building of a distinct Samaritan identity. From a historical point of view, it is irrelevant to consider the people of Shechem as the offspring of native Israelites, foreign immigrants, or dissident Judeans.[41] Culturally and socially, at the beginning of the Persian period they became the citizens of the province of Samaria, the legitimate heir of the pre-exilic state of Israel. In their newly-organized homeland they developed a religious system closely related to, but not to be identified with, the Judaism of their southern cousins. They certainly entertained exchanges and relations with them, but they probably never considered themselves other than "Israelites." Gerizim and Zion were two competing holy places for two different peoples, the Samaritans and the Judeans. This situation dramatically changed in 142 BCE, when Judah became an independent state, and especially after John Hyrcanus conquered the region and destroyed the Temple on Mount Gerizim as well as the Samaritan large city built on its top towards the end of the second century BCE. In spite of their political submission, the Samaritans neither adhered to nor split from Judaism. They kept a distinct and specific profile with their own holy places, scriptures, synagogues, clergy, liturgy, halakhah and sectarian movements, both in their communities in Samaria and in the Diaspora.[42] They were able to resist the Roman, Byzantine, Persian, and Muslim persecutions. Technically, they did not become a Jewish sect until 1841 when the chief Rabbi of Jerusalem had to intervene on their behalf and certify that they were a branch of the Children of Israel in order to protect them from religious intolerance. Without such a long-term perspective – from the formative Persian period to, at least, the end of Late Antiquity – we could easily but mistakenly believe that the Samaritans were but a strange sect "within the spectrum of Judaism."

In fact, I would even argue that we could not fully understand Second Temple religious turmoil unless we placed it into the long-term perspective of the Mediterranean culture.[43] In the end, it seems to me that in such a family, clan, village and region-based culture, sectarianism was a logic centrifugal response to the centripetal pressure exerted by the globalizing ideologies and institutions of the day. After all, competition for the power among different groups and resistance to the assimilation are still providing the bedrock for the outburst of sectarian behaviours among peoples that should – theoretically – share the same cultural and religious values. This is one of the main paradoxes of the three great monotheistic religions.

At the beginning of my research, I was attracted by the possibility of identifying multiple sectarian phenomena not only during the Achaemenid and Ptolemaic periods but also all through the history of the Second Temple and beyond. Accordingly, I began to wonder if Judaism and Christianity in particular or all the monotheistic religions in general offer a propitious milieu to the flourishing of sects and sectarian groups. Of course, after a rapid glance at other religious cultures and traditions, I realized how naive such an impression was. Nonetheless, no other symbolic and/or social construction of the reality displays such a contradiction in terms of a multiplicity of claimants that boldly declare to monopolistically hold the right Place, the only Way, and the essential Truth. In a certain way, monotheism and sectarianism have been the two faces of the same coin from the post-exilic "triumph of Elohim."

As with many other social phenomena, religious sectarianism can be either a positive force, in its more reformist variants, driving the society towards evolution and change, or a negative power, in its more introversionist aspects, leading the world to destruction and chaos. Like many other intellectuals after 9/11, in his recent book *Le Feu sacré* (2003), the French philosopher and specialist of religious studies Régis Debray has tackled the delicate question of the relationships that exist between religions and violence. In regards to the question of whether Islam is intrinsically more violent than Christianity, Debray's unequivocal answer is no. However, sadly enough, in his opinion, if it is true that no religion is more violent than another one, it is also true that no religion is *less violent.* The same considerations can be applied to sectarianism, which can be, to a certain extent, either the luminous or the dark side of any attempt to construct and/or to maintain cultural identities. Identities are always based on differences and constructed against the other.

At the International Meeting of the Society of Biblical Literature, held in Groningen, the Netherlands, 25-28 July, 2004, in his inaugural speech Frans Zwarts, the Rector Magnificus of the University of Groningen, made the point of the public utility of studying the human sciences. Both Baumgarten and Cohen's books certainly match such a need. Baumgarten stated in the introduction to his *The Flourishing of Jewish Sects* that in the Spring of 1996 he "recorded a series of lectures based on the arguments of [his] book for Israel Army Radio, as part of their 'Broadcast University' Series" (1997: xii),[44] and Cohen declared that one of the purposes of his monograph *The Beginnings of Jewishness* was "to illuminate the beginnings of Jewishness" on behalf of contemporary North American Jews who are experiencing a major identity crisis: "Once upon a time we knew who was a Jew, who was a Black, what was a red wolf, and what was a rodent. Now we are not so sure" (1999: 10).[45]

Personally, I believe that our most important task as historians, biblical scholars, specialists of religious studies, theologians, philosophers and intellectuals *tout court* is to deconstruct and to demystify the productions of past and present sectarian ideological constructions. Hopefully, the critical re-examination and re-reconstruction of our Jewish and Christian history will enable us to modify our collective memories that – as Yosef Hayim Yerushalmi (1982) and Paul Ricoeur (2000) have abundantly demonstrated – are the true core of our identities.

Endnotes

1. Interestingly enough, both Baumgarten and Cohen were students of Smith. As popular wisdom acknowledges, a good tree brings forth good fruit.

2. One should note that the scholars that discard the applicability of Weberian models frequently also reject the usefulness of Freudian approaches. The switch from such European models to new concepts developed on the basis of North American experiences is also questionable.

3. For a critique of Weber's work from a postcolonialist perspective, see Blaut (2000: 19-30). For a critical introduction to Weber's methodology, see Eliaeson (2002).

4. For a discussion of such limitations, see Hamilton (1995: 193-96), as well as David Chalcraft's contribution to the present volume.

5. Compare Saldarini's synthetic definition, "Sect: a religiously based group which is either actively involved against society or withdrawn in reaction to it. Such groups are often political forces. In its classical Christian definition sect is contrasted with the dominant religious force, church" (1988: 313). Contrast Baumgarten's broader – and perhaps too encompassing – description, "I would therefore define a sect as a *voluntary association of protest, which utilizes boundary marking mechanisms – the social means of differentiating between insiders and outsiders – to distinguish between its own members and those otherwise normally regarded as belonging to the same national or religious entity.* Ancient Jewish sects, accordingly, differentiated *between Jews who were members of their sect and those not*" (1997: 7). This sounds more like a special interest group or a political party than a religious movement at odds with the rest of the society. Also see the comments of Elliott (2000: 48-52, 188-91).

6. The "historical" examples are taken from Wilson (1970: 48-188; 1973: 35-48, 53-69). He seems to make a distinction between the closely related thaumaturgical and spiritualistic categories only in one work (1970: 45-46).

7. For a useful and up to date presentation of the Jewish movements, see Grabbe (2000: 183-209). More difficult to apply to ancient phenomena is the distinction between "sects" and "cults" proposed by Stark and Bainbridge (1987: 121-93; 1996: 103-28). According to Stark and Bainbridge, both sects and cults are deviant religious organizations, the former emerging through a process of schism (e.g. Hicksite Quakerism) and the second being the result of an innovation (e.g. Shakerism, Mormonism, Neo-Paganism, or the Unification Church). In the case of the majority of the Second Temple movements it is, however, impossible to exactly ascertain if they came into existence in one way or the other. This is also true for the beginnings of Christianity that Stark analyzed in his insightful book on *The Rise of Christianity* (1996).

8. Thus, Saldarini (1988: 71-73, 286-87) considers early Christians as a conversionist sect, apocalyptic groups as revolutionists, Essenes and Qumranites as introversionists, the Gnostics as manipulationists, magicians and healers as thaumaturgists, the Jesus movement and the Pharisees as reformists, the latter with introversionist and revolutionist tendencies (also see Saldarini, 2000). For Baumgarten (1997: 13) both Sadducees and Pharisees belong to the reformist category, the Qumranites being introversionists.

9. A practice obviously inherited from Josephus's use of the Greek term *hairesis* – originally meaning, "*system of philosophic principles, or those who profess such principles, sect, school*" (Liddell and Scott, 1973, *sub voce*) – to designate the main Jewish religious and political movements of the late Second Temple period. Josephus, however, was an ancient historian, not a specialist of religious studies or a contemporary sociologist. Therefore, it is questionable to argue, as Baumgarten does, that the Sadducees "must be included within the compass of ancient Jewish sects, as Josephus listed them with Pharisees, Essenes and the Fourth Philosophy as part of the same cultural, religious and social phenomenon" (1997: 11 n. 29).

10. According to Niebuhr (1957) a second-generation sect could develop into a denomination. Such an assumption is, however, unwarranted. See the criticism of Wilson (1990: 107-109); Hamilton (1995: 196-97).

11. Saldarini (1988: 298-308) reaches a similar conclusion.

12. We could speculate that, after the destruction of the Second Temple and before totally disappearing, the few surviving Sadducees eventually became an introversionist sect. This was certainly the case of the Jewish Christian groups – the so-called Nazoreans and Ebionites – in the aftermath of the Second Jewish War (132–135 CE).

13. For a critical assessment of the rabbinic traditions, see Neusner (1971; 1973), Sanders (1992: 380-451, 532-39). For Josephus, see Mason (1991).

14. In this connection, it is important to understand that the aim of the different decisions taken in Yavneh was to gather the people together, not to exclude some groups under the pretext of heterodoxy. For the *Birkat ha-Minim*, see now the seminal essay by Vana (2003).

15. Some specialists are still hesitating to consider the Pharisees as a sect. See, for example, the arguments of Sanders (1977: 156-57, 425-26) and, even more cogently, Luomanen (2002: 123-24). Luomanen rightly points out that what is at stake are the issues of the debate between Sanders' "common Judaism" and Jacob Neusner's variety of "Judaisms" (2002: 114-19).

16. "A party – as Sanders aptly defines it – is a group which believes itself to be right and which wishes others to obey or agree, but which does not exclude dissenters from 'Israel'" (1977: 156 n. 52).

17. The study of Second Temple Jewish and early Christian religious groups in the context of other voluntary associations in Antiquity is a very promising one. Besides Saldarini (1988: 59-70) and Belayche and Mimouni (2003), see Kloppenborg and Wilson (1996); Ascough (2000; 2003); Harland (2003).

18. Concerning the elusive group of the Hasidim and its relationship with the circles that produced the book of Daniel, see the contributions of Rainer Albertz, Stefan Beyerle, Lester L. Grabbe, Philip Davies, and Daniel Smith-Christopher in Collins and Flint (2001: I, 171-290). Horsley (1985) has insightfully studied the Zealots, the Sicarii, and the different prophetic and/or messianic movements.

19. For the Jesus movement, see Gager (1975: 20-37, 57-62); Allison (1998).

20. The Christian exception is more apparent than real. In fact, the primitive community that the followers of the historical Jesus created in Jerusalem was not primarily involved in the missionary activities that the Hellenists and Paul progressively developed in Palestine and the Diaspora. In theory, however, the role of fostering such a missionary response could be attributed to the historical Mary of Magdala. See Schaberg (2002: 300-56); Piovanelli (2003: 123-24).

21. For an assessment of García Martínez and Boccaccini's complementary hypotheses, see van Peursen (2000).

22. The sectarianism of the Qumran community is clearly reaffirmed, for example, by Walker-Ramisch (1996), Marcus (1996) and Regev (2004). Also see the methodological caveat of Jokiranta (2001) and the comments of Piovanelli (2005b).

23. The spiritualist aspects were already present in the earliest Enochic writings. See Piovanelli (2002). The phenomenon of spirit possession is also associated with the Jesus movement by S. L. Davies (1995).

24. For the community of Matthew, see Overman (1990), Stanton (1992), Saldarini (1994), Sim (1998), as well as Luomanen (1998; 2002) and, for its interpretation as a voluntary association, Ascough (2001). For the community of John, see Brown (1979), Zumstein (1990) and Wahlde (1997).

25. For the community of Luke, see Esler (1987), Moxnes (1997). For the Valentinian communities, see Williams (1996: 96-115, 284-88), Markschies (1997).

26. One should note that Sacchi's work is based on an intellectual and literary approach. For a social history of the Yehud province in the Persian period, see Berquist (1995).

27. On the ideology of the exile and its consequences, see Carroll (1992), Barstad (1996), Grabbe (1998), Blenkinsopp (2002). In the case of Ezra-Nehemiah, Grabbe does not hesitate to speak of "apartheid attitude toward the native inhabitants" (2000: 15).

28. One more time, the history of Christianity offers many examples of similar discriminating processes, beginning with the marginalization and persecution of the late antique Donatist Church in North Africa. More recently, at their arrival in Israel from Ethiopia the Falashas experienced the difficulties of integrating a Western society and Rabbinic Judaism. As it is usually the case, after the enthusiasm of the first generation newcomers the second and third generations are expected to suffer some identity

troubles. We could speculate that, in spite of all their efforts to assimilate, if they had the feeling of being rejected and had to take the decision of retrieving their distinct Jewish-Ethiopian identity, they could eventually develop a new sectarian movement in contemporary Israeli society. See Westheimer and Kaplan (1992).

29. For the question of their ethnical identity, see Hamilton (2001). For a historical and religious assessment, see Bolin (1995), Frey (1999).

30. Concerning the editorial history of the book of Jeremiah, see Piovanelli (1997).

31. See Ackerman (1993; 1997), Kletter (1996), Binger (1997), van der Toorn (1999), Hadley (2000).

32. Today Guidi's opinion is considered as an antiquarian curiosity. The Falashas call themselves *Byetä Israel*, "House of Israel," and claim descent from those who migrated from Jerusalem with the son of King Solomon and the Queen of Sheba. According to Halévy (1874: 129-31), they could be the heirs of the Jewish prisoners that the Emperor Kaleb brought back from Hymiar – corresponding to modern Yemen – in 525 CE. However, their origins are still a matter of speculation. For an overview, see Kaplan (1992: 13-41, 168-78) and Quirin (1992: 7-27, 214-23).

33. See Blenkinsopp (1981; 1990), Rofé (1985), Redditt (1986a; 1986b; 1989), Talmon (1986; 1991a), Cook (1995).

34. Those who consider that the societies and religions of ancient Israel and Judah were models of "internal cohesion" adopt a very idealistic – and sometimes ideological – reading of the biblical texts. They also seem to disregard the archeological and cross-cultural data that contradict such an idyllic picture. For a healthy criticism see, for example, the hermeneutical reflections of Lemche (1994; 1999), Elayi and Sapin (1998: 97-109).

35. On the literary career of Enoch within Judaism, see VanderKam (1995), Alexander (1998), Nickelsburg (2001: 71-82).

36. The *Book of the Watchers*, the *Book of Dreams*, and the *Epistle of Enoch*: 4Q201, 202, 204–207, 212; the *Book of the Luminaries*: 4Q208–211; the *Book of Giants*: 1Q23, 24, 26, 4Q203, 530–533. According to Beyer (1984: 227-30, 259; 1994: 117) the literary idiom in which were written the oldest manuscripts of *1 Enoch* (4Q201, 202, 208) was the *Jüdisch-Altpalästinisch*, or, more exactly, *Jüdisch-Altostjordanisch*, while the language of its latest copies clearly belongs to the *Hasmonäisch* variety of Aramaic, which was also used in other documents from Qumran.

37. I am especially thinking of the prescriptions against necromancy in Deut. 18:10-11 and Lev. 19:31; 20:6, 27.

38. On the geography of *1 Enoch* 17–19, also see Bautch (2003).

39. On such Enochic legacy, see VanderKam (1996).

40. To this we could also add Joseph M. Baumgarten's equally insightful conclusion, "we should bear in mind that in religious history one rarely finds phenomena which totally lack precedents" (1991: 158).

41. On the difficult and still debated issue of the Samaritan origins, see Coggins (1975; 1999), Dexinger (1981; 1992), Macchi (1994), Nodet (1997: 122-201), Hjelm (2000; 2003; 2004).

42. Of special interest are the related Dustan and Dosithean schismatic movements. Their halakhah was very strict and, in certain regard, comparable to the

halakhah of the Qumranites, while their feast reckoning was closer to the Pharisaic ruling. See Isser (1976), Fossum (1989).

43. Among the most influential representatives of the *long durée* approach as opposed to *l'histoire événementielle* we could mention the renowned historians Mikhail Rostovtzeff, Henri Pirenne, Shlomo Dov Goitein and Fernand Braudel. The existence of a Mediterranean geographical and anthropological specificity in the long-term has recently been confirmed by the authoritative inquiry of Peregrine Horden and Nicholas Purcell, *The Corrupting Sea* (2000).

44. I dare to suggest that the message implicitly addressed to young Israelis in arms was – especially a few months after the murder of Prime Minister Yitzhak Rabin, on 4 November, 1995 – that sectarian divisions could lead a successful nation to its ruin.

45. In this connection, one should not overlook the process of creating a new Jewish identity through the combination of mystical Jewish approaches and Eastern spiritual techniques in what is called, in North America, the "Jewish Renewal Movement." See, for example, Salkin (2003).

REFERENCES

Ackerman, S. 1993. "The Queen Mother and the Cult in Ancient Israel." *Journal of Biblical Literature* 112: 385-401. Reprinted in A. Bach, ed., *Women in the Hebrew Bible: A Reader*: 179-94. London: Routledge, 1999.

—1997. "The Queen Mother and the Cult in the Ancient Near East." In K. L. King, ed., *Women and Goddess Traditions in Antiquity and Today*: 179-209. Minneapolis: Fortress Press.

Alexander, P. S. 1998. "From Son of Adam to Second God: Transformations of the Biblical Enoch." In M. E. Stone and T. A. Bergren, eds, *Biblical Figures outside the Bible*: 87-122. Harrisburg, PA: Trinity Press International.

Allison, D. C. 1998. *Jesus of Nazareth: Millenarian Prophet*. Minneapolis: Fortress Press.

Ascough, R. S. 2000. "The Thessalonian Christian Community as a Professional Voluntary Association." *Journal of Biblical Literature* 119: 311-28.

—2001. "Matthew and Community Formation." In D. E. Aune, ed., *The Gospel of Matthew in Current Study: Studies in Memory of William G. Thompson, S.J.*: 96-126. Grand Rapids, MI: Eerdmans.

—2003. *Paul's Macedonian Associations: The Social Context of Philippians and 1 Thessalonians*. Tübingen: Mohr Siebeck.

Barstad, H. M. 1996. *The Myth of the Empty Land: A Study in the History and Archaeology of Judah during the "Exilic" Period*. Oslo: Norwegian University Press.

Baumgarten, A. I. 1997. *The Flourishing of Jewish Sects in the Maccabean Era: An Interpretation*. Leiden: E. J. Brill.

Baumgarten, J. M. 1991. "Recent Qumran Discoveries and Halakhah in the Hellenistic-Roman Period." In Talmon, 1991b: 147-58.

Bautch, K. C. 2003. *A Study of the Geography of 1 Enoch 17–19: "No One Has Seen What I Have Seen."* Leiden: E. J. Brill.

Belayche, N., and S. C. Mimouni, eds. 2003. *Les communautés religieuses dans le monde gréco-romain: Essais de définition*. Brepols: Turnhout.

Berquist, J. L. 1995. *Judaism in Persia's Shadow: A Social and Historical Approach*. Minneapolis: Fortress Press.

Beyer, K. 1984. *Die aramäischen Texte vom Toten Meer samt den Inschriften aus Palästina, dem Testament Levis aus der Kairoer Genisa, der Fastenrolle und den alten talmudischen Zitaten.* Göttingen: Vandenhoeck & Ruprecht.

—1994. *Die aramäischen Texte vom Toten Meer. Ergänzungsband.* Göttingen: Vandenhoeck & Ruprecht, 2nd edn, 2004.

Binger, T. 1997. *Asherah: Goddesses in Ugarit, Israel and the Old Testament.* Sheffield: Sheffield Academic Press.

Blaut, J. M. 2000. *Eight Eurocentric Historians.* New York: Guilford Press.

Blenkinsopp, J. 1981. "Interpretation and the Tendency to Sectarianism: An Aspect of Second Temple History." In Sanders, Baumgarten and Mendelson, 1981: 1-26, 299-309.

—1990. "A Jewish Sect of the Persian Period." *Catholic Biblical Quarterly* 52: 5-20.

—2002. "The Bible, Archaeology and Politics, or The Empty Land Revisited." *Journal for the Study of the Old Testament* 27: 169-87.

Boccaccini, G. 1998. *Beyond the Essene Hypothesis: The Parting of the Ways between Qumran and Enochic Judaism.* Grand Rapids, MI: Eerdmans.

—2002a. *Roots of Rabbinic Judaism: An Intellectual History, from Ezekiel to Daniel.* Grand Rapids, MI: Eerdmans.

Boccaccini, G., ed. 2002b. *The Origins of Enochic Judaism: Proceedings of the First Enoch Seminar (University of Michigan, Sesto Fiorentino, Italy, June 19–23, 2001).* Turin: Zamorani.

Bolin, T. M. 1995. "The Temple of YHW at Elephantine and Persian Religious Policy." In D. V. Edelman, ed., *The Triumph of Elohim: From Yahwisms to Judaisms*: 127-42. Kampen: Kok Pharos.

Brown, R. E. 1979. *The Community of the Beloved Disciple.* New York: Paulist Press.

Carroll, R. P. 1992. "The Myth of the Empty Land." In D. Jobling and T. Pippin, eds, *Ideological Criticism of Biblical Texts*: 79-93. Semeia, 59; Atlanta, GA: Scholars Press.

Coggins, R. J. 1975. *Samaritans and Jews: The Origins of Samaritanism Reconsidered.* Oxford: Blackwell.

—1999. "Issues in Samaritanism." In J. Neusner and A. J. Avery-Peck, eds, *Judaism in Late Antiquity.* III. *Where We Stand: Issues and Debates in Ancient Judaism*: 63-77. Leiden: E. J. Brill.

Cohen, Sh. J. D. 1999. *The Beginnings of Jewishness: Boundaries, Varieties, Uncertainties.* Berkeley, CA: University of California Press.

Collins, J. J., and P. W. Flint, with the assistance of C. VanEpps, eds. 2001. *The Book of Daniel: Composition and Reception.* 2 vols.; Leiden: E. J. Brill.

Cook, S. L. 1995. *Prophecy and Apocalypticism: The Postexilic Social Setting.* Minneapolis: Fortress Press.

Davies, P. R. 1998. *Scribes and Schools: The Canonization of the Hebrew Scriptures.* Louisville, KY: Westminster/John Knox Press.

Davies, S. L. 1995. *Jesus the Healer: Possession, Trance, and the Origins of Christianity.* New York: Continuum.

Davila, J. R. 2001. *Descenders to the Chariot: The People behind the Hekhalot Literature.* Leiden: E. J. Brill.

Debray, R. 2003. *Le Feu sacré: Fonctions du religieux.* Paris: Fayard.

Dexinger, F. 1981. "Limits of Tolerance in Judaism: The Samaritan Example." In Sanders, Baumgarten and Mendelson, 1981: 88-114, 327-38.

—1992. "Der Ursprung der Samaritaner im Spiegel der frühen Quellen." In F. Dexinger and R. Pummer, eds, *Die Samaritaner*: 67-140. Darmstadt: Wissenschaftliche Buchgesellschaft.

Elayi, J., and J. Sapin. 1998. *Beyond the River: New Perspectives on Transeuphratene.* Trans. J. E. Crowley. Sheffield: Sheffield Academic Press.

Eliaeson, S. 2002. *Max Weber's Methodologies: Interpretation and Critique.* Cambridge: Polity Press.

Elliott, M. A. 2000. *The Survivors of Israel: A Reconsideration of the Theology of Pre-Christian Judaism.* Grand Rapids, MI: Eerdmans.

Esler, P. F. S. 1987. *Community and Gospel in Luke–Acts: The Social and Political Motivations of Lucan Theology.* Cambridge: Cambridge University Press.

Fossum, J. 1989. "Samaritan Sects and Movements." In A. D. Crown, ed., *The Samaritans*: 293-389. Tübingen: Mohr-Siebeck.

Frey, J. 1999. "Temple and Rival Temple – the Cases of Elephantine, Mt. Gerizim, and Leontopolis." In B. Ego, A. Lange and P. Pilhofer, eds, *Gemeinde ohne Tempel – Community without Temple: Zur Substituierung und Transformation des Jerusalemer Tempels und seines Kults im Alten Testament, antiken Judentum und frühen Christentum*: 171-203. Tübingen: Mohr Siebeck.

Gager, J. G. 1975. *Kingdom and Community: The Social World of Early Christianity.* Englewood Cliffs, NJ: Prentice-Hall.

García Martínez, F. 1988. "Qumran Origins and Early History: A 'Groningen' Hypothesis." *Folia Orientalia* 25: 113-36.

García Martínez, F., and J. Trebolle Barrera. 1995. *The People of the Dead Sea Scrolls: Their Writings, Beliefs and Practices.* Trans. W. G. E. Watson. Leiden: E. J. Brill.

García Martínez, F., and A. Simon van der Woude. 1990. "A 'Groningen' Hypothesis of Qumran Origins and Early History." *Revue de Qumrân* 14.4: 521-44.

Goodman, M. 1994. *Mission and Conversion: Proselytizing in the Religious History of the Roman Empire.* Oxford: Clarendon Press.

Grabbe, L. L. 1995. *Priests, Prophets, Diviners, Sages: A Socio-historical Study of Religious Specialists in Ancient Israel.* Valley Forge, PA: Trinity Press International.

—2000. *Judaic Religion in the Second Temple Period: Belief and Practice from the Exile to Yavne.* London: Routledge.

Grabbe, L. L., ed. 1998. *Leading Captivity Captive: "The Exile" as History and Ideology.* Sheffield: Sheffield Academic Press.

Guidi, I. 1932. *Storia della letteratura etiopica.* Rome: Istituto per l'Oriente.

Hadley, J. M. 2000. *The Cult of Asherah in Ancient Israel and Judah: Evidence for a Hebrew Goddess.* Cambridge: Cambridge University Press.

Halévy, J. 1874. *Mélanges d'épigraphie et d'archéologie sémitiques.* Paris: Imprimerie nationale.

Hamilton, M. 2001. "Who Was a Jew? Jewish Ethnicity during the Achaemenid Period." *Restoration Quarterly* 37: 102-17.

Hamilton, M. B. 1995. *The Sociology of Religion: Theoretical and Comparative Perspectives.* London: Routledge.

Harland, P. A. 2003. *Associations, Synagogues, and Congregations: Claiming a Place in Ancient Mediterranean Society.* Minneapolis: Fortress Press.

Hjelm, I. 2000. *The Samaritans and Early Judaism: A Literary Analysis.* Sheffield: Sheffield Academic Press.

—2003. "Brothers Fighting Brothers: Jewish and Samaritan Ethnocentrism in Tradition and History." In T. L. Thompson, ed., *Jerusalem in Ancient History and Tradition*: 197-222. London: T&T Clark.

—2004. *Jerusalem's Rise to Sovereignty: Zion and Gerizim in Competition.* London: T&T Clark.

Horden, P., and N. Purcell. 2000. *The Corrupting Sea: A Study of Mediterranean History.* Oxford: Blackwell.

Horsley, R. H., with J. S. Hanson. 1985. *Bandits, Prophets, and Messiahs: Popular Movements in the Time of Jesus*. Minneapolis: Winston Press.

Isser, S. J. 1976. *The Dositheans: A Samaritan Sect in Late Antiquity*. Leiden: E. J. Brill.

Jokiranta, J. M. 2001. " 'Sectarianism' of the Qumran 'Sect': Sociological Notes." *Revue de Qumrân* 20.2: 223-39.

Kaplan, S. 1992. *The Beta Israel (Falasha) in Ethiopia: From Earliest Times to the Twentieth Century*. New York: New York University Press.

Kingsbury, J. D., ed. 1997. *Gospel Interpretation: Narrative-Critical and Social-Scientific Approaches*. Harrisburg, PA: Trinity Press International.

Kletter, R. 1996. *The Judean Pillar-Figurines and the Archaeology of Asherah*. Oxford: Tempus Reparatum.

Kloppenborg, J. S., and S. G. Wilson, eds. 1996. *Voluntary Associations in the Graeco-Roman World*. London: Routledge.

Lemche, N. P. 1994. "Is It Still Possible to Write a History of Ancient Israel?" *Scandinavian Journal of the Old Testament* 8: 165-90.

—1999. "Are We Europeans Really Good Readers of Biblical Texts and Interpreters for Biblical History?" *Journal of Northwest Semitic Languages* 25: 185-99.

Liddell, H. G., and R. Scott. 1973. *A Greek-English Lexicon*. Ed. H. S. Jones *et al.* Oxford: Clarendon Press.

Luomanen, P. 1998. "Corpus Mixtum – an Appropriate Description of Matthew's Community?" *Journal of Biblical Literature* 117: 469-80.

—2002. "The 'Sociology of Sectarianism' in Matthew: Modeling the Genesis of Early Jewish and Christian Communities." In I. Dunderberg, C. Tuckett and K. Syreeni, eds, *Fair Play: Diversity and Conflicts in Early Christianity*: 107-30. Leiden: E. J. Brill.

Macchi, J.-D. 1994. *Les Samaritains: Histoire d'une légende: Israël et la province de Samarie*. Geneva: Labor et Fides.

Marcus, J. 1996. "Modern and Ancient Jewish Apocalypticism." *The Journal of Religion* 76: 1-27.

Markschies, C. 1997. "Valentinian Gnosticism: Toward the Anatomy of a School." In J. D. Turner and A. McGuire, eds. *The Nag Hammadi Library after Fifty Years: Proceedings of the 1995 Society of Biblical Literature Commemoration*: 401-38. Leiden: E. J. Brill.

Mason, S. 1991. *Flavius Josephus on the Pharisees: A Composition-Critical Study*. Leiden: E. J. Brill.

Moxnes, H. 1997. "The Social Context of Luke's Community." In Kingsbury, 1997: 166-77.

Neusner, J. 1971. *The Rabbinic Traditions about the Pharisees before 70*. 3 vols.; Leiden: E. J. Brill.

—1973. *From Politics to Piety: The Emergence of Pharisaic Judaism*. Englewood Cliffs, NJ: Prentice-Hall.

Neusner, J., and A. J. Avery-Peck, eds. 2003. *George W. E. Nickelsburg in Perspective: An Ongoing Dialogue of Learning*. 2 vols.; Leiden: E. J. Brill.

Nickelsburg, G. W. E. 1981. "Enoch, Levi, and Peter: Recipients of Revelation in Upper Galilee." *Journal of Biblical Literature* 100: 575-600. Reprinted in J. Neusner and A. J. Avery-Peck, 2003: II, 427-57.

—2001. *1 Enoch 1: A Commentary on the Book of 1 Enoch, Chapters 1–36; 81–108*. Minneapolis: Fortress Press.

—2003. *Ancient Judaism and Christian Origins: Diversity, Continuity, and Transformation*. Minneapolis: Fortress Press.

Niebuhr, H. R. 1957 [1929]. *The Social Sources of Denominationalism*. New York: Meridian Books.

Nodet, É. 1997. *A Search for the Origins of Judaism: From Joshua to the Mishnah*. Sheffield: Sheffield Academic Press.

Overman, J. A. 1990. *Matthew's Gospel and Formative Judaism: The Social World of the Matthean Community*. Minneapolis: Fortress Press.

Piovanelli, P. 1995. "La condamnation de la diaspora égyptienne dans le livre de *Jérémie* (*JrA* 50,8–51,30/*JrB* 43,8–44,30)." *Transeuphratène* 9: 35-49.

—1997. "JrB 33,14–26, ou la continuité des institutions à l'époque maccabéenne." In A. H. W. Curtis and T. Römer, eds, *The Book of Jeremiah and its Reception – Le livre de Jérémie et sa réception*: 255-76. Leuven: Peeters.

—2002. "A Theology of the Supernatural in the *Book of Watchers*? An African Perspective." In Boccaccini, 2002b: 87-98.

—2003. "Pre- and Post-Canonical Passion Stories: Insights into the Development of Christian Discourse on the Death of Jesus." *Apocrypha* 14: 99-128.

—2005a. "Jesus' Charismatic Authority: On the Historical Applicability of a Sociological Model." *Journal of the American Academy of Religion* 73: 395-427.

—2005b. "Some Archeological, Sociological and Cross-cultural Afterthoughts on the 'Groningen' and the 'Enochic/Essene' Hypotheses." In G. Boccaccini, ed., in collaboration with J. H. Ellens and J. Waddell, *Enoch and Qumran Origins: New Light on a Forgotten Connection*: 366-72. Grand Rapids, MI: Eerdmans.

Quirin, J. A. 1992. *The Evolution of the Ethiopian Jews: A History of the Beta Israel (Falasha) to 1920*. Philadelphia: University of Pennsylvania Press.

Redditt, P. L. 1986a. "Once Again, the City in Isaiah 24–27." *Hebrew Annual Review* 10: 317-35.

—1986b. "The Book of Joel and Peripheral Prophecy." *Catholic Biblical Quarterly* 48: 225-40.

—1989. "Israel's Shepherds: Hope and Pessimism in Zechariah 9–14." *Catholic Biblical Quarterly* 51: 631-42.

Regev, E. 2004. "Comparing Sectarian Practice and Organization: The Qumran Sects in Light of the Regulations of the Shakers, Hutterites, Mennonites and Amish." *Numen* 51: 146-81.

Ricoeur, P. 2000. *La mémoire, l'histoire, l'oubli*. Paris: Seuil.

Rofé, A. 1985. "Isaiah 66:1–4: Judean Sects in the Persian Period as Viewed by Trito-Isaiah." In A. Kort and S. Morschauser, eds, *Biblical and Related Studies Presented to Samuel Iwry*: 205-17. Winona Lake, IN: Eisenbrauns.

Sacchi, P. 2000. *The History of the Second Temple Period*. Trans. T. Kirk. Sheffield: Sheffield Academic Press.

Saldarini, A. J. 1988. *Pharisees, Scribes, and Sadducees in Palestinian Society: A Sociological Approach*. Wilmington, DE: Michael Glazier.

—1994. *Matthew's Christian Jewish Community*. Chicago: University of Chicago Press.

—2000. "Sectarianism." In L. H. Schiffman and J. C. VanderKam, eds, *Encyclopedia of the Dead Sea Scrolls*: II, 853-57. 2 vols.; Oxford: Oxford University Press.

Salkin, J. K. 2003. "New Age Judaism." In J. Neusner and A. J. Avery-Peck, eds, *The Blackwell Companion to Judaism*: 355-70. Oxford: Blackwell.

Sanders, E. P. 1977. *Paul and Palestinian Judaism: A Comparison of Patterns of Religion*. London: SCM Press.

—1992. *Judaism: Practice and Belief 63 BCE – 66 CE*. London: SCM Press.

Sanders, E. P., A. I. Baumgarten, and A. Mendelson, eds. 1981. *Jewish and Christian Self-Definition*. II. *Aspects of Judaism in the Graeco-Roman Period*. Philadelphia: Fortress Press.

Schaberg, J. 2002. *The Resurrection of Mary Magdalene: Legends, Apocrypha, and the Christian Testament*. New York: Continuum.

Sim, D. C. 1998. *The Gospel of Matthew and Christian Judaism: The History and Social Setting of the Matthean Community*. Edinburgh: T&T Clark.

Smith, M. 1971. *Palestinian Parties and Politics That Shaped the Old Testament*. New York: Columbia University Press.

Stanton, G. N. 1992. *A Gospel for a New People: Studies in Matthew*. Edinburgh: T&T Clark.

Stark, R. 1996. *The Rise of Christianity: A Sociologist Reconsiders History*. Princeton, NJ: Princeton University Press.

Stark, R., and W. S. Bainbridge. 1987. *A Theory of Religion*. New York: Lang.

—1996. *Religion, Deviance, and Social Control*. London: Routledge.

Suter, D. W. 1979. "Fallen Angel, Fallen Priest: The Problem of Family Purity in 1 Enoch." *Hebrew Union College Annual* 50: 115-35.

—2002. "Revisiting 'Fallen Angels, Fallen Priests.'" In Boccaccini, 2002b: 137-42.

—2003. "Why Galilee? Galilean Regionalism in the Interpretation of *1 Enoch* 6–16." *Henoch* 25: 167-212.

Talmon, S. 1986. "The Emergence of Jewish Sectarianism in the Early Second Temple Period." In S. Talmon, *King, Cult and Calendar in Ancient Israel: Collected Studies*: 165-201. Jerusalem: Magnes Press.

—1991a. "The Internal Diversification of Judaism in the Early Second Temple Period." Revised version of Talmon (1986), printed as 1991b: 16-43.

Talmon, S., ed. 1991b. *Jewish Civilization in the Hellenistic-Roman Period*. Philadelphia: Trinity Press International.

Van der Toorn, K. 1999. "Goddesses in Early Israelite Religion." In L. Goodison and C. Morris, eds, *Ancient Goddesses: The Myths and the Evidence*: 83-97. Madison, WI: University of Wisconsin Press.

Van Peursen, W. 2000. "Qumran Origins: Some Remarks on the Enochic/Essene Hypothesis." *Revue de Qumrân* 20.2: 241-53.

Vana, L. 2003. "La *Birkat ha-minim* est-elle une prière contre les judéo-chrétiens?" In Belayche and Mimouni, 2003: 201-41.

VanderKam, J. C. 1995. *Enoch: A Man for All Generations*. Columbia, SC: University of South Carolina Press.

—1996. "Enoch, Enochic Motifs, and Enoch in Early Christian Literature." In J. C. VanderKam and W. Adler, eds. *The Jewish Apocalyptic Heritage in Early Christianity*: 33–101. Assen: Van Gorcum.

Wahlde, U. C. von. 1997. "Community in Conflict: The History and Social Context of the Johannine Community." In Kingsbury, 1997: 222-33.

Walker-Ramisch, S. 1996. "Graeco-Roman Voluntary Associations and the Damascus Document: A Sociological Analysis." In Kloppenborg and Wilson, 1996: 128-45.

Weinberg, J. 1992. *The Citizen-Temple Community*. Trans. D. L. Smith-Christopher. Sheffield: Sheffield Academic Press.

Westheimer, R. K., and S. Kaplan. 1992. *Surviving Salvation: The Ethiopian Jewish Family in Transition*. New York: New York University.

Williams, M. A. 1996. *Rethinking "Gnosticism": An Argument for Dismantling a Dubious Category*. Princeton, NJ: Princeton University Press.

Wilson, B. R. 1961. *Sects and Society: A Sociological Study of Three Religious Groups in Britain*. London: Heinemann.

—1967 [1959]. "An Analysis of Sect Development." In B. R. Wilson, ed., *Patterns of Sec-*

tarianism: Organisation and Ideology in Social and Religious Movements: 22-45. London: Heinemann.

—1970. *Religious Sects: A Sociological Study*. London: Weidenfeld & Nicolson.

—1973. *Magic and the Millennium: A Sociological Study of Religious Movements of Protest among Tribal and Third-World Peoples*. London: Heinemann.

—1982. *Religion in Sociological Perspective*. Oxford: Oxford University Press.

—1990. *The Social Dimensions of Sectarianism: Sects and New Religious Movements in Contemporary Society*. Oxford: Clarendon Press.

Yerushalmi, Y. H. 1982. *Zakhor: Jewish History and Jewish Memory*. Seattle: University of Washington Press.

Zumstein, J. 1990. "La communauté johannique et son histoire." In J.-D. Kaestli, J.-M. Poffet and J. Zumstein, eds, *La communauté johannique et son histoire: La trajectoire de l'évangile de Jean aux deux premiers siècles*: 359-74. Geneva: Labor et Fides.

Atonement and Sectarianism in Qumran: Defining a Sectarian Worldview in Moral and Halakhic Systems

Eyal Regev

Since the early stages of the study of the scrolls found in Qumran, scholars have noticed the central place of atonement in the belief-system of the writers of the scrolls.[1] The attention given by Christian scholars of theology to the concept of atonement was natural, but by no means overstated. I regard atonement as the major aim of both the members of *yahad* and the *Damascus Covenant*. Here I would like to discuss the ideological background for the concept of atonement in Qumran as well as its relevance to the understanding of its halakhic system. I would like to approach it from rather unconventional perspectives: the study of sectarianism in the sociology of religion, and what I call "comparative sectarianism."

Almost everyone would agree that writings such as the *Community Rule*, the *Damascus Document*, the *Hodayot* and the *Pesharim* were composed by a sectarian movement, that is sometimes called "the Qumran Community" (though actually referring to several different communities with considerable differences) or "the Qumran sectarians." It is therefore quite obvious that we should study these sources in a way similar to those that are used in the study of the sociology of religion in relation to sects in general. In order to do so we should first define what is the most essential feature of sectarian worldview, namely, what is the major point of departure that characterizes sectarian worldview (or ideology). Consequently, we should trace the particular expressions of this feature in the scrolls, that is, the sectarian ethos,[2] and try to find its parallels among other sects of the same type. If such a parallelism succeeds, the result will enable us to conclude that such expressions or ethos are not unique to the Qumran sects, but are an integral part of the sectarian worldview.[3]

In the present article I will try to follow this general methodology, limiting myself to one general feature of the sectarian ideology – tension towards the world, namely, viewing the world as evil. I will also concentrate on one general expression of the tension towards the world – the idea of atonement. I will suggest that the quest for atonement is characteristic of many other sects, and it is therefore an integral part of the sectarian worldview. I will proceed by showing that the obsessive search for atonement is related not only to the moral order of the Qumran sects, but is already embedded in the halakhic system of the *Temple Scroll* and *Miqsat Maase Ha-Torah* (henceforth: MMT). That is, the very general characteristics of the halakhah in the *Temple Scroll* and MMT actually resemble the religious pre-suppositions regarding tension and atonement in the *Community Rule*, the *Damascus Document* and the *Hodayot*. I will therefore suggest that the sectarian worldview and the formation of the sectarian social system of the Qumran sects was developed due to the emergence of the concepts of tension towards the world and the quest for atonement among the circles who established those sects.

The Sectarian Worldview: Tension with the Evil World

If the sectarian worldview is reduced to one major feature from which all others result, it is the view of tension towards the world. According to Stark and Bainbridge, a sect is a religious group in a state of tension towards the surrounding environment. Sects are dissatisfied with the world, reject the world as it seems, and feel that the material world is not rich enough unless supplemented by the supernatural.[4] The idea of tension with the world is also acknowledged by Bryan Wilson, who asserted that among the characteristics of sectarian societies are hostility or indifference to the outside society, and the fact that the sect is a protest group. In fact the pattern of tension is implicit in other characteristics that Wilson enumerated: (1) a self-conception of an elect, a gathered remnant, possessing special enlightenment; (2) a claim that the sect has a monopoly of the complete religious truth, which others do not enjoy. This truth provides the framework for all aspects of belief, religious worship, social practice, ethics, politics, and all areas of human affairs. It may also embrace the understanding of the natural world, and the purposes and order that are thought to underlie the universe, (3) Personal perfection is the expected standard of aspiration.[5] Common to these ideas is the belief that all truth and human perfection are found among the sect, while the outside world is negated and resisted, as if there is nothing good, true or worthy of pursuing in it.

All these characteristics of the sect's tension with the world are related to a grave dissatisfaction with the actual reality in the outside society. The ideological origin of this dissatisfaction was discussed by Wilson in his classification of "responses to the world," namely, types of sectarian ideologies (among the responses: introversionist, revolutionist, reformist, conversionist).[6] Common to all these responses is the coping with the belief that the world is disrupted by evil, stressing the nature of salvation men seek. The responses are complex orientations to the wider society, its culture, values, and cultural goals and the experience of evil (which together may simply be referred to as "the world"), as well as the means of escaping it and attaining salvation.[7] All of them reject the world and its cultural arrangements and suggest a way by which men might be saved. They differ from each other in their conceptions of the source of evil and the way it will be overcome.[8]

According to Wilson's classification, it is possible to conclude that the sectarian tension with the world derives from viewing the world as evil, and (as will be shown further below) the concept of human sinfulness. This can be attested to by several examples from the writings of some well-known sects. Peter Rideman, one of the earliest Hutterite leaders, asserted that "Evil hath now taken the upper hand in the world and still increases daily, so that men proceed from iniquity to iniquity, because they have yielded and committed their members to serve sin." He also claimed that "all men save Christ only have a sinful nature," that "all of us have by nature a tendency towards sin," and thus called for remorse and repentance.[9] The Puritans also discussed sin at length, aiming to introduce a new religious and governmental system.[10] The early Quakers coped with the problem of evil, especially within the Church.[11] The Salvation Army was "an army organized for the deliverance of mankind from sin and the power of the devil."[12] For the Shakers, deliverance from the power of sin was the prominent issue. The Shakers viewed both Roman Catholics and Protestants as "miserable sinners."[13]

Indeed, the degree of the evilness attributed to the world is relative, as much as the degree of tension with the world varies. A reformist response/sect that aims to amend the world from within and change the hearts or minds of people outside the sect, or a conversionist sect which aims to cause them emotional transformation, may feel relatively less tension and view the world in a more positive light. In contrast, an introversionist sect that withdraws from the world, or a revolutionist sect that foresees the world's destruction and its overturning, hoping for the creation of a new order bear higher tension. Since the Qumran sects (namely, the *Community Rule*, the *Damascus Covenant* and the authors of the *Hodayot*) held positions characteristic of introversionist and revolutionist sects,[14] one may expect to find in their writings high tension with the outside society and an emphasis on the evilness of the world.

Many attestations can be found in the writing of the *yahad* and the *Damascus Covenant* to the tension with the outside world and the belief that it is full of wickedness.[15] The author of the *Damascus Document* opens with the claim that "the last generation" is "a congregation of traitors" (CD 1.12). He views his period of time as the years when "Belial will be set loose against Israel," with its three nets – fornication (or lack of chastity), wealth (or arrogance) and the defilement of the temple" (CD 4.12-18). The members of the outside society are called "the builders of the wall" and they are accused of transgressing laws of matrimony and in speaking against the laws of the sect, and thus are portrayed as those who "have no intelligence" (CD 4.19–5.17). Such people are sentenced to death by God since they "all are rebels because they have not left the path of traitors and have defiled themselves in the path of licentiousness, and with wicked wealth, avenging themselves, and each one bearing resentment against his brother, and each one hating his fellow. Each one becomes obscured by blood relatives and approached for debauchery and bragged about wealth and gain. Each one did what was right in his eyes and each one has chosen the stubbornness of his heart" (CD 8.4-8; cf. 19.16-21). The author is also condemning the "sons of the pit" for stealing from the poor of his people, preying upon widows and murdering orphans (CD 6.11-17; 4Q266 3.2).

In the *Community Rule*, the members declare that they "shall separate from the congregation of the men of injustice" (1QS 5.1-2; cf. 8.13), who "walk along the path of wickedness" (5.10-11). Elsewhere (9.8) they are called "men of deceit" who are set against the sect's "men of holiness." The members are committed to "love all the sons of light...and to detest all the sons of darkness according to their guilt in God's vindication" (1.9-11). As for anyone who declines to enter the sect's covenant "his soul loathes the discipline of knowledge of just judgment...and shall not be counted with the upright...he ploughs in the mud of wickedness" (1QS 2.26–3.3). In *Pesher Habbakuk*, the Wicked Priest (usually identified with the Hasmonean high priest) is condemned for sinning by stealing and collaborating with evil people and he is also defiled by impurity (1QpHab 8.8-13). The Wicked Priest is also blamed for acting in violence against the towns of Judaea and the stealing of the property of the poor (1QpHab 12.7-10).

Self-Guilt and the Quest for Atonement in Qumran

In the view of the Qumran sectarians, not only have these unrighteous and evil people outside their sects sinned. Quite surprisingly, a strong sense of guilt and sin is shared by the sectarians themselves. The following evidence indicates that the Qumran sectarians presupposed that the world is a place where even good people fail to walk in the way of righteousness. The *Damascus Document* opens with the prehistory of the sect, arguing that the sect's forerunners "realized their iniquity and knew that they were guilty [men]; they were like blind persons and like those who grope the path for twenty years" (CD 1.8-9). The *Damascus Document* also concludes with the call for the members to "confess before God: 'Assuredly, we have sinned, both we and our fathers, walking contrary to the ordinances of the covenant; just[ice] and truth are your judgments against us'" (CD 20.28-30). Moreover, those who joined the *Damascus Covenant* were supposed to confess their sins against the Torah before joining the sect and to justify divine punishment of all transgressing Jews (CD 20.27-32).

This notion of self-blame is explicit in the confessing rituals of entry into the covenant and the prayer of the *yahad* (*Community Rule* 1.24–2.1; 11.9-10). The authors of the *Hodayot* expresses their feelings of self-guilt time and time again: "the [pardon]ing of my former offences, to [bow] low and beg your favor for [my sins and the evilness] of my deeds and the depravity of my heart. Because I defiled myself with impurity, and I was crea[ted] from the foundation [of lewdness]."[16] In this passage and many others, the world, the human experience, is portrayed in very dark colours. Finally, the notion of repentance is attested to in the sectarian's self-designation as *shavei pesha* "those repent from sin/convert from iniquity."[17]

Naturally, such guilt and iniquities require atonement. The *yahad's raison d'être* was to "to lay a foundation of truth for Israel, for the community of the eternal covenant. They should make atonement for all who freely volunteer for the holiness of Aaron and for the house of truth in Israel" (1QS 5.5-6). The term "to atone for the land" is mentioned twice in the so-called manifesto of the *yahad* (1QS 8.6, 10). Upon cursing of the one who declines to enter the covenant it is stated that he shall not attain atonement (1QS 3.4). The authors of the *Hodayot* repeatedly emphasize the idea of atonement and heavenly forgiveness when they praise God: "And all the sons of your truth you bring to forgiveness of your presence, you pu[ri]fy them from their offences by the greatness of your goodness, and by the abundance of your com[pas]sion to make them stand in your presence, for ever and ever."[18]

In the *Damascus Document*, the forefathers of the present Covenanters are referred to as those whom "God, in his wonderful mysteries, atoned for their iniquity and *pardoned their sin*. And he built for them a safe home in Israel... (CD 3.18-19). The passage concluding the *Damascus Covenant* announces that

> those who remain steadfast in these rules [co]ming and going in accordance with the law...and are instructed in the first ordinances in conformity with which the men of the *yahid* (read: yahad) were judged; and led their ears to the voice of the Teacher of Righteousness; and do not reject the just regulation when they hear them; these shall exult and rejoice and their hearts will be strong, and they shall prevail over all the sons of the world. *And God will atone for them,* and they shall see his salvation, for they have taken refuge in his holy name (CD 20.27-34).

Atonement, however, was not only proclaimed, but was actually perceived due to practices, regulation, and rituals.[19] The Qumran sectarians view their communities and social lives as modes of atonement and as a solitary island of righteousness. The members of the *yahad* are committed to "justice and uprightness, compassionate love and seemly behavior...lawsuit and judgment to proclaim as guilt all those who trespass the decree" (1QS 5.4, 6-7). Also, the members of the *Damascus Covenant* are called to "walk perfectly on his [i.e. God's] paths and not allow yourself to be attracted by the thought of guilty inclination and lascivious eyes, for many have gone astray due to these" (CD 2.15-17). The author of the *Hodayot* is addressing God with gratitude: "[You, my God] have opened my ears for the instruction of those who rebuke with justice [and saved me] from the assembly of futility and from the counsel of violence...[and cleansed me] from guilt. And I know that there is hope for whoever turn from offence and relinquish sin...to walk on the path of your heart without injustice" (1QH^a 14.[Sukenik 6]3-7).

This quest for moral behaviour was translated into scrupulous actions in the penal codes of the *Community Rule* and the *Damascus Document*.[20] In order to illustrate the rigorousness of this system of transgression and punishment, the penalties may be classified as three types: (1) expulsion was used in cases such as informing outsiders about the sect, voicing complaints about its teaching, and betrayal of the sect; (2) exclusion or separation from full membership, preventing the member from participating in meetings or communal sect meals. This was the penalty for lying about financial issues or gossiping about other members; (3) rationing of food supply by a half for a period of several days, months or even a year or two. This was the most lenient and common type of punishment and it was used in cases such as improper behaviour in the council of the community, answering one's fellow stubbornly, addressing him impatiently, or bearing a grudge. There were also many combinations of the second and third types, which were applied in cases such as when "one whose spirit swerves from the authority of the Community by dealing treacherously with the truth and by walking in the stubbornness of his heart, if he returns [i.e. repents]" (1QS 7.18-21).

This moral code was accompanied by a unique perception concerning the sect's autonomous coping with sin and attaining atonement. According to the *Community Rule*, justice and righteous behaviour atone for sin and treachery as substitutes for the corrupt sacrifices in the Temple: "these [men] become in Israel a foundation of the Holy Spirit in eternal truth, they shall atone for iniquitous guilt and sinful unfaithfulness, so that [God's] favor for the land [is obtained] without flesh of burnt offerings and without the fat of sacrifices...*the perfect of the Way [are as] a pleasing freewill offering* (1QS 9.3-5). A further analogy between the communal punishment and the sacrifices of atonement and purgation of the sin from the altar is attested to in two fragments of the *Damascus Document* from Cave 4: "Any[one] who [...] shall enter and make it known to the priest [in cha]rge over the many, and he shall receive his judgment with goodwill as he has said through Moses concerning the one who sins unintentionally that they shall bring his *hattat* and his *asham*" (4QD[e] 7.1 and 4QD[a] 11).

The ultimate atonement, however, was saved for the future. According to 11QMelchizedek the coming of Melchizedek (identified as the priestly messiah by some scholars) "in the first week of the jubilee which follows the ni[ne] jubilees. And the d[ay of aton]ement is the e[nd of]the tenth jubilee in which *atonement shall be made* for all the sons of [light and] for the men [of] the lot of Melchizedek."[21]

Until now we have discussed two major phenomena: the consciousness of the threat of sin and evilness, also apparent in the dualistic thinking such as the *Instruction of the Two Spirits* (1QS 3.13–4.26),[22] and the endless pursuit for atonement. These two interrelated conceptions may lie at the base of the *yahad*'s self-conception as "a dwelling place for the holy of holies" (1QS 8.8), or "a house of holies for Israel and of the holy of holies in Israel for Aharon" (1QS 8.5-6) or the Damascus Covenanters self-image as members of a new covenant with God. Their holiness and closeness to God were not only a matter of predestination, but of a continuous endeavor of moral behaviour and strict halakhic observance.[23]

But here we discern a paradox. If the *yahad* is a holy community and the *Damascus Covenant* is very close to this category; if the sectarians are all pardoned by God, either due to the divine predestinate plan or because they follow God's moral ways and true laws, why do they continue to confess their sins and feel guilty? Were not the regulations mentioned above supposed to bring relief from their self-blame? I think that this paradox is related to the basic notion of the evilness of the world that may lie at the basis of any sectarian worldview. The members of the Qumran sects held humans in low esteem: "What is someone born of woman…a structure of dust fashioned with water, his counsel is the [iniquity] of sin shame of dishonor and so[urce of] impurity, and depraved spirits rule over him."[24] Here the nothingness of all humans is expressed, and we finally realize that the problem of evil in the world is also related to the carnal character of man. Man is naturally afflicted with physical incompleteness, imperfection, falling short, and surfeit of human desires.

To overcome these grave shortcomings of man since his creation, divine intervention is necessary. Thus, the sectarian's presumption to overcome imperfect or evil nature of humans cannot be detached from the supernatural. Divine election and guidance are the keys to escaping from sin. The Qumran sectarians believed that God had predestinated them to be righteous.[25] But they also understood their ability to become righteous as a divine grace: "Only on Your Goodness is man acquitted (*yitsdak*, will be righteous)."[26] Namely, God elected specific individuals and redeemed them from afflictions with his grace.[27] Nonetheless, although this idea solves the paradox of the spiritual merits of the members and the problem of their senseless flesh, it cannot fully explain why those who attained God's grace still feel guilty and ask for forgiveness. Indeed, they were elected to be the just ones, but their righteousness is incomplete, and they may be tempted to sin. The election is an opportunity, but its fulfillment is not self-evident.

As the *Instruction of the Two Spirits* reveals, there is a concept of psychological dualism, that is, each person contains both good and evil: (T)he spirits of truth and injustice feud in the heart of man: they walk in wisdom or in folly… (1QS 4.23-25).[28] Just as the Israelites were elected by God and designated as holy, but then disobeyed him repeatedly and were exiled, similarly the election of the sectarians would not ensure them from sin and punishment. It seems that the fact that the sectarians regarded themselves as chosen did not lead them to view themselves as self-righteous. Their belief in their own election was only the basis of their acts of atonement. They must atone with just deeds and complete observance of God's true commands.

To conclude this section, the members of the Qumran sects believed that only within the sect is it possible to accomplish penitence, penance and atonement and hence also redemption and salvation. Their main means of achieving atonement was a system of moral behaviour and punishments. The rest of the people outside the *yahad* and the *Damascus Covenant* would continue to be wicked, whereas the sectarian moral code was the only way of righteousness. Interestingly, some significant component of this distinctive belief-system can be found among other sects.

Confession and Atonement in Other Sects: Shakers and Amish

As noted above, the *yahad* and the *Damascus Covenant* were introversionist sects. They withdrew from the world in order to create a civilization where righteousness rules. They believed that the only remedy for the evil of the outside society is by replacing it with an alternative one. In this section I would like to show that other introversionist sects (and perhaps also other types of sects) approach the problem of sin and atonement in a way similar to the one discerned in Qumran. Introversionist sects maintain strict boundaries that separate them from the world: boundaries of commerce (common property among the Hutterites and Shakers), marriage (celibacy among the Shakers), resistance to contemporary material culture and technology (Amish) and residing in separate communities (Amish) or colonies (Shakers and Hutterites). The purpose of the following "comparative sectarianism" between the Qumran sects and the Shakers and Amish is to comprehend the ideological background and the social function of the Qumranic idea of atonement. I suggest that the sense of self-guilt and the intensive quest for atonement, translated into different regulations and rituals, is characteristic of some of the interversionist sects.[29]

The Shakers and the Amish followed a path similar to the one of the Qumran sects: in order to overcome sin and accomplish atonement, they practiced special rituals of confession. The Shaker practice of overcoming sin through confession goes back to Ann Lee, founder of the Shakers, who first confessed, and taught it "as the first act of a repentant soul, and as being absolutely essential to the reception of the power to forsake sin."[30] For Ann Lee, confession emerged as an immediate and emotional response to her feelings of self-guilt, as she testified: "I felt such a sense of my sins that I was willing to confess them before the whole world. I confessed my sins to my elders, one by one... When my elders reproved me, I felt determined not to be reproved twice for the same thing, but to labor to overcome the evil for myself."[31]

According to Shaker laws, a member who discovered a violation of "the law of Christ or any thing contrary to the known doctrine of the gospel...is bound to make it known to the Ministry," or the Elders. Shaker "Laws and Orders" (1860) add that if the member failed to reveal the matter of sin and transgression to the Elders, "they [i.e. the Elders] participate in the guilt and condemnation thereof." Furthermore, transgressing Shakers confessed before assembling for worship, and reproach led to open "trials."[32] In his confession, the Shaker convert was required to describe his past life and sins in great detail. When Shaker Elders were asked: "Are you perfect? Do you live without sin?" the Elders answered: "The power of God, revealed in this day, does enable souls to cease from sin; and we have received that power; we have actually left off committing sin, and we live in daily obedience to the will of God."[33] The confession always included all one's sins and was made in a fervour of repentance. For those who underwent the ritual it constituted both baptism in the Spirit and a vow to enter the church, thereby also implying a commitment to the future.[34] Confessions were frequently deemed insincere or insufficient and had to be repeated. Confession was believed to expiate sins and to purify the convert, while symbolizing his rejection of the world and its temptations. The act of confession mortified the convert and so encouraged the development of humility and submissiveness, qualities that the Shaker leaders held as essential for the believers.[35]

An Amish member confesses his sins either on his or her own initiative or as a procedure of punishment (the latter's function is quite similar to the admonitions discussed above). According to Amish legislation "church confession is to be made, if practical, where transgression was made. If not, a written request of forgiveness should be made to said [sic] church. All manifest sins to be openly confessed before church before being allowed to commune."[36] There are four different levels of confession, depending on the severity of the offense, the strictest of which leads to a six-week ban from the congregational meal and fellowship.[37] Shunning (Meidung) is the Amish equivalent to the Qumranic expulsion (shunning had great significance in the formation of the Anabaptist and especially the Amish movements). An Amish member would feel helpless coping with isolation from his or her friends and relatives and, therefore, would either repent or leave the community.[38]

An additional practice of confession is to be found in the Amish baptism rite (the Amish, like the other Anabaptists, namely, the Mennonites and Hutterites, reject infant baptism and view baptism as a conversion ceremony).[39] A similar act of remission of one's sins before baptism was already demanded by the Hutterite leader Peter Rideman.[40]

The Danger of Desecration and the Quest for Atonement in the Temple Scroll and MMT

I turn now from theology and moral systems to the realm of halakhah and sacrificial rituals. Sacrifices in general and a sacrificial cult in the so-called priestly-code in particular are sensitive to desecration and aimed to bring about atonement. I would like to show that in the laws of the *Temple Scroll* and MMT, the danger of sacrilege and the means of atonement are extended and become more significant. They are accomplished in manners that go beyond scriptural requirements and are in opposition to rabbinic halakhah.[41] My suggestion is that this emphasis on defending the sacredness of the cult and on rituals of atonement is related to the sectarian worldview that the world is full of evilness and to the sectarian ethos of an extensive search for atonement. Thus, the halakhah of the *Temple Scroll* and MMT is not detached from the general worldview and the moral system found in the *Community Rule*, the *Hodayot* and the *Damascus Document*. The tendencies of the Qumranic cultic laws may be classified into four major categories (for the sake of brevity, only a few examples will be given in each category).[42]

1. *Strengthening Purity Boundaries*

This tendency presupposes that impurity lies everywhere and endangers the sanctity of the cult. For example, the bones and skin of unclean ("non-kosher") animals are defiling (*Temple Scroll* 51.1-4; MMT B 21–23), whereas the rabbis declared them as clean (m. Hul 9.1). MMT prohibits the entrance of Ammonite, Moavite, *mamzer*, and men who are sexually disabled into the Temple (B 39–49), while rabbinic halakha does not mention such taboos at all. The explicit motivation for this Qumranic rigorousness is the suspicion of desecration of the cult's sanctity by the force of impurity (*ibid.*, 48–49). MMT further prohibits the entrance of the blind and the deaf into the Temple since they cannot restrict themselves from defilement and uncleanness (B 49–54; for the blind see also *Temple Scroll* 45.12-14). This strictness in purity laws presupposes that the sacredness is in constant danger of pollution and hence it is necessary to restrict contacts between the holy and the suspected impurities.

2. *Elevating the Holiness of Sacred Food from the Realm of the Laity to the Realm of the Priesthood*

The rabbis insist that the animal tithe, the fruits of the fourth year, and the arm, cheek and stomach of the *shelamim* sacrifice should be eaten by the lay owners; the *Temple Scroll* and MMT maintain that the holy food should be given to the priests and eaten by them.[43] The purpose of restricting the consumption of sacred foods (originally belong to God Num. 18:9–14, 19) to the priests derives from the fact that they are more sacred than the lay Israelites. Limiting the use of these holy foods by the laity protects them from defilement and sacrilege by the common people. The *Temple Scroll* (35.10-15; 37.8-12) also orders separating between the sacrifices of the priests (and especially the *hattat* and *asham*, the sacrifices of atonement) and those of the laity. Clearly, the authors of the scroll view the priests as more sacred than the laity, and believe that sacredness requires separation. Again, the separation aims to reduce the threat of defilement and desecration.

3. *Spatial Boundaries of Holiness in the Temple Mount*

According to MMT "Jerusalem is the camp of holiness... For Jerusalem is capital of the camps of Israel" (B 59–61). This probably means that impurity should be restricted as much as possible within the city. Thus, MMT prohibits non-sacral slaughtering in Jerusalem as well as raising dogs in the city (since they might eat the remains of the sacrifices) (MMT B 17–20, 27–35; 58–59). Thus, the holiness of Jerusalem results in additional purity restrictions of separating the sacred from the non-sacred/ suspected as impure, in order to avoid defilement.

The main aim of the plan of the Temple courts in the *Temple Scroll*[44] is to separate between the priestly and lay realms, that is, to create a "graded holiness." For instance, the priestly cult and priestly meals of sacrifices and cereal-offerings should take place in the inner court. The priests must not eat them outside the inner court since their priestly share of the sacrifices and offerings must be spatially separated from those of the laity that are eaten in the middle court (*Temple Scroll* 37.4-12). Furthermore, the middle court was designated for eating sacrificial food by the lay males. Women, children and proselytes (until the fourth generation) were not allowed to enter it (39.4-9). Wearing priestly garments was forbidden in the middle court (40.1-4) since it was not as holy as the inner court. All these gradations of sacredness are aimed (among other things) to protect from sacrilege.

4. *Special Rituals of Atonement*

The *Temple Scroll* more than once orders that the he-goat (*s´eir*) that is sacrificed as sin-offerings (*hattat*) should precede the burnt-offering (*'olah*). This rule is mentioned in relation to first day of the first month (where its atoning function is stressed), the wood offering, and the Day of Atonement (where atonement is stressed following Leviticus 16). The rabbis agreed that the blood of the sin-offerings precedes the blood of the burnt-offering, "since it makes atonement" (*meratseh*). However, they also ruled that the limbs of the burnt-offering precede the sacrificial portions of the sin-offering because they are considered more sacred. Here the *Temple Scroll* expands the atoning function of the he-goat from the blood to the limbs, and also emphasized the idea of atonement.[45]

The Qumranic calendar was distinctive not only due to its reckoning of 364 days, but also because it consisted of special festivals or rituals. The first is the annual days of *milluim* (inauguration), in which the priests were sanctified (*Temple Scroll* 15.3–17.5). Quite similar to the original *milluim* in Exodus 29 and Leviticus 8–9, this was a long and complex ritual in which the priests were consecrated and reappointed, a rite of passage which transferred them from a profane state to sacred one.[46] Among other things, two bulls were sacrificed as *hattat*, one atoning for the priests, and the other ("the bull of the public") for the rest of the people of Israel. The conclusion of the passage indicates on the purpose of the ritual: "[the] priests, and they shall place cro[wns...]...and they shall rejoice because *atonement has been made for them...*" (17.2-3).

Two additional sacrificial rituals are the festivals of the first fruits of wine and oil, both were celebrated in order to attain atonement. The *Temple Scroll* mentions the root *kipper* in these rituals (21.8; 22.14-16). It seems that the purpose of these rituals is to redeem the sanctity of the new crop of grapes and olives (apparently the usual bringing of first fruits, *bikkurim*, to the Temple did not satisfy the authors). Their taboo of sanctity was thus released and eating them, as God's own crop, was not considered sinful anymore. Obviously, the rabbis did not find any need for such additional atoning rituals. Since atonement is aimed at eliminating pollution or guilt and constituting sanctity, it follows that in comparison to the Qumranic tendency, the rabbis were less interested in these ritualistic or cultic ideas.

Sectarian Worldview in the Laws of the Temple Scroll *and MMT*
Why did the *Temple Scroll* and MMT stress the need to protect the sacred from pollution and sacrilege and create additional rituals of atonement?[47] What negative force requires the protection of the sacred? Why should the means of atonement be extended? The halakhic evidence surveyed above may be parallel to the sectarian perception that the world is immersed in evil and that man's major aim should be overcoming this sinfulness and atoning for his sins. Both have similar cosmological and anthropological premises regarding evil/impurity, sin and atonement. Therefore, I suggest that the worldview behind the laws of the *Temple Scroll* and MMT is also sectarian. It presupposes tension between the sacrificial cult and "the world" and it seeks atonement more than any other Jewish cultic system.

In fact, it is possible to reach the same conclusion in a slightly different manner. In a previous study I have tried to explain why the *Temple Scroll* and MMT hold more rigorous views than the rabbis.[48] I concluded that the intensive pursuit of purity, sanctity and atonement in relation to the Temple cult derives from the idea that the sancta is extremely sensitive to the threat of pollution and desecration, and any violation of the cultic holiness bears guilt upon Israel and thus causes divine wrath and punishment. I have called this perception "dynamic holiness," meaning that holiness is very vulnerable. Any violation may transform it or cause its desecration, and the additional taboos and rituals were designated to preventing such a situation or restoring sanctity as a reaction to it. If one does not do his best to protect it, holiness (or the Divine Presence, namely, the earthly aspect of God's holiness) will vanish or at least be reduced, and human action will be divinely viewed as sinful and punishable.

In contrast, the rabbis view the sancta and holy food as not as sensitive to pollution and desecration as the Qumranic halakhah. The regarded holiness is not as vulnerable as in the *Temple Scroll* and MMT. I suggested that holy is only a status for the rabbis, not an entity. It is only an etiquette that God named for certain cultic objects or activities that relate to the worship of God. Holiness is thus static and may be approached more overtly by the non-priests, for example. Desecration is only an unwelcome change of this status and not a real cosmic or natural event. Its implications are limited to, at worst, impiety or non-disciplined behaviour. Thus, for the rabbis, holiness is static.

The main point which I would like to stress is that the theological, or rather, cosmological presuppositions that lie behind this perception which I termed "dynamic holiness" recall the general sectarian worldview as defined by Bryan Wilson and others: the world is a hostile environment where negative forces are dominant. Unless special efforts are made, the outcome will be sin, guilt and the departure of the heavenly presence and grace. Such a worldview was described by three anthropologists, Thompson, Ellis and Wildavsky, in their *Cultural Theory* as "Nature Ephemeral" which they associated with a sectarian social system. "Nature Ephemeral" views the world as terrifying or fragile and God as unforgiving. The smallest jolt may trigger a complete collapse. Therefore, it requires setting up effective sanctions to prevent such a collapse from happening and encourages managing institutions (or rituals) that would treat an ecosystem (or cultic system) with great care. This perception may be described as an Omega in which the ball must stay on top.[49]

In order to illustrate the basic worldview of the *Temple Scroll* and MMT it is possible to compare the laws of ritual impurity and sacrificial ritual with the moral code of the *Community Rule* and the *Damascus Document*. The different cultic boundaries parallel the social boundaries of separation from the wicked. Both create an enclave, a restricted social or religious realm. The atoning rituals parallel the penal code, the confessions and the other rituals, since they are all aimed at repairing sin and transgression. They elevate the enclave to a higher sphere of sacredness and closeness to God. Both are behavioural means to achieve a spiritual moment of salvation.

Of course, there are also many phenomenological differences between these moral and cultic systems. However, I think that the basic similarity between the two is hardly coincidental. It cannot be regarded simply as a consequential interpretation of the laws of Scripture. The circles that created the *Temple Scroll* and MMT already had in mind a worldview in which there is tension between the cult and the outer world and between God and man (or between nature and humanity). This worldview seems to be a result of some social or religious pressures that encouraged it.

Reflections on the Early Development of Sectarianism in Qumran: The Temple Scroll *and MMT as the Forerunners of the* Yahad *and the* Damascus Covenant

If this interpretation of the worldview of the *Temple Scroll* and MMT is accepted, one may go a bit further and try to reconstruct the social and chronological relationship between the moral and the cultic sectarian ideologies. Is it possible that the same circles are responsible for both of them? The general accordance between the two, and the plausibility that the members of the *yahad* and the *Damascus Covenant* not only read the *Temple Scroll* and MMT but also felt obliged to follow their laws, increases the possibility of a certain historical linkage between them.

I would suggest that the cultic laws incorporated in the *Temple Scroll* and MMT reflect an earlier phase, when the sectarian worldview was still limited to the cosmological realm. Later on, due to historical and social developments it was extended to the social realm and became more extreme. There are several reasons for reconstructing such a sequence: First, the *Community Rule* and the *Damascus Covenant* are more radical in their sectarian outlook; they bear wider behavioural consequences and the social construction for their groups is far more developed. Second, the cultic sectarian worldview still depends on the classification system of the priestly code (purity-impurity, sacred-profane, laity-priesthood, atonement-divine punishment) whereas, the moral one has no actual base in scripture and seems to be a complete innovation. Third, a stark dualistic worldview and a complex system of social boundaries and regulations do not emerge abruptly. They are built on against a certain background that presupposes that the world is evil and so on. Such a gradual development is present if one follows the suggestion that the sectarian cultic ideology preceded the moral one. Fourth, the *Book of Jubilees* shares some of the major ideological and halakhic views of the *Temple Scroll* – especially the emphasis of atonement.[50] Unlike the *Temple Scroll* and MMT, it is possible to date *Jubilees* according to external criteria, since the polemic against nudity and the negligence of circumcision echoes the reality in 175–164 BCE.[51] Since the laws of the *Temple Scroll* and MMT are more elaborate than those of *Jubilees*, and since their religious ideology is much more explicit and developed,[52] they should be dated later then *Jubilees*, but still within the same generation.

Therefore, it is possible to conclude that the cultic laws preceded the moral code of the *Community Rule* and the *Damascus Document* as pre-Qumranic, meaning that they preceded the social and theological constructions which we usually associate with the so-called "Qumran movement." Although it is impossible to point to clear-cut evidence, I think that the movement behind the sacrificial laws of the *Temple Scroll* (and, in a certain sense, already behind *Jubilees*) and later on also behind MMT, coped with the problem of evil in its general, "cosmological" sense, and found solutions in the halakhic realm. Certain unclear histori-cal occurrences led to the development of this heritage by a subsequent movement (descending groups) into a social system, later known as the *yahad* and the *Damascus Covenant*. All this may support prevailing schol-arly opinions that view the *Temple Scroll*, and to certain extent also MMT as being composed before the so-called "sectually explicit" documents such as the *Community Rule* and the *Damascus Document*.[53]

Conclusion

This article discussed the framework of sectarian ideology and ethos as defined by sociologists of religion and was confirmed by comparisons with other sects. This framework was used here as a classification tool in order to point to the central place of sectarian characteristics in the life of the members of the Qumran sect, as well as to show that two differ-ent realms in the scrolls – the moral, the cultic – are interrelated. They are all connected to the view that there is tension between God and the human world, between righteousness and evil, and the search for atone-ment through separation and rituals.

Historians tend to appreciate chronological sequence, and aim to point to the origins and consequences of phenomena. This creates a sense of order and control of the past. In order to satisfy this need, it is possible to suggest that the Qumranic sectarian worldview originated from the cultic realm of the *Temple Scroll* and MMT. Later on, it evolved and was strengthened in the realm of morality, which later resulted in the construction of social systems that directed and executed this worldview.

There are many questions regarding the essence and development of these phenomena that still require further study. I think that along with the textual study of the documents, we should also examine the different components of sectarian ideology and social practices in Qumran and compare them to other sects. This may enable us to understand not only which characteristics in the scroll are related to the phenomenon of sectarianism, but also to define which types of sectarianism are present in Qumran.[54]

Endnotes

1. E.g. B. Gartner, *The Temple and the Community in Qumran and the New Testament* (Cambridge: Cambridge University Press, 1965), 16-30, 44-46; G. Klinzing, *Die Umdeutung des Kultus in der Qumrangemeinde und im NT* (Göttingen: Vandenhoeck & Ruprecht, 1971); P. Garnet, *Salvation and Atonement in the Qumran Scrolls* (Tübingen; Mohr-Siebeck, 1977); H. Lichtenberger, *Studien zum Menchenbild in Texten der Qumrangemeinde* (Göttingen: Vandenhoeck & Ruprecht, 1980b), 93-98, 209-12; *idem*, "Atonement and Sacrifice in the Qumran Community," in W. S. Green (ed.), *Approaches to Ancient Judaism: Theory and Practice* (BJS, 9; Chico, CA: Scholars Press, 1980), II, 159-71.

2. I have purposely differentiated between the terms worldview, ideology and ethos. Anthropologists tend to view ethos as an (emotional) attitude towards the self or the world, whereas worldview is regarded as the more comprehensive perception of society and nature as a whole. Ideology is defined by sociologists in terms that recall a sectarian worldview: it is an ideal realization of cognitive and moral values which are fuller or purer than those existing in that contemporary society. It insists on the realization of the ideal, which is contained in the sacred, through "total transformation" of society. See C. Geertz, "Ethos, World View, and the Analysis of Sacred Symbols," in *The Interpretation of Cultures* (New York: Basic Books, 1973), 126-41; E. Shils, "Ideology: The Concept and Function of Ideology," in D. L. Sills (ed.), *International Encyclopedia of the Social Sciences* (London: Macmillan, 1968), VII, 66-75, esp. 67.

3. For such an effort see E. Regev, "Comparing Sectarian Practice and Organization: The Qumran Sect in Light of the Regulations of the Shakers, Hutterites, Mennonites and Amish," *Numen* 51 (2004): 146-81.

4. R. Stark and W. S. Bainbridge, *The Future of Religion: Secularization, Revival and Cult Formation* (Berkeley, CA; Los Angeles: University of California Press, 1985), esp. 23, 49-60. This concept was applied to Qumran by A. I. Baumgarten, "The Rule of the Martian as Applied to Qumran," *Israel Oriental Studies* 14 (1994): 179-200; *idem, The Flourishing of Jewish Sects in the Maccabean Era: An Interpretation* (JSJSup, 55; Leiden: E. J. Brill, 1997).

5. B. Wilson, "An Analysis of Sect Development," *American Sociological Review* 24 (1959): 3-15, esp. 4; *idem, Religion in Sociological Perspective* (Oxford and New York: Oxford University Press, 1982), 91-93.

6. B. Wilson, *Magic and the Millennium: A Sociological Study of Religious Movements of Protest among Tribal and Third-World Peoples* (London: Heinemann, 1973), esp. 18-30. Aiming to avoid the traditional Christian conception of a sect in discussing third-world religions, Wilson did not directly discuss the phenomenon of sectarianism. He noted that the responses do not necessarily represent organized movement or well-established sects, but rather activities, life-styles and ideologies (*ibid.*, 20). Nevertheless, his typology also applies to such sects.

7. Wilson, *Magic and the Millennium*, 12-19.

8. Wilson, *Magic and the Millennium*, 21. Note also that Yinger concluded that established sects develop because they emphasize the evil nature of society. See J. M. Yinger, *Religion, Society, and the Individual* (New York: Macmillan, 1957), 151-52.

9. P. Rideman, *Confession of Faith: An Account of our Religion, Doctrine and Faith, Given by Peter Rideman of the Brothers Whom Man Call Hutterians* (Rifton, NY: Plough Publishing House 1970 [1545]), 56, 57, 59-61, respectively. See also Jacob Hutter's letter to the ruler of Moravia: "...we have left the world and all its wrong and ungodly ways...leave behind all sin and evil," in *The Chronicle of Hutterian Brethren* (Rifton, NY: Plough Publishing House, 1987), I, 137. Evil, wickedness and sin repeat many times in another letter of Hutter (dated 1533) concerning internal debates (ibid., 110–26). Elsewhere in the Chronicle (ibid., 193-94) it is stated that the pope and the priests live sinful lives, are idolatrous and commit abominations.

10. P. Miller and T. H. Johnson (eds), *The Puritans: A Sourcebook of their Writings* (New York: Harper & Row, 1963), I, 202, 218-19, 272, 297, 291-314, 329-31, 336-40, 348-50. For Increase Mather, for example, "the nature of man is woefully corrupted and depraved" (*ibid.*, 348).

11. W. C. Braithwaite, *The Beginnings of Quakerism* (London: Macmillan, 1923), 55, 63-65, 120-21, 206, 466.

12. Quoted in R. Sandall, *The History of the Salvation Army* (London: Nelson, 1947), I, 237. Cf. R. Robertson, "The Salvation Army: The Persistence of Sectarianism," in B. Wilson (ed.), *Patterns of Sectarianism* (London: Hienemann, 1967), 49-105.

13. F. W. Evans, *Ann Lee (the Founder of the Shakers): A Biography with Memoirs of William Lee, James Whittaker, J. Hocknall, J. Meacham, and Lucy Wright; also a Compendium of the Origin, History, Principles, Rules, and Regulations, and Government and Doctrines of the United Society of Believers in Christ's Second Appearing* (London and Mount Lebanon, NY: J. Burns, 1858), 63-64, 77, 88-90. The early Shakers are depicted as "taking up of a full and final cross against all evil in their knowledge, they were thereby endowed with great power of God over sin." See F. W. Evans, *Testimonies of the Life, Character, Revelations and Doctrines of Mother Ann Lee and the Elders with Her, through who the Word of Eternal Life Was Opened in This Day, of Christ Second Appearing, Collected from Living Witnesses, in Union with the Church* (Albany: Weed and Parsons, 2nd edn, 1888), 3.

14. For the Damascus Covenant as a sect according to Wilson's categories of sectarianism, see J. W. Martens, "A Sectarian Analysis of the Damascus Document," in S. Fishbane and J. N. Lightstone (eds), *Essays in the Social Scientific Study of Judaism*

and Jewish Society (Montreal: University of Concordia, 1990), 27-46. For the Qumran sects as introversionist see Baumgarten, *Flourishing of Jewish Sects*, 13-15; P. F. Esler, "Introverted Sectarianism at Qumran and in the Johannine Community," in *idem*, *The First Christians in their Social World: Social Scientific Approaches to New Testament Interpretation* (London/New York: Routledge, 1994), 79-84. For messianism and eschatology in Qumran, which in my view should be labelled under the category or revolutionist sect, see J. J. Collins, *The Scepter and the Star: The Messiahs of the Dead Sea Scrolls and other Ancient Literature* (New York: Doubleday, 1995). For a more elaborate discussion see E. Regev, *Sectarianism in Qumran: A Cross-cultural Perspective* (Religion and Society Series; Berlin: Walter de Gruyter, 2007), ch. 1.

15. All this is related to the moral dualism of the Qumran sects, which was first developed in documents such as *Enoch*, *Jubilees*, etc. Cf. J. Frey, "Different Patterns of Dualistic Thought in the Qumran Library: Reflections on their Background and History," in M. Bernstein *et al.* (eds), *Legal Texts and Legal Issues: Proceedings of the Second Meeting of the International Organization for Qumran Studies, Cambridge, 1995* (STDJ, 23; Leiden: E. J. Brill, 1997), 275-335. However, here the tension is higher, and the accusations are much more specific. The following translation of citations from the scrolls is adopted from F. García Martínez and E. J. C. Tichelaar, *The Dead Sea Scrolls Study Edition* (2 vols.; Leiden: E. J. Brill; Grand Rapids and Cambridge; Eerdmans, 1997–98).

16. 1QH[a] 4[Sukenik17].18-20 following the restorations of J. Licht, *The Thanksgiving Scroll* (Jerusalem: Bialik Institute, 1957), 210. See also 1QH[a] 9[1].21-23; 12[4].34-35; 20[12].24-26.

17. 1QS 10.20; CD 2.5; 1QH[a] 10[Sukenik 2].9; 6[14].24. Cf. Isa. 59.20. See also M. Knibb, "Exile in the Damascus Document," *JSOT* 25 (1983): 99-117.

18. 1QH[a] 15[Sukenik 7].29-31; see also, *inter alia*, 1QH[a] 4[17].14-19; 14[6].5-6.

19. See E. Regev, "Abominated Temple and a Holy Community: The Formation of the Concepts of Purity and Impurity in Qumran," *DSD* 10.2 (2003): 267-78.

20. See L. H. Schiffman, *Sectarian Law in the Dead Sea Scrolls: Courts, Testimony and Penal Code* (BJS, 33; Chico, CA: Scholars Press, 1983); *idem*, *Law, Custom and Messianism in the Dead Sea Scrolls* (Jerusalem: Zalman Shazar, 1993), 136-267; C. Hempel, *The Laws of the Damascus Document: Sources, Tradition, and Redaction* (STDJ, 29; Leiden: E. J. Brill, 1998), 140-48.

21. 11QMelchizedek 2.7-9 (DJD 23, 225). The passage continues describing "the time for the Year of Grace of Melchizedek" "of [his] armi[es the nat[ions] of the holy ones of God, of the rule of judgment," "Melchizedek's revenge of God's judgment, [and on that day he will fr]e[e them from the hand of] Belial and from the hand of all the sp[irits of his lot]" (2.9-13). Note that in *1 Enoch* 10:20-22 the eschatological purification and purgation of the world is designated to take place by the angel Michael.

22. See a survey of dualistic documents in J. J. Collins, *Apocalypticism in the Dead Sea Scrolls* (London and New York: Routledge, 1997), 35–51.

23. The role of halakhic practices in achieving atonement will be discussed below. This is implicit in the *Community Rule*'s concept of following the revelations to the Sons of Zadok or any other members (1QS 5.2–9; 8.15–16), but is apparent in the laws of the *Damascus Document* from the Geniza and the Qumran caves.

24. 1QH[a] 5.20-22 [Sukenik 13.14-16]. This passage corresponds with the characterization of evil as physical incompleteness, imperfection, falling short, and surfeit of human desires, whose harmful effects are denounced by a system of moral rules and prohibitions. Cf. D. Parkin, "Introduction," in D. Parkin (ed.), *The Anthropology of Evil* (Oxford and New York: Basil Blackwell, 1985), 13. Although I am unable to find further explicit attestations to this idea, I think it is implicit in the evidence regarding confessions and self-guilt feelings discussed above.

25. For the general belief that God predestines people to be evil or righteous, see: 1QS 3.13–4.26; 1QH[a] 7[Sukenik 15].13-22; 5.7-16[Sukenik 13.1-10]. The flaws of all men and the election of the holy people are also discussed in 1QS 9.1-15, esp. 7-10; 11.7-9. In the *Damascus Document*, the theme of election is applied to the sect forefathers in CD 1.7; 2.11; 6.2-3.

26. 1QH[a] 5.22-23 [Sukenik 13.16-17].

27. 1QH[a] 11[3].19-25; 19[11].3-34. See H.-W. Kuhn, *Enderwartung und gegenwärtinges Heil* (Göttingen: Vandenhoeck & Ruprecht, 1966). This concept is attested to in the belief that God's spirit cleansed the member from his iniquities (1QS 3.6-12; 4QS[a] II; 4QS[c] III) and is ritualized in the liturgies of immersion (4Q284, 4Q414, and 4Q512). See J. M. Baumgarten, "The Purification Liturgies," in P. W. Flint and J. C. VanderKam (eds), *The Dead Sea Scrolls after Fifty Years* (Leiden: E. J. Brill, 1999), II, 200-12. For the moral purifications, see Regev, "Abominated Temple", 272-77.

28. See Frey, "Different Patterns," 290-94. For other attestations of this concept, see J. Licht, "Legs as Signs of Election," *Tarbiz* 35 (1965): 18-26 (Hebrew); F. Schmidt, "Astrologie juive ancienne – Essai d'interprétation de 4QCriptique (4Q186)," *RQ* 28 (1997): 97-113.

29. Although coping with the problem of evil and sin is common to all religions, the emphasis on atonement is not self-evident. Atonement is dominant in the priestly-code and the Pauline corpus, but is absent from Deuteronomy and is less significant in most prophetic literature, *1 Enoch*, the gospels and rabbinic literature in general.

30. Evans, *Ann Lee*, 116 (italics original). Ann believed that in the second appearing of Christ (which, according to the Shakers, already occurred with the leadership of Ann Lee), the confession of sins was again restored and established in perfect order.

31. Evans, *Ann Lee*, 122. See also Evans, *Testimonies of the Life*, 3-4.

32. T. E. Johnson, "Rule and Orders for the Church of Christ's Second Appearing," *The Shaker Quarterly* 11.4 (1971): 148. Compare the orders in CD 9.2-8 and 1QS 5.24–6.1, and especially the danger of the "bearing of sin" already introduced in Lev. 19:17. In contrast to the Qumranic regulation, in the Shakers' laws the reproached person was not allowed to discover the identity of the person who complained about his or her behaviour. See T. E. Johnson, "The 'Millennial Laws' of 1821," *The Shaker Quarterly* 7.2 (1967): 46-47.

33. Evans, *Testimonies of the Life*, 14.

34. H. Desroche, *The American Shakers: From Neo-Christianity to Presocialism* (trans. J. K. Savacool; Amherst: University of Massachusetts Press, 1971), 147.

35. J. Mckelvie Whitworth, *God's Blueprints: A Sociological Study of Three Utopian Sects* (London and Boston: Rouledge & Kegan Paul, 1975), 18.

36. "Ordung of a Christian Church" of Amish Church of Pike Country Ohio (1950), cited in A. Hostetler, *Amish Society* (Baltimore: The Johns Hopkins University Press, 1968), 61.

37. D. B. Kraybill, *The Riddle of Amish Culture* (Baltimore and London: The Johns Hopkins University Press, 1989), 111-14.

38. For the practice of shunning and its history, see Hostetler, *Amish Society*, 29-32, 62-65, 241-44, 306f. For Amish sanctions, confession to the church, excommunication (shunning) and expulsion, see *ibid.*, 14.

39. S. M. Nolt, *A History of the Amish* (Intercourse, PA: Good Books, 1992), 53.

40. Rideman, *Confession of Faith*, 174-75. Another ritual that is related to atonement is the admonition of one's sins, found in CD and among the Shakers, Amish and Hutterites. See Regev, "Comparing Sectarian Practice," 160-62. For the Hutterites, see *Chronicle of Hutterian Brethren*, 178.

41. For a more detailed presentation of the halakhic evidence and further bibliography, see E. Regev, "Different Halakhic Perceptions between the Qumran Sectarians and the Pharisees-Rabbis: Dynamic Holiness and Static Holiness," *Tarbiz* 72 (2003): 113-32 (Hebrew); *idem*, "Reconstructing Qumranic and Rabbinic Worldviews: Dynamic Holiness vs. Static Holiness," in S. Fraade, A. Shemesh and R. A. Clements (eds), *Rabbinical Perspectives: Rabbinic Literature and the Dead Sea Scrolls* (StDJ; Leiden: E. J. Brill, 2006), 87-112.

42. For the problem of desecration cf. P. P. Jenson, *Graded Holiness: A Key to the Priestly Conception of the World* (JSOTSup, 106; Sheffield: JSOT Press, 1992). For sacrifices and atonement, see: E. Leach, "Ritual," *International Encyclopedia of the Social Sciences* (New York: McMillan, 1968), XIII, 523; F. H. Gorman., *The Ideology of Ritual: Space, Time and Status in the Priestly Theology* (Sheffield: JSOT Press, 1990). See also Lev. 17:11; J. Milgrom, *Leviticus 17–22* (AB, 3A; New York: Doubleday, 2000), 440-41, 1474-78.

43. Animal tithe: MMT B 63–64; m. Zeb 5.8. Fruits of the fourth year: MMT B 62–63; *Temple Scroll* 60.3-4; 4Q266 2.2.6 in J. M. Baumgarten, *Qumran Cave 4, XIII, the Damascus Document (4Q266–273)* (DJD, 18; Oxford: Clarendon Press, 1966), 144-45; m. Ma´aser Sheni 5.1-5; Sifrei Numbers 6 (ed. Horovits 6); j. Peah. 7.6 (20b-20c). Arm, cheek and stomach of the *shelamim* sacrifice: *Temple Scroll* 20.14-16, 22.8-11 11QT[b] 8 I in E. Qimron, *The Temple Scroll: A Critical Edition with Extensive Reconstructions* (Beer-Sheva/Jerusalem: Ben Gurion University of Negev Press/Israel Exploration Society, 1996), 32; m. Hul 10.11; Sifrei Shoftim 165 (ed. Finkelstein, 214); Y. Yadin, *The Temple Scroll* (Jerusalem: Israel Exploration Society and the Shrine of the Book, 1977), I, 120-21.

44. See Yadin, *Temple Scroll*, I, 154-247; L. H. Schiffman, "Exclusion from the Sanctuary and the City of the Sanctuary in the Temple Scroll," *Hebrew Annual Review* 9 (1985): 301-20.

45. *Temple Scroll* 14.9-12; 23.10-13; 26.5–27.4; m. Zeb. 10.2; b. Zeb. 89b; See Yadin, *The Temple Scroll*, I, 116-17; II, 44 (Hebrew); Note that on the Day of Atonement, the *Temple Scroll* 26.7ff. reversed the sacrificial sequence of Lev. 16:21ff.: the offering of the he-goat to the Lord precedes the confession on the he-goat which is sent to the desert as well as the burnt offerings. In *Jubilees* 7:4 Noah offered the he-goat before the burnt-offerings in order to make atonement for himself and his sons. Yadin noted that this sequence was inspired by Lev. 8:14-18; 14:19; Ezek. 43:19-24. The rational of the *Temple Scroll* seems compatible with Marx's theory of the sin-offering as a *rite de passage* and Baumgarten's theory of its function as restoring the sanctity of the altar

which was diminished by sin (without rejecting Milgrom's theory of the sin offering as purgation of the latter from the defiling force of sin). See A. Marx, "Sacrifice pour les péchés ou rite de passage? Quelques réflexions sur la fonction du *hattat*," *RB* 96 (1989): 27-48; J. Milgrom, "The *HATTAT*: A Rite of Passage?" *RB* 98 (1991): 120-24; A. I. Baumgarten, "*Hattat* Sacrifice," *RB* 103 (1996): 337-42.

46. For the ritual in Exodus 29 and Leviticus 8–9, see Jenson, *Graded Holiness*, 65-55, 119-21; Gorman, *Ideology of Ritual*, 103-139. Gorman comments that this ritual may protect the holiness and constitute the Divine dwelling in the sanctuary (*ibid.*, 26, 39-60).

47. These two phenomena are attested to in different argumentation in these scrolls, explaining the need to follow these laws scrupulously. See, Regev, "Different Halakhic Perceptions," 124-25; *idem*, "Reconstructing Qumranic and Rabbinic Worldviews."

48. See the articles cited in n. 30 above.

49. M. Thompson, R. Ellis and A. Wildavsky, *Cultural Theory* (Boulder, CO; San Francisco; Oxford: Westview Press, 1990), esp. 25-29. They introduced a classification of the social construction of nature that is based on the cultural model of Mary Douglas' theory of grid-and-group. See M. Douglas, *Natural Symbols: Explorations in Cosmology* (London and New York: Routledge, 3rd edn, 1996).

50. For the halakhic affinities between *Jubilees* and the *Temple Scroll* (above all, the 364-day calendar!), see J. C. VanderKam, "The Temple Scroll and the Book of Jubilees," in G. J. Brooke (ed.), *Temple Scroll Studies* (JSPSup, 7; Sheffield: JSOT Press, 1989), 211-36. See also the law regarding the priority of sacrificing the he-goat in *Jub.* 7:4. For the idea of atonement in *Jubilees*, see: 1:23-24; 5:17-18; 6:1-4; 16:22; 23:26-31; 30:10; 33:13; 34:8; 41:23-24.

51. *Jub.* 3:31; 7:20; 15:26, 33-34. Cf. 1 Macc. 1:15, 48, 60-61; 2.46; *Ant.* 12.241; J. A. Goldstein, *I Maccabees* (AB; Garden City, NY: Doubleday, 1976), 200. For dating *Jubilees* between 163–152 BCE, see J. C. VanderKam, *Textual and Historical Studies in the Book of Jubilees* (HSM, 14; Missoula, MT: Scholars Press, 1977), 214-85. I would also add that the hostility towards gentiles and the condemnation of cooperation with them corresponds to the very same period. Later on, throughout the Hasmonean period, there was a consensus regarding the struggle with the local gentiles. See also Regev, *Sectarianism in Qumran*, ch. 6.

52. I am fully aware of the constraints of *Jubilees'* genre as a rewritten bible in presenting a detailed and coherent worldview. However, I think that the author's preference for this genre indicates that his cultic ideas were premature in comparison to the *Temple Scroll*.

53. I follow the terminology and main reasoning of C. Newsom, " 'Sectually Explicit' Literature from Qumran," in W. Propp, B. Halpern and D. N. Freedman (eds), *The Hebrew Bible and its Interpreters* (Winona Lake, IN: Eisenbrauns, 1990), 167-87. For dating 4QMMT to 158–152 BCE and the related debate, see Regev, "Abominated Temple," 252-56 and bibliography. For different views regarding the date of the *Temple Scroll*, see M. O. Wise, *A Critical Study of the Temple Scroll from Qumran Cave 11* (Chicago: The Oriental Institute of the University of Chicago, 1990).

54. For a broader discussion see Regev, *Sectarianism in Qumran*.

Bibliography

Brethren, Hutterian. *The Chronicle of Hutterian Brethren*. Vol. 1; Rifton, NY: Plough Publishing House, 1987.

Baumgarten, A. I. "The Rule of the Martian as Applied to Qumran." *Israel Oriental Studies* 14 (1994): 179-200.

—"*Hattat* Sacrifice." *RB* 103 (1996): 337-42.

—*The Flourishing of Jewish Sects in the Maccabean Era: An Interpretation*. JSJSup, 55; Leiden: E. J. Brill, 1997.

Baumgarten, J. M. *Qumran Cave 4, XIII, The Damascus Document (4Q266–273)*. DJD, 18; Oxford: Clarendon Press, 1966.

— "The Purification Liturgies." In P. W. Flint and J. C. VanderKam, eds, *The Dead Sea Scrolls after Fifty Years*: 200-212. Leiden: E. J. Brill, 1999.

Braithwaite W. C. *The Beginnings of Quakerism*. London: Macmillan, 1923.

Collins, J. J. *The Scepter and the Star: The Messiahs of the Dead Sea Scrolls and Other Ancient Literature*. New York: Doubleday, 1995.

—*Apocalypticism in the Dead Sea Scrolls*. London and New York: Routledge, 1997.

Desroche, H. *The American Shakers: From Neo-Christianity to Presocialism*. Trans. J. K. Savacool. Amherst: University of Massachusetts Press, 1971.

Douglas, M. *Natural Symbols: Explorations in Cosmology*. London and New York: Routledge, 3rd edn, 1996.

Esler, P. F. "Introverted Sectarianism at Qumran and in the Johannine Community." In P. F. Esler, *The First Christians in their Social World: Social Scientific Approaches to New Testament Interpretation*: 79–84. London/New York: Routledge, 1994.

Evans, F. W. *Ann Lee (the Founder of the Shakers): A Biography with Memoirs of William Lee, James Whittaker, J. Hocknall, J. Meacham, and Lucy Wright; also a Compendium of the Origin, History, Principles, Rules, and Regulations, and Government and Doctrines of the United Society of Believers in Christ's Second Appearing*. London and Mount Lebanon, NY: J. Burns, 1858.

—*Testimonies of the Life, Character, Revelations and Doctrines of Mother Ann Lee and the Elders with Her, through who the Word of Eternal Life Was Opened in This Day, of Christ Second Appearing, Collected from Living Witnesses, in Union with the Church*. Albany: Weed and Parsons, 2nd edn, 1888.

Frey J. "Different Patterns of Dualistic Thought in the Qumran Library: Reflections on their Background and History." In M. Bernstein *et al.*, eds, *Legal Texts and Legal Issues: Proceedings of the Second Meeting of the International Organization for Qumran Studies, Cambridge, 1995*: 275-335. STDJ, 23; Leiden: E. J. Brill, 1997.

García Martínez, F., and E. J. C. Tichelaar. *The Dead Sea Scrolls Study Edition*. 2 vols.; Leiden: E. J. Brill; Grand Rapids and Cambridge: Eerdmans, 1997–98.

Garnet, P. *Salvation and Atonement in the Qumran Scrolls*. Tübingen: Mohr-Siebeck, 1977.

Gartner, B. *The Temple and the Community in Qumran and the New Testament*. Cambridge: Cambridge University Press, 1965.

Geertz, C. "Ethos, World View, and the Analysis of Sacred Symbols." In C. Geeertz, *The Interpretation of Cultures*: 126-41. New York: Basic Books, 1973.

Goldstein, J. A., *I Maccabees* (AB; Garden City, NY: Doubleday, 1976)

Gorman, F. H. *The Ideology of Ritual: Space, Time and Status in the Priestly Theology*. Sheffield: JSOT Press, 1990.

Hempel, C. *The Laws of the Damascus Document: Sources, Tradition, and Redaction*. STDJ, 29; Leiden: E. J. Brill, 1998.

Hostetler, A. *Amish Society*. Baltimore: The Johns Hopkins University Press, 1968.

Jenson, P. P. *Graded Holiness: A Key to the Priestly Conception of the World*. JSOTSup, 106; Sheffield: JSOT Press, 1992.

Johnson, T. E. "The 'Millennial Laws' of 1821." *The Shaker Quarterly* 7.2 (1967): 46-47.

—"Rule and Orders for the Church of Christ's Second Appearing." *The Shaker Quarterly* 11.4 (1971): 148.

Klinzing, G. *Die Umdeutung des Kultus in der Qumrangemeinde und im NT*. Göttingen: Vandenhoeck & Ruprecht, 1971.

Knibb, M. "Exile in the Damascus Document." *JSOT* 25 (1983): 99-117.

Kraybill, D. B. *The Riddle of Amish Culture*. Baltimore and London: The Johns Hopkins University Press, 1989.

Kuhn H.-W. *Enderwartung und gegenwärtinges Heil*. Göttingen: Vandenhoeck & Ruprecht, 1966.

Leach, E. "Ritual." In Sills, 1968: XIII, 523.

Licht J. *The Thanksgiving Scroll*. Jerusalem: Bialik Institute, 1957.

—"Legs as Signs of Election." *Tarbiz* 35 (1965): 18-26 (Hebrew).

Lichtenberger, H. "Atonement and Sacrifice in the Qumran Community." In W. S. Green, ed., *Approaches to Ancient Judaism: Theory and Practice*: II, 159-71. BJS, 9; Chico, CA: Scholars Press, 1980a.

—*Studien zum Menschenbild in Texten der Qumrangemeinde*. Göttingen: Vandenhoeck & Ruprecht, 1980b.

Martens, J. W. "A Sectarian Analysis of the Damascus Document." In S. Fishbane and J. N. Lightstone, eds, *Essays in the Social Scientific Study of Judaism and Jewish Society*: 27-46. Montreal: University of Concordia, 1990.

Marx, A. "Sacrifice pour les péchés ou rite de passage? Quelques réflexions sur la fonction du *hattat*." *RB* 96 (1989): 27-48.

Mckelvie Whitworth, J. *God's Blueprints: A Sociological Study of Three Utopian Sects*. London and Boston: Rouledge & Kegan Paul, 1975.

Milgrom, J. "The *HATTAT*: A Rite of Passage?" *RB* 98 (1996): 120-24.

—*Leviticus 17–22*. AB, 3A; New York: Doubleday, 2000.

Miller, P. and T. H. Johnson, eds. *The Puritans: A Sourcebook of their Writings*. Vol. I; New York: Harper & Row, 1963.

Newsom, C. " 'Sectually Explicit' Literature from Qumran." In W. Propp, B. Halpern and D. N. Freedman, eds, *The Hebrew Bible and its Interpreters*: 167-87. Winona Lake, IN: Eisenbrauns, 1990.

Nolt, S. M. *A History of the Amish*. Intercourse, PA: Good Books, 1992.

Parkin, D. "Introduction." In D. Parkin, ed., *The Anthropology of Evil*: 13. Oxford and New York: Basil Blackwell, 1985.

Qimron, E. *The Temple Scroll: A Critical Edition with Extensive Reconstructions*. Beer-Sheva/ Jerusalem: Ben Gurion University of Negev Press/Israel Exploration Society, 1996.

Regev, E. "Abominated Temple and a Holy Community: The Formation of the Concepts of Purity and Impurity in Qumran." *DSD* 10 (2003): 267-78.

— "Comparing Sectarian Practice and Organization: The Qumran Sect in Light of the Regulations of the Shakers, Hutterites, Mennonites and Amish." *Numen* 51 (2004): 146-81.

— "Different Halakhic Perceptions between the Qumran Sectarians and the Pharisees-Rabbis: Dynamic Holiness and Static Holiness." *Tarbiz* 72 (2003): 113-32 (Hebrew).

—"Reconstructing Qumranic and Rabbinic Worldviews: Dynamic Holiness vs. Static Holiness." In S. Fraade, A. Shemesh and R. A. Clements, eds, *Rabbinical Perspectives: Rabbinic Literature and the Dead Sea Scrolls*: 87-112. STDJ; Leiden: E. J. Brill, 2006.

—*Sectarianism in Qumran: A Cross-cultural Perspective*. Religion and Society Series; Berlin: Walter de Gruyter, 2007.

Rideman, P. *Confession of Faith: An Account of our Religion, Doctrine and Faith, Given by Peter Rideman of the Brothers Whom Man Call Hutterian*. Rifton, NY: Plough Publishing House, 1970 [1545].

Robertson, R. "The Salvation Army: The Persistence of Sectarianism." In B. Wilson, ed., *Patterns of Sectarianism*: 49-105. London: Hienemann, 1967.

Sandall, R. *The History of the Salvation Army*. Vol. 1; London: Nelson, 1947.

Schiffman L. H. *Sectarian Law in the Dead Sea Scrolls: Courts, Testimony and Penal Code*. BJS, 33; Chico, CA: Scholars Press, 1983.

—*Law, Custom and Messianism in the Dead Sea Scrolls*. Jerusalem: Zalman Shazar, 1993.

— "Exclusion from the Sanctuary and the City of the Sanctuary in the Temple Scroll." *Hebrew Annual Review* 9 (1985): 301-20.

Schmidt, F. "Astrologie juive ancienne—Essai d'interprétation de 4QCriptique (4Q186)." *RQ* 28 (1997): 97-113.

Shils, E. "Ideology: The Concept and Function of Ideology." In Sills, 1968: VII, 66-75.

Sills, D. L. *International Encyclopedia of the Social Sciences* (London: Macmillan, 1968).

Stark R., and W. S. Bainbridge. *The Future of Religion: Secularization, Revival and Cult Formation*. Berkeley, CA; Los Angeles: University of California Press, 1985.

Thompson, M., R. Ellis and A. Wildavsky. *Cultural Theory*. Boulder, CO: Westview Press, 1990.

VanderKam, J. C. *Textual and Historical Studies in the Book of Jubilees*. HSM, 14; Missoula, MT: Scholars Press, 1977.

—"The Temple Scroll and the Book of Jubilees." In G. J. Brooke, ed., *Temple Scroll Studies*: 211-36. JSPSup, 7; Sheffield: JSOT Press, 1989.

Wilson, B. R. "An Analysis of Sect Development." *American Sociological Review* 24 (1959): 3-15.

—*Magic and the Millennium: A Sociological Study of Religious Movements of Protest among Tribal and Third-world Peoples*. London: Heinemann, 1973.

—*Religion in Sociological Perspective*. Oxford and New York: Oxford University Press, 1982.

Wise, M. O. *A Critical Study of the Temple Scroll from Qumran Cave 11*. Chicago: The Oriental Institute of the University of Chicago, 1990.

Yadin, Y. *The Temple Scroll*. Jerusalem: Israel Exploration Society and the Shrine of the Book, 1977.

Yinger, J. M. *Religion, Society, and the Individual*. New York: Macmillan, 1957.

GROUPS IN TENSION: SECTARIANISM IN THE
DAMASCUS DOCUMENT AND THE *COMMUNITY RULE*[1]

Cecilia Wassen and Jutta Jokiranta

It is commonplace for Qumran scholars to use the terms "sect" and "sectarian" in a general way in connection to the community, or voluntary association, that produced and preserved the Dead Sea Scrolls. Nevertheless, not all texts that are considered to be composed by the Qumran movement[2] are viewed as similar in their "sectarian" nature.[3] The *Damascus Document* (D) is commonly understood as a rule book (*serek*) that circulated among married members living in "camps" in towns or villages, while the *Community Rule* (S) is seen as the foundational rule in the *yahad*, which scholars associate with a group of celibate members living at Qumran.[4] Although several aspects of this model are problematic and the historical reality was likely much more complex than this,[5] we will assume for this study that the documents were composed within different Essene communities.[6] Scholars in general consider S to be the primary example of a document produced by a sect. The document reveals a group or groups that distanced themselves from the rest of the society. Commonly, the assumed celibacy and the desert location are seen as indicators of sectarian authorship, but strict qualifications for membership, stringent purity rules and rigid discipline are also clear and perhaps more undisputable markers. Although a few scholars describe the "Damascus community" as a sect,[7] most consider this community[8] only mildly – or not at all – sectarian. For example, Joseph Baumgarten and Daniel Schwartz, in the introduction to their translation of D, consider the document to be a product of the same general movement that produced S, but point out that "its laws take account of a sectarian framework which, in comparison to that of the *Rule of the Community*, was less completely separated from the outside world and its norms."[9] Similarly, Michael Knibb, in his entry "Community Organization" in the *Encyclopedia of the Dead Sea Scrolls*, makes the following conclusion about the laws in D:

> The Laws section provides legislation for a community of Jews who lived among other Jews and gentiles, were married and had children, had male and female slaves, practiced agriculture, engaged in trade, had private income from which they were expected to contribute the wages of at least two days per month to support members of the community who were in need. They adopted a positive attitude toward the Temple, in that they were concerned about maintaining its purity and participated in its cult. In short, the legislation was intended for a group of Jews who were not cut off from society, even though they formed a separate community.[10]

Few Qumran scholars have discussed the different environments behind D and S from a social-scientific perspective, using established sociological criteria and definitions of a sect. Nevertheless, there are some exceptions. The most frequently applied sociological framework in Qumran scholarship is that of Bryan Wilson whose classic typology identifies seven types of sects according to their specific "responses to the world."[11] These include the introversionist sect that withdraws from the world, the conversionist type whose members actively engage in proselytizing and the reformist sect, which tries to reform the world and save humankind. Anthony Saldarini, for example, defines all the branches of the Essenes as sects, but he distinguishes between the Qumran group and those who lived in towns. Concerning the Qumran group, he states, "...its response to society is marked by withdrawal and apocalyptic expectation of divine intervention and thus may be typed as an introversionist, revolutionary (to a limited extent) sect with an alienative, expressive response to society. The Essene groups that lived in towns may have been more reformist and instrumental in their orientation."[12] By definition, a reformist type of sect is more interactive with outsiders than an introversionist one, or to use the terminology of Albert Baumgarten, "...in terms of walls a group erects around itself, those of an introversionist sect are higher, wider, and less permeable, while those of a reformist group are the opposite."[13] Eyal Regev considers "Qumran sectarians" as introversionist but sees a difference between D and S: "In comparison to the *yahad* group, members of the Damascus Covenant maintained rather permeable boundaries between themselves and the outside world. They maintained private property, they married and raised children."[14] In response to these views that consider the "Damascus community" somehow less sectarian than the community behind S, this study evaluates the evidence of the two documents using a model by contemporary sociologists and offers a somewhat different understanding. We will particularly draw attention to features consistent with a sectarian setting in D that have previously gone largely unnoticed.

1. *Literary Development*

In analyzing the evidence in the texts, it is important to take into account the literary development of the documents, D in particular. For our discussion, Charlotte Hempel's literary critical study of the legal section of D offers a well-grounded basis.[15] Hempel divides the laws and regulations into two main sections, which she calls "Halakhah" and "Community Organization."[16] She proposes a different *Sitz im Leben* for the two main strata: the Halakhah, she speculates, originated within priestly circles since there is an interest in issues related to the priesthood; it is characterized by having a "national frame of reference" and is not directed towards a particular organized community.[17] This legal tradition developed prior to the development of an organized community.[18] The Community Organization layer, in contrast, presupposes a certain organized community, which we will call the "Damascus community." This distinction is important to keep in mind when we evaluate the evidence in comparison to S. The earliest layer reflects a time prior to the life of the "Damascus community," and though important for our investigation because it contains laws that probably were observed within the community, it does not tell us directly about the legal inventions of the "Damascus community."[19]

The *Community Rule* too has gone through substantial literary development. The manuscript evidence and the material reconstruction made by Sarianna Metso testify to at least four stages of literary growth.[20] For our discussion, it is relevant that some copies of S contained a shorter form of only Columns 5–9 of 1QS, addressed to the *maskil* (without a parallel to 1QS 8.15b–9.11). Scriptural proof-texts and other additions were presumably included in 5–9 later, as well as the final hymn (1QS 10–11)[21] and Columns 1–4. Columns 1–4 preserve one of the introductory sections of the document, including the liturgy for the annual Renewal of the Covenant ceremony, and the discourse on the two spirits (3.13–4.26). It is noteworthy that the dualism reflected in the discourse has a non-Qumranic pre-history of its own;[22] thus it cannot be taken to represent the core ideology of S.[23]

Furthermore, S and D closely resemble each other in various sections, implying either parallel redactional activity or common sources.[24] However, the purpose of this analysis is not to reconstruct the literary or organizational development but to evaluate the nature of the rules within the wider context of society.[25]

2. *Definition of Sect*

The sociology of sectarianism is a wide research field of its own. One has to choose a model that can be articulated to address the specific questions one is posing. Since we are interested in measuring the *degree* of sectarianism we require a model that allows us to do that. Rodney Stark and William Bainbridge have criticized common typological models that compare and contrast a sect versus a church for not being able to distinguish between the *defining criteria*, those features that are present in *every* case, and *correlates*, those features that may or may not be present.[26] On the other hand, Bryan Wilson has continued to list typically sectarian characteristics,[27] but has emphasized that this ideal type applies only in Western Christian context and that a single sect may not include all the characteristics of the ideal type. It is the divergences from the ideal type that are especially interesting for a sociologist.[28] Wilson has, however, wished to move away from the sect-church model and sought to explain different kinds of sects.[29] The seven types are briefly described according to their solution to the evil in the world: "introversionists" seek a purified community; "conversionists" seek a transformed self; "manipulationists" seek a transformed perception of evil; "thaumaturgists" seek specific dispensations and miracles; "reformists" seek to reform or change the world; "revolutionists" seek a world transformed (by God); and "utopists" seek a reconstruction of the world (by men).[30] Yet, these types do not exist in pure forms, as Wilson admits, and sects change in terms of their response to the world.[31] In the case of S, we may recognize several types of responses in it. A "conversionist" ideal is present in that the individual has to "convert" (turn away from the world) voluntarily and prove to be "converted" by his or her righteous deeds (1QS 5.1, 4b-5). A "revolutionist" view is reflected in the limitation of deceit: in the future, God will remove all evil (1QS 5.10-13a). A "manipulationist" aspect is seen in the discourse of the two spirits, which powerfully transforms the members' perception of the world; evil is ultimately outside.[32] Thus, S offers at least a potential for many kinds of responses to the evil: to abandon the world (introversionist) but also to "convert" individuals, to view one's life in a new positive light, to overturn the world, and even to reform and reconstruct it (1QS 8.5-10). As the types are not pure and not on a continuum either, it makes any comparison difficult.[33] For the purpose of this paper, one cannot make use of typologies since what is at stake in those typologies is not degree of sectarianism but rather types of sectarianism. This does not mean that typological approaches should be abandoned entirely.

The "responses to the world" may serve as heuristic tools in becoming aware of the sectarian features and in accounting for the primacy of one type over another; however, in our opinion, mixed types are probable in the case of the rule documents. In this study, we also refer to Wilson's general analysis of sects where this is relevant.

Sociologists' attempts to find a definition that is applicable cross-culturally resulted in a dramatic reduction in the set of variables in the past century.[34] Stark and Bainbridge, among many others,[35] adopted the variable of *tension* as a central feature of their definition: "a *sect movement* is a deviant religious organization with traditional beliefs and practices." "Deviance" is explained as tension with the socio-cultural environment.[36] By their definition, they see a "continuum running from high to low tension," whereby a sect is found at one pole where the tension is high, and a church – or in a non-Christian context any other established religious institution – at the opposite pole where there is no tension.[37]

Stark and Bainbridge are two of the few scholars who argue that the tension can be clearly measured.[38] They further define tension as *subcultural deviance* and argue that it can be measured by three elements: *difference, antagonism, and separation.*[39] In the examples of measurements they give, difference means especially *deviant norms*, antagonism means *particularistic beliefs and attitudes* (belief that only one's own religion is legitimate), and separation is manifested in favouring *social relations* amongst insiders as well as restricting social interaction with outsiders.[40] Stark and Bainbridge stress that these are not three different variables but three elements that function within tension, "each is directly implied by the other two."[41] This specification of tension is indeed useful: the variable is clear and allows for variety in degree, not type.[42] Therefore, tension is about deviant behaviour, not just deviant opinions.[43] Other models have been successfully used to describe large-scale *changes* in one religious movement on *two* dimensions, "tension" and "claim for monopoly."[44] Since our focus is quite limited, we believe that here the tension continuum suffices. Nevertheless, the "claim for monopoly" is included within "tension."[45]

Stark and Bainbridge also raise an important point concerning deviance: the standard of "normal" is often set by the powerful elite, not by the *average* of population as a whole.[46] This leads to an important specification: the context in which we view tension has to be defined. The degree of "sectarianism" in D and S might look very different depending on whether we focus on Graeco-Roman culture in general, or a narrower context. Meredith McGuire argues that the model of religious collectivities requires specification of (1) societal context, (2) level of analysis (national, regional, local), and (3) time period.[47] Our focus may thus be defined as: (1) Hasmonean society, (2) Palestinian rather than the entire diaspora Judaism, (3) some time during the late second and first century BCE.[48] Despite the pluralism that characterized Jewish beliefs and practices of this time, we believe that deviance from some "common" norms can be detected.[49] Stark and Bainbridge also note the significance of societal change. According to their theory, some religious groups adapt to change while others seek to cause or prevent social change.[50] Consequently, tension should not be seen as a static concept but a dynamic one: deviance is something that "swims upstream" in societal change, or something that moves at different "speeds," either slower or faster.[51] Low-tension groups would be close to the no-tension end (represented by the elite/the average of the population), and would adapt to societal change.

We acknowledge that Stark and Bainbridge's definition of sect movements belongs to their larger theory of religion, which we will use selectively.[52] Statistical measuring of tension in the way outlined above would, of course, demand information that we do not have. We hope to show that, in spite of the limited amount of information, the documents contain enough evidence that we can speak of "measuring" tension in an indirect way. Of course, measuring of tension is only one aspect of sectarian analysis. It is important to note that our interest is not whether a group can be designated a sect or not; the question is how the features in the documents (S and D) can be properly described and interpreted in their wider settings. In the following, we shall focus on the *common* sectarianism in S and D, analyzing the degree of tension as it appears in three elements, antagonism, difference and separation. Since there is broad consensus among scholars of the sectarian nature of S, we will focus more on D in order to highlight the level of tension implied within it.[53] Subsequently, we will focus on the *differences* between the documents, as these relate to sectarian traits.

3. *Common Sectarianism in S and D*

3.1. *Antagonism: Particularistic Claims*[54]
The degree to which the group expresses and holds particularistic claims influences its degree of tension. By claiming to possess the truth, a sect professes to provide an exclusive way to salvation. The assertion of possessing an exclusive truth permeates S. Members know the truth because God has revealed his statutes to them (1QS 1.8-13). They can live perfectly, according to his will, loving what God loves and hating what God

hates (1.3ff.).[55] In the discourse on the two spirits (3.13–4.26), the insiders represent the only light in an otherwise dark and deceitful world.[56] This portion of S exclaims that true knowledge is only possible amongst the Sons of Light who are guided by the Prince of Lights – or, as he is also called, the Angel of His Truth – as opposed to the rest of humanity who are guided by the Angel of Darkness.[57] In the other, and probably more original sections of S, particularistic beliefs are also evident: there is no redemption outside the community (e.g. 1QS 5.7-13).

The theology of D is outlined primarily in the Admonition, the first third of D which is sermon-like in character. It seems reasonable to assume that the bulk of the Admonition, although stratified in itself,[58] is approximately contemporary with the Community Organization layer.[59] The Admonition shares a strict, dualistic outlook on the world with S as well as the exclusive claim of possessing the truth (CD 2.14-17; 3.12-17; 6.2-5). The author(s) of the Admonition underscore the supreme status of the audience(s) by identifying it (them) as a "remnant" (CD 2.11), those who enter the covenant, and "those who walk in [ordinances] in perfect holiness" (7.4-5). Furthermore, the audience is told it possesses true knowledge, so that – parallel to S – it can *choose* what God wants and despise what he hates (CD 1.1; 2.14-15). God has revealed hidden things about his laws to the elect (CD 3.13-14). There are thus two distinct ways of life (ethical dualism): to follow God's will or to stray from it.

That the dualistic outlook in D is not only a rhetorical device to exhort *anybody* to act in the right way in his/her life is evident from the demand to "enter" the covenant and from the explicit regulations for admission in the law section. A new community (a new covenant! ברית חדשה) is needed in order to escape the coming judgment (CD 7.9; 8.1-2).[60] Those who observe God's law are a minority; that is, the insiders; the rest of Israel is evil and ruled by Belial (CD 4.12–5.15; 7.4 ff.). The outsiders, their fellow Jews, have unwittingly been caught in the nets of Belial (CD 4.12–5.15). As in S, redemption is possible only within the group.[61] Although the Admonition lacks a theological treatise similar to that on the two spirits in S (1QS 3.17–4.1), there is a reference to [ב]ני אור "[so]ns of light" in the first line of the document, preserved in 4QDᵃ (1 a–b 1), which suggests a similar dichotomy in D between light and darkness (cosmic dualism).[62] There is no indication in the Admonition that the community is interested in reforming outsiders; instead, the document is aimed at reinforcing the commitment and loyalty of the insiders to the Covenantal Community.

In sum, both documents express the strong belief that the insiders possess exclusive knowledge, available only to those within the group.

The firm dualistic outlook in both S and D that divides the world into "us-versus-them" reflects tension between the insiders and the outsiders. The boundary between the two is absolute in that the documents describe the outside world in terms of belonging to the devil, or "the Prince of Darkness." This dualistic perspective is coupled with a fervent apocalyptic worldview, according to which the members live at the end of times, "the period of wickedness" (CD 6.10, 14), awaiting the eschaton when God will visit the world to destroy the wicked and reward the faithful.

3.2. *Difference: Deviant Norms*[63]

Differences between the norms of D and S communities to that of the society at large range from minor issues that would create minor tension, to norms that would create high tension, or "deviance," with the outside world. Deviance in areas that the society values, or has an opinion about, is what matters most.

As we know both from D and S, the demands placed on members were high. The *Damascus Document* provides stringent interpretations of biblical laws, indicating that the members were to strive for religious perfection.[64] For example, the Sabbath laws (CD 10.14–11.18) from the Halakhah layer of D forbid aiding an animal to deliver its young, helping an animal up from a pit on the Sabbath (CD 11.13-14),[65] or helping a human who has fallen into water by using an object (CD 11.16-17).[66] Other examples include the requirement that fish be ritually slaughtered (CD 12.13-14) and the prohibition against sexual intercourse in the city of Jerusalem, "the city of the sanctuary" (CD 11.1-2)[67] – although these halakhot come from the earlier layers of D, their adherents would be in a deviant position. Whereas S does not provide the halakhah for the community, community regulations are notable for high demands on the members: the "*rabbim*" had to commit substantial time to studying texts and praying (1QS 6.7); a lower ranking member was obliged to obey a higher ranking one (5.23). The 364-day calendar that is reflected in 4QOtot of 4QS[e] – which differed from the calendar observed in the temple – would place the members at odds with the wider society.

The importance of purity rules in creating differences between groups in ancient Judaism in general, and forming unity within groups, cannot be overstated.[68] In his sociological study on Jewish sects, Albert Baumgarten explains that the Essenes applied mechanisms of separation that other Jews normally applied to non-Jews "as a way of protesting against those Jews, and/or against Jewish society at large."[69] The Essenes thereby set up elaborate and efficient boundaries against fellow Jews, in order to protect themselves from the outsiders' "defiling" presence, as well as to express their disapproval of the outsiders' way of life. To consider fellow Jews, who on average observed general purity rules,[70] as impure, would be offensive and create tension with outsiders. Whereas the Pharisees, for example, observed stringent purity laws, their level of tension remained lower due to their less demanding, or less "deviant," rules in combination with more open social relation patterns as well as their ability to gain power occasionally.

A heightened concern about purity is evident throughout the whole legal section of D in both the main strata, as well as in the Admonition. The ability to properly differentiate between what is pure and impure is one of the key qualities that distinguishes the "Damascus community" from the greater society (CD 6.17).[71] Both S and D reflect stringent views on purity and describe outsiders as impure; not only are those persons impure, but so is their property (CD 6.15; 1QS 5.16-20).[72] We can assume that the communities behind these documents were prohibited from extensive social interaction with outsiders because of their purity laws.

One issue deserves special attention. Purity laws concerning food created a particular difference to outsiders. Both documents refer to the common food of the community as "the purity," טהרה and a common punishment in both communities was exclusion from "the purity" of the community.[74] The initiation process in S centres on gradual access to pure food and drink. This suggests that only within the community was food considered pure. Consequently, neither of these communities accepted table fellowship with outsiders.[75] If one could not eat with an outsider, one could not interact with anyone on a deeper level outside of the in-group. Purity laws concerning food that we find in both documents thereby marked a distinction between insiders and outsiders and affected the degree of tension.

3.3. *Separation: Restriction of Social Relations*[76]
By creating strict boundaries between members and non-members, a sect encapsulates itself and expresses tension with the outside world. This encapsulation – restriction of social relations to inside members – is also related to deviant norms, which were the focus of the previous section. The point regarding a sect's distancing itself from others is where Qumran scholars often are mistaken. They see the physical isolation that is reflected in S as clear evidence of a sectarian stance while failing to detect other strategies sects can develop in order to create firm boundaries and distinguish themselves from outsiders. In a general way, the Admonition states unequivocally that the members should distance themselves from the outsiders. CD 8.8 lists as a sin that each one "did

not separate (נזרו) himself from the people" (cf. 19.20b-21a), and CD 6.14-15 warns the readers or listeners "to separate (להבדל) (themselves) from the sons of the pit," that is, the outsiders. Similarly, S emphasizes the "us-versus-them" mentality by having the new members promise to separate themselves from outsiders as 5.10-11 reads: "He shall take upon his soul by covenant to separate from all the men of deceit who walk in the way of wickedness" (cf. 5.14-15). This separation may, in the first place, be separation in terms of *norms*, that is, keeping the laws which the outsiders did not keep (thus reflecting difference). But it also clearly penetrates into patterns of social relations, as is seen in the idealistic exhortation to withdraw to the desert (1QS 8.13), and will be also seen with respect to D.

The most explicit way the groups behind the documents distinguished between insiders and outsiders was through formal initiations rituals; only through this process could outsiders become insiders. According to S, new members who joined the sect had to prove themselves worthy through a two-year probation during which time they were gradually allowed access to pure food, drink and property (1QS 6.13-23). The entrance ritual in D, which Hempel places in the Community Organization layer, describes how the children of members also marked their formal initiation by this ritual when they reached an age of maturity (CD 15.5-15).[77] In both groups, new members were formally initiated by taking a binding oath, promising to live by the laws of the covenant (CD 15.8-10; 1QS 5.8). The initiation ritual was designed to affirm the self-identity of the sect, by accepting new members as "part of us."[78]

Both groups, in typical sectarian fashion, had mechanisms for expelling members, again, clearly controlling the social place of the members (4QDᵃ 11.5-16; 1QS 7.17, 22-25).[79] It is revealing that both documents consider among the most serious offences that of disputing persons in authority which results in expulsion.[80] In other words, any evidence that the allegiance of a member of the group was weak was unacceptable. The expulsion ceremony for rebellious members in D follows immediately after the penal code and is preserved in 4QDᵃ. Importantly, according to the text, not only were members expelled, but any contact with them afterwards was strictly forbidden, as the text reads, "anyone who eats from that which belongs to him [the expelled], or who inquires about his welfare, or derives benefit from him, shall have his action inscribed by the Examiner (*mebaqqer*) permanently, and his judgment will be complete" (4QDᵃ 11.14-16). This stance is paralleled in 1QS 7.24-25, which prescribes expulsion for anyone who is aiding an expelled member.[81] Thus both communities demanded total allegiance from their members, controlling social interactions with outsiders. Obviously, expelled members posed a special kind of threat to faithful members, and therefore the groups could not tolerate any further contact with them.[82]

As an important part of a sect's tendency to advance its separation from the society at large, a sect needs to develop firm control over its members, a phenomenon that is apparent in both S and D. The total grip a sect has over its members is especially apparent in the way violation of norms is addressed. Penal Codes are found in both texts (in the Community Organization in the *Damascus Document*). The documents include several parallel offences, such as insulting another, interrupting another member, sleeping during the assembly, and laughing foolishly.[83] Both Penal Codes impose punishments ranging from exclusion from "the purity" and food reduction, to expulsion.[84]

In his sociological study on the Essenes, A. Baumgarten has uncovered an informant system amongst the Essenes.[85] He bases his conclusion on Josephus's claim that at "initiation" the Essene swore to expose liars and to conceal nothing from the members of the sect (*War* 2.141). In addition, information about members' shortcomings was recorded, as evidenced by 4Q477. In our opinion, the Penal Codes in D and S, which mandate punishments for transgressions such as insulting someone, showing oneself naked, and the serious offence of dissent, are likely to rely on an informant system as well, whereby members reported each other's wrongdoings to the communal authority. Furthermore, D explicitly states that the offences were reported to the Examiner who subsequently recorded them (4QD[a] 11.16; CD 9.16-22). Such an informant system manifests members' firm loyalty to the sect rather than to individual members.

In summary, both texts reflect groups in which social relations were highly restricted. Crossing the membership boundary in either direction – to enter or to be expelled – was marked by a ritual to explicitly confirm the change in status. Purity rules affected many areas of social interaction with others. By having initiation rites, strict criteria for membership, ongoing monitoring of members' commitment to sectarian rules and loyalty to the sect, as well as rules for expulsion, both S and the later literary layer in D clearly reflect communities that fit the definition of high tension sects.

4. *Differences between D and S*

Finally, we will consider those features of D that are not found in S. These suggest to some scholars that the "Damascus community" was less isolated from mainstream society than the "S community." Knibb (see above) presents precisely those features that are often understood to suggest much interaction and a less controlled relationship between the "Damascus community" and others, namely, that they married and had children, they had interactions with gentiles, they owned slaves, they engaged in trade and had private incomes and, finally, that they had a positive attitude toward the Temple, participating in its cult.[86] In short, his description suggests that the group was highly integrated within the society and in low tension with it. We will analyze these traits one by one and discuss whether or not they reflect a sectarian tension: whether they reflect separation, antagonism and difference.[87]

The first issues are marriage and having children. Celibacy, which distinguished some Essene groups from the general society, constitutes a deviant norm on one level: celibacy rejects the common societal pattern of marriage and discards the most basic expectations of sons (and daughters), namely to reproduce and continue the family line. Nevertheless, we have evidence of respect for those who choose such a lifestyle.[88] Therefore, celibacy alone would perhaps not create too much tension, if it were the only deviant norm. Furthermore, several of the laws concerning marriage and purity rules within marriage in D are examples of "deviant" norms that differ from those of the surrounding society. The discourse on the *Nets of Belial* (CD 4.12–5.15) deals with transgressions committed by Israel, that is, the general Jewish population, two of which concern marital unions. The narrative presents polygamy (CD 4.20-21)[89] and marriage between an uncle and his niece (CD 5.7-11) as primary examples of "fornication" (זנות, CD 4.17), one of Belial's Nets with which he ensnares the people. According to the text, Belial is successful because he makes the sins appear as "righteousness" (4.16-17), which indicates that the rest of the people disagreed with the "Damascus community" concerning these laws. It is revealing that both polygamy, especially in the form of bigamy, and the uncle-niece marriage were common marital configurations throughout the Second Temple period.[90] Since the marital laws of D represent the minority position, they are presented with exegetical evidence: the ban on polygamy uses three biblical proof-texts that limit the number of partners within intimate unions among humans (as well as animals); the prohibition against an uncle-niece marriage is based on a gender-inclusive reading of Leviticus 18:13 that clarifies a law that could be seen as uncertain.[91] Halakhic differences between the community and the surrounding society are presented in D as evidence of an existing, fundamental divide between good and evil and as proof that the majority of the population was under Belial's regime. Such a polarized view expresses sharp antagonism toward the surrounding socio-cultural environment.

Within the Halakhah stratum of D, there are additional laws regulating marital unions; one passage prohibits marriage to a woman who has had sexual intercourse before marriage and to a widow who has had sex after widowhood; the same section prohibits marriage to a woman who is suspected of not being a virgin (4QD^f 3.10-15). In this case, female experts, who are called "trustworthy" and "knowledgeable" and presumably were mid-wives, would examine a woman to determine her virginal status. The laws are similar to those concerning priests in Leviticus 21 who are prohibited from marrying "defiled" women or divorcees. On the one hand, these laws in D concurred with general societal attitudes that valued female virginity and sexual modesty, but on the other, the laws in D represent a perspective that differed from the general society in that these norms were made into laws and applied not only to priests, but to all men.

Moreover, there are several regulations in D concerning family that give strong evidence of the tension of the group. The "Damascus community" developed strategies to control and exert authority over families to ensure commitment of the family members to the sect, as well as to restrict the social relations between members and outsiders. Children within sects are usually socialized to remain within the sects, but they have to show their allegiance explicitly when they are old enough to make a choice. They also have to prove that they are worthy of belonging to the sect.[92] As mentioned above, children of members of the Damascus community, probably both young men and women, entered on the same terms as outsiders and had to demonstrate their commitment and prove their eligibility. Such an entrance ritual for children that we find in the Community organization layer of D is thus consistent with a sectarian ethos.

Furthermore, passages from the Community organization layer indicate that the group had extensive control of the family through its leader, the Examiner. The extent of his power over individual members has largely gone unnoticed in the debate about the sectarian nature of the "Damascus community." The Examiner provided theological instruction and examined prospective members (CD 15.7-15; 13.11). His leadership of the group is described as that of a father who looks after his children and as a shepherd looking after his flock (13.9). The lower part of Column 13 is damaged, but fortunately the text can be restored based on 4QD^a 9.3:

> Let no man do anything involving buying or selling unless he informs the Examiner who is in the camp and acts [with counsel] so that they do not err. Likewise for anyone who tak[es a wife] let it be with counsel, and likewise let him (the Examiner) guide a man who divorces (CD 13.15-17/4QDᵃ 9.3.1-5).

The passage indicates that the Examiner exerted power over matters of marital unions, as well as divorce. Although the text does not explicitly explain what kind of influence the Examiner had, it is clear that neither marital unions nor divorces could take place without his supervision. Based on how the term עצה "counsel" is used elsewhere in D (4QDʰ 6 "counsel of the Torah"; CD 12.7-8), the term is likely to carry the meaning of "permission." Thus, the group – through the Examiner – exerted power over some of the most important decisions by members, namely, whom to marry and if to divorce. The Examiner, thereby, took over the role that traditionally belonged to parents.[93] Marriage in that period involved not only joining two persons, but, more importantly, two families.[94] The fact that the Examiner had considerable influence over such important decisions illustrates the extent to which sectarian members allowed their personal lives to be governed by the sect.

Additional evidence of the sect's power over families is apparent in the mechanism for expelling members. Expulsion of straying members sometimes breaks up families.[95] Any social contact with that person is cut off, including that between the expelled member and his or her family. There is good reason to believe that expulsion in the "Damascus community" would in fact separate family members. One offence that led to expulsion was for-nication with a wife: "Anyone who comes near to fornicate with his wife contrary to the law shall depart and return no more" (4QDᵉ 7.1.12-13). There has been considerable debate about the exact nature of this transgression. We side with those scholars who argue that it concerns sexual intercourse in a way or at a time which made conception impossible, for example during pregnancy, which is explicitly prohibited elsewhere in the document (4QDᵉ 2.2.15b-16).[96] It is interesting to note that only the husband appears to be expelled for this transgression, not the wife. He is seen as responsible and thus he alone is punished. This is an obvious case where the family is split up as the result of what was considered unlawful behaviour according to sectarian rules. Furthermore, by going beyond common sexual laws that put restrictions on sexual intercourse in relation to purity, this regulation reflects the sect's power over the family that extends into the intimate relationship between husband and wife. The regulation concerning fornication with a wife also exemplifies the sect's stringent discipline.

This kind of legislation begs the question: how could such a rule be enforced? How would the sect know whether a couple had intercourse during a time when it was forbidden? Perhaps it is most reasonable to assume that anyone – particularly family members who would sleep close by – who knew about a couple's improper sexual conduct, or suspected something to that effect, was encouraged to come forward.[97] Evidently, such a rule would encourage members to report each others' transgressions and would foster a general climate of suspicion, in accordance with the general informant system of the sect (see above).

A second difference between D and S that Knibb notes is the issue of slavery. D is unique among the Qumran documents in that it includes laws about the treatment and sale of slaves. However, none of the references to slaves belong to the Community Organization layer, but to the earlier layer, Halakhah.[98] When we recall that both Philo and Josephus agree that the Essenes did not own slaves, it becomes possible to think that the Essene movement as a whole moved from accepting slavery to rejecting it. What, then, is the stance of the "Damascus community" on this issue? Even though it preserved the earlier references to slaves, its attitude towards slaves seems to be somewhat deviant in its environment. Biblical laws in general testify to a particular concern about subjecting a fellow Israelite to slavery: the length of time for keeping slaves was restricted (Exod. 21:2-6; Deut. 15:12-18) and the use of forced labour or gentiles slaves was preferable (Lev. 25:39-46).[99] The obligation to redeem a fellow Israelite from foreigners implies that selling another Israelite to foreigners was regarded as forbidden (Lev. 25:47-55).[100] Several passages suggest, however, that these laws were not followed (e.g. Amos 2:6; Jer. 34:8-22; Neh. 5:3-5).[101] According to biblical legislation, foreign slaves could be held for their lifetimes, but they had to be circumcised (Gen. 17:12-13; Exod. 12:44). This is what D also implies in the prohibition of selling a servant or a maidservant to gentiles by stating that "they have entered the covenant of Abraham" (CD 12.10-11), that is, they were converted and males were circumcised. For our discussion, it is significant that this prohibition wishes to prevent selling *gentile* slaves (though converted to Judaism) to gentiles, thus expanding or clarifying scriptural legislation.[102]

During the Second Temple period, the Graeco-Roman slave system, which was a significant part of the economy, also became common in Palestine. The slavery was a common practice and Judeans were also exported as slaves.[103] Reports by Josephus indicate that the Hasmoneans enslaved people from the areas they conquered.[104] In this context, the prohibition against selling slaves to gentiles (CD 12.10-11) and the command not to "press" one's servant or maidservant or employee on the Sabbath (CD 11.12) testify to halakhic restrictions in D that the society in general did not follow. Whereas D does not include any prohibition against owning slaves, its legislation seems to testify to the biblical ideal of having no "oppressed" among its congregation.[105] According to Josephus, the reason why the Essenes did not own slaves comes very close to this: the practice of having slaves contributes to injustice (*Ant.* 18.21).[106] On the other hand, Josephus refers to some kinds of servants that the Essenes appointed among themselves (*Ant.* 18.22; *War* 8.123). Therefore, we may conclude that slavery in the "Damascus community" – if it existed – stands in some degree of deviation from the common practices by introducing restrictions and promoting the biblical ideals rather than considering slavery as an inherent part of their world.

Similarly, all references to gentiles, which we find in the Sabbath code and in laws concerning sending offerings to the Temple, belong to the earliest layer, the Halakhah. At the same time, most references to gentiles occur within rules limiting interactions, such as in the prohibition against selling clean animals and produce to gentiles (CD 12.9-11), and do not signify an openness to society.[107] Rather, the rules concerning gentiles result in restrictions of social relations with outsiders.

The third main difference between the organizations behind S and D to which Knibb draws attention is the issue of private property. Members of the "Damascus community" were to give the earnings of at least two days per month to the Examiner and the judges; this pool of money was used to help the poor and vulnerable in the group (CD 14.12-16). In contrast, according to S (1QS 6.20-24), new members "mingled" their property with that of the community when they were accepted into the community.

A closer look reveals that the differences between the systems may not have been as great as they first appear. Both documents refer to property within the context of entrance into the group (CD 13.11; 1QS 1.11-13; cf. 1QS 3.2-3).[108] Although new members made their property available for the community according to S, there are indications that their private property was still retained to some extent, such as the law that limits members' business transactions with outsiders to cash transactions (1QS 9.8-9), which indicates that the communal ownership was not absolute and that properties of individual members were marked off within the communal pool.[109] In comparison, members of the "Damascus community" were restricted in their business transactions with outsiders. As we have seen in 4QD^a 9.3.1-3, all members had to inform the Examiner about prospective business deals and probably needed his approval before entering into any deal. Further restrictions appear in a law prohibiting members from engaging in trade with each other; instead they had to give according to need, which also shows a communal aspect of property within the "Damascus community" (CD 13.14).[110] Thus, there was also supervision over members' property by the sect in the "Damascus community" and conversely, although the sect behind S had extensive rights over members' property, it did not have full ownership. In the matter of property, the demands were high in both groups, thus reflecting their tension with the rest of the society.

In terms of property, however, Catherine Murphy's study gives reason to detect further implications of these high demands. As we saw, property is associated with *entering* the covenant in both documents (CD 13.11; 1QS 5.1-3; 1.11-13). Murphy, however, sees a difference between D and S, and phrases it in this way: "Whereas in the Damascus Document the emphasis is on socio-economic critique, in the Rule priority is given to the alternative ideal community where a different economy reigns."[111] Whereas D seems to be concerned with the "biblical" ideal of taking care of the disadvantaged, S does not state this concern so clearly. The *mebaqqer* in D should have pity on the "many" and unbind all their bonds so that "there will be neither harassed nor oppressed in his congregation" (CD 13.7-10),[112] and thus is concerned with the welfare of the insiders. S also includes "biblical" ideals of justice and righteousness (1QS 5.3-4; alluding to Mic. 6:8). Nevertheless, in agreement with Murphy's statement,[113] property is emphatically presented as part of the *covenantal* relationship with Yahweh in S: instead of sacrifices to the Temple, the member brings into the covenant community his pure walk, obedience, knowledge and property. The *language* of S expresses more strongly the adoption of the Temple's functions by the community and thus the group's claim to be uniquely legitimate. This element of tension seems to be higher in comparison to D.

This brings us to the final difference between the communities, which Knibb mentions: the attitude towards the Temple. We agree with Knibb that the "Damascus community" took part in the Temple cult (see, e.g., CD 11.17-23). Nevertheless, in this respect the sectarians were also quite deviant in their social setting by viewing the Temple and its priests as defiled and asserting that only those within the sect could validly use the Temple services (CD 6.11-16).[114] Furthermore, the institutions of the community partly replaced the functions of the Temple.[115]

In sum, this section has addressed the features that scholarship has emphasized to demonstrate that the "Damascus community" was integrated within society. But upon closer examination, those features do not support this view. Instead, in spite of living among other Jews and gentiles, the members had mechanisms in place to preserve distinct boundaries with outsiders, Jews and gentiles alike. Although the members may have participated in the Temple cult, they considered the Temple defiled.[116] Furthermore, we noted that the layer of the Community Organization lacks any references to gentiles and slaves. It is possible that by the time a specific Community had developed, interaction with gentiles may have decreased and its members may have renounced slave ownership. Perhaps such community was more in line with the later Essenes who, according to Josephus and Philo, did not own slaves. In addition, many rules in the Community Organization layer show that the "Damascus community" had a strong hold over its members' social interaction, typical of a sect, including supervision over business deals by members and decisions about marriage and divorce.

5. *Conclusion*

Based on our investigation into the characteristics in S and D, we submit that both S and D contain regulations, norms, and ideology that display high tension with the greater society and thus a sectarian stance. According to Stark and Bainbridge, sectarianism is defined as being in high tension with the socio-cultural environment and it consists of three elements in particular: antagonism, separation, and difference. All three elements are connected to each other and add to tension in close interplay. Therefore, *antagonism*, the claim to be on the right and manifesting hostility towards outsiders, often arises from being different, that is, following deviant norms, which in turn lead to *separation*, a sort of social encapsulation. Yet, a particularistic worldview – apocalyptic beliefs about the present as an evil age, or belief in a specific divine revelation, for example – may also give rise to *separation*, whereby members are keeping to themselves, or shutting themselves off from some normal institution of society. Such a worldview may also increase a deviant lifestyle, or "*difference*," because of particular norms, attitudes, or behaviour that label one as nonconformist. The *context* in which this tension comes to the fore is crucial in understanding the dynamic relationship between a religious movement and the surrounding society. Stark and Bainbridge's model of sectarianism enabled us to demonstrate what it means to be "in tension." The model has hopefully facilitated making comparisons and making relevant matters visible. Our conviction is that a dimensional model – one in which variables are set on a continuum – allows for a more nuanced and a clear picture than models which distinguish sects based on variety of characteristics.

We discovered that *antagonism* towards outsiders is channelled into dualistic language, and is present in both documents. The world is divided into two opposite spheres, one ruled by God, the other by Satan. Both documents also firmly claim to possess exclusive knowledge that is supernatural in origin. Only within the group is redemption possible because only the members know the will of God. Thus, with regard to ideology, a sectarian stance is obvious in both documents.

A close examination of the regulations also confirms the sectarian nature of the communities behind these documents. *Separation* from open social relations is created by formal initiation into the community and its regulations, and by the resultant social interaction with the insiders more than with outsiders. Closely related to separation are *deviant* norms and behaviour, which themselves create separation, and aid in the formation of a distinct group of people. Both communities had initiations based on merits and marked by a ritual, rituals for expelling wayward members, prohibitions against contact with expelled members, and stringent purity rules that may suggest that outsiders were considered ritually impure. Strict purity rules are the most manifest case of norms that often go beyond what other religious groups demanded. In this context, the concept of pure food is important; members would not share food with outsiders. The claim that insiders live in "perfection" provides evidence of how religion was assumed to be the dominant factor in the members' lives. The penal codes in both documents, which are based on an informant system, show that members were subjected to harsh penalties for infringements of communal laws.

The various forms of *separation* have to be understood correctly. Whereas the community behind S, or some part or stage of it, appears to have promoted physical isolation, the "Damascus community" created its own ways of achieving separation, some of which correspond to those found in S, and some were unique to D. The special strategies of D include control over marital and family relations, which is evident in both the Admonition and the Law section of the D. Although the "Damascus community" was made up of families, the boundary between communal and private spheres was blurred by laws that gave the Examiner far-reaching power over the family and created an authoritarian environment. The Examiner supervised important decisions in matters of marriage, divorce and finances, reflecting the firm hold the sect had over its members. Such supervision of the most private aspects of the members' lives was part of an overall means of retaining members and distancing outsiders. Communal regulation restricting sexual intercourse to times when a woman could conceive was part of the same system of control. In addition, it is likely that the group, in extreme cases, would separate families by expelling transgressing family members. This also shows the high level of control that the sect exerted over the individuals. Thus, although not physically isolated from the world like the community behind S may have been, the "Damascus community" kept apart from the surrounding society in terms of ideology and religious praxis, as well as by following its own regulations and having its own leadership and officials, in effect, creating a society within society. Sectarianism can indeed, now as well as then, exist even in a local family setting.

Nevertheless, when it comes to D, the sectarian features appear most strongly in the later layers, the Community Organization and parts of the Admonition. Distinguishing between an early layer and those strata that reflect a specific Community allows the sectarian stance to stand out clearly. Two of the features that are often taken to indicate a non-sectarian stance, namely interaction with gentiles and slave-ownership, belong to the earliest layer and perhaps do not reflect the practices of the "Damascus community" per se. The early halakhah of D serves, in many cases, as clarifications and restrictions to the biblical laws, which result in a stance more stringent than the norms in general or in other religious groups (e.g. oil transmitting impurity to dust and wood, strict Sabbath rules). Yet, as Hempel notes, many halakhot were shared with others and they did not mark the group as distinct. The laws about slaves and gentiles, however, introduce mostly restrictions: they demand that slaves be treated in accordance with the Torah, and they limit contacts with gentiles in order to safeguard the purity of the covenanters and to avoid involvement in a pagan cult. The ideology behind these restrictions was possibly held in high esteem in general Jewish society, but the extent that ordinary people were willing to follow these kinds of ideals is difficult to tell.

It is important to remark that the tension we have studied does not necessarily mean an open conflict with society, or open hostility to outsiders in *all* everyday matters. Rather than attempting to reform the society using power, the Qumran movement seems to have formed an inward society where these ideals could be fulfilled. Hence, tension is manifested in the distinctiveness of these groups in comparison to other groups and in the high demands that not all in the society were able to fulfil. Tension is also apparent in the relationship to power institutions of society which is evident in the criticism of the Temple and the priesthood, and the leaders in general. Nevertheless, such tension is not always detected by outsiders. We have studied the rule documents, which are designed to demonstrate distinctiveness in all possible ways. They *promote* antagonism, difference and separation. It is another matter whether the outsiders necessarily viewed the members as deviant and hostile. The matters that were most crucial to the inside members may have been unknown by many outsiders and thus have gone unnoticed.

Endnotes

1. This article is based on the paper "Sectarianism in the Damascus Document and the Community Rule" that Cecilia Wassen gave at the annual symposium of the Nordic Network in Qumran Studies in Oslo 2004, and is the result of our joint effort to substantially expand and revise that presentation.

2. The groups behind the Scrolls are here called "the Qumran movement," without the idea that they were necessarily restricted to the settlement at Qumran, but assuming that since the large corpus of texts and the settlement were at Qumran, this location played an important role in the movement.

3. To clarify our position, we regard the Qumran movement Essene, but our analysis will not rely on the Greek and Roman descriptions of the Essenes more than in a cursory way since these are written much later than the Qumran documents by authors who did not belong to the movement. We refrain from using the common term "sectarian texts" for those documents that were written within the group since we follow a strict definition of "sectarian" in this study.

4. Both documents have been preserved in multiple copies. Ten copies of the *Damascus Document* were found at Qumran – 4QD[a-h], 5QD, 6QD; the Cave four manuscripts are the most substantial: Joseph M. Baumgarten, *Qumran Cave 4 XIII: The Damascus Document (4Q266–4Q273)* (DJD, 18; Oxford: Clarendon Press, 1996), and two medieval copies of D come from Cairo (CD A, B; Elisha Qimron, "The Text of CDC," in Magen Broshi, *The Damascus Document Reconsidered* [Jerusalem: The Israel Exploration Society, 1992], 9–49; Joseph M. Baumgarten and Daniel R. Schwartz, "Damascus Document [CD]," in James H. Charlesworth *et al.*, [eds] *The Dead Sea Scrolls: Hebrew, Aramaic and Greek Texts with English Translations.* II. *Damascus Document, War Scroll, and Related Documents* [Tübingen: J. C. B Mohr, 1995], 4-57). The *Community Rule* has been preserved in twelve copies, 1QS, 4QS[a-j], 5QS; Elisha Qimron and J. H. Charlesworth, "Rule of the Community (1QS)," in James H. Charlesworth *et al.*, *The Dead Sea Scrolls. Hebrew, Aramaic, and Greek Texts with English Translations.* I. *Rule of the Community and Related Documents* (Tübingen: J. C. B. Mohr, 1994), 1-51; P. Alexander and G. Vermes, *Qumran Cave 4 XIX: 4QSerekh Ha-Yahad* (DJD, 26; Oxford: Clarendon Press, 1998). D was composed over a long period with a completion around 100 BCE. S was also compiled around this time: the most extensive copy, 1QS, comes from 100–75 BCE, and 4QS[a] (a few fragments on papyri) is dated to second half of the second century BCE. Both documents – or some versions of them – continued to be used and copied within the Qumran movement throughout its history (based on palaeography, 4QD[b] and 4QD[d] are dated to late first century BCE, and 4QD[e] to the first half of the first century CE [Baumgarten, *Qumran Cave 4 XIII*, 96, 124, 138]; 4QS[b] and 4QS[d] were written in the last third of the first century BCE [Alexander and Vermes, *Qumran Cave 4 XIX*, 45, 89].

5. One problem with the traditional model is chronology: Jodi Magness, *The Archaeology of Qumran and the Dead Sea Scrolls* (Grand Rapids, MI: Eerdmans, 2002),

47-69, dates the origin of the Qumran settlement to 100–50 BCE. If the *final* composition of S already existed c. 100–75 BCE (see the note above), this eliminates the possibility that S was first written for the desert community at Qumran. Furthermore, there are many uncertainties concerning the application of the term *yahad*; importantly, Baumgarten has reconstructed this term in one of the D copies, 4QD^e 3.3.19.

6. E. P. Sanders points out the legal incompatibility between the two documents ("The Dead Sea Sect and Other Jews: Commonalities, Overlaps and Differences," in Timothy H. Lim with Larry W. Hurtado, A. Graeme Auld and Alison Jack, [eds], *The Dead Sea Scrolls in their Historical Context* [Edinburgh: T&T Clark, 2000], 35-36). Philip Davies searches for the systems of Judaisms in D and S, and sees differences in their ideology on "Israel," the Torah and the Temple (Philip R. Davies, "The Judaism(s) of the Damascus Document," in Joseph M. Baumgarten, Esther G. Chazon and Avital Pinnick, [eds], *The Damascus Document: A Centennial of Discovery. Proceedings of the Third International Symposium of the Orion Center for the Study of the Dead Sea Scrolls and Associated Literature, 4-8 February, 1998* [STDJ, 34; Leiden: E. J. Brill, 2000], 27-40).

7. E.g. Davies uses the term sect ("The 'Damascus' Sect and Judaism," in John C. Reeves and John Kampen, [eds], *Pursuing the Text: Studies in Honor of Ben Zion Wachholder on the Occasion of his Seventieth Birthday* [JSOTSup, 184; Sheffield: Sheffield Academic Press, 1994], 70-73), and Lawrence H. Schiffman calls the group behind the scrolls (including the *Damascus Document*) the "Dead Sea sect" or "Qumran sect," with the note that the term is used nonspecifically, referring to all Jewish groups in the Second Temple period (*Reclaiming the Dead Sea Scrolls. The History of Judaism, the Background of Christianity, the Lost Library of Qumran* [Philadelphia: The Jewish Publication Society, 1994a], 73, 90).

8. We will refer to the "Damascus community" in the singular – the primary term of its self-identification is עדה, congregation. However, D refers to "camps" both in the plural (7.6-9; 12.23; 13.20; 14.3, 9), and in the singular (e.g. 9.11; 13.3-19; 15.14). The members of the D community were likely to have lived in several towns and villages (12.19), but the exact form of the organization is outside the focus of this paper. The redactional histories of both D and S reflect changes in the community structures, so "community" should not be taken too rigidly to refer to a single group.

9. Baumgarten and Schwartz, "Damascus Document (CD)," 7.

10. Michael Knibb, "Community Organization in the Damascus Document," in L. Schiffman and J. VanderKam, (eds), *Encyclopedia of the Dead Sea Scrolls* (New York: Oxford University Press, 2000), I, 136-38 (136).

11. For a description of these types, see Bryan R. Wilson, *Religious Sects: A Sociological Study* (New York: McGraw-Hill, 1970), 35-47; idem, *Magic and the Millennium: A Sociological Study of Religious Movements of Protest among Tribal and Third-World Peoples* (London: Heinemann, 1973), 18-26.

12. Anthony J. Saldarini, "Sectarianism," in Schiffman and VanderKam, *Encyclopedia of the Dead Sea Scrolls*, II, 853-57 (855). Philip Esler also employs Wilson's typology in his chapter "Introverted Sectarianism at Qumran and in the Johannine Community," in *The First Christians in their Social Worlds: Social-Scientific Approaches to New Testament Interpretation* (London: Routledge, 1994), 70-91. Esler argues that the *Community Rule* was produced by a sect that is appropriately described as introverted while the *Damascus Document* – which reflects camps around Palestine – was

written for a reform movement. The *Damascus Document* has elements of isolationism, but other evidence, such as attendance at the Temple services and interaction with gentiles, point to a reform movement. In addition, the *Community Rule* contains stronger dualistic language than the *Damascus Document* does. Some difficulties with this view were discussed by Jutta Jokiranta, " 'Sectarianism' of the Qumran 'Sect': Sociological Notes," *RQ* 20 (2001): 223-39.

13. A. I. Baumgarten, "Finding Oneself in a Sectarian Context: A Sectarian's Food and its Implications," in A. I. Baumgarten, J. Assmann and G. G. Stroumsa, (eds), *Self, Soul and Body in Religious Experience* (Leiden: E. J. Brill, 1998), 125-47 (125 n. 1). A. I. Baumgarten also employs the terminology of Bryan Wilson. Baumgarten, however, interprets the *Damascus Document* as expressing introversionist sectarianism (and full maturity of sectarianism in its final form), whereas he considers the Pharisees and the Sadducees as examples of reformist sects (Albert I. Baumgarten, *The Flourishing of Jewish Sects in the Maccabean Era: An Interpretation* [JSJSup, 55; Leiden: E. J. Brill, 1997], 13, 90, 105).

14. Eyal Regev, "Comparing Sectarian Practice and Organization: The Qumran Sects in Light of the Regulations of the Shakers, Hutterites, Mennonites and Amish," *Numen* 51.2 (2004): 14681. Elsewhere Regev argues that the *yahad* and the Damascus Covenant share similar theology and introversionist markers, but yet they have dissimilar organizations and they "maintained distinctive boundaries and ways of life" (Eyal Regev, "The *Yahad* and the *Damascus Covenant*: Structure, Organization and Relationship," *RdQ* 82 [2003]: 233-62).

15. Charlotte Hempel, *The Laws of the Damascus Document: Sources, Tradition and Redaction* (Leiden: E. J. Brill, 1998).

16. In addition, Hempel detects various interpolations and miscellaneous material that are not especially relevant for the present study (*Laws of the Damascus Document*, 153-62, 189-90).

17. Hempel uses four criteria to distinguish various literary layers: frame of reference, vocabulary, form, and polemical/ideological stance. In the study of the "Damascus community," the frame of reference – whether the laws were associated with the society at large, or with a particular group – is somewhat vulnerable to circular reasoning: distinguishing laws according to their association to a particular community and then studying this community according to those laws. Hempel's cautious side comment is appropriate: "One gains the impression that this material [i.e. the Halakhah] is intended – *at least in theory* – to be of general application" (*Laws of the Damascus Document*, 18; italics ours). See also the study on the literary development of the laws in D by Robert Davis, "The History of the Composition of the 'Damascus Document' Statutes" (PhD dissertation, Harvard University, 1992). He detects four layers, the earliest being very similar to Hempel's Halakhah stratum. Hempel's formal characteristics of the earliest layer are similar to Davis' (i.e. the common introduction formula על + topic for groups of laws, and extensive referencing to the Hebrew Bible often using an introductory formula). In addition, Hempel highlights the common form of the halakhic exposition: אל + jussive + איש. Unfortunately, Davis did not have access to the 4QD fragments at the time of writing. For a comparison between the two compositional theories, see Cecilia Wassen, *Women in the Damascus Document* (Society of Biblical Literature Academia Biblica Series, 21; Atlanta, GA: SBL/Leiden: E. J. Brill, 2005).

18. According to Hempel (*Laws of the Damascus Document*, 70), the legal tradition of the Halakhah stratum originated "before the emergence of the *yahad* and probably also prior to the emergence of the parent movement of the *yahad*."

19. While Hempel argues that this stratum lacks sectarian features, we wish to leave open the degree of tension reflected by this early halakhah. The more these halakhic rulings were deviant in their setting, the more tension they would have caused (see below). Halakhic issues are at the centre of Jewish sectarianism as Lawrence H. Schiffman states in "Halakhah and Sectarianism in the Dead Sea Scrolls," in Timothy H. Lim with Larry W. Hurtado, A. Graeme Auld and Alison Jack, (eds), *The Dead Sea Scrolls in their Historical Context* (Edinburgh: T&T Clark, 2000), 123-42. In the Qumran corpus, we have examples of both strict and moderate halakhic rulings; e.g. Wassen (*Women in the Damascus Document*) highlights examples of both with regards to halakhah relating to women.

20. Sarianna Metso, "The Textual Traditions of the Qumran Community Rule," in Moshe Bernstein, Florentino García Martínez and John Kampen, (eds), *Legal Texts and Legal Issues: Proceedings of the Second Meeting of the International Organization for Qumran Studies, Cambridge 1995* (STDJ, 23; Leiden: E. J. Brill, 1997), 141-47. Metso notes, however, that the material evidence is not the only means to reconstruct the literary development of the document – traditional exegetical methods are needed too. See also Sarianna Metso, *The Textual Development of the Qumran Community Rule* (STDJ, 21; Leiden: E. J. Brill, 1997a).

21. In another tradition, represented by 4QS[e], a calendrical Otot text was included instead of the final hymn. This text provides a list of the weekly service of the priestly families in the temple (Metso, "Textual Traditions," 144).

22. Armin Lange, *Weisheit und Prädestination: Weisheitliche Urordnung und Prädestination in den Textfunden von Qumran* (ed. F. García Martínez and A. S. van der Woude; STDJ, 18; Leiden: E. J. Brill, 1995), 127-28, and Jörg Frey, "Different Patterns of Dualistic Thought in the Qumran Library: Reflections on their Background and History," in Berstein *et al.*, *Legal Texts and Legal Issues*: 275-335.

23. Recently, Carol Newsom makes a contribution in discussing the "pre-texts" of the two-spirits-treatise and the function of this section in S; Carol A. Newsom, *The Self as Symbolic Space: Constructing Identity and Community at Qumran* (STDJ, 52; Leiden: E. J. Brill, 2004), 85-87, 127-34.

24. Many parallels have been observed. For connections between the discourse on the two spirits and CD 2, see Frey, "Different Patterns," 302-305; for connections between 1QS 6.1-8 and CD 12.22–13.7 (groups of ten or more members), see Sarianna Metso, "Whom Does the Term Yahad Identify?" in Charlotte Hempel and Judith M. Lieu, (eds), *Biblical Traditions in Transmission: Essays in Honour of Michael A. Knibb* (JSJSup, 111; Leiden: E. J. Brill, 2006), 213-35; for connections between 1QS 8–9 and CD 19.33b–20.34 (e.g. the "first rules"), see Philip R. Davies, "Communities at Qumran and the Case of the Missing 'Teacher,' " *RdQ* 15.57-58 (1991): 275-86; for parallel penal codes and organizational structures in S and D, see Charlotte Hempel, "Community Structures in the Dead Sea Scrolls: Admission, Organization, Disciplinary Procedures," in Peter W. Flint and James C. VanderKam, (eds), *The Dead Sea Scrolls after Fifty Years: A Comprehensive Assessment* (Leiden: E. J. Brill, 1999), II, 67-92, and Sarianna Metso, "The Relationship between the Damascus Document and the Com-

munity Rule," in Baumgarten *et al.*, *The Damascus Document*: 85-93. Other "rules" are also relevant for a comparison of S and D, e.g., 1QSa and 4Q*Serek Damascus*. For our purposes, the S and D material suffices in order to establish the understanding of "sectarianism" in the largest rule documents.

25. The recent suggestion by John Collins makes the comparison between D and S even more challenging. He argues that *yahad* is an umbrella term for many local groups and that, in addition to the *yahad*, the *Community Rule* applies to an elite group (which probably lived at Qumran); John J. Collins, "Forms of Community in the Dead Sea Scrolls," in Shalom M. Paul *et al.*, (eds), *Emanuel: Studies in Hebrew Bible, Septuagint, and Dead Sea Scrolls in Honor of Emanuel Tov* (VTSup, 94; Leiden: E. J. Brill, 2003), 97-111; idem, "The Yahad and 'the Qumran Community,' " in Hempel and Lieu, *Biblical Traditions in Transmission*: 81-96. See a different view by Metso, "Whom Does the Term Yahad Identify?" It does have an impact on our interpretations of the documents, whether we consider S and D as reflecting the life of a "commune" or scattered local groups – for example, everyday contacts with outsiders may be reduced in a closed setting. However, determining the *form of organization* of these groups is outside of the scope of this study. Our working hypothesis is the assumption that groups associated with D consisted of several smaller groups in various villages and towns and were united under the same organization, whereas S may reflect fewer groups in a more permanent setting.

26. Rodney Stark and William Sims Bainbridge, *The Future of Religion. Secularization, Revival and Cult Formation* (Berkeley, CA: University of California Press, 1985), 19-24; idem, *A Theory of Religion* (Toronto Studies in Religion, 2; New York: Peter Lang, 1987), 15-17. For the Troeltschian model, see the table by Jutta Jokiranta, "Sectarianism," 227.

27. E.g. exclusiveness, claim for monopoly, lay organization, rejection of religious division of labour, voluntarism, accession by merit, total commitment; Bryan Wilson, *Religion in Sociological Perspective* (Oxford: Oxford University Press, 1982), 91-95. See also Bryan Wilson, *The Social Dimensions of Sectarianism: Sects and New Religious Movements in Contemporary Society* (Oxford: Clarendon Press, 1990), 1-2, and cf. Lorne Dawson, *Comprehending Cults: The Sociology of New Religious Movements* (Oxford/New York: Oxford University Press, 1998), 30: sects are voluntary organizations, homogenous in their membership, radical and strict in their beliefs; they espouse feelings of being elect, have personal organizational structures, and are sometimes anti-ritualistic.

28. Wilson, *Religion*, 95, 100-105. Ernest Gellner's study in an Islamic context has a very different set of typological characteristics. Rural tribal religion has a tendency to be hierarchical and have religious specialists but it is also mystical and expressed in perceptual images, whereas the urban central religion is characterized by egalitarianism, puritanism, observance of rules, and scriptural revelation, Ernest Gellner, "A Pendulum Swing Theory of Islam," in Roland Robertson, (ed.), *Sociology of Religion* (New York: Penguin, 1969), 127-39. This example was pointed out by Kimmo Ketola from the Department of Comparative Religion, University of Helsinki, at an interdisciplinary seminar in Helsinki. For limitations of the ideal type in non-Christian cultures, see also A. I. Baumgarten, *Flourishing of Jewish Sects*, 5.

29. Therefore, for Wilson, it was already clear that the groups in question were

"sectarian," and this sectarianism was characterized by responses to the world that included tension: "The sectarian movement always manifests some degree of tension with the world, and it is the type of tension and the ways in which it is contained or maintained that are of particular importance," Wilson, *Magic and the Millennium*, 19. The "responses to the world" were designed to facilitate comparative study, "without postulating all the various specific characteristics that are true for Christian sects" (Wilson, *Religion*, 103). However, the actual definition of sect in Wilson's work remains somewhat obscure; as far as we see, it arises from the ideal (Christian) type. In later work, Wilson prefers the term "new religious movements."

30. Wilson, *Magic and the Millennium*, 22-27.

31. Wilson, *Magic and the Millennium*, 26, 35. The responses to the world are not only classificatory tools but aimed at explaining the conditions in which particular types of sects emerge and the consequences of particular responses, Wilson, *Religion*, 103.

32. In light of the assumed celibacy of the *yahad*, the discourse of the two spirits (1QS 3.13–4.26) is noteworthy in its promise of fruitful *offspring* to the sons of truth (4.7). It was noted above that the discourse does not represent the original teaching of the *yahad*. In its present context in the *Community Rule*, the list of rewards to the sons of truth (4.6-8, e.g., healing, peace, blessings, offspring, eternal enjoyment) may well change the members' *perception* of themselves: the insider would definitely count his successes as rewards and *not* view any misfortunes as punishments but rather as a testing. Also elsewhere in S, evil is perceived to be controlled by the new way of life; members possess counsel, spiritual supremacy and material goods (1QS 6.22).

33. Cf. a similar kind of criticism about the "responses" in the study of early Christianity by Petri Luomanen, "The 'Sociology of Sectarianism' in Matthew: Modeling the Genesis of Early Jewish and Christian Communities," in Christopher Tuckett, Ismo Dunderberg and Kari Syreeni, (eds), *Fair Play: Diversity and Conflicts in Early Christianity. Essays in Honour of Heikki Räisänen* (Leiden: E. J. Brill, 2002), 107-30 (119-20).

34. An illustrative table of the defining characteristics in various models is provided by Keith Roberts, *Religion in Sociological Perspective* (Belmont, CA: Wadsworth, 1990), 192-93.

35. Tension is also central to Wilson's conceptualization of sects, and "new religious movements," Wilson, *Social Dimensions*, 46-68.

36. Stark and Bainbridge, "Sects: Emergence of Schismatic Religious Movements," in *A Theory of Religion*, 121-28. For doubts about the usefulness of this variable, see Roberts, *Religion in Sociological Perspective*, 188-89. Roberts notes that, although many sects seem to be in conflict with the surrounding society, they often function in ways that result in the socialization of members into the values of the society. We acknowledge that no single variable works without difficulties, but we hold that "tension" in the continuum, as Stark and Bainbridge have it, works better in our context than "complexity of organization," for example, which has been also suggested (sects having less complexity); see Roberts, *Religion in Sociological Perspective*, 189-90. It is important to remember that "tension" does not mean tension in every aspect of life and it is not necessarily expressed in conflict. For this point, Stark and Bainbridge's analysis of measuring tension is very relevant, see below.

37. According to Stark and Bainbridge, cults are also at the high tension end: a cult is "a deviant religious organization with *novel* beliefs and practices"; Stark and Bainbridge, *A Theory of Religion*, 124. See the application of this in the interpretation of Matthew's community by Luomanen, "The 'Sociology of Sectarianism' in Matthew."

38. Stark and Bainbridge, *Future of Religion*, 48-67. Wilson describes tension with modern Western societies in his chapter "Sects and Society in Tension" (in *Social Dimensions*, 46-68) by taking up seven "institutions" in which sects deviate from common norm: defence, polity, economy, status, education, recreation, and health. In addition, he distinguishes three areas, in which sects not only reject society's norm but affirm their own practices: public comportment (e.g. dress, speech, diet), proselytizing, and family relations. As such, these are not suitable in the ancient context (e.g. there was no public defence system, or public education), but they could be used as heuristic tools for looking at ancient sects.

39. Stark and Bainbridge adopt the concept of "tension" rather than "deviance" since tension has also the other side: not only rejecting the surrounding society but being *rejected* by it (*Future of Religion*, 48-49).

40. Wilson's distinction of areas in which tension occurs (above, n. 37) conforms well to these three elements: deviant norms concerning the central institutions of society stand for *difference*; proselytizing and other particularistic beliefs and behaviour mark *antagonism*; family relations reveal *separation* (and potentially other areas as well, e.g., economy or recreation, if sect members are denied common social intercourse in these areas in their everyday life). What Stark and Bainbridge's analysis of tension perhaps lacks, is Wilson's notion that tension is greater when a community – not merely an individual – "sponsors" a certain lifestyle (affirmative action, as opposed to exemption from some activity). Also, recognition of areas in which exemption is pursued may help to distinguish central matters that cause greater tension from less central matters about which society is indifferent.

41. Stark and Bainbridge, *Future of Religion*, 66. This fluidity between the concepts becomes apparent in our analysis below; some features in the text concern more than one of the three elements.

42. According to Stark and Bainbridge, "...the utility of concepts can be judged by two criteria. First, they must be adequate for *classification*... [Secondly], concepts are to be preferred to the extent that they facilitate theorizing – increase the scope, precision, accuracy, or simplicity of a theory" (Stark and Bainbridge, *Theory of Religion*, 15-17). The variable of "tension" offers the best tool for our purposes. For criticism of "tension" and defence for the Weberian "mode of membership," see Lorne L. Dawson, "Creating 'Cult' Typologies: Some Strategic Considerations," *Journal of Contemporary Religion* 12.3 (1997): 363-81. Dawson provides an overview of sect typologies and argues for uni-dimensional models instead of taxonomies. For a positive view of Stark and Bainbridge's definition of sects, see, e.g., John H. Simpson, "The Stark-Bainbridge Theory of Religion," *JSSR* 29 (1990): 367-71. Malcom B. Hamilton seems to simplify their definition to concern *schismatic* movements, primarily (*The Sociology of Religion: Theoretical and Comparative Perspectives* [London: Routledge, 1995], 200-202), but according to our understanding, it is the surrounding society, not a schism from an established religious institution, that Stark and Bainbridge emphasize.

43. Albert Baumgarten's definition of sects comes very close to this understanding. He defines a sect as "a voluntary association of protest, which utilizes boundary marking mechanisms – the social means of differentiating between insiders and outsiders – to distinguish between its own members and those otherwise normally regarded as belonging to the same national or religious entity" (*Flourishing of Jewish Sects*, 7). He notes that the definition has to include the *practical* consequences of being involved in a voluntary association of protest. In his earlier work, he has also utilized Stark and Bainbridge's analysis and the "level of tension" to compare Qumran and the Essenes ("Rule of the Martian as Applied to Qumran," *IOS* XIV [1994]: 121-42 [134]). We acknowledge that *marking* boundaries (against *normal* group-boundaries) is very close to our understanding of "tension," but one could argue that every group, if it has a distinctive social identity, has some sorts of boundaries. Baumgarten's definition of sects includes a wide variety of groups, which is useful for his description of Second Temple sectarianism. The need to distinguish between different sects is resolved by using Wilson's typology (Pharisees being reformists and the Qumran group introversionist). The continuum of "tension," together with Stark and Bainbridge's analysis of it, could, in our opinion, also elucidate some of the differences between these groups.

44. See, e.g., stances of the Roman Catholic Church by Meredith B. McGuire, *Religion in Social Context* (Belmont: Wadsworth, 4th edn, 1997), 150, or development of the Salvation Army by Ronald Robertson, *The Sociological Interpretation of Religion* (Oxford: Basil Blackwell, 1972), 128. The "claim for monopoly" derives from the model by Roy Wallis, who distinguished between *sect* and *cult*: sects regard themselves as uniquely legitimate whereas cults are pluralistic; Roy Wallis, "The Cult and its Transformation," in idem (ed.), *Sectarianism: Analyses of Religious and Non-Religious Sects* (Contemporary Issues Series, 10; London: Peter Owen, 1975), 35-49. See also McGuire, *Religion in Social Context*, 144-50, and Jokiranta, "Sectarianism," 229. Instead of tension, Robertson has the membership principle as the other variable (exclusive/inclusive).

45. Distinguishing the "claim for monopoly" as another variable may serve some purposes, as we shall see in the case of property in D and S.

46. Stark and Bainbridge, *Future of Religion*, 50-51. One apparent application could be monasteries: these followed deviant norms and ways of life but were not in tension with the larger society since they were approved by the Church or had power themselves.

47. McGuire, *Religion in Social Context*, 150.

48. For the dates of the documents, see above n. 4.

49. No society is entirely homogeneous, and Palestine in the later part of the Second Temple period was diverse and pluralistic with several groups (e.g. Pharisees, Sadducees, Essenes) competing against each other for influence and power. Whereas some scholars speak of "Judaisms" for this time, others, notably E. P. Sanders, argue in favour of an underlying common religious ideology (see Sanders' concept of "covenantal nomism" in his *Judaism: Practice and Belief 63 BCE–66 CE* [London: SCM Press, 1992]). In terms of deviance, which requires that behaviour or norms differ from the surrounding society, we hold that, in spite of the pluralistic Jewish society, certain laws and regulations in D and S do appear to be at odds with common norms. These will be highlighted below.

50. Stark and Bainbridge, *Theory of Religion*, 126.

51. See a graphical representation of this idea by Luomanen, " 'Sociology of Sectarianism' in Matthew," 129. Change in society is seen as central in A. I. Baumgarten's analysis of ancient Jewish sectarianism, e.g., Baumgarten, *Flourishing of Jewish Sects*, 14. In contrast to this, Regev, "Comparing Sectarian Practice," argues that the Qumran sectarian rules did not develop in response to Hellenistic influence or as a result of specific scriptural exegesis, but because of a particular worldview, "an endless fear of sin, an aim for redemption, and a necessity for maintaining discipline and moral stance." Although Regev succeeds in highlighting many important insights from modern parallels, this argument seems to overlook the dynamism involved in a sectarian relationship to the society.

52. This theory is an exchange theory, according to which it is part of human nature to seek rewards. These rewards exist in limited quantity in the ordinary day-to-day life. Religion, then, is a system of general compensators (postulations of rewards) based on supernatural assumptions; Stark and Bainbridge, *Theory of Religion*, 36-39. For general reviews and criticism of their theory, see, e.g., Simpson, "The Stark-Bainbridge Theory of Religion," 367-71; Randall Collins, "Book Review: A Theory of Religion," *JSSR* 32 (1993): 402-406; Hamilton, *The Sociology of Religion*, 183-92, 202-206.

53. Despite the level of tension, it is important to bear in mind the common characteristics with the rest of Jewish religion, see Sanders, "The Dead Sea Sect and Other Jews."

54. Stark and Bainbridge measure antagonism in a Christian setting by people's responses to various propositions like "Being of the Hindu religion would definitely prevent salvation" or "Tithing is absolutely necessary for salvation," and by their willingness to convert outsiders (*Future of Religion*, 58-59).

55. A certain hostility toward outsiders is noticeable; see, e.g., 1QS 1.10; 2.5-7. Note that, as the group claims to be uniquely legitimate and deals with outsiders with a sense of hostility, it runs the risk of decreasing its power to attract outsiders and may be gaining fewer converts (cf. Stark and Bainbridge, *Future of Religion*, 56, 60). The rule documents tell us little about how new members decided to join the group and whether new members were recruited or not. The *Rule of the Congregation* (1QSa), like D, seems to reflect socialization of children into the movement.

56. See the discussion of the forms of dualism in the discourse by Frey, "Different Patterns." According to Frey, the discourse represents cosmic, ethical and psychological dualism. On the other hand, the strong psychological dualism (good and evil are competing *within* an individual) reflected in the discourse is quite unique in comparison with other Qumran texts.

57. Particularistic claims are thus expressed in S, using the terms of Frey (see n. 53 above), by the belief that humankind is divided into exclusive groups according to their conduct (ethical dualism) and according to their relationship to cosmic forces (cosmic dualism), connected to the belief that the right conduct and good cosmic forces are manifested in a sociologically defined group.

58. See the concise presentation of suggested redactions by Charlotte Hempel, *The Damascus Texts* (Companion to the Qumran Scrolls, 1; Sheffield: Sheffield Academic Press, 2000), 44-49.

59. Hempel refers to the possibility that both the Admonition and the Laws went through a "Qumranic recension" or a "Serekh redaction" (*Damascus Texts*, 87-88). Hempel sees two kinds of accounts about the community's origins in the beginning of the Admonition, one possibly going back to the "parent group" ("Community Structures," 316-29).

60. Cf. Frey, "Different Patterns," 304: "Now the ethical criteria of good and evil seem to be firmly related to definite social groups."

61. John Martens highlights expressions of protest and tension *vis-à-vis* the general society in the Admonition ("A Sectarian Analysis of the Damascus Document," in Simcha Fishbane and Jack Lightstone, [eds], *Essays in Social Scientific Study of Judaism and Jewish Society* [Canada-Israel Conference on the Social Scientific Study of Judaism; Concordia University, 1990], 27-46).

62. Cf. Frey, "Different Patterns," 303-307, for the emphasis on cosmic dualism in CD 4.12–6.11.

63. Stark and Bainbridge stress that the content of deviant norms depends on the society. They measure difference mostly by behaviour that is permitted by society but prohibited by high tension groups. The reverse is also possible: sects promote behaviour which society regards as harmful or avoidable (*Future of Religion*, 51-56). Stark and Bainbridge define norms as "rules governing what behavior is expected or prohibited in various circumstances" (*Theory of Religion*, 328).

64. Both documents describe the life of members using terms of holiness and perfection, for example, in the expression "men of holiness who walk perfectly" in 1QS 9.8 (cf. 1QS 8.13), and in the Admonition, "the congregation of perfect holiness" in CD 20.2 (cf. CD 20.6-7; 7.5).

65. Cf. Mt. 12:11.

66. Additional stringent laws from the Halakhah section include disqualifying priests who have been in captivity among gentiles, as well as those who have served outside of the country, from officiating in the Temple (4QD[a] 5.2.4-9; Hempel, *Laws of the Damascus Document*, 41) and the requirement of paying tithes on gleaning, which is in contrast to rabbinic law (4QD[e] 3.2.18-19; see Baumgarten, *Qumran Cave 4 XIII*, 148-49). Laws such as these suggest that tension with the surrounding society may have begun already in the earliest stage, within the early "priestly circles," contrary to Hempel's assertion.

67. These belong to "miscellaneous halakhah," see n. 15.

68. Many studies have explored this subject: e.g. Eyal Regev, "The Idea of Non-Priestly Purity in Ancient Judaism," *JJS* 31 (2000): 176-202 (188); Colleen M. Conway, "Toward a Well-Formed Subject: The Function of Purity Language in the Serek-ha-Yahad," *JSP* 21 (2000): 103-20.

69. A. I. Baumgarten, *Flourishing of Jewish Sects*, 9, 91. Baumgarten's study gives valuable insights into many areas of norms and provides the background against which we look at "deviant" norms.

70. E. P. Sanders points to archaeological evidence, such as a large number of *mikvaot*, in favour of a general observance of purity laws; see, *Judaism*, 223-30; cf. Hannah K. Harrington, *The Purity Texts* (Companion to the Qumran Scrolls, 5; London: T&T Clark International, 2004), 7. On *mikvaot*, see E. P. Sanders, *Jewish Law from Jesus to the Mishnah* (London: SCM Press, 1990), 214-27; Ronny Reich, "The

Hot Bath-House (balneum) the Miqweh and the Jewish Community in the Second Temple Period," *JJS 39* (1988): 102-107; Mark A. Chancey, *The Myth of a Gentile Galilee* (Society for New Testament Studies Monograph Series, 118; Cambridge: Cambridge University Press, 2002), 65-68.

71. There are many purity laws in D that are stringent compared to the general Jewish halakhah which confirms the impression created by the Admonition (CD 6.15) that the purity status of ordinary Jews could not be trusted. D insists that a person, after having been ritually impure, must wait until sunset on the last day of his or her purification until that person is considered pure (4QDᵃ 6.2.4); this view rejects the Pharisaic concept of *tevul yom*, according to which a person is considered pure in certain respects after washing him- or herself in the morning of the final day of his or her purification period; see Joseph Baumgarten, "The Pharisaic-Sadducean Controversies about Purity," *JJS* 31 (1980): 157-70. See also Regev, "Idea of Non-Priestly Purity," 188-89; Lawrence Schiffman, "Pharisaic and Sadducean Halakhah," *DSD* 3 (1994b): 285-99. Oil has the capacity to transmit impurity onto wood, stones, and dust (CD 12.15-17; this corresponds with Josephus's claim that the Essenes avoided using oil [*War* 2.8.3, 123]); see J. Baumgarten, "The Essene Avoidance of Oil and the Laws of Purity," in *Studies in Qumran Law* (Studies in Judaism in Late Antiquity, 24; Leiden: E. J. Brill; 1977), 88-97. The impurity status of a *zavah* is imposed after only one day's bleeding outside of normal menstruation (4QDᵃ 6.2.2-3). The concern about preserving purity on the Sabbath is unique to the sect; CD 11.3-4 prohibits wearing soiled clothes on the Sabbath, and the prohibition "let no one intentionally intermingle [יתערב] on the Sabbath" (CD 11.4-5) is likely to refer to sexual intercourse (Lutz Doering, "Purity Regulations Concerning the Sabbath in the Dead Sea Scrolls and Related Literature," in Lawrence Schiffman, Emanuel Tov and James VanderKam, [eds], *The Dead Sea Scrolls Fifty Years after their Discovery: Proceedings of the Jerusalem Congress, July 20-25, 1997* [Jerusalem: Israel Exploration Society in cooperation with the Shrine of the Book, Israel Museum, 2000], 600-609).

72. 1QS 5.13–14 explicitly states that outsiders are impure: "For they cannot be cleansed unless they turn away from their wickedness, for (he remains) impure (טמא) among all those who transgress his words" (cf. 1QS 3.4-5); Baumgarten comments on this law: "This is to be taken not as a metaphor, but as a law declaring all pagans and Jews outside the *yahad* ritually unclean" ("The Essene Avoidance of Oil," 96; for a similar understanding, see Jonathan Klawans ("The Impurity of Immorality in Ancient Judaism," *JJS* 48 [1997]: 1-16 [8-10]) and Harrington (*Purity Texts*, 116-18). Based on the purity laws concerning liquid and solid food and the admission process in S, Schiffman argues that a non-member was "impure at the highest level of impurity possible. Only a dead body had greater impurity" (*Reclaiming the Dead Sea Scrolls*, 102). According to Davies, the "Damascus sect" was formed in the first place because of disputes concerning the calendar and purity ("The 'Damascus' Sect and Judaism," 80-82).

73. The term טהרה, "the purity," carries a wide range of meanings; for general studies on the term, see Saul Lieberman, "The Discipline in the So-Called Dead Sea Manual of Discipline," *JBL* 71 (1951): 199-206; Jacob Licht, *The Rule Scroll: A Scroll from the Wilderness of Judaea: 1QS, 1QSa, 1QSb, Text, Introduction, and Commentary* (Jerusalem: Bialik Institute, 1965 [Hebrew]), 294-303; idem, "Some Terms and Concepts

of Ritual Purity in The Qumran Writings," in J. M. Grintz and J. Liver, (eds), *Studies in the Bible Presented to Professor M. H. Segal* (Publications of the Israel Society for Biblical Research, 17; Jerusalem: Kiryat Sepher, 1964), 300-309; Friederich Avemarie, "'Tohorat Ha-rabbim' and 'Mashqeh Ha-rabbim': Jacob Licht Reconsidered," in Bernstein *et al.*, *Legal Texts and Legal Issues*: 215-29.

74. See 1QS 6.25; 7.3, 16; CD 9.21, 23; 4QD[a] 10.1.15 [partly reconstructed]; 4QD[e] 7.1.6. Whereas only S explicitly connects this punishment with food, it is likely that the punishment of being separated from purity in D (CD 9.21, 23) also refers to pure food; see Klawans "Impurity of Immorality," 9; Hempel, *Laws of the Damascus Covenant*, 99; Florentino García Martínez and Trebolle Barrera, *The People of the Dead Sea Scrolls: Their Writings, Beliefs and Practices* (trans. Wilfred G. E. Watson; Leiden: E. J. Brill, 1995), 151. At times the texts do not explicitly specify to what exclusion refers (e.g. 1QS 7.5; 4QD[a] 10.2.2, 4, 6, 10, 12 [these are partly reconstructions]).

75. Sharing food with outsiders appears to be prohibited in 1QS 5.16-17, and the gradual admission with access to pure food only after a full year (1QS 6.16-17) presumes that only members could partake of the pure food of the community. The expulsion ritual in D, moreover, explicitly prohibits a member from eating food belonging to a former member (4QD[a] 11.15), which suggest that members did not share food with non-members. For a full discussion of sectarian food laws as boundary-marking laws, see Baumgarten, "A Sectarian's Food" (especially p. 134 concerning 1QS 5). In addition, food laws in D express a stringent view: selling clean animals or agricultural products to gentiles is prohibited, which presumes that buying any food from gentiles is also banned (CD 12.8-11); and as noted, fish had to be ritually slaughtered (CD 12.13-14).

76. Stark and Bainbridge measure separation by the degree that relations with other insiders are favoured. For example, "...members of sects are more than twice as likely to say they fit in very well with their church congregation than are members of low tension dominations." High tension groups tend to disapprove of marriages with outsiders more often than low tension groups (*Future of Religion*, 60-61).

77. Hempel, *Laws of the Damascus Covenant*, 73-90, 189.

78. See the analysis of the covenant ritual by Carol Newsom in her chapter "How to Make a Sectarian" in *Self as Symbolic Space*, 117-27.

79. Wilson explains that, because sects make rigorous demands on their members in combination with them "being voluntary, intense and in insisting on merit in their members," it follows that they "have procedures for expulsion of the wayward" (*Religious Sects*, 27).

80. See 1QS 7.16 (slandering the community), 7.17 (murmuring against the authority); 4QD[e] 7.1.11 (despising communal law); 4QD[e] 7.1.13-14 (murmuring against the Fathers).

81. "And the man from the men of the communi[ty] (היחד) [w]ho shares with him (the expelled) his pure-food or his property wh[ich...] the Many, his judgment shall be the same: he shall be expe[lled]."

82. Note that various Graeco-Roman voluntary associations also had means to punish inappropriate behaviour by fines or expulsion, but their norms and structures reflected that of the *polis* (Sandra Walker-Ramisch, "Graeco-Roman Voluntary Associations and the Damascus Document: A Sociological Analysis," in John S. Kloppenborg and Stephen G. Wilson, [eds], *Voluntary Associations in the Graeco-Roman World*

[London: Routledge, 1996], 128-45). Walker-Ramisch compares these associations to D and concludes that, despite many similarities, D's exclusivism and language of separation are not found in collegia.

83. For a comparison between the penal codes, see Joseph M. Baumgarten, "The Cave 4 Versions of the Qumran Penal Code," *JJS* 43.2 (1992): 268-76. See also Charlotte Hempel, "The Penal Code Reconsidered," in Bernstein *et al.*, *Legal Texts and Legal Issues*: 337-48; Metso, "Relationship between the Damascus Document," 89-91.

84. While נֱעֱשׁ "be punished" in S clearly refers to food reduction by a quarter, D never specifies the meaning of the term. Exclusion from pure food and drink for two years, which would effectively impose the level of a novice on the member, was enforced for severe violations of "foundations" or halakhic rulings (1QS 7.18-25, 8.21–9.1).

85. Baumgarten states, "An Essene was to be a permanent spy on activities of fellow members, and I suppose that the information provided by Essenes about each other was used by the leadership to control the lives of members" (*Flourishing of Jewish Sects*, 110-11).

86. Knibb, "Community Organization," 136.

87. While not equating the Qumran group with the Essenes, A. I. Baumgarten holds that both marriage and living in towns, characteristics of one branch of Essenes, indicate a lower level of tension compared to a celibate, desert group ("Rule of the Martian," 132, 134).

88. See, e.g., Josephus, *War* 2.129; Philo, *Hypothetica* 11.14; 1 Cor. 7:1-9.

89. The exact meaning of the phrase "taking two wives in their lives" has been debated; Jerome Murphy-O'Connor and Davies take the literal meaning at face value, i.e., in addition to polygamy, any second marriage (e.g. after divorce), even after the death of the first wife, is prohibited (Murphy-O'Connor, "An Essene Missionary Document? CD II, 14–VI, 1," *RB* 77 [1970]: 201-29 (220); Davies, *Behind the Essenes: History and Ideology in the Dead Sea Scrolls* [BJS, 94; Atlanta, GA: Scholars Press, 1987], 73-85; ibid, *The Damascus Covenant: An Interpretation of the "Damascus Document"* [JSOTSup, 25; Sheffield: JSOT Press, 1983], 116). Joseph Fitzmyer argues that the prohibition concerns any second marriage, including that after divorce, for either husband or wife as long as the other is alive ("Divorce among First-Century Palestinian Jews," *ErIsr* 14 [1978]: 106-10). We agree with Geza Vermes ("Sectarian Matrimonial Halakhah in the Damascus Rule," *JJS* 25 [1974]: 197-202) and others, who argue that the passage refers to polygamy alone – and not remarriage after divorce – which is indicated by the proof-texts, e.g., "male and female created he them," that is, one male and one female. Moreover, in light of a fragment from Cave 4 that mentions children (4QD[a] 9.3.5), it is now clear that the word למגרש in CD 13.17 (within a very fragmentary passage) refers to divorce, i.e., "one who divorces." Thus, divorce apparently was accepted in the community. For a detailed bibliography of studies on this passage, see Adiel Schremer, "Qumran Polemic on Marital Law: CD 4:20–5:11 and its Social Background," in Baumgarten *et al.*, *The Damascus Document*: 147-60.

90. See, Tal Ilan, *Jewish Women in Greco-Roman Palestine: An Inquiry into Image and Status* (Peabody, MA: Hendrickson, 1995), 76 (concerning uncle and niece), 85-88 (concerning polygamy).

91. The law concerning uncle-niece marriages is an example of the exegetical tendency among sectarians to harmonize biblical laws; Jacob Milgrom calls this principle "homogenization" ("The Scriptural Foundations and Deviations in the Laws of Purity of the Temple Scroll," in Lawrence Schiffman, [ed.], *Archaeology and History in the Dead Sea Scrolls: The New York University Conference in Memory of Yigal Yadin* [JSPSup, 8; Sheffield: JSOT Press, 1990], 83-99 [91, 95]).

92. Wilson explains that children and outsiders "enter on the same terms and all are subject to the same continuing tests of eligibility and the same sanctions for misconduct" (*Social Dimensions*, 180).

93. In contrast, a marriage law in the halakhah section takes for granted that the father decides to whom he shall give his daughter (4QD^f 3.4b-15).

94. Marriage was "a social contract negotiated between families, with economic, religious, and (occasionally) political implications beyond the interests of sexuality, relationship, and reproduction" (K. C. Hanson, "BTB Readers Guide: Kinship," *Biblical Theological Bulletin* 24 [1994]: 183-94 [188]).

95. Cf. Wilson, *Social Dimensions*, 64-65.

96. Joseph Baumgarten (*Qumran Cave 4 XIII*, 165) argues that the legislation concerns "unnatural intercourse" that prevents procreation. According to Lilliana Rosso Ubigli ("Il Documento Di Damasco e L'Etica Coniugale: A Proposito di un Nuovo Passo Qumranico," *Henoch* 14 [1992]: 3-10), the issue is intercourse without the intention of procreation. For a similar view based on rabbinic texts, see Menahem Kister, "Notes on Some New Texts from Qumran," *JJS* 44 (1993): 280-90 (280-81).

97. Perhaps even a wife was encouraged to testify about her husband's sexual behaviour since, according to 1QSa 1.11, wives would be testifying about their husbands; see the proposal by Wassen (*Women in the Damascus Document*).

98. References to slaves appear in a section outlining general commercial laws (CD 12.10-11), in the Sabbath code (CD 11.11-12), and in a passage concerning intercourse with a slave woman (4QD^e 4.12-21). It is notable that *Jubilees* (11:2) introduces the selling of male and female slaves in the thirty-fifth jubilee as one example of corruption of humankind.

99. For the relationship between these biblical laws, see Gregory C. Chirichigno, *Debt-Slavery in Israel and the Ancient Near East* (JSOTSup, 141; Sheffield: JSOT Press, 1993), 344-57.

100. Cf. also Exod. 21:7-8; Deut. 23:16-17.

101. Dexter E. Callander Jr, "Servants of God(s) and Servants of Kings in Israel and the Ancient Near East," *Semeia* 83/84: Slavery in Text and Interpretation (1998): 67-82 (74-80).

102. We find later the same prohibition in Tannaitic halakhah, see L. H. Schiffman, "Legislation Concerning Relations with Non-Jews in the Zadokite Fragments and in Tannaitic Literature," *RdQ* 43 (1983): 379-89 (388). Non-Jewish slaves were given one year to accept conversion to Judaism; if they did not, they were to be sold. See, however, doubt about distinguishing between "Hebrew" and "Canaanite" slaves in practice by Dale B. Martin, "Slavery and the Ancient Jewish Family," in Shaye J. D. Cohen, (ed.) *The Jewish Family in Antiquity* (Brown Judaic Studies, 289; Atlanta, GA: Scholars Press, 1993), 113-29 (115-16). Josephus complains about Herod's practice of

selling criminals to foreigners as punishment as being against Jewish customs (*Ant.* 16.1-5). Nevertheless, Josephus does not distinguish between Jewish and non-Jewish slaves in his terminology (Martin, "Slavery," 127 n. 47).

103. Martin, "Slavery," 118-29; Benjamin G. Wright III, " 's *Ebed/Doulos*: Terms and Social Status in the Meeting of Hebrew Biblical and Hellenistic Culture," *Semeia* 83/84: Slavery in Text and Interpretation (1998): 83-111 (88); Morton Smith, "The Gentiles in Judaism 125 BCE–CE 66," in William Horbury, W. D. Davies and John Sturdy, (eds), *The Cambridge History of Judaism* (Cambridge: Cambridge University Press, 1999), 192-266 (194-99). Judean slaves were exported during the Ptolemaic and Seleucid invasions (e.g. 2. Macc. 8:9-11).

104. Smith, "Gentiles," 194-99, 211. That the tension is defined often in relation to the powerful elite, as Stark and Bainbridge note, also applies in our case. One example of this could be the ambiguous issue of slavery. Whereas the Hasmoneans seem to have ignored or bypassed the biblical legislation concerning slaves, D displayed a concern atypical of its day. On the other hand, in the context of Roman Palestine, the Essene practice of not keeping slaves is shown in a different light. It is still regarded by Josephus as unusual, but also highly regarded. The dynamics of sectarianism is a crucial matter: tension has to be studied in its contemporary context and setting.

105. It is even possible that slaves were not part of the functional system of the "Damascus community." Evidence of this may be found in the instruction for the Examiner of the camp in CD 13.9-10. The *mebaqqer* is to have pity on the members of his congregation "like a father to his sons" and to "show concern (for them) in all their distress." Catherine Murphy discusses the meaning of this phrase and, based on a parallel in 4QInstructions[b] 2.1.1 4, argues that the member would "be freed from service to a master outside the community and enter the care of a new master, the Examiner." This freedom would have concerned a number of matters, including contract labour and slavery. See also Matthew J. Goff, *The Worldly and Heavenly Wisdom of 4QInstruction* (STDJ, 50; Leiden: E. J. Brill, 2003), 159-62, for the possible economic nature of the term "distress." Furthermore, according to CD 14.12-16, the members were obliged to give two days' wages to the Examiner and the judges in order to help the poor and needy and to support "the one imprisoned by a foreign people." This phrase may refer to cases in which an Israelite would have sold himself into debt slavery (Catherine M. Murphy, *Wealth in the Dead Sea Scrolls and in the Qumran Community* [STDJ, 40; Leiden: E. J. Brill, 2002], 40-44, 83-84 n. 156).

106. Interestingly, the attitude of the *maskil* should, according to 1QS 9.21-23, be like that of a slave, who leaves "goods and hand-made items" to his master. The context suggests that the *maskil* should not openly show his hatred towards the "men of the pit," until the day of vengeance. This metaphor suggests that slavery was by no means strange to the S community either.

107. In addition, CD 11.14-15 prohibits resting near gentiles on the Sabbath; CD 12.8b-11 bans the sale of slaves to gentiles; CD 12.6-8 aims at protecting the life and property of gentiles.

108. Murphy, *Wealth*, 97-99, 120-30.

109. Another rule requires that a member refunds what he has wasted of communal property (1QS 7.6). Schiffman explains that the system was a two-tiered economic system in which members made their property available to the community while not surrendering it (*Reclaiming*, 110).

110. CD 13.14: "None of those who have entered the covenant of God shall buy or sell to the sons of dawn; rather, [let them give] from hand-to-hand." However, the reading בני השחר is uncertain. Textually, the reading בני השחת, "the sons of the pit," is also possible. In its favour, see Charlotte Hempel ("The Community and its Rivals According to the *Community Rule* from Caves 1 and 4," *RdQ* 81 [2003]: 47-81 [66-67]). We agree with Joseph Baumgarten ("Damascus Document [CD]," 55 n. 203; ibid, "The 'Sons of Dawn' in *CDC* 13:14-15 and the Ban on Commerce among the Essenes," *IEJ* 33 [1983]: 81-85) that the expression "Sons of Dawn" refers to members rather than novices (Stephen Pfann argues for novices in "Sons of Dawn," in Schiffman and VanderKam, *Encyclopedia of the Dead Sea Scrolls*, II, 891.

111. Murphy, *Wealth*, 162.

112. See Murphy, *Wealth*, 40-44 for the economical nature of this statement. Nevertheless, the passage is likely to refer to the welfare of the inside members. In particular, the reference to "the association" or "communal house" in 14.16 suggests that this is an internal charity system.

113. Murphy, *Wealth*, 141-43.

114. For defilement of the Temple, see CD 4.17-18; 5.6-7. CD 6.11-14 indicates that only those who observe the Torah correctly will not "light his altar in vain"; see Philip Davies, "The Judaism(s) of the Damascus Document," 34-35. Davies argues that the "Damascus sect" used the Temple to a limited extent ("The 'Damascus Sect,'" 79; "The Ideology of the Temple in the Damascus Document," *JJS* 33 [1982]: Essays in Honour of Yigael Yadin: 287-301).

115. See, e.g., discussion by Joseph Baumgarten about 4QD^a 11.1-5 and the punishments of the community replacing the sacrifices ("A 'Scriptural' Citation in 4Q Fragments of the Damascus Document," *JJS* 43 [1992]: 95-97).

116. However, it remains true that, as this attitude did not result in total rejection of the Temple, the tension can be seen lower in this respect.

BIBLIOGRAPHY

Alexander, P., and G. Vermes. *Qumran Cave 4 XIX: 4QSerekh Ha-Yahad*. DJD, 26; Oxford: Clarendon Press, 1998.

Avemarie, Friederich. " 'Tohorat Ha-rabbim' and 'Mashqeh Ha-rabbim': Jacob Licht Reconsidered." In Bernstein *et al.*, *Legal Texts and Legal Issues*: 215-29.

Baumgarten, Albert I. "Rule of the Martian as Applied to Qumran." *IOS* XIV (1994): 121-42.

—*The Flourishing of Jewish Sects in the Maccabean Era: An Interpretation*. JSJSup, 55; Leiden: E. J. Brill, 1997.

—"Finding Oneself in a Sectarian Context: A Sectarian's Food and its Implications." In A. I. Baumgarten, J. Assmann and G. G. Stroumsa, eds, *Self, Soul and Body in Religious Experience*: 125-47. Leiden: E. J. Brill, 1998.

Baumgarten, Joseph M. *Studies in Qumran Law*. Studies in Judaism in Late Antiquity, 24; Leiden: E. J. Brill, 1977.

— "The Pharisaic-Sadducean Controversies about Purity." *JJS* 3 (1980): 157-70.

—"The 'Sons of Dawn' in CDC 13:14-15 and the Ban on Commerce among the Essenes," *IEJ* 33 (1983): 81-85.

—"A 'Scriptural' Citation in 4Q Fragments of the Damascus Document." *JJS* 43 (1992): 95-98.

—"The Cave 4 Versions of the Qumran Penal Code," *JJS* 43.2 (1992): 268-76.

—*Qumran Cave 4 XII: The Damascus Document (4Q266–4Q273)*. DJD, 18; Oxford: Claren-don Press, 1996.

Baumgarten, Joseph M., Esther G. Chazon and Avital Pinnick, eds. *The Damascus Document: A Centennial of Discovery. Proceedings of the Third International Symposium of the Orion Center for the Study of the Dead Sea Scrolls and Associated Literature, 4-8 February, 1998*. STDJ, 34; Leiden: E. J. Brill, 2000.

Baumgarten, Joseph M., and Daniel R. Schwartz. "Damascus Document [CD]." In James H. Charlesworth *et al.*, eds, *The Dead Sea Scrolls: Hebrew, Aramaic and Greek Texts with English Translations*. II. *Damascus Document, War Scroll, and Related Documents*: 4-57 Tübingen: J. C. B. Mohr, 1995.

Bernstein, Moshe, Florentino García Martínez and John Kampen, eds. *Legal Texts and Legal Issues: Proceedings of the Second Meeting of the International Organization for Qumran Studies, Cambridge 1995*. STDJ, 23; Leiden: E. J. Brill, 1997.

Callander, Dexter E., Jr. "Servants of God(s) and Servants of Kings in Israel and the Ancient Near East." *Semeia* 83/84 (1998): Slavery in Text and Interpretation: 67-82.

Chancey, Mark A. *The Myth of a Gentile Galilee*. Society for New Testament Studies Mono-graph Series, 118; Cambridge: Cambridge University Press, 2002.

Chirichigno, Gregory C. *Debt-Slavery in Israel and the Ancient Near East*. JSOTSup, 141; Sheffield: JSOT Press, 1993.

Collins, John J. "Forms of Community in the Dead Sea Scrolls." In Shalom M. Paul, Robert A. Kraft, Lawrence H. Schiffman and Weston W. Fields, eds, *Emanuel: Studies in Hebrew Bible, Septuagint, and Dead Sea Scrolls in Honor of Emanuel Tov*: 97-111. VTSup, 94; Leiden: E. J. Brill, 2003.

—"The Yaḥad and 'the Qumran Community.'" In Hempel and Lieu, *Biblical Traditions in Transmission*: 81-96.

Collins, Randall. "Book Review: A Theory of Religion." *JSSR* 32 (1993): 402-406.

Conway, Colleen M. "Toward a Well-Formed Subject: The Function of Purity Language in the Serek-ha-Yahad." *JSP* 21 (2000): 103-20.

Davies, Philip R. "The Ideology of the Temple in the Damascus Document." *JJS* 33 (1982) (Essays in Honour of Yigael Yadin): 287-301.

—*The Damascus Covenant: An Interpretation of the "Damascus Document."* JSOTSup, 25; Sheffield: JSOT Press, 1983.

—*Behind the Essenes: History and Ideology in the Dead Sea Scrolls*. BJS, 94; Atlanta, GA: Scholars Press (1987).

— "Communities at Qumran and the Case of the Missing 'Teacher.' " *RdQ* 15.57-58 (1991): 275-86.

— "The 'Damascus' Sect and Judaism." In John C. Reeves and John Kampen, eds, *Pursuing the Text: Studies in Honor of Ben Zion Wachholder on the Occasion of his Seventieth Birthday*: 70-84. JSOTSup, 184; Sheffield: Sheffield Academic Press, 1994.

—"The Judaism(s) of the Damascus Document." In Baumgarten *et al.*, *The Damascus Document*: 27-43.

Davis, Robert. "The History of the Composition of the 'Damascus Document' Statutes." PhD dissertation, Harvard University, 1992.

Dawson, Lorne L. "Creating 'Cult' Typologies: Some Strategic Considerations." *Journal of Contemporary Religion* 12.3 (1997): 363-81.

—*Comprehending Cults: The Sociology of New Religious Movements*. Oxford/New York: Oxford University Press, 1998.

Doering, Lutz, "Purity Regulations Concerning the Sabbath in the Dead Sea Scrolls and

Related Literature." In Lawrence Schiffman, Emanuel Tov and James VanderKam, eds, *The Dead Sea Scrolls Fifty Years after their Discovery: Proceedings of the Jerusalem Congress, July 20-25, 1997*: 600-609. Jerusalem: Israel Exploration Society in cooperation with the Shrine of the Book, Israel Museum, 2000.

Esler, Philip F. *The First Christians in their Social Worlds: Social-Scientific Approaches to New Testament Interpretation*. London: Routledge, 1994.

Fitzmyer, Joseph. "Divorce among First-Century Palestinian Jews." *ErIsr* 14 (1978): 106-10.

Frey, Jörg. "Different Patterns of Dualistic Thought in the Qumran Library: Reflections on their Background and History." In Bernstein *et al.*, *Legal Texts and Legal Issues*: 275-335.

García Martínez, Florentino, and Julio Trebolle Barrera. *The People of the Dead Sea Scrolls: Their Writings, Beliefs and Practices*. Trans. Wilfred G. E. Watson. Leiden: E. J. Brill, 1995.

Gellner, Ernest. "A Pendulum Swing Theory of Islam." In Roland Robertson, ed., *Sociology of Religion*: 127-39. New York: Penguin, 1969.

Goff, Matthew J. *The Worldly and Heavenly Wisdom of 4QInstruction*. STDJ, 50; Leiden: E. J. Brill, 2003.

Hamilton, Malcolm B. *The Sociology of Religion: Theoretical and Comparative Perspectives*. London: Routledge, 1995.

Hanson, K. C. "BTB Readers Guide: Kinship." *Biblical Theological Bulletin* 24 (1994): 183-94.

Harrington, Hannah K. *The Purity Texts*. Companion to the Qumran Scrolls, 5; London: T&T Clark International, 2004.

Hempel, Charlotte. "The Penal Code Reconsidered." In Bernstein *et al.*, *Legal Texts and Legal Issues*: 337-48.

—*The Laws of the Damascus Document: Sources, Tradition and Redaction*. Leiden: E. J. Brill, 1998.

— "Community Structures in the Dead Sea Scrolls: Admission, Organization, Disciplinary Procedures." In Peter W. Flint and James C. VanderKam, eds, *The Dead Sea Scrolls after Fifty Years: A Comprehensive Assessment*: II, 67-92. Leiden: E. J. Brill, 1999.

—*The Damascus Texts*. Companion to the Qumran Scrolls, 1; Sheffield: Sheffield Academic Press, 2000.

— "The Community and its Rivals According to the 'Community Rule' from Caves 1 and 4." *RdQ* 81 (2003): 47-81.

Hempel, C., and Judith M. Lieu, eds. *Biblical Traditions in Transmission: Essays in Honour of Michael A. Knibb*. JSJSup, 111; Leiden: E. J. Brill, 2006.

Ilan, Tal. *Jewish Women in Greco-Roman Palestine: An Inquiry into Image and Status*. Peabody, MA: Hendrickson, 1995.

Jokiranta, Jutta. " 'Sectarianism' of the Qumran 'Sect': Sociological Notes." *RQ* 78.20 (2001): 223-39.

Kister, Menahem. "Notes on Some New Texts from Qumran." *JJS* 44 (1993): 280-90.

Klawans, Jonathan. "The Impurity of Immorality in Ancient Judaism." *JJS* 48 (1997): 1-16.

Knibb, Michael. "Community Organization in the Damascus Document." In Schiffman and VanderKam, *Encyclopedia of the Dead Sea Scrolls*: I, 136-38.

Lange, Armin. *Weisheit und Prädestination: Weisheitliche Urordnung und Prädestination in den Textfunden von Qumran*. STDJ, 18; Leiden: E. J. Brill, 1995.

Licht, Jacob. "Some Terms and Concepts of Ritual Purity in the Qumran Writings." In J. M. Grintz and J. Liver, eds, *Studies in the Bible Presented to Professor M. H. Segal*: 300–309.

Publications of the Israel Society for Biblical Research, 17; Jerusalem: Kiryat Sepher, 1964.

—*The Rule Scroll: A Scroll from the Wilderness of Judaea: 1QS, 1QSa, 1QSb, Text, Introduction, and Commentary.* Jerusalem: Bialik Institute [Hebrew], 1965.

Lieberman, Saul. "The Discipline in the So-Called Dead Sea Manual of Discipline." *JBL* 71 (1951): 199-206.

Lim, Timothy H., Larry W. Hurtado, A. Graeme Auld and Alison Jack, eds. *The Dead Sea Scrolls in their Historical Context.* Edinburgh: T&T Clark, 2000.

Luomanen, Petri. "The 'Sociology of Sectarianism' in Matthew: Modeling the Genesis of Early Jewish and Christian Communities." In Christopher Tuckett, Ismo Dunderberg and Kari Syreeni, eds, *Fair Play: Diversity and Conflicts in Early Christianity. Essays in Honour of Heikki Räisänen*: 107-30. Leiden: E. J. Brill, 2002.

Magness, Jodi. *The Archaeology of Qumran and the Dead Sea Scrolls.* Grand Rapids, MI: Eerdmans, 2002.

Martens, John. "A Sectarian Analysis of the Damascus Document." In Simcha Fishbane and Jack Lightstone, eds, *Essays in Social Scientific Study of Judaism and Jewish Society*: 27-46. Canada-Israel Conference on the Social Scientific Study of Judaism; Concordia University, 1990.

Martin, Dale B. "Slavery and the Ancient Jewish Family." In Shaye J. D. Cohen, ed., *The Jewish Family in Antiquity*: 113-29. Brown Judaic Studies, 289; Atlanta, GA: Scholars Press, 1993.

McGuire, Meredith B. *Religion in Social Context.* Belmont: Wadsworth, 4th edn, 1997.

Metso, Sarianna. "The Relationship between the Damascus Document and the Community Rule." In Baumgarten *et al.*, *The Damascus Document*: 85-93.

—*The Textual Development of the Qumran Community Rule.* STDJ, 21; Leiden: E. J. Brill, 1997a.

—"The Textual Traditions of the Qumran Community Rule." In Bernstein *et al.*, *Legal Texts and Legal Issues*: 141-47.

—"Whom Does the Term Yaḥad Identify?" In Hempel and Lieu, *Biblical Traditions in Transmission*: 213-35.

Milgrom, Jacob. "The Scriptural Foundations and Deviations in the Laws of Purity of the Temple Scroll." In Lawrence Schiffman, ed., *Archaeology and History in the Dead Sea Scrolls: The New York University Conference in Memory of Yigal Yadin*: 83-99. JSPSup, 8; Sheffield: JSOT Press, 1990.

Murphy, Catherine M. *Wealth in the Dead Sea Scrolls and in the Qumran Community.* STDJ, 40; Leiden: E. J. Brill, 2002.

Murphy-O'Connor, Jerome. "An Essene Missionary Document? CD II,14–VI, 1." *RB* 77 (1970): 201-29.

Newsom, Carol A. *The Self as Symbolic Space: Constructing Identity and Community at Qumran.* STDJ, 52; Leiden: E. J. Brill, 2004.

Pfann, Steven. "Sons of Dawn." In Schiffman and VanderKam, *Encyclopedia of the Dead Sea Scrolls*: II, 891.

Qimron, Elisha. "The Text of CDC." In Magen Broshi, ed., *The Damascus Document Reconsidered*: 9-49. Jerusalem: The Israel Exploration Society, 1992.

Qimron, Elisha, and J. H. Charlesworth. "Rule of the Community (1QS)." In James H. Charlesworth, F. M. Cross, J. Milgrom, E. Qimron, L. H. Schiffman, L. T. Stuckenbruck and R. E. Whitaker, eds, *The Dead Sea Scrolls. Hebrew, Aramaic, and Greek Texts with English Translations*. I. *Rule of the Community and Related Documents*: 1-51. Tübingen: J. C. B. Mohr, 1994.

Regev, Eyal. "The Idea of Non-Priestly Purity in Ancient Judaism." *JJS* 31 (2000): 176-202.

— "Comparing Sectarian Practice and Organization: The Qumran Sects in Light of the Regulations of the Shakers, Hutterites, Mennonites and Amish." *Numen* 51.2 (2004): 146-81.

—"The *Yahad* and the *Damascus Covenant*: Structure, Organization and Relationship." *RdQ* 82 (2003): 233-62.

Reich, Ronny. "The Hot Bath-House (balneum) the Miqweh and the Jewish Community in the Second Temple Period." *JJS* 39.1 (1988): 102-107.

Roberts, Keith. *Religion in Sociological Perspective*. Belmont, CA: Wadsworth, 1990.

Robertson, Ronald. *The Sociological Interpretation of Religion*. Oxford: Basil Blackwell, 1972.

Rosso Ubigli, Lilliana. "Il Documento Di Damasco e L'Etica Coniugale: A Proposito di un Nuovo Passo Qumranico." *Henoch* 14 (1992): 3-10.

Saldarini, Anthony J. "Sectarianism." In Schiffman and VanderKam, *Encyclopedia of the Dead Sea Scrolls*: II, 853-57.

Sanders, E. P. *Jewish Law from Jesus to the Mishnah*. London: SCM Press, 1990.

—*Judaism: Practice and Belief 63 BCE–66 CE*. London: SCM Press, 1992.

— "The Dead Sea Sect and Other Jews: Commonalities, Overlaps and Differences." In Lim et al., *The Dead Sea Scrolls in their Historical Context*: 7-43.

Schiffman, Lawrence H. "Legislation Concerning Relations with Non-Jews in the Zadokite Fragments and in Tannaitic Literature." *RdQ* 43 (1983): 379-89.

—*Reclaiming the Dead Sea Scrolls: The History of Judaism, the Background of Christianity, the Lost Library of Qumran*. Philadelphia: The Jewish Publication Society, 1994a.

—"Pharisaic and Sadducean Halakhah." *DSD* 3 (1994b): 285-99.

—"Halakhah and Sectarianism in the Dead Sea Scrolls." In Lim et al., *The Dead Sea Scrolls in their Historical Context*: 123-42.

Schiffman, L., and J. VanderKam, eds. *Encyclopedia of the Dead Sea Scrolls*. New York: Oxford University Press, 2000.

Schremer, Adiel. "Qumran Polemic on Marital Law: CD 4:20–5:11 and its Social Background." In Baumgarten et al., *The Damascus Document*: 147-60.

Simpson, John H. "The Stark-Bainbridge Theory of Religion." *JSSR* 29 (1990): 367-71.

Smith, Morton. "The Gentiles in Judaism 125 BCE–CE 66." In William Horbury, W. D. Davies and John Sturdy, eds, *The Cambridge History of Judaism*. III. *The Early Roman Period*: 192-266. Cambridge: Cambridge University Press, 1999.

Stark, Rodney, and William Sims Bainbridge. *The Future of Religion: Secularization, Revival and Cult Formation*. Berkeley, CA: University of California Press, 1985.

—*A Theory of Religion*. Toronto Studies in Religion, 2; New York: Peter Lang, in association with the Centre of Religious Studies at the University of Toronto, 1987.

Vermes, Geza. "Sectarian Matrimonial Halakhah in the Damascus Rule." *JJS* 25 (1974): 197-202.

Walker-Ramisch, Sandra. "Graeco-Roman Voluntary Associations and the Damascus Document: A Sociological Analysis." In John S. Kloppenborg and Stephen G. Wilson, eds. *Voluntary Associations in the Graeco-Roman World*: 128-45. London: Routledge, 1996.

Wallis, Roy. "The Cult and its Transformation." In Roy Wallis, ed., *Sectarianism: Analyses of Religious and Non-Religious Sects*: 35-49. Contemporary Issues Series, 10; London: Peter Owen, 1975.

Wassen, Cecilia. *Women in the Damascus Document*. Society of Biblical Literature Academia Biblica Series, 21; Atlanta, GA: SBL Publications/Leiden: E. J. Brill, 2005.

Wilson, Bryan R. *Religious Sects: A Sociological Study.* New York: McGraw-Hill, 1970.

—*Magic and the Millennium: A Sociological Study of Religious Movements of Protest among Tribal and Third-World Peoples.* London: Heinemann, 1973.

—*Religion in Sociological Perspective.* Oxford: Oxford University Press, 1982.

—*The Social Dimensions of Sectarianism: Sects and New Religious Movements in Contemporary Society.* Oxford: Clarendon Press, 1990.

Wright, Benjamin G., III. " 's *Ebed/Doulos*: Terms and Social Status in the Meeting of Hebrew Biblical and Hellenistic Culture." *Semeia* 83/84 (1998): Slavery in Text and Interpretation: 83-111.

Information Processing in Ancient Jewish Groups

Albert I. Baumgarten

> Any fruit, even a lemon
> Must have a beautiful rind
> But if this lemon's a lemon
> It's a scholar's prerogative to change her (his) mind
> (With apologies to Johnny Mercer)[1]

When we lived in Canada I was a member of the Education Committee of the school my children attended. My responsibilities included interviewing candidates for teaching positions and over the years I must have met dozens of teachers. I developed a standard question that I asked of them all. It had a double virtue: it was one for which no one seemed to have a canned answer, hence it allowed committee members to see the candidate thinking on his/her feet. Second, the way the candidate framed the answer told us a good deal about that person, much more than the reply to usual questions. My question was: tell me about your successes and your failures, with special emphasis on the failures, rather than the successes.

In this chapter I want to take up the challenge of answering my own question. At conferences and in published papers we rarely present our failures, only what we believe to be our successes (how we feel after the discussion of our paper is another matter). And yet, our failures have a lot to teach us.[2] Why do we consider certain ideas successes and others failures? What distinguishes a success from a failure? What, if anything, can we learn from our failures? Why does someone – the same scholar, working with the same tools at resolving the same questions – succeed at times, fail at others? These are only a few of the issues raised by a willingness to discuss failures candidly. Accordingly I would like to devote this paper to a consideration of an idea that did not work out as I had hoped it would, and contrast that failure with what I believe to have been more successful efforts. The larger context is my efforts, now almost over two decades, to enhance the understanding of ancient Jewish groups with the help of the social sciences. Specifically, I would like to begin by discussing "Information Processing in Ancient Jewish

Groups," the topic originally announced as the subject of my presentation at the conference in Groningen.

There are a number of different ways of characterizing movements, by their openness to or withdrawal from the larger world, or by asking what sorts of behaviour they consider risky, to name but two of many examples. Information processing is another way. How is information processed in a particular movement? Who has access to information? Who controls its diffusion? Who is allowed to know which things, and who is forbidden? Who are reliable as opposed to illicit or discredited sources of information? These are among the questions one should ask when trying to understand the dynamics of a group. In order to achieve a fully significant appreciation of the patterns of information processing in any particular group, its answer should also be compared to that of others at their time and place, as the features of one particular answer are often clearest only when compared to others. Ultimately, the effort is worth the trouble, as it is by means of information processing that groups create their specific definition of truth and falsehood, at times very different from the definitions held by others and extra-ordinarily immune to refutation.

The analysis of information processing has been proposed as a window of insight into modern enclaves by Douglas and Mars.[3] Building on prior work on enclaves by Douglas and others,[4] Douglas and Mars propose to track the trajectory of enclaves at crucial turning points such as the death of the founder or the transition from first to second generation with the assistance of a focus on information processing. As the insights of Douglas and other cultural theorists into enclaves were a significant source of inspiration in my previous work on ancient Jewish sectarianism[5] it seemed natural to see how much better one could understand the ancient Jewish evidence with the assistance of a focus on information processing in enclaves.

The results thus far, unfortunately, are meagre. In marked contrast to my previous attempts to explain ancient Jewish sects better with the assistance of the social sciences, in this case little that was not unknown or poorly understood before is now clearer. Yes, CD has regulations that place control of instruction in the hands of the sectarian leadership, as many of the roles traditionally the province of parents are transferred from the biological parent to the sectarian "father." Discussing these texts from the perspective of the shift of loyalty from biological family to sectarian "brothers" is significantly insightful. The additional vantage point of information processing adds only a little extra. Having discussed these passages in the past, I would have little to add were I to rewrite that article to take account of the perspective of information processing.[6]

An Essene, according to Josephus, had numerous obligations. Some of these concern information processing. Thus, an Essene was sworn not to reveal certain secrets to outsiders (*War* 2.141-42). Here too, the perspective of information processing adds little extra value, as the fear being faced in this regulation was that members would clone the movement, a point that has been recognized for some time. On a parallel line, Essenes were expected to expose liars and conceal nothing from other members of the sect (*War* 2.141). This turned every Essene into a permanent spy on the activities of fellow Essenes. I presume that this information was used by the leadership to control the lives of members and punish offenders. In previous work I discussed this aspect of the movement in light of the regulations of other voluntary groups, and as an effective consequence of the voluntary nature of these groups. In particular I compared the Essenes to the Epicureans, as analyzed by De Witt.[7] As Epicureans formulated their rules, it was considered a mark of genuine friendship to report an "evil friend and a friend to evil" to the authorities. Failure to do so was serious. The environment was such that even seniors had to accept "constructive criticism" from their inferiors. I know of at least one other instance of spying as a means of control in a voluntary group: Shakers were encouraged to report misdeeds that required the purge of confession.[8] Unfortunately, the perspective of information processing adds little to understanding these cases over what I offered previously.

One well-known text describes the establishing of Rabbinic authority in the aftermath of the Bar Kochba revolt (135 CE).

> At the end of the great persecution our teachers met together at Usha, namely, R. Judah and R. Nehemiah, R. Meir, R. Yosi, R. Simon b. Yohai, R. Eliezer son of R. Yosi the Galilean, and R. Eliezer b. Jacob. They sent to the elders of the Galilee saying: "Whoever has learnt, let him come and teach, and whoever has not learnt, let him come and learn." They came together, taught and studied, and took all the necessary steps (*CantR* 2.5).[9]

This passage may be profitably considered from the angle of information processing. The invitation to meet at Usha supposedly was formulated as addressed to all who could teach and to all who wanted to learn. Students and teachers met at Usha, each side fulfilling its role, so that the goal of instruction and learning was perfectly met. To what extent is this account idealized? Was the Rabbinic movement always characterized by this degree of openness in exchange of information? These seem useful questions to ask, as part of the comparison of ideal to reality as lived, but the Rabbinic movement was a successor to the sectarianism of the Second Temple era. If anything, its professed attitude to information processing as expressed in the passage just cited was open and free, unlike the pattern expected in a sect. Rabbinic attitudes towards information processing may be one aspect among others of the contrast between Rabbinic Judaism and the experience of Jewish sectarianism pre 70 CE. These attitudes may also be connected with an important contrast between the Jewish world before and after the destruction. Before 70 CE legal disagreement had important social consequences, while in the world of the Rabbis legal disagreements abounded, but seemed to have lost their social sting. Authorities who disagreed with each other seemed to have found it easier to agree to disagree.[10] And yet, while investigation of information processing in the world of the Rabbis is a topic worth pursuing it lies outside investigations of the nature of Second Temple sectarianism. Pursuit of the Rabbinic aspects of information processing is thus, at best, an unintended beneficial consequence of asking about the nature of information processing among ancient Jews.[11] As useful as it may be to have our eyes opened to the new topic, turning to the Rabbis is a sign of failure of the approach to enlighten us concerning the sects of the Second Temple period.

A Contrasting Success Story

It is easy to blame our sparse evidence for the Second Temple era for the lack of success this time round, but that is too easy an excuse. The evidence is equally fragmentary when asking about the replacement of biological family by sectarian brotherhood among the Second Temple groups. Yet, after an initial insight that allowed better comprehension of Josephus's remark concerning the Essenes that they can give charity to people in need as they see fit, but assistance to relatives requires the permission of the leaders of the group (*War* 2.134), numerous other pieces fell into place. The terms employed by several groups to call their members brothers, as well as the features of the cemetery at Qumran now became clearer.[12]

Failure and Success from a Philosophical Perspective

According to Lakatos a scientific research program will often overlook inconsistencies and anomalies that might seem to challenge it. At some later point in the life of that program these overlooked matters will be taken up and explained, but until then they pose no bar to continued work under the auspices of that program. For Lakatos, the real challenge to any program comes not from falsifications but from other programs. The competition is which program can more fully explain what is known, while predicting and successfully illuminating what will first be known in the future. Victory of one program over another may not be clear for a generation or more. During that time both programs will continue to generate meaningful work; neither will be discarded.[13] The key to success or failure, only to be known in the future, is which program will predict and successfully illuminate what will first be known in the future. This criterion is formulated in terms appropriate to the natural sciences, but it has its equivalent in the human sciences. All concepts are limited to some extent by the examples on which they were based, yet an idea that can explain as many cases as possible, over and above those on which the idea was based, has achieved meaningful success. Yet, even following Lakatos, what can one say about a research approach that does not achieve minimal success? The intuitive sense that an idea that can illuminate many examples is more powerful than an idea can only explain a few is also good philosophy.

Why We Often Fail in Applying the Social Sciences to Movements in the Past

The nature of history is such that one should not expect too high a rate of success in applying ideas from the social sciences to the study of the past. This connection between past and present is one of the continuing themes in the work of many historians, including one of the giants of the twentieth century, Christopher Hill:

> That is why history has to be rewritten in each generation; each new act in the human drama necessarily shifts our attitude towards the earlier acts... We ourselves are shaped by the past; but from our vantage point in the present we are continually reshaping that past which shapes us.[14]

History is what interests people of the present in the past. Anachronisms and misunderstandings lurk at every turn in such an effort. Much of what will be written will be the intellectual boilerplate of one generation to be questioned and rejected immediately by the next. Few works will overcome the numerous handicaps inherent in the process, and will attain the status of longer term contributions to the discipline, but some do.

Yet, if history is what interests the people of one time in the lives of their predecessors then employing the insights of the social sciences is one way to ask new questions about the past in doing history. And yet, the context on which these social-scientific studies are based is very different than the world of the past that a historian might seek to understand with the assistance of the social-scientific perspectives. I therefore suggest that some degree of eclecticism in taking up social-scientific ideas for analysis of the past is inevitable, maybe even desirable. The fit between the two will never be perfect. Some aspects of the social-scientific theory will prove beneficial for history, others will not. Those circumstances are effective acknowledgement that notions based on such a different world cannot be transferred whole to another time and place. Eclecticism in employing social-scientific insights in writing history, as I see it, is not a flaw, a sign of inconsistency and sloppy thinking. It is not evidence of being misled by superficial similarities that fade on closer analysis. Rather it is a sign of genuine appreciation of difference between the two things being compared, between the source of insight and its application to new material. Indeed, if a historian ever claimed to have found a perfectly consistent and thorough point-by-point equivalence between some historical data and a social-scientific model I would take that claim as evidence of history gone awry, that has overlooked important differences.[15]

Perhaps the best way to put this point is to return to Christopher Hill's thoughts on writing history, as expressed in his last published substantial work, the crowning achievement of a lifetime of study, on the role of the English Bible in the seventeenth-century revolution. Hill compared history and poetry, citing T. S. Eliot:

> A poet's mind...is constantly amalgamating disparate experience. The ordinary man...falls in love, or reads Spinoza, and these two experiences have to do with each other, or with the noise of the typewriter or the smell of cooking: in the mind of the poet these experiences are always forming new wholes.[16]

The amalgamations that interest Hill cross a range of sources of different types (ballads, plays, pamphlets, etc.). They include a focus on many social groups (alchemists, astrologers, bishops and rioters, males as well as females, for example). The disciplines to be employed are those of political history, social analysis and literary criticism. Is it possible to work in this way without some degree of eclecticism? A new whole constructed from such disparate experiences is inevitably eclectic in its origins and based on partial overlaps. And yet, if the effort is successful those experiences that began with no connection to each other become parts of a new whole, thus overcoming the stigma of eclecticism that might attach to the effort if it had not been successful.

I conclude this section with the statement of the anthropologist, Clifford Geertz, also taking a comment of T. S. Eliot as his point of departure:

"Bad poets borrow," T. S. Eliot has said, "good poets steal." I have tried in what follows to be, in this respect anyway, a good poet, and to take what I have needed from certain others and make it shamelessly my own. But such thievery is in great part general and undefined, an almost unconscious process of selection, absorption and reworking, so that after a while one no longer quite knows where one's argument comes from, how much of it is his and how much is others.[17]

Both history and anthropology begin as "eclectic," yet (at their best) fusing their several points of departure into a new creation, that illuminates experience in hitherto unknown ways.[18] Along the way, in such an eclectic enterprise, some percentage of failures is inevitable, perhaps even desirable.

Lemons into Lemonade

What can unsuccessful attempts, such as mine concerning information processing, teach us? When comparing an unsuccessful attempt with another that yielded a more productive result one needs to learn why one effort succeeded while the other did not. What about the nature of the evidence might help explain the different result?

Jewish Second Temple sects were relatively small, based on a small segment of the population as a whole. They were based on an educated elite, as opposed to the mass movements of lower-class origins and educational level typical of many modern groups. Some of the most extreme ancient communities, such as at Qumran, were places where everyone knew each other. They had a strong egalitarian streak. If the explanation of several difficult passages in 1QS and the parallel fragments from Cave Four that I proposed is accepted there was a period with a strong sense of *communitas* at one of the earlier phases in the history of the group.[19] I suggest that these might be the reasons that information processing was not as tightly controlled in ancient Jewish groups, such as the Qumran community, as one might expect based on the experience of modern enclaves. The relative failure of an approach based on information processing to yield significant insights into Second Temple groups is thus a reminder of difference between them and the sects of modern times.

Endnotes

1. "A Woman's Prerogative"; Lyrics – Johnny Mercer, Music – Harold Arlen. St Louis Woman, 1946.

2. The great Rabbinic scholar, Professor Saul Lieberman, suggested that on the occasion of reaching mature old age, say eighty, when a Jubilee Volume might be

planned, the honoree him/herself should publish a volume of corrections of ideas proposed that were wrong, and that should be withdrawn as a result of more mature reflection. Many would rush to read such a volume, Lieberman concluded. Lieberman then offered a series of corrections to suggestions he had made in the past. See S. Lieberman, "Divrey Siyyum," *Mehkarim ba-sifrut ha-Talmudit: yom `iyun le-regel melot shemonim shanah le-Sha'ul Liberman 8-9 be-Sivan 5738* (Jerusalem: National Academy of Sciences, 1983 [Hebrew]), 225-28. On Lieberman's willingness to acknowledge and then correct his own errors see also M. Bar Ilan, "Saul Lieberman: The Greatest Sage in Israel," in M. Lubetski, (ed.), *Saul Lieberman (1898–1983), Talmudic Scholar* (Lewiston, NY, and Lampeter: Edwin Mellen Press, 2002), 82-87.

3. M. Douglas and G. Mars, "Terrorism: A Positive Feedback Game," *Human Relations* 56 (2003): 763-86.

4. M. Douglas, *In The Wilderness: The Doctrine of Defilement in the Book of Numbers* (Sheffield: Sheffield Academic Press, 1993), 42-62; E. Sivan, "Enclave Culture," in G. Almond, R. S. Appleby and E. Sivan, (eds), *Strong Religion* (Chicago and London: University of Chicago Press, 2003), 1-89.

5. See A. I. Baumgarten, *The Flourishing of Jewish Sects in the Maccabean Era: An Interpretation* (JSJSup, 55; Leiden: E. J. Brill, 1997).

6. See A. I. Baumgarten, "The Perception of the Past in the Damascus Document," in J. M. Baumgarten, E. G. Chazon and A. Pinnick, (eds), *The Damascus Document: A Centennial of Discovery. Proceedings of the Third International Symposium of the Orion Center for the Study of the Dead Sea Scrolls and Associated Literature 1998* (Leiden: E. J. Brill, 2000), 1-15.

7. See Baumgarten, *Flourishing of Jewish Sects*, 110-12; N. De Witt, "Organization and Procedure in Epicurean Groups," *Classical Philology* 31 (1936): 206-207.

8. See L. Coser, *Greedy Institutions: Patterns of Undivided Commutment* (New York: Free Press; London: Collier Macmillan, 1974), 145-46.

9. For the end of this passage I follow the readings of MSS. Vat. 76 and 249, rather than that of the *editio princeps*.

10. See further A. I. Baumgarten, " 'But Touch the Law and the Sect Will Split': Legal Dispute as the Cause of Sectarian Schism," *The Review of Rabbinic Judaism* 5 (2002): 301-15.

11. If one were to investigate this question seriously there would be much to learn from C. Hezser, *The Social Structure of the Rabbinic Movement in Roman Palestine* (Tübingen: Mohr Siebeck, 1997). Much of the data and analysis she presents would need to be reformulated only slightly to focus the inquiry on the issue of information processing.

12. See further A. I. Baumgarten, *Second Temple Sectarianism – A Social and Religious Historical Essay* (Tel Aviv: Israel Ministry of Defence, 2001 [Hebrew]), 21-32.

13. I. Lakatos, *The Methodology of Scientific Research Programmes: Philosophical Papers* (ed. J. Worrall and G. Currie; Cambridge and New York: Cambridge University Press, 1978), I, esp. 33-36.

14. C. Hill, *Change and Continuity in 17th Century England* (New Haven, CT, and London: Yale University Press, 1991), 284.

15. My argument in this paragraph derives important inspiration from the essay by W. Doniger, "Post-modern and –colonial –structural Comparisons," in K. C. Patton

and B. C. Ray, (eds), *A Magic Still Dwells: Comparative Religion in the Postmodern Age* (Berkeley, CA, and London: University of California Press, 2000), 63-76.

16. T. S. Eliot, *Selected Essays* (1932), 287, as cited by C. Hill, *The English Bible and the Seventeenth Century Revolution* (London: Allen Lane, 1993), 437.

17. C. Geertz, *Islam Observed: Religious Development in Morocco and Indonesia* (Chicago and London: University of Chicago Press, 1968), ix.

18. It is for this reason that I disagree with the arguments of P. Buc, *The Dangers of Ritual* (Princeton, NJ: Princeton University Press, 2001). For a further evaluation of Buc's essay, from a perspective different than mine above, see A. Walsham, "The Dangers of Ritual," *Past and Present* 180 (2003): 277-87. For example, both Walsham and I find Buc nihilistic, but for somewhat different reasons. Walsham finds Buc nihilistic because: (1) according to Buc one may only employ analytic tools based on the "native" culture to understand it. One may not think thoughts the subjects would not have understood. (2) Yet, at the same time, if the analytic concepts employed are too close to that of the world of the subjects (the fatal flaw of social scientific notions, as Buc's reconstruction of the history of these disciplines is intended to show) then the results are seductively circular but likely meaningless. The same thing is being used to explain itself, and while equation is interesting it is far from explanation. If Buc's limitations are accepted, as Walsham notes, no explanation is ever possible, and thus she rightly accuses Buc of nihilism.

19. A. I. Baumgarten, "The Zadokite Priests at Qumran: A Reconsideration," *Dead Sea Discoveries* 4 (1997): 137-56.

BIBLIOGRAPHY

Baumgarten, A.I. "The Zadokite Priests at Qumran: A Reconsideration." *Dead Sea Discoveries* 4 (1997a): 137-56.
—*The Flourishing of Jewish Sects in the Maccabean Era: An Interpretation.* JSJSup, 55; Leiden: E. J. Brill, 1997b.
— "The Perception of the Past in the Damascus Document." In J. M. Baumgarten, E. G. Chazon and A. Pinnick, eds, *The Damascus Document: A Centennial of Discovery. Proceedings of the Third International Symposium of the Orion Center for the Study of the Dead Sea Scrolls and Associated Literature 1998*: 1-15. Leiden: E. J. Brill, 2000.
—*Second Temple Sectarianism – a Social and Religious Historical Essay.* Tel Aviv: Israel Ministry of Defence, 2001 [Hebrew].
— " 'But Touch the Law and the Sect Will Split': Legal Dispute as the Cause of Sectarian Schism." *The Review of Rabbinic Judaism* 5 (2002): 301-15.
Bar Ilan, M. "Saul Lieberman: The Greatest Sage in Israel." In M. Lubetski, ed., *Saul Lieberman, (1898–1983), Talmudic Scholar*: 82-87. Lewiston, NY and Lampeter: Edwin Mellen Press, 2002.
Buc, P. *The Dangers of Ritual.* Princeton, NJ: Princeton University Press, 2001.
Coser, L. *Greedy Institutions: Patterns of Undivided Commitment.* New York: Free Press/ London: Collier Macmillan, 1974.
De Witt, N. "Organization and Procedure in Epicurean Groups." *Classical Philology* 31 (1936): 205-11.
Doniger, W. "Post-modern and -colonial -structural Comparisons." In K. C. Patton and B. C. Ray, eds, *A Magic Still Dwells: Comparative Religion in the Postmodern Age*: 63-76. Berkeley, CA, and London: University of California Press, 2000.

Douglas M., and G. Mars. "Terrorism: A Positive Feedback Game." *Human Relations* 56 (2003): 763-86.

Douglas, M. *In The Wilderness: The Doctrine of Defilement in the Book of Numbers*. Sheffield: Sheffield Academic Press, 1993.

Geertz, C. *Islam Observed: Religious Development in Morocco and Indonesia*. Chicago and London: University of Chicago Press, 1968.

Hezser, C. *The Social Structure of the Rabbinic Movement in Roman Palestine*. Tübingen: Mohr Siebeck, 1997.

Hill, C. *Change and Continuity in 17th Century England*. New Haven, CT, and London: Yale University Press, 1991 [first published London: Weidenfeld & Nicholson, 1974).

— *The English Bible and the Seventeenth Century Revolution*. London: Allen Lane, 1993.

Lakatos, I. *The Methodology of Scientific Research Programmes: Philosophical Papers*, Vol. 1. Ed. J. Worrall and G. Currie. Cambridge and New York: Cambridge University Press, 1978.

Lieberman, S. "Divrey Siyyum," *Mehkarim ba-sifrut ha-Talmudit: yom `iyun le-regel melot shemonim shanah le-Sha'ul Liberman 8-9 be-Sivan 5738*: 225-28. Jerusalem: National Academy of Sciences, 1983 [Hebrew].

Sivan, E. "Enclave Culture." In G. Almond, R. S. Appleby and E. Sivan, eds, *Strong Religion*: 1-89. Chicago and London: University of Chicago Press, 2003.

Walsham, A. "The Dangers of Ritual." *Past and Present* 180 (2003): 277-87.

INDEX OF AUTHORS

Roberts, K. 230
Robertson, R. 197, 229, 232
Rofé, A. 172
Rostovtzeff, M. 173

Sacchi, P. 163, 171
Saldarini, A. J. 156, 166, 169-71, 206, 226
Salkin, J. K. 173
Sandall, R. 197
Sanders, E. P. 127, 141, 170, 171, 226,
    232-34
Sapin, J. 172
Scaff, L. 46
Schaberg, J. 171
Schiffman, L. H. 138, 152, 198, 200, 226,
    228, 235, 238-40
Schluchter, W. 46
Schmidt, F. 199
Schremer, A. 237
Schürer, E. 59
Schwartz, D. 205, 225, 226
Schwartz, S. 149
Schweitzer, A. 141
Scott, C. A. 57, 58
Scott, H. M. 57
Scott, R. 170
Sennett, R. 50
Shemesh, A. 200
Shils, E. 196
Sica, A. 46
Sievers, J. 149
Silber, J. 73
Sills, D. L. 196
Sim, D. C. 171
Simpson, J. A. 130
Simpson, J. H. 231, 233
Sivan, E. 253
Smith, M. 152, 156, 164, 239
Smith-Christopher, D. 171
Southern, R. W. 91
Stanton, G. N. 26, 171
Stark, R. 2, 3, 6, 14, 15, 17-19, 26, 170,
    196, 208-10, 222, 229-34, 236, 239
Steck, O. H. 141
Sterling, G. E. 146
Stock, B. 73
Stroumsa, G. G. 227
Sturdy, J. 239
Suter, D. W. 165
Swedburg, R. 46

Sydie, R. A. 104
Syreeni, K. 230

T. K. 59
Talmon, S. 153, 164, 172
Tarrow, S. 127
Tenbruck, F. H. 27
Thompson, M. 16, 193, 201
Tichelaar, E. J. C. 198
Toennies 48, 90, 104
Torrey, C. C. 142, 152
Tov, E. 235
Troeltsch, E. 12, 26, 36, 42, 47, 48, 120,
    124, 129, 130, 133
Tuckett, C. 230

Ubigli, L. R. 238

Van der Toorn, K. 172
van der Woude, A. S. 161, 228
Van Peursen, W. 171
Vana, L. 170
VanderKam, J. C. 172, 199, 201, 226, 228,
    235, 240
Vermes, G. 85, 103, 225, 237
Vico, G. 166
Vincent, J. 127

Wahlde, U. C. von 171
Walker-Ramisch, S. 171, 236, 237
Wallis, R. 9, 134, 232
Walsham, A. 254
Wassen, C. 5, 13, 17-20, 85, 225, 227,
    228, 238
Weber, M. 2-6, 8-12, 14, 15, 17-19, 23,
    26-62, 64-84, 86-94, 96, 98, 100-
    104, 129, 130, 133, 134, 142, 153,
    169
Weinberg, J. 164
Weiner, E. S. C. 130
Westheimer, R. K. 172
Whimster, S. 46
Whitworth, J. M. 199
Whyte, W. H. 50
Wildavsky, A. 16, 193, 201
Williams, M. A. 171
Wilson, B. R. 2, 3, 5-8, 11-15, 18, 19, 22,
    23, 26, 47, 124-130, 133, 135, 157-
    59, 169, 170, 181, 182, 193, 197, 206,
    208, 209, 226, 227, 229-32, 236, 238